MENDING *broken* HEARTS

MENDING
broken HEARTS

ONE CARDIOLOGIST'S
JOURNEY THROUGH
A HALF CENTURY OF DISCOVERY
AND MEDICAL CHANGE

by Donald C. Harrison, M.D.

ORANGE FRAZER PRESS
Wilmington, Ohio

ISBN 978-1933197-61-6
Copyright © 2008 by Donald C. Harrison, M.D.
All Rights reserved

Additional copies of *Mending Broken Hearts*
Orange Frazer Press
P.O. Box 214
Wilmington, OH 45177

Telephone 1.800.852.9332 for price and shipping information.
Website: www.orangefrazer.com

Back cover photograph by Muli Tang

Library of Congress Cataloging-in-Publication Data

Harrison, Donald Carey.
  Mending broken hearts : one cardiologist's personal journey through a half century of discovery and medical change / by Donald C. Harrison.
      p. cm.
  Includes bibliographical references and index.
  ISBN 978-1-933197-61-6 (alk. paper)
  1. Harrison, Donald Carey. 2. Cardiologist--United States--Biography.
I. Title.
  RC666.72.H37A3 2008
  616.1'20092--dc22
  [B]
                              2008043329

I dedicate this book to Laura, my companion on most of the journeys presented here. We have known each other since we were three years old. We competed with each other in school and have shared life's adventures for the last fifty-three years. She supports me to meet challenges, helps me make difficult decisions, praises me when I deserve it, and is always there to encourage me through failures and disappointments.

ACKNOWLEDGMENTS

There are many colleagues, patients, friends, and associates who, over the past fifty years, have helped to make my life full of adventure, challenge, and joy. This book is about my life and the changes in medicine that have occurred as I have been enmeshed in it. It is my purpose to acknowledge a few of those people who have helped me with the book and my life's adventures.

Most recently, my daughter, Beth Harrison, and Jeff Lueders, who copy edited the manuscript, certainly helped to make the book more readable, and I greatly appreciate their efforts. The expert production of the book by Orange Frazer Press and the encouragement of Marcy Hawley to persevere to complete the book, even when I became discouraged, are gratefully acknowledged.

To all those colleagues, associates and friends at the University of Cincinnati Academic Health Center who helped me to accomplish my vision there, I owe a debt of gratitude for seventeen challenging years. My daily interaction with this cadre of people helped me to keep focused and to move on in a persistent way to accomplish a greater goal. Finding my way in a new city was difficult, but many colleagues and friends smoothed the pathway.

The pinnacle of my cardiology career occurred during my twenty-three years at Stanford University and Stanford Hospital. There I had the exciting experience of working with 156 extremely talented postdoctoral trainees who helped me achieve success. I also had Norman Shumway, one of the country's most talented cardiovascular surgeons, as a colleague during those years. He helped build one of the overall best cardiovascular programs in the country. I also would like to acknowledge the help of many of my teachers and mentors in college, medical school, and post-graduate training, especially Drs. Tinsley Harrison and Eugene Braunwald, who did much to stimulate me to be a scientist, clinician and teacher. I am also grateful to Braunwald for an insightful foreword.

My mother, Sovola, who had other career plans for me but still gave me the drive to achieve success, and my father, Walter, who taught me to persevere even in the toughest times, are acknowledged for what they contributed to my life as I grew up in Appalachia. My children have all played prominent roles in my life and have encouraged me in my endeavor to create this book. Beth especially helped encourage me to spend a week at the Iowa Writers Conference in 2003. This experience helped give me the focus to continue writing this book.

Finally, I could not have succeeded in meeting challenges and taking advantage of opportunities without the support of my devoted wife, Laura. We have shared all of our experiences over the last fifty-two years, from growing up in Appalachia to the present.

I owe her much of the credit for my success and certainly the encouragement to finish this book.

When one writes such intimate details of many of the events in this book, there are certain to be mistakes and exaggerations. This probably results from my faulty memory of events that took place in my life. For any oversights and errors I hope I will be forgiven, and I take full responsibility for them.

TABLE OF CONTENTS

Foreword   xv

Introduction   xvii

Part I. Up from Appalachia (1934–1954)

One The early years   2

Two Our move to Garden City   8

Three Formative early school years   14

Four World War II: parent separation   18

Five Junior and senior high school   24

Six Career choice and uncertainty   34

Seven Leaving Appalachian life   38

Eight Choosing a lifelong partner   42

Part II. Career building (1954–1963)

Nine Mystique of medicine   46

Ten A real doctor—finally!   64

Eleven The joy of family   72

Twelve Meeting challenges   78

Thirteen A career stepping-stone   84

Part III. The Stanford era (1963–1986)

Fourteen Stanford—unbridled enthusiasm   94

Fifteen The critical decision   102

Sixteen California family activities   106

Seventeen Stanford's challenges   116

Eighteen Becoming a young chief   128

Nineteen Restructuring cardiology　　　　134

Twenty The heart transplant　　　　144

Twenty-one Raising the flag　　　　152

Twenty-two Surrogate parents　　　　156

Twenty-three Knighting party　　　　158

Twenty-four Family escapade　　　　162

Twenty-five Bahrain connection　　　　166

Twenty-six Exploring Hawaii's paradise　　　　172

Twenty-seven South American adventures　　　　176

Twenty-eight A happy consultant　　　　180

Twenty-nine Cardiologist for a Chinese leader　　　　184

Thirty A full year of my life　　　　190

Thirty-one Changing face of national meetings　　　　196

Thirty-two African adventures　　　　200

Thirty-three Famous patients and friends　　　　204

Thirty-four Scare of our lives　　　　210

Thirty-five Our Tahoe retreat　　　　214

Thirty-six Medical education and consultation　　　　216

Thirty-seven Falk Cardiovascular Center　　　　220

Thirty-eight Return to China　　　　224

Thirty-nine My female guides　　　　232

Forty East trips with Frank Jones　　　　236

Forty-one Career mistake: Michigan　　　　240

Forty-two Last days at Stanford　　　　244

Forty-three Radical career move　　　　248

Forty-four Stanford legacy　　　　254

Part IV. Cincinnati: a career change (1986–2003)

Forty-five Cincinnati challenges   256

Forty-six Laura adapts to Cincinnati   274

Forty-seven The Holy Grail   280

Forty-eight Recruiting the knights   286

Forty-nine The hassle of politics   290

Fifty Medical system restructuring   300

Fifty-one Life at Seven Knolls   314

Fifty-two Parade of dignitaries   322

Fifty-three Medicine and wine   324

Fifty-four Gateway with Frank Gehry   330

Fifty-five Roadmap for a decade   340

Fifty-six Legacy at Cincinnati   344

Fifty-seven Return to my roots   348

Part V. Retirement? What retirement? (2003–2008)

Fifty-eight Retirement emotions   350

Fifty-nine A fourth career   356

Sixty Fun life: retired living   360

Sixty-one Aging and vulnerabilities   364

Sixty-two Honors and giving back   368

Sixty-three Summing up   370

Appendix——Parade of companies   *372*

Index   *378*

FOREWORD

Mending Broken Hearts is the clearly written, frank, autobiography of Donald Harrison, a leader of contemporary academic medicine. It is the story of the American dream, in which a boy from humble beginnings in Appalachia applies his very substantial talents—superior intelligence, grit and sheer determination—to reach the apex of his field. In this book, Don intertwines the two key themes of his life. The first, his personal life, particularly his successful marriage (fifty-three years and counting) to his childhood sweetheart, Laura. The other is his professional life, and he shows how each has had a profound effect on the other. The result is a fascinating story for anyone interested in understanding the extraordinary events occurring in American academic medicine during the second half of the twentieth century, and how they were shaped by one of its important leaders.

As a medical student at the University of Alabama, Donald Harrison came under the influence of his namesake, the great Tinsley Harrison (no relation) who recognized Don's promise and persuaded him to apply for internship to the (then) Peter Bent Brigham Hospital, where the elder Harrison, also from Appalachia, had himself trained. The Brigham was not a likely destination for someone with Don's background. To his amazement, Don was accepted, and his outstanding performance at that Harvard hospital turned out to be the key that unlocked the door to a world that gave him the opportunity to live up to his enormous potential.

His next stop was the cardiology department at the NIH that I headed at the time. Don was an apt trainee, a self starter, an original thinker, and hard-driving researcher who accomplished an enormous amount in just two years at the Institute. Just as his outstanding performance at the Brigham had led to his acceptance at the NIH, so did his notable accomplishments there lead him to Stanford, where he was appointed chief of cardiology at the age of 32!

Don rapidly elevated the reputation of what had been a somewhat sleepy program to the top ranks of cardiology divisions in the world. The success of the program was based on Don's personal involvement in, and leadership of, the three legs of the academic medical tripod—patient care, research, and teaching; he was equally strong in all three areas. He soon added a fourth important quality, a knack for academic administration, thus becoming a fabled "quadruple threat."

Donald Harrison's spectacular growth continued. He became active in the affairs of the American Heart Association and served that organization brilliantly as its president. He became the cardiologist to important personages around the world.

The next step in Don's professional life was inevitable. He was destined to direct an entire academic medical center and took the reins of the University of Cincinnati Medical Center as the university's senior vice president and provost for health science. Like his earlier experience at Stanford, he was cut out for this position. And as at Stanford, he successfully overcame many obstacles. He was forced to play on a much larger stage—becoming a master of constructive academic medical politics. He engaged successfully and simultaneously with diverse power centers such as the National Institutes of Health, state and local governments, hospital administrators, private practice groups, faculty unions, powerful department chairs, and the deans of three professional schools who reported to him. Don had to deal with the most important issues of late twentieth century medicine in the U.S. —managed care, the development of integrated health care delivery systems, the emptying of hospital beds, the merger of hospitals that had been long-standing rivals, the need to develop strategies to deal with the NIH, and the evolution of medical education.

Laura's advice to Don—"step aside while you're on top"—was, as had been the case at every critical juncture of their lives, supremely wise. It has allowed him to develop yet another career—that of a life science venture capitalist, which makes use of his vast experience, many acquaintances, sound judgment, and ample common sense.

Mending Broken Hearts is both a fascinating autobiography as well as the story of the varied currents of American academic medicine during the past half century. Don navigated these turbulent waters successfully, placing his personal imprint on this important segment of the history of our profession.

> —*Eugene Braunwald, M.D.*
> *Distinguished Hersey Professor of Medicine*
> *Harvard Medical School*
> *Chair, TIMI Study Group*
> *Brigham and Women's Hospital*
> *Boston, MA*

INTRODUCTION

I am a physician, and for the past fifty years have been involved with many segments of the field of medicine. This story of my life is a series of short stories occurring in my life, as I took part in and watched many of the events that have shaped and changed medicine over five decades. I experienced the health care system as a child, student, resident, research fellow, junior academic faculty member, professor, practicing cardiologist, productive researcher, and department head, culminating as chief executive for a large medical center. My stories tell of my life struggle to receive total acceptance by my mother of my chosen career. I was a major disappointment to her by becoming a doctor, even though she alone probably contributed more to my success than any other single person.

One Tuesday night in 1980 at my home in Los Altos, California, I was finishing my dinner when the phone rang with an ominous tone. It was my mom, Sovola, calling. I had not heard from her in many months.

"Don," she said, "I'm having trouble breathing, my chest hurts, and I am hot and sweaty." She continued, "Now I don't want to bother you, but I am suddenly afraid."

After a couple of questions, I suspected instantly that she had pneumonia and needed to see a physician. Because I lived 2,500 miles away, I responded, "Mom, you are ill. I want you to see one of my former colleagues from my house staff training, Dr. Richard Russell, who is in Birmingham now."

"You know how I hate doctors. I see no reason to visit one. I'll probably be better tomorrow."

The discourse continued. When I suggested I would come and care for her she just shouted, "You are just one of them, always taking advantage of people. I detest how you treat people." But being quite fearful for her health, I collected my stethoscope, a sampling of antibiotics, some intravenous fluid, and made plane reservations to go to Garden City, the small rural Alabama town where my parents had lived for forty-three years, and where I had grown up.

On my arrival twelve hours later, I was again subjected to her verbal abuse, which had become common in my relationship with her over the prior twenty-five years. "You should never have become a doctor. That wasn't my wish for you. You know that. Why don't you just go away?"

I had a cup of coffee with my dad while she continued to express more agitation. Finally, she calmed down and it was apparent that she was gravely ill. After some persuasion, she permitted me to examine her and I was able to confirm my opinion that she had a lobar pneumonia, severe enough to be life threatening. It took some further convincing before she allowed me to administer antibiotics intravenously, but I finally succeeded in doing so. To combat the dehydration, I gave her fluid all through the evening.

The next day she was better but still had difficulty in rising from the bed. She said, "Don, you did a nice job with me, but you should know I haven't changed my mind. I still do not approve of you being a doctor. I had higher ambitions for you. I wanted you to do those things I did not have the opportunity to do. You had the luxury of going to college and I wanted you to be a famous politician—even the governor of Alabama. Now it's too late. I only wish we could roll back time."

The next day I was able to convince her to go see my colleague Richard Russell, where an x-ray confirmed the diagnosis. She recovered from the pneumonia, but then withdrew from everything and rarely responded to my phone calls.

It is clear that I was a major disappointment to my mom. She felt she had made so many sacrifices for me and had expended so much effort in bringing me up. Her influence on my life took a strange twist, though. As I reached maturity, she unknowingly became my stimulus to succeed. This will become clearer as this tale unfolds.

MENDING *broken* HEARTS

THE EARLY YEARS

For everything there must be a beginning. For me it was in Blount County, Alabama, on the edge of Sand Mountain at the lower end of Appalachia.

My birth in 1934 took place in inconspicuous Forrest Gap, two miles from any settlement and located along the edge of U.S. Highway 31, a main route south from the Midwest to Florida. My mother, Sovola, describes my birth as difficult, and I was delivered at home by a local general practitioner, who had only a sponge soaked with ether to ease her pain, as she breathed through the sponge. Though unknown to me at the time, this was my first encounter with the medical system of our country.

My mother, who had been married to my father for only a year, expressed that she had not really wanted to be pregnant and did everything to rid herself of me by walking the high hills near Forrest Gap, which were totally isolated and in many instances covered with rattlesnakes. I can only presume why my mother wanted to abort. She was a beautiful woman, but she had watched what pregnancy could do to a woman's body and had a fear resulting from the death of her sister through childbirth. She also had ambition for Forrest Gap and did not want the inconvenience of a child, although I believe she did want a family—evident by the effort she spent in shaping my early life. She wished it to be later.

DON HARRISON IN FORREST GAP'S
ONLY GAS STATION IN 1935.

Forrest Gap was located two miles from Bangor to the north, a railroad town, and two miles from Blount Springs to the south, which ten years earlier had been a local Roaring Twenties tourist area. It was simply a collection of buildings hung over the edge of a ravine leading down to a large creek. One building had a living area and a section that was the speakeasy. It had a single gas pump, and the gas at that time was pumped by hand

and frequently spilled. I well remember its smell, leaking down the side of a car when it overflowed onto the gravel driveway. But I am getting ahead of the story, for I must describe how my parents came to settle in this forsaken place.

Life for my father had been rather difficult. His mother died when he was about three. His father, Walter Carey Harrison, for whom dad was named, moved into an orphanage as a caretaker with my dad, his sister, and his younger brother. The family running the orphanage invited my father to live in the house with them as a house boy. He did not attend school beyond the third grade. With the menial chores he was assigned, he had no time for school. When he reached his teenage years, he started going to a local gym where he was noticed for being very quick and light on his feet. He was enticed by a trainer into boxing and soon became known as the local champ. He also played sandlot baseball and was known in the area as a good ball player.

When he reached 18, he gave up baseball, acquired a manager and became a professional boxer. He fought professionally as a bantam weight all over the south and even as far north as Cincinnati. And as he described it, did very well, except on occasion when he was fighting individuals who later became national champs— they "beat my brains out," he said. Later I came to know through talking with other boxing fans that he was considered a southern champ. Other men told stories of my dad's boxing career. His fighting name had been "Bud" and they remembered newspaper articles about his fights. He shielded me from knowing about his boxing until I was grown. He destroyed all his

DON AND HIS FATHER, 1937.

equipment, scrapbooks, and news clippings the day I was born. Dad was always reluctant to talk about this stage in his life, but as I became a teenager he told me that boxing was not something he wanted for me—I should strive for an education.

However, his ability as a boxer proved to be useful when he was running a tavern. I was told that on occasion if someone became unruly, one lick from my dad would bounce the person out onto the street. He was always reluctant to talk about these issues and never attempted to teach me anything about boxing. This was the Great Depression, and a time when it was difficult to make a living. He was, in fact, usually paid $100 for a major fight. I've tried to imagine how my dad with no education must have felt traveling to New

Orleans, Nashville, and Cincinnati to fight in front of large crowds. No doubt he was nervous, but also determined to win. It was just part of his character to persevere and to win.

Because he was so poor and needed money, in about 1931, the height of the Great Depression, he heard that labor was needed in the wheat fields of Nebraska. He became a hobo on the train to Nebraska, only to find that hundreds of other people had preceded him and there was no work. He returned to Alabama on the train and luckily got a job with his uncle who had a franchise for delivering the *Birmingham News*, the largest newspaper of the state. My dad delivered the paper from Birmingham all the way north to the Tennessee line. It was on one of these trips that he stopped at the cafe where my mom worked as a waitress. This soon became a regular stop for him, and they courted as he delivered the newspapers every day. My dad ate lunch at the café on his return trips after delivering the papers. My grandfather, mom's dad, who was a bit unstable, probably watched them both like a hawk. He may well have been looking, though, for someone to take my mom off his hands. When dad married my mom they went to a Justice of the Peace and my great uncle and aunt stood for them as witnesses.

> *The family running the orphanage invited my father to live in the house with them as a house boy. He did not attend school beyond the third grade.*

Soon after they were married, he gave up the newspaper delivery job, and together they had to find a place to live and make a living. My mother had experience working in her father's speakeasy, so they chose Forrest Gap, which was about three miles north of where she had lived with her father, and there they established their own speakeasy. The buildings were already available at Forrest Gap and they rented at first, but then purchased and modified the property. This was during prohibition and the rural area in this part of Blount County was near Birmingham and friendly to speakeasy operations.

As I reminisce about my father it seems to me that we were never really close, although we did many things together. One of the things that I enjoyed most was that he taught me to play baseball. Even though I was not wildly talented he was persistent—working with me for many hours and teaching me how to catch the ball and throw it effectively. This made me a reasonably good baseball player and I was selected to play on a championship American Legion team later in my high school days. Dad was proud.

Persistence was one of the things he possessed and he taught me to value it, too. His persistence resulted in his learning to read on his own, and he developed good math skills as well. He was truly a self-educated and self-made man who had few helpers to guide him along his way. Even though I made errors in my career, the lessons of persistence that my dad imprinted on my brain made it possible to put mistakes behind me and move on.

My mom, Sovola, was a very intelligent woman who grew up in a dysfunctional family with a coal miner father who was alcoholic, had a bad temper, frequently got into terrible fights, and moved incessantly from one mining camp to another. He moved the family from Birmingham and the mining areas of Sayre, Alabama to Colorado or some other new place almost yearly. Mom attended school in many of the places they lived but by high school the family was settled in an area near where she met my father. She attended Hanceville High School, later the same school I attended. She was an excellent student and well liked. She had many friends and I've seen photos of her and her friends in those 1930s baggy dresses. She was a beautiful woman, usually the prettiest woman in the pictures. She became the Salutatorian of her 1931 graduating class and wanted to go to school or college.

But in 1931 there was no money and her father was not able to send her. She attempted to go to secretarial school in Birmingham but did not have the funds. She went to work in her dad's café in Blount Springs, met my dad, they courted, married, and she convinced him they could be successful in the speakeasy business, which she had observed when her father had tried to establish one but it failed after a year. In contrast to my dad, she graduated from high school near the top of her class, had good business sense, and she was extremely interested in books. My dad had more persistence than Mom, and while he was interested only in the practical news of the day, she seemed to have more desire to read anything she could get her hands on.

My mom was much more outgoing in a group than my dad. She loved to dance and since he didn't, she chose other partners. She could talk to anyone who came to the party. Dad always seemed shy and uncertain of what he might say, whereas my mom knew more about the happenings in the world, and what we children were doing.

My parents' Blount County speakeasy was certainly not the Chicago variety, where there would be a special door on which one knocked softly and then stated a special code to enter. No codes were required, but there was liquor, music, usually jazz, and gambling with slot machines—that part all very like the Chicago speakeasies I've seen in movies. To keep the law at bay, my dad paid off the county sheriff who came weekly to collect about $25 and for that amount, they were left

DON WITH HIS MOTHER, SOVOLA, BY THEIR 1936 CHRYSLER.

to do as they pleased. The speakeasy business of Forrest Gap attracted many people from Birmingham which was thirty miles away. There was gambling, liquor, and beer even in the height of prohibition.

Although my memory is a little vague, I recall the speakeasy's smoky atmosphere. The lights were low and the colors danced off the walls. The music was not loud, and some people were dancing while others pulled the handles on the slot machines. The guests seemed to be enjoying themselves as though they had not a care in the world. Speakeasies were a very popular destination for nighttime entertainment during this period of prohibition. They were frequently located in a rural area but near to a large city.

There was a unique but competitive speakeasy only five miles away from Forrest Gap. Bangor Cave was a limestone cave of almost a mile in length. The entrance and first two large caverns had been converted into a night club. The entrance to the cave was covered with a large door. Inside, the caverns were brightly lit, and many of the rocks and the walls of the cavern were covered with carpet. Seating had been carved into the walls. There was a dance floor, a bar, and slot machines and card tables all around.

After operating for about a year there was a terrible fire that destroyed Bangor Cave Night Club. It was always considered a suspicious fire, possibly set by some of the fundamental religious groups in the area. Years later I explored the full-mile length of the cave; there were few remains of its grandeur but farther back in the darkness there were bats, and at its termination a small exit hole through which I could crawl out onto a creek bed.

My first memory of Forrest Gap is of a large steam shovel parked on the roadway across from our house. It was large and imposing. I have vague memories of it working to clear an embankment. My next early memory is when I was just past three years old. My sister, Ann, was born. I don't remember this being very traumatic. I think I welcomed a new playmate into the family. Although Ann captured my mother's attention, she still spent time playing and reading to me. I can't recall being jealous, but I surely had to feel my world had changed.

Two black couples lived in shacks near us, one across the creek from where the speakeasy was located, and one about a half-mile up the creek that ran by our property. Archie and Carrie, who lived just across the creek, were my favorites. They were extremely poor. They looked after me and thought a lot of me and I loved them too. My dad employed them to do odd jobs.

———————— ⊰⊱ ————————

About twenty years ago, my dad and I were sorting through a shoe box of old faded photographs. We came upon pictures of a small boy in bedraggled clothes in the arms of a wizened black man, and another of a boy wading up to his waist in the creek. "Who's that?" I pointed, thinking it must be one of the hired hands catching a trespassing neighbor boy.

"That's you," my dad chuckled. "We was so relieved when Old Archie drug you out of the creek that day, we didn't even spank you." He went on to explain how I had wandered into the creek, and luckily the handyman had rescued me.

I can almost picture myself, then, at about three and a half years old. My dad said it was early spring, a season when great thunderstorms rolled through the hills, producing torrents of rain. That day, April 9, there had been a tremendous "gully washer," and my mom would have told me, "Don't you go near that creek today, Donald."

Oblivious to her command, I waddled down the steep banks anyway, in search of the soft sand where I'd often watch minnows swimming or see turtles climb out onto rocks to sun themselves. As I made my way down the creek bed, I talked with my imaginary playmates Juju and Jaja, not paying any attention to the water rising around me. Soon the water was up to my waist, and panicking, I cried out, "Help! Someone help me." Choking on tears, I thought I was about to be pulled down into the deep pools just behind the speakeasy.

Mom wanted a better life for me and she tried to live her dreams through me, by always manipulating me to meet her expectations.

Suddenly, at that moment, Old Archie appeared on the bank like a black apparition and shouted, "Master Don, for God's sakes, hold on! I'm a-comin'!" He scrambled down the bank into the rapidly flowing muddy water, carrying brush and small logs to grab me in his arms and carry me to safety. Whether this is the way it happened I'll never know but it seems feasible. Long afterwards, Mom said, "Don, that creek incident makes me want to teach you to swim."

Mom spent as much of her time as possible with my sister and me while working full time. Every evening she read books to us such as *Billy Whiskers*, the *Four Little Blossoms at Brookside Farm*, and many others. She was very interested in showing us more of the world outside of our rural area and took us to movies in Birmingham. She wanted to ensure that we had a better opportunity for an educated start in life.

Mom wanted a better life for me and she tried to live her dreams through me, by always manipulating me to meet her expectations. This started early in my life although as a child I did not recognize it, but later understood it. The manipulation was something subtle. She would say, "Don, you did not apply yourself" when I was not the top of my class or she would advise, "Don, you should read more if you are to go to college." We hear frequently that many men who succeed have a driving mother behind them. I can certainly say that my mother was that driving force.

Our move TO GARDEN CITY

In 1937 as I approached my fourth birthday, prohibition was repealed.

My dad began to plan moving the family to a county just north of us,

Cullman County, which had a sizable German population, long accustomed

to having their beer and wine.

Since there was local option whether or not alcoholic beverages could be sold, Cullman County had voted "wet"—a term meaning the sale of alcoholic beverages was legal. My dad wanted to get into a legitimate business there. In order to do so, he bought twenty-one acres from his mother, my grandmother, who was now separated from my grandfather as he had been committed to the insane asylum in Tuscaloosa. This time he was committed for bashing in a man's head with a baseball bat in a drunken fight at a ball game. Grandfather had many encounters with drunkenness, selling moonshine and frequent fights at public events. Grandmother had moved to Garden City

GARDEN CITY HOUSE YEARS LATER.

in Cullman County, a town about six miles from Forrest Gap, a few years earlier.

My parents were improving their status in the world as they too prepared for their move to Garden City. I remember going to the new house up on a large hill that Mom and Dad were building. It was brick and had nice grass-covered terraces. My parents were trying to make a statement about their acquired wealth, which had been earned legitimately in their minds even though it had been by an illegal business. This wealth was not great, only several thousand dollars, but in 1937 that was enough to build a substantial house.

The brick house was not large by modern standards but it had hardwood floors, a furnace, a basement, modern kitchen and modern bathroom, and we each had our own bedroom. By all standards, it was a showplace in the community. The house was built on a hill near the Mulberry River and looked over the tavern that my parents now operated. The yard was terraced. A series of steps lead up to the house and large oak trees, transplanted from the nearby woods, were planted in the yard near the house. The brick terrace faced east and extended to a covered patio leading to the garage. There was a small separate dining room adjoining the kitchen, which had an electric stove, almost unheard of in our community. We had a large tub for bathing and an indoor toilet, which was quite different from most houses nearby with their classic outhouses. I remember being quite proud to live in this house—especially when I visited with others and saw how they lived. My parents were seeking a better life for themselves and for my sister and me. My sister, Ann, was just a year old when we moved to Garden City. My parents employed two black maids from Birmingham, both of whom spent much of their time raising Ann and me, since my mother worked in the tavern. I remember many days sitting at Emma's feet, and being told ghost stories about witches and voodoo magic. Emma was very black, middle aged,

DON WITH HIS SISTER, ANN, IN 1938.

with graying hair and a missing front tooth. Her vivid imagination and stories were about haunted houses, murders, and supernatural happenings. I can still hear her voice today, telling stories that have been handed down for generations, reflecting her African heritage. The stories were troubling and frightening enough to cause bad dreams and to affect my sleep at night. Marilla, our second maid, was much younger, but was very efficient with the housework, taking care of us and preparing our meals. She was very light brown with frizzy hair that was always well kept. Marilla had a high school education and could even read stories to us at bedtime when my mom was not home. She was gentle with us, yet taught us to mind and to go to bed on time. She also taught us the well-known child's nightly prayer: "Now I lay me down to sleep, I pray the Lord my soul to keep, if I should die before I wake, I pray the Lord my soul to take." I remember that the words frightened me, and I wasn't sure I wanted to go to sleep.

During the years prior to WWII, my parents had many parties and invited many of their friends into our home. One of their friends was "Big Jim Folsom," who later became Governor of Alabama and was known as "Kissing Jim." I remember seeing him strolling across our lawn on Sunday afternoon, thinking he surely was a giant, since he was 6'9" tall. My parents hosted many people of influence from the area, their way of trying to gain status.

Mom and Dad did not shop in the local stores but went to Birmingham to purchase their clothes. Even in my early years I remember noticing that they both liked to dress quite differently from other moms and dads. I never saw my dad in overalls, which was the common dress for men in Garden City. Years later, I received a box of old family photographs and saw they were quite dapper in their dress. They took Ann and me to Birmingham for our clothes and even we were dressed quite differently from the other Appalachian children in the area. I had knickers and short pants while other boys wore overalls, so they often made fun of me. We frequently went about barefooted in summer and some kids had no shoes. Though we always had nice shoes, we pleaded to go barefoot to be like our playmates.

DON WITH GRANDMOTHER THOMPSON, AFTER SNOW IN 1936.

I remember my first introduction to movies—*Snow White and the Seven Dwarfs*—at the Alabama Theater in Birmingham. The theater had a large organ that arose up on a platform above the seated audience, and Stan Mallott played happy music before the movie and during the intermission, a carryover from the silent movie era. It was a wonderful treat for Ann and me that none of our schoolmates enjoyed. I suspect it was the fantasy of the movies that inspired me to have imaginary playmates—Juju and Jaja. When I grew older my parents described how I invented many stories about these imaginary playmates, even giving them superhuman characteristics. My grandmother considered them a spiritual blessing. She was a spiritualist and always told me I was blessed and destined for great things in my life. This became wonderful encouragement for me.

One barrier to gaining respect in the community was that neither my mother nor my father was very religious. Church was an important part of family life in our community, but they did not attend. To be respected in Garden City, a town of 500 people and two churches, one needed to worship regularly at his church. The fact that my parents operated the only tavern in Alabama which sold alcoholic beverages on Sunday seemed a black mark on their lives, though it was a very busy place. People came from miles around and carried away beer in gallon jugs. This did not endear them to the church-going community.

Though they did not go to church themselves, they sent us to Sunday School to try to ensure our acceptability in the community. While I have no memory of it, I later learned that a girl named Laura McAnnally was in my Sunday School class. As children we learned many Bible stories, some of which I still remember. The one I remember most is "In order to enter the Kingdom of Heaven one must come as a little child." I certainly wanted to go to heaven as it was presented to us.

Over the years, I have attempted to analyze why my parents were motivated to have me be accepted in the community where they were such nonconformists. They did not go to church even though they lived in a community deeply rooted in fundamental religious beliefs. They operated a tavern when alcohol was considered a sin. Worst of all, they sold beer and worked on Sunday against the Bible's instructions to rest on the Sabbath. It is no wonder they were not well accepted. I have speculated my own account for their lack of community concern: they had no roots or family in the community and my dad was only concerned about making a good living for his family.

Polio was epidemic in our area during my childhood and it was thought that one caught it from swimming...

Mom never experienced any religious education, as she moved with her family so frequently. Together their ambition for me was to make me respected and accepted. It never really worked, for I often heard people talking about me, saying, "That's Bud's boy; wonder why he is here." Many times I felt likean outcast. For me there was considerable ambivalence—liking my home and conveniences but always feeling somewhat a loner. Now I realize how this separateness influenced my temperament and career path. I was willing to be a maverick; my parents were my teachers in that regard. I both cared and didn't care about others' opinions.

While my mom and dad were busy, they still gave us considerable attention. Mom read to us almost every night at bedtime. When I was about five, she began to teach me to read, which I found quite easy. I am sure that the time with my mom was the beginning of my love of books. I still have some of my books that I treasured as a child, though the pages have yellowed with age. These early experiences were part of her mission to have me excel at whatever I was doing. She frequently asked me to repeat the stories she had just read and always questioned me on the ones I had begun to read.

Around age six, I was having some trouble learning to swim. Our house was located on the banks of the Mulberry Fork of the Warrior River, and after a rain the river was usually quite muddy. In summer the water quickly cleared but the rocks still had mud on them and were quite slick. I was told that if I did not learn to swim that year I would not be able to go to the river. We were able to swim in the river for at least seven months each year.

Both my parents could swim, but probably only about a third of the local people could swim. My father tried to teach me but was not good at instruction in the water. My mom was an excellent swimmer, took up the task and taught me better strokes, and even offered the reward of new books if I would try harder. I rose to the challenge and learned to swim and have always enjoyed the activity. She loved books, whether they were for her or for me, so that was a good bribe for us both. Polio was epidemic in our area during my childhood and it was thought that one caught it from swimming, so that curtailed some of our summer fun but did not keep us from the river. It was only later that I learned of polio's devastating effects.

Just before my sixth birthday, I had my second encounter with the health care system available in rural Alabama. While I do not remember the first one at my birth, I have vivid memories of this next encounter. It demonstrates some of the major changes which have occurred in health care for children over the past fifty years. I had experienced several severe sore throats and high fever and had been given over-the-counter medicines to gargle. At that time there were no antibiotics for treating sore throats. Our local family physician pointed out to my parents that I had enlarged tonsils and that it was customary for tonsils to be removed since it was not clear that they served any function in the human body. Rather than have that take place at the local hospital in Cullman, which was near our home in Garden City, I was taken to a clinic in Birmingham for an examination and evaluation. This clinic was for children in north Birmingham, known as the Carraway Clinic. I was seen by a pediatrician who concurred that my tonsils should be removed and he noted that I had not been circumcised. He recommended circumcision at the same time.

It was arranged for me to come to the pediatric unit of the hospital and have these procedures done the following week. Obviously a six-year-old was quite frightened by all this, but the doctors seemed to be very kind and reassuring. My mom and dad took me to the hospital on the appointed morning. I was taken to the operating room and had ether anesthesia, and when I awoke I had an awful sore throat and my penis hurt terribly. It was wrapped in gauze. I had a very kind nurse but do not remember being given any type of pain-killing medication. I vomited a great deal and it contained blood, which apparently came from the tonsils being removed. My throat got better over the ensuing days, but I had a great deal of pain from the circumcision, which normally is carried out at birth and not when someone is nearly six years old. This hurt for several weeks, but finally all healed.

Today in medicine there is a recognized purpose for tonsils, and it is uncommon to have them removed routinely, unless they are accompanied by severe throat infections. The common knowledge is that they help provide immunity and are excellent lymphoid tissue. As one grows older they will shrink, even if they are enlarged in childhood. The argument about circumcision is that circumcision is not necessary since it is carried out to prevent penile cancer, and that with modern hygiene penile cancer is very rare. However, most male babies now born in the U.S. still are circumcised. In any case, I was a frightened young child and remember well the pain that occurred from both surgical procedures.

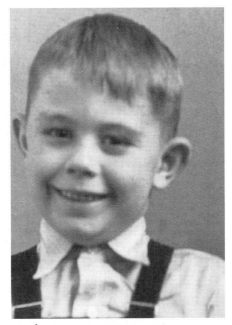

DON'S FIRST GRADE SCHOOL PHOTO.

I was taken to the Carraway Clinic for my medical care because my parents believed that the big city was the place for better care. They did their shopping there for food and clothes and frequently drove the thirty-five miles to Birmingham. One of my pleasures was to await my mom and dad's return to see what they would bring home. Because we did not have much fresh produce then, bananas were always a treat. But they brought many other toys, books, and new clothes as well.

I started school and remember this was a happy time with my parents, bonding closer to my mother, as she enjoyed sharing my learning experiences. They had a new car, many friends, and weekends were frequently times of frivolity and fellowship. Perhaps of all my childhood years, this time period represents the greatest happiness for me and for my family. There was little sign of the discord that was to come several years later.

EARLY SCHOOL YEARS

There was no kindergarten in Garden City so I started school in the first grade the fall after I turned six. I found one friend in my first grade class, Laura McAnnally, who was in my Sunday school class, and we started school together.

I remember being happy that I knew someone in my class at the start, and during our after-lunch rest periods we placed our oil cloth resting mats side by side. We both played in the Kitty Band, a small group of first-, second-, and third-grade children who received a modicum of musical education. Musical programs were sponsored by our school and the band participated in the Cullman County parade at the annual Strawberry Festival. Our county raised lots of strawberries and had a parade and festival to celebrate the harvest each May.

DON AND ANN WITH THER DOG IN 1943.

Our school building was relatively new for rural Alabama in the 1940s and was pretty well equipped. The school was built by the WPA in an attempt to bring the Appalachian area of the south up to some national educational norm. The first grade room was large, with high windows through which nice natural light filtered in. There were no indoor toilets, however, and we had to go about a hundred yards to the outdoor pit toilets. Its academic standards and the quality of teachers were considered far below national standard. For these reasons, we were required to take all types of academic tests to determine if Appalachian kids could compete.

There were serious questions among the educational professionals about the intelligence of children raised in the poverty of this region. I.Q. and achievement tests continued through several years of our schooling. These tests were very upsetting and stressful for all of us, since we knew we were being compared. My mom was wary of these tests and she, too, must have been stressed. We were never told our scores but we were able to guess who did well. It was clear, too, that certain children were singled out as more likely to be successful in school. Both Laura McAnnally and I were among that group and the fact that we completed the second and third grade together in a single year was considered a double promotion. We were the only children to be doubly promoted. Later I was offered a double promotion for the fifth and sixth grades, but my mother wisely refused. I was not as large as other boys in these classes and she knew that I was not socially ready to be a teenager. Our school year was only eight months long and we were really encouraged to learn and to be socialized.

My major worry during this time was the concern about polio, which was still rampant. We saw people who had been crippled by the dreaded disease and it was frightening.

The pleasant life of my early years continued throughout my primary school days. We went to school and to weekly Sunday school. As part of getting ready for school we were subjected to various inoculations. For the impoverished South, school admission required vaccinations for diphtheria, smallpox, and whooping cough or pertussis. Children then did not get the series of vaccinations that are now required beginning at six months and continue through age six for diphtheria, pertussis, tetanus (the DPT inoculations) plus hepatitis A and B, measles and rubella. The vaccines for most of these diseases had not been discovered. Our school inoculations were given in an open auditorium with everyone in a long line. I almost fainted when it came my turn. These remarkable discoveries have resulted in less infant and pediatric morbidity and mortality. Quite clearly the wide array of antibiotics that were not available until after World War II also help make childhood less risky.

My major worry was the concern about polio, which was still rampant. We saw people who had been crippled by the dreaded disease and it was frightening. My mother thought one might acquire polio from swimming in the river. She allowed us to swim, cautiously, and we were not to get any water into our mouths. As the years passed, the probability of infection seemed to decrease, but each summer the fear was present. When the Salk polio vaccine became available in 1954, we received the vaccine by intramuscular injection. A few years later the Sabin oral vaccine, ingested on a sugar cube, became available and my mom insisted we get this, too. She always feared that someone in the family would get polio.

It is ironic that many years later I became a friend and colleague of Dr. Albert Sabin, who developed the oral vaccine while he was a faculty member at the University of Cincinnati. He was always friendly with me, but though a tall, pleasant-looking, white-haired man, he was quite an authority figure among the faculty. Sabin was famous worldwide but still lived in the shadow of Salk. The Salk and Sabin vaccines have essentially eradicated polio as a threat worldwide, and their development is a great example of basic research leading to a product that eradicates a threat to human life and health.

Soon after I turned six, I began to develop ear infections. They usually cleared without any therapy except symptomatic relief provided by aspirin and some type of anesthetic gargle. On one occasion, however, I developed a severe ear infection, with terrible, throbbing pain. I was taken to an ear, nose, and throat specialist who said I had a severe form of otitis media and that I was about to develop a potentially life-threatening mastoiditis, an infection of the bony parts of the skull behind the ear. He recommended puncturing my eardrum to drain the pus. He did this as an office procedure, and I remember well the relief I got with the pus draining, though pain in the ear did persist for several more days.

On one occasion, however, I developed a severe ear infection, with terrible throbbing pain.

The doctor considered my situation quite serious. There were no antibiotics at that time, but sulfa drugs had just been approved and were available. I was given a sulfa drug for several days, and over that time my fever went away and the pain in my ear disappeared, but it took a month for my eardrum to heal. I eventually gained back hearing in that ear. Today there are effective antibiotics given to children when they have severe ear infections that clear them up without having to have the eardrum opened, and without the risk of mastoiditis. Common then, mastoiditis is a rare diagnosis today, showing what major advances have occurred with the discovery and appropriate use of antibiotics. However, today antibiotics are thought to be too frequently administered to young children with earaches, resulting in the development of drug-resistant organisms. I was fortunate because, had the sulfa drugs not been available, I might have developed mastoiditis and severe skull infection with complications that could have led to death.

PARENT SEPARARTION

Chapter Four

During my second year in school the bombing of Pearl Harbor occurred—I remember it as if it were today. I was at my friend Billy Hoagland's house and on the Sunday afternoon of December 7, 1941, I heard the news on the radio that changed my life abruptly.

Even though I was young, I understood that we were soon to be at war and that my dad might become a soldier. I rushed to tell my parents, who were working at the tavern and had not heard the news. My dad's words, "Oh God, this means war," were ominous. That Sunday was a watershed in the lives of many throughout the country but had particular meaning in Garden City, where most 18-year-old young men, including the two McAnnally boys, were drafted or enlisted into the military. Sam and Red McAnnally were the older brothers of my school playmate Laura. The war would bring major changes in my life and our town's life that I could not foresee on that afternoon. Clearly we had an evil enemy, and the first reaction of my parents and my friends' parents was, "We got to get those Japs."

The news, of course, did mean war. My dad, rather than being drafted as a soldier, volunteered for "war work." War work for him was to help construct airplanes at a plant in Birmingham. In order to be trained for this work he attended an eight-week course in Memphis. As a family we drove him to Birmingham to catch his bus to Memphis. It was a tearful separation and to compensate, my mom let Ann and me buy a small present. I remember that a bag of multicolored marbles was my choice. As we started the drive home it began to rain.

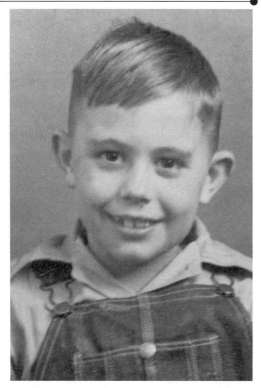

DON'S SECOND AND THIRD GRADE SCHOOL PHOTO IN 1943.

What was once called just a good hard rain became a very dark and frightening night without my dad. There were almost no cars on the two-lane road that curved through the rural and isolated Alabama countryside. No businesses or homes existed on the road for miles, and there was nothing but darkness. Ann and I became frightened, and my mother tried to display her strong resolve and reassured us, "We are going to be all right. Just sit still and when we get home I'll give you some ice cream." As I remember, we probably did not move so much as a finger, and we did make it home safely. The ice cream was a delicious treat, but with every bite, I missed my dad.

My parents were distraught during an eight-week separation, having never been apart for even a day during their marriage. My mom wrote letters and was tearful. Ann and I were afraid to be alone without our dad and wondered if he would come back. We had seen many fathers leaving for military service, and did not understand the difference. Later he was joined at work by my mother at the same aircraft factory, but she did not have to go to Memphis for training. I am not sure what motivated her, for few southern women worked. When Mom started to work Ann and I were too young to be left alone, and so we were moved from our new house to our grandmother's house across the road. This unsettling move created anxiety on my part and I was unable to sleep. I relied on my mother for so many of my everyday thoughts and actions. I suddenly felt terribly alone!

She experienced nightmares and visions, which was a horror to us as young children. These visions were about visiting angels and devils.

My cousin Melvin also lived in the house with my grandmother and my great-grandmother, who was then in her eighties. Great-grandmother had crippling arthritis and was confined to bed. She experienced nightmares and visions, which was a horror to us as young children. These visions were about visiting angels and devils. She would often scream out and could relate these dreams to us when we visited her in her bedroom, and especially when we took her meals to her. She had badly deforming arthritis for which there was no medical care at that time, and had to be lifted out of bed for bodily functions, which seemed "gross" to us as children.

In this era, rheumatoid arthritis was managed with bed rest, resulting in joints that became frozen and further crippled. There were no walkers or wheelchairs that could accommodate their disabilities, and in the advanced stage, people were often invalids. Treatment today includes anti-inflammatory drugs, monoclonal antibodies and extensive physiotherapy administered early in the course of the disease, and these kinds of deformities are not often seen. Granny had a good appetite but was always thin and gaunt. It was only when she passed a large tapeworm in her stool that this was understood. The idea of a tapeworm frightened us as children. Worm infestation was common in the rural south in the early to mid-part of the last century and resulted in malnutrition for both children and adults. While we never had worms, many of my classmates in grammar school did and were treated. My mom thought purging once a year protected us, and she gave us castor oil and another harsh laxative. It caused severe diarrhea for a day and was a horrible experience.

During the nearly four years I lived with my grandmother, from age 8 to age 11, I continued to do quite well in school and took part in many of the school plays. I had some wonderful teachers whom my parents wanted to know better and to have them understand their desire for me to be challenged. The teachers were invited to our house for a meal, since my mom was a good cook. It was unusual for teachers to go to their students' home, but my parents insisted, and since they did not have invitations to other students' homes, they accepted. In my opinion, this unusual effort by my parents was an attempt to overcome the low esteem in which they were held in the community, and in my mom's mind, to help me get extra attention for learning.

DON AND ANN BAREFOOT
WITH SCHOOL BOOKS.

I remember my fourth grade teacher, Miss Teem, smoked at a reception at our house. I was shocked, since we did not think a teacher would, or should, smoke. My parents had one day each week when they did not have to drive to work in Birmingham, and we planned our time with them and the visits by teachers. They worked the evening shift, and one of my tasks was to go from my grandmother's house to our house and "bank" the furnace by putting in extra coal and limiting the air intake, so it would be warm when they came home at 3 a.m., after driving forty miles from Birmingham at the end of their work shift. The heating for my grandmother's house was much more primitive than my parents' house. In the main living room there was a large space heater which kept it relatively warm. The kitchen was heated by an upright cook stove which burned wood and was our cooking unit for all food preparation. Our bedroom had no heat so we left the door open to get what warmth we could. It was cold at night but we hunkered down under feather bedding.

It was during this time of my life that my interest in the nature of the area grew, and this curiosity has carried on through my life. I fished for brem, now known as blue gills, in the small creek near our house and where it ran into the Mulberry River. I had to dig worms in the garden and be very patient sitting on the bank to catch little three- to five-inch bream. I often explored the nearby creek, catching crawfish which I used for bait to fish for larger catfish, though I was usually not very successful. I was also given an air rifle that took copper-coated lead bullets, which were hard to get during World War II, and on cold Saturday mornings I remember going out to hunt small birds. While this may seem cruel, it was part of the culture of that time in the South to be a hunter. I became a very good shooter with my air rifle and would bring the killed birds home to feed to our cat. My favorite bird target was the blue jay and they were quite plentiful in central Alabama.

While I have hundreds of memories of those years living with my grandmother, four vivid memories stand out. The first was that the bathroom of the house, which had been built a bit earlier, was not heated. We heated water for the tub on the cook stove on Saturday night and everyone had a bath. That was a ritual that we went through for almost three years.

The second was that we raised our own hogs. They were slaughtered while the weather was quite cold and hung up from a tree to let the blood drain. The fat was cut away and rendered for our grease, since there was rationing of grease for cooking during World War II. This was quite an ordeal for a 10-year-old, since I was expected to actively participate.

Thirdly, I was angry once at my grandmother over her harsh discipline and wanted to run away. I remember her pulling me back and sitting on me to keep me from running. That was a clear message also to my sister not to run away. I was angry because she had assigned me the chore to "slop the pigs." We were also expected to clean the chicken house. The smells from both chores were terrible, so I decided to leave. But I made the mistake of telling her and she pounced on me.

My fourth memory is of my grandmother's "boyfriend." My grandmother never divorced my grandfather, even though he spent several periods in the insane asylum and never came into our lives. However, my grandmother had a man friend who visited many Sunday evenings. She was a spiritualist and they had séances which we had to peek to see. My grandmother and her friend seemed to talk to spirits, usually someone who had died many years earlier. She told me about communicating with her dead relatives. I had no reason to doubt her and was reassured by her explanation and attention. My grandmother considered my imaginary playmates, Juju and Jaja, as spiritual blessings, assuring me of momentous accomplishment in my life. She would say, "Don, ain't it a blessing that you are so chosen by God?" I wondered in my mind what all this meant and I'm sure I was only confused by it all.

My grandmother's house was relatively large but my cousin and I slept in the same bed. He was several years older than I, and escorted me to and from my Saturday morning haircuts or the market in Garden City, a mile away. By this time I was riding a bike and was able to go by bike for trips to town. In Garden City there were three very successful merchants.

To attract crowds on Saturday mornings they had lottery drawings for baskets of groceries and small amounts of money for people who had the tickets acquired by purchasing things at the stores. Saturday mornings in town were big gatherings and almost everyone was there. I never won anything but I did meet up with many of my friends from school. By this time Cullman County had voted "dry," but there was moonshine available that people bought from bootleggers in the nearby hills. Moonshine was easily available because it could be made from corn mash and yeast in the "hollers" without being detected. A discarded car radiator was used in the process and the product had a high lead content. There were instances of lead poisoning reported.

During my second year in school I became acquainted with death firsthand. I was taken to the funeral of an older boy in the community who was killed while setting off dynamite to dig a well. Every family had a well since that was our only source of water. In many instances they had to be blasted out of sheer rock. The funeral service was long and the casket was open. Seeing someone dead and watching them lower the casket into the ground at the cemetery kept me awake for several nights. Although he had been killed by a dynamite blast, his face had been reconstructed and he almost looked alive. It was too much for me, just nine at the time. Even though I had been told in Sunday School that one went to heaven or hell after death, that concept was beyond me, and wondered where this boy would wind up. It was a shock for me.

Elementary school was a joy. I delighted in every minute of it and I had some excellent teachers. I learned all about the countries of the world, their people and geography, and states in our country, including all the state capitals. My curiosity about the world out there grew. But my cursive handwriting was so poor that in the sixth grade when I had a substitute teacher, she insisted that I begin a standard handwriting training program all over again. Though I was dismayed, irritated, and even angry then, it proved of great value to me after I became a doctor. Everyone could, and still can, read my prescriptions, meeting notes, and manuscripts.

As we finished elementary school, it was clear that Laura McAnnally and I were the top two students in our classes and were destined to compete. We were singled out and given every opportunity and encouragement by the teachers. As you might imagine, we became rivals for the top class spots and the attentions of our teacher. We were competitive, but in retrospect, I feel sure that I was the one driving any competition. I'm sure I boasted when I was ahead, but doubt she ever did. We remained friends, and since we lived in the same direction we frequently walked home together along the L&N railroad tracks.

Even though I was living with my grandmother, who was very concerned about my studies, I was usually allowed in the afternoon to listen to the radio and my favorite program, *The Lone Ranger*. The Lone Ranger and Tonto easily caught the bad guys. The ending of each episode, and I remember it like it was yesterday, was the shout to his horse, Silver, "Hi-yo Silver, away!" In the evenings we listened to radio programs such as *Inner Sanctum*, which started with a scary "screeching door." I can still hear it today, although at the time it caused me to have nightmares.

There, of course, were no televisions, but we did have what I considered excellent radio, and I was frequently mesmerized by the programs. I also read many books, which were given to me by my parents and the school, and my love of books continued to grow. Many of these books were chosen by my mother to teach me about history and the lives of great men. My Aunt Minnie, who lived in Washington, D.C., also gave me a lot of books. She had never married, and worked as a secretary in the Commerce Department. She chose educational books for us, usually of historical significance. I remember one about Abraham Lincoln but the most memorable one in my memory was Dickens' *A Tale of Two Cities*. I was appalled to read of the plight of youngsters in England. I remember this period of time with my books, the woods and Mulberry River, the radio programs, and my beginning days at school as a happy time in my life.

HIGH SCHOOL

Junior high school started with the seventh grade and extended through the ninth grade. Even though I entered junior high school at a relatively young age, I began to notice girls by the time I was in the eighth and ninth grade.

Laura McAnnally no longer appeared just as a competitor, but was becoming a focus of my eye, though she showed no interest in me. If anything, she had a disdain for me. I

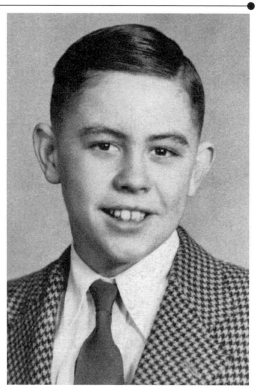

DON'S JUNIOR HIGH GRADUATION AS VALEDICTORIAN.

was also interested in Zania White, but she seemed to only care for older boys. I no longer was walking the mile to school but was riding with Mrs. Ruby Marcum, the teacher who was the instructor for grades seven and eight. Mrs. Marcum was a relatively hard taskmaster and worked us as a group in English and math quite diligently. Laura continued to walk to school and I missed the opportunity to accompany her.

During this time I continued to excel in the class, and in the ninth grade ,which was our graduation year from junior high school, I was the valedictorian of the class. I was nervous at the presentation of my speech, but with some adult help, I talked about an economic revolution for America. Our class had fourteen graduates and almost all of them were relatively bright. Those who were not had previously dropped out of school. Forty years later we had a class reunion. Many of them came and were living quite successful lives. By this time several had begun to experience health problems and much of the discussion was on the medical care system. Their feeling was that it did not serve those with chronic illness very well, and with this I concurred.

By this time my newly developed interest was pursuing girls. Mothers were very protective of their daughters but would let them participate in activities with adult supervision; thus they were permitted to participate with my Boy Scout troop, of which I was a very active member, especially when we went on night "possum hunting" trips. These trips included both girls and boys and obviously were an opportunity to spark. We actually did have dogs and we even caught opossums. There seemed to be no raccoons in our area during this time, but this was great fun and was a night outing for all of us. I remained an active Boy Scout and in high school I went on to become a member of the senior scout troop. I had a thoughtful scoutmaster, Alton Tidwell. I worked through many merit badges, with Tidwell becoming almost my second father. I spent many exhilarating afternoons and longer periods of time with him.

Part of our scout experience included building a log cabin in a very remote area along the banks of the Mulberry River. A man named Hugo Kretchmar, who was the coach for our baseball team, supervised us through two summers of this building project. He owned the land and the trees we needed. We cut the pine trees, stripped the bark from them and mounted them to construct walls. We then filled the spaces between with hand-mixed mortar. Little did I know then how many more building projects loomed in my future, but I learned the great lesson about the persistence necessary to successfully complete a structure. Since we built this log cabin near the Mulberry River, we had to be certain we were above the flood level. This was another lesson I learned on the Mulberry River, to be sure we evaluated the flooding potential properly.

DON AS A BOY SCOUT IN 1948.

We had other Boy Scout projects. One of the summer projects for the Boy Scouts was cotton farming, to raise money for our programs. During the summer of 1947 we planted three acres of cotton. We borrowed a small tractor for preparing the field and doing the planting. We "chopped" cotton or thinned the stand to permit maximal growth. At the time of maturity we picked the cotton, took it to the gin, and sold it, making almost $300 for our effort.

I had learned to pick cotton as a young child during what was called "cotton picking

DON BEING TAUGHT PERSISTENCE AT AN EARLY AGE, 1937.

time" at school. We began school in July and after six weeks of classes, were out for six weeks to assist in cotton picking with local farmers. The harvest of cotton was a big economic gain in our area and I picked cotton, working very hard from daylight to dark on occasions from age 11 to 13. I struggled hard to pick up to 200 pounds of cotton a day. For this we were paid $6 for almost twelve hours of very strenuous work. As I became older and stronger, I was designated the weigher of the picked cotton on one of the farms where I worked. The cotton farms were small and there were no mechanical pickers. By the time I entered high school the cotton picking school recess had disappeared.

As a young child, my dad had helped me learn to bat and throw, and I became relatively proficient. When I was about 12, I began playing organized baseball. Although I was

DON IN HIS AMERICAN LEGION BASEBALL UNIFORM.

younger than other boys playing on the team, they would let me play in right field in the late innings of the game. I was pretty good at getting hits and eventually became the lead-off batter. This led to more exploits in baseball in high school and eventually with the Cullman American Legion baseball team. For four years I played second base on the Legion team. We traveled around the state to play and in 1950 we were the state champs. There were several very good players on the team and one of my teammates, Robert Anderton, later made it to the majors with the Pittsburgh Pirates. All summer we practiced and played baseball. If anyone today saw how we traveled to our games in the back of a pick-up truck with sideboards they would be appalled and probably call the authorities.

My interest in nature and being in the woods continued throughout my youth, and I spent more time on the Mulberry River and in the woods. My dad gave me a rifle, a single-shot .22, and I was very aggressive at hunting squirrels. I often hunted in the afternoons after school, and learned a great lesson from those squirrels. I once saw six red squirrels in one tree out in the middle of the field. I approached and shot the first one. Since it fell into a large area of weeds I wanted to pick it up before I shot the others. I spent some time hunting the one I shot, and while I was looking around on the ground, the remaining squirrels escaped from my sight. Trying for perfection was too much and I lost the other five squirrels. This, I observed, was a real problem.

Fishing on the river in my flat-bottomed boat became another pastime. We always planted trot lines, which were long lines with multiple hooks to catch catfish. We baited this with smaller fish that we would catch in nets. Sometimes I would shoot fish called gars with my rifle off the side of the boat. The gars ate up the other fish and kept our river void of

DON DISPLAYING A LARGE FISH CATCH.

bass and trout and many of the game fish that we sought. Occasionally I also went with some of our neighbors, who were real hillbillies, to the Tennessee River to fish for crappie. A family of real hillbillies, defined by not working jobs, but hunting, trapping and fishing for a living, lived nearby.

The Hoaglands took me on these fishing trips. They hunted, fished, and trapped for animal furs for a living. We fished with minnows and carried the fish home in a tote sack. I remember catching at least thirty fish on one successful day. We also enjoyed the adventure of catching frogs. With a three-pronged gig and carbine lanterns, we went out at night in my boat and gigged frogs—even while they were alive we cut their legs off, skinned them, and cooked them in hot grease. It was a wonderful delicacy, and my family was delighted when I returned home with enough for my mom to cook. While this may seem cruel, it was part of growing up in the rural south. The river was full of water moccasins and I have a distinct memory of gigging a large snake and not being able to get it off the gig until I shot it.

My hunting adventures took me all over the area, an extensive woodland covering some large hills. I remember once getting lost late in the evening before sunset and not being able to find my way home until the moon rose to provide light. My dad was exasperated, came hunting for me, and found me at Whaley Creek, many miles from home. What followed was one of the serious reprimands I got for being lost in the woods.

DON WITH BILLY HOAGLAND
AT FAMILY TAVERN IN 1948.

Another vivid memory of a hunting trip was the day I wandered into a working still where a car radiator was being used to make moonshine whiskey. Four men wearing overalls and looking very mean came out pointing guns at me. I was shaking with fright but had enough wit to say I was lost and could not find my way back. They let me go and I ran for several miles to escape. They apparently believed that I was just a kid and even if I knew where they were I would be too frightened to report them. It was true!

During the war years, I became acquainted with the incredible impact of religion in the South. Every summer our Baptist church had an evangelical revival lasting about two weeks. During revival we had intense preaching by very powerful speakers and at age 12 everyone was supposed to be "saved" and baptized in the river. "Being saved" was the most important event in one's young life and the preachers threatened us with "going to hell" if we did not come forward. The gospel music also helped to set the tone. All of my friends, including Laura McAnnally, responded and accepted the calling. But I was a skeptic and I remained unrepentant for the whole summer when I was 12. While it was emotionally troubling to not "go along," I really wanted to stand up for what I believed, something I learned from my mother. I did not accept all the emotional conversions within my mind and sought something rational for reasons to believe. During the next year at Sunday School and at Baptist Training Union, which was every Sunday night, I was the focus of intense pressure by all of the others based on the concept that if I did not accept Jesus Christ as my savior, I would surely go to Hell and be alone while they were all in heaven.

Finally after two years of this I could resist no longer. I accepted the concept of

Christianity, and was baptized by a dunking in the river in an area where I fished and near an area where I hunted. I remember being led with about a dozen others holding hands into the middle of the Mulberry River—about waist deep while those on the shore were singing the Gospel song, "Just as I am." When it came my turn to be dunked three times I held my nose to keep water out, since we were dunked backwards. The words were: "I baptize you in the name of the Father," one dunk! "The Son," dunked again, "and the Holy Ghost," dunked the third time. Many of those with me were frightened since they could not swim. We were fully clothed and looked like drowned rats on emerging from the river. Strangely, I did not feel any different, and surely not "saved." This was an important event in my life that later led to much of my skepticism about religion and vows that were made under such pressure. However, after baptism I was able to rejoin the group on their terms.

I remember this period of my life as being one of growing, developing new ideas, creating friendships, and becoming more mature. I had anxieties about my future because through my reading I recognized there was a bigger world out there and I needed to begin preparing for it. My mother encouraged me and pushed me to create larger goals for myself. She continued to urge me to read widely and to keep abreast of current events.

From our junior high at Garden City, the fourteen of us who finished moved on to the consolidated high school at Hanceville, Alabama. We joined a class of sixty or seventy other students from around our Appalachian area. We had individual classes in English, biology, physics, chemistry, and math with individual teachers for each. I found my physics, chemistry, and biology classes quite interesting and I enjoyed those studies a great deal. However, soon after beginning my physics class, my teacher, Mr. Fanning, gave me his college physics book and told me he could not teach me anymore—I was already far more advanced than he. His degree from a teachers' college was in education and the only physics course he had was a summer course for his post-graduate teaching certificate. He suggested that I read the book and work through its problems independently.

Fortunately, and in contrast, Joyce

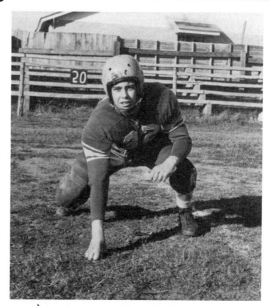

DON'S HIGH SCHOOL FOOTBALL PHOTO.

Lamont, our math teacher, was outstanding. She took us through much of the algebra and geometry that would be needed later for college. We had one young English teacher who was just out of teachers' college named Pamela Perry. She could not control the class; many students made fun of her and we learned very little English in that class. Our social studies and American history classes were much more exciting, and Howard Holley, our teacher, helped me recognize a real interest in history. I remember a course in business math where several of the older students who had been in WW II joined us. They had difficulty because of a deficiency in math skills, but I found this to be one of the more exciting and stimulating classes I took, and I was able to help these war veterans pass the course. I also took bookkeeping, learned well, and soon began to take care of the bookkeeping for my parents' business.

Early in the morning the boys were separated from the girls in home rooms when we arrived at the school. The boys met in the agricultural classroom. There we had boxing contests every morning, with two being chosen to box each day. I participated frequently and remembered that my dad had said, "I got my brains beat out" a great deal. Football was the premier sport in high school. Even though I was only 165 pounds, I played right guard and was captain of the team in my junior year. Football practice was every afternoon at the end of school and was quite strenuous.

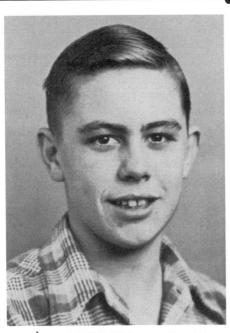

DON'S PHOTO FOR THE *BIRMINGHAM NEWS* ORATORICAL CONTEST.

We had a new concrete block locker room with few amenities. Games against nearby rural high schools were played on Friday nights and attended by everyone—great rivalries developed. Many of the boys on the team were "rough and ready country boys" who played football on Friday nights and partied on Saturday nights—drinking moonshine whiskey and fighting with the boys from rival schools. In my senior year our football team was undefeated and several members of the team received college scholarship consideration, but even then I was too small to be considered for college football.

I participated in many activities during high school. One the most significant was an oratorical contest that was sponsored by the *Birmingham News*, the largest paper of the state. With a lot of coaching from my home room teacher, Clara Mae Burkhart, I managed to win the contest for the school, and I later won the contest for Cullman County. When I was chosen to participate in the regional my mother was so impressed she bought a new car to take us to the competition. She was extremely proud of me and had me practice with her on many occasions and offered helpful comments.

The competitors were five young women and I was the only man. Each delivered a more erudite and expressive speech for their memorized entry but did not do well on the second part, which was to speak extemporaneously from one of the subjects listed in the prepared speech. My ability to speak extemporaneously was strengthened by my intense study of the subject and by my ability to remember almost anything I had read. We all had deep Southern accents and our words like "night" and "right" were spoken with a true hillbilly twang, the long "I" sounding like an "A" in rat, for example. Although the young women were prettier, I won the regional and went on to participate at the state level.

I was barely 15 and was off to Birmingham Southern College to participate at the state level. My competitors were older students with what I perceived as a much higher achievement scholastically than I, and it turned out to be quite a challenge. I prepared for weeks and did quite well, winning a scholarship for one year to Birmingham Southern College where I attended later. I will never forget getting the topic I was assigned to speak on, and in the preparation time of the thirty minutes, alone in a quiet room upstairs in Munger Hall at Birmingham Southern College—I felt a deep anxiety.

But I fashioned a convincing extemporaneous speech, "Using the Natural Resources of the South." The two main points I emphasized were the fast-growing pine forests of the South and its vast underutilized other natural resources such as oil, coal and water. In many ways the persistence I had learned from my dad helped, and the confidence I felt from my mother's continual encouragement carried me through, and also the personal experience of living and playing among the natural resources. Later when I attended college, I made several speeches on that same stage and as an alumnus I have been back to speak to college students on several occasions. The stage was not so frightening then.

During my high school years I became an even more avid hunter with my trusty .22 rifle which had been given to me when I reached age 12. I can never forget the fear I felt when I was on a late fall trip walking through the woods and heard the rattle of a rattlesnake. I jumped a fence and started to take off, but went back, found the snake, and killed it.

I often fished in the Mulberry River and found that in the fall in small pools, I could catch lots of blue catfish, which were excellent eating. Two things I learned about risk taking took place with the fishing. Handling the blue catfish had to be done carefully, for they had sharp fins containing a toxin, which when injected caused great pain. There were also many poisonous moccasin snakes that had to be avoided. Turtledoves were also one of my favorite prey for my hunting expeditions. We baited the fields with corn and I became an excellent shot with my double-barrel L.C. Smith shotgun, which my dad had given me for my 15th birthday. This was great sport, though many people consider it very cruel. Being able to hit a fast-flying dove was considered by hunters to be a major challenge, and I was good at it.

On one occasion when I was fishing on the Mulberry River, I vividly remember being called to help at what was called the "round hole," a deep hole in the river. Someone had drowned there in the middle of the night. I was an excellent swimmer and joined in the hunt for this person, but we were unsuccessful at finding him or pulling him up. The group had grappling hooks and later found the body.

During that night on my way home through the deeply wooded area, I heard bobcats cry in the bush. This was the first time I had heard them, and while they did not frighten me, it seemed something of an omen that night. I also recognized that wildlife in the area was increasing. It had once been depleted by hunters who really needed the game for food during World War II. Later in my life, living in Ohio, we have many deer, but by this time they have been hunted so much that none exist in this back area of Alabama.

I continued to fish with Laura's cousin Billy McAnnally, who was a medical student while I was in college but now had moved from bank fishing to a boat on the Tennessee River below Guntersville Dam. One windy day my glasses were blown off into the water. This generated many stories about big fish wearing my glasses being caught. Laura's brothers were the ones to tease me the most and spread the story around the county. By this time Laura and I were becoming friendly competitors but also taking a more serious notice of each other.

To return to an earlier time, when my parents returned, having ended their war work in 1945, they opened a tavern and dance hall in the same building where they had sold beer before the war. The county was still dry, and my dad often paid off the local county authorities to leave him alone, but he was still harassed by the state authorities. Most everyone else sold moonshine liquor but my dad insisted on selling only bonded whiskey from commercial vendors. It seemed easy to placate the local authorities but the state officers were relentless in enforcing state liquor laws. Federal agents were not concerned if one sold bonded whiskey since there was no Federal law broken and all the taxes were collected. The Federal officials focused enforcement on moonshine, which avoided federal tax. Dad bought his liquor in Birmingham and transported it illegally to Cullman County.

After he picked up a load he had many hiding places—in a covered tub under a trap door in the chicken house under the chicken droppings, and in special compartments under the bed in the house. Once when three state officers raided him he had his last two bottles under the counter. Luckily a customer came in and bought the last two bottles while the officers were searching elsewhere, and the state guys found nothing—to their dismay. Despite these clever escapes, Ann and I were dreadfully afraid they would catch my dad and send him to prison—luckily they never did.

The dance hall, which was part of the tavern, attracted a large and rowdy crowd every Saturday night. I have been told that my dad bounced many a large guy out when he became unruly. My mom was a steady hand and did the hiring of local help and managed the preparation of barbecue, which she sold in abundance. After these Saturday nights, I would help clean up the rubbish. Once I found a $20 bill and I was allowed to keep it. This was big money to a teenager. Unfortunately though, our dance hall business was again bringing our family into disfavor in the community and I resented it. I wondered how my mom and dad could do this to me. In 1948 my dad stopped running the dance hall and decided to build a motel to accommodate tourists on their way from the Midwest to Florida. We lived on U.S. Highway 31, which was a main route back and forth to Florida. He thought this would be a good business and wanted to stop the risk of a state prison term for his liquor sales.

Luck was with us when, by chance, my parents managed to recruit two unemployed builders from Pennsylvania who had left home seeking work away from the harsh winters. They lived in my grandmother's house and worked to build a six-cabin motel in a single winter. I worked with them and learned some builders' techniques, and even after they left, I continued to lay some of the concrete blocks and put tile up in the bathroom. The motel turned out to be quite a success and we added six more rooms the following year.

My dad and my mother operated the café, and even though I was not old enough for a driver's license at age 14 or 15, I drove the car to school every day and then went to Cullman to pick up all of the supplies, such as chicken, doughnuts, and produce. This was grueling work because after school I worked from 5 until 9 at night and then we sat down as a family to have our evening meal. My sister, my mother, my dad, and I all worked. I ran the front and Ann and my mother took care of the kitchen. We then arose early the next morning to prepare breakfast for all of our guests at the motel, and after breakfast Ann and I went to school.

CHOICE AND UNCERTAINTY

My decision to become a physician did not come in an instant. Near the end of high school we all had to be tested for syphilis, a dreaded disease for the medical profession.

It could result from being transmitted in pregnancy to the infant, or it could be acquired through sexual encounters. Public health measures were being instituted to obliterate it with penicillin if it was detected. The testing for syphilis also included the measurement of blood sugars, and mine was reported to be high.

I knew enough about diabetes from my science reading to be extremely frightened. While everyone encouraged me to wait for other tests I reacted by not eating, losing sleep and being very withdrawn. It was like a period of situational depression. Today we know much more about diabetes and understand that lifelong treatment with insulin can prevent the dreaded complications of heart disease, loss of vision, and blood vessel disease that causes loss of limbs and end-stage kidney disease.

I was not aware of this then and was horrified. Finally I went to my family doctor, George Rowe, who was very kind, personally taking me to Cullman Hospital and doing a glucose tolerance test, the method used then to confirm the diagnosis or to rule it out. My test was negative and I developed a great respect for Dr. Rowe. He

DON AND LAURA ON FIRST DATE.

began to invite me to come to his office to learn about medicine and took me on rounds at the hospital. I was awed with the knowledge he had and the suffering he relieved. I wanted to be like him. Much later when I knew more my awe disappeared. As I learned the newer methods of diagnosis and treatment in medical school I recognized that Dr. Rowe was not an up-to-date medical doctor. He had not kept up with the advances. I understood why, though, since he was so busy seeing forty or fifty patients each day with no time to read or attend conferences.

The final event that made medicine my career choice came at the end of my high school senior year. As part of a sociology course we took aptitude tests and I scored high in both science and history. Career choices were recommended based on our scores—medicine became my number one recommendation and choice. My mother, who wanted me to study law, was not overly concerned. She must have anticipated I would change once in college.

During these years I had little time for homework except for late at night, but I found the work in high school very easy and continued to be at the top of my class. Laura McAnnally and I graduated one-two, as the top of the class in high school. I spent considerable time with other girls in a group, but I had not started dating. As time for the annual football banquet drew near, I had no date. Clara Mae Burkhart, my home room teacher, sensed my concerns and bashfulness and encouraged me to invite Laura McAnnally. Even

We had many of the same values and aspirations. We went to the drive-in movies, and even though naïve, found we could smooch.

though I had interest in other girls, I always had my eye on her. Mrs. Burkhart must have sensed this. Laura was pretty, smart, and also had not begun to date. I invited her but she had to have the permission of her dad. It seems he accepted me since she agreed to be my date. Laura's family was very strict with their daughters and Laura's three older sisters had not been allowed to date while in school. She accepted and we attended the football banquet together.

We enjoyed each other's company and began to date regularly. We had many of the same values and aspirations. We went to the drive-in movies, and even though naïve, found we could smooch. Afterward we would go to Cullman for cokes and hamburgers. In 1950, Christmas came and I ventured to visit her at home with a gift of a Whitman's Sampler of Chocolates. She was not at home but was visiting with girlfriends across the railroad tracks. I can hardly believe it now but I went there to see her—my knees knocked as I approached the door. I was at first embarrassed but had a fine evening playing bingo with Laura and the girls she was visiting. Our romance blossomed and we began seeing each other with increasing frequency. On the last day of high school we took a long drive together and made a pledge to "go steady" and date only each other. Going steady at such an early age was acceptable in our rural south and was a rite to adulthood. After that we dated on the weekends frequently. We graduated a young 17 years old from high school, being only two or three months into the seventeenth year. At the time I was still keeping the financial books for my parents, helping them run the motel, and feeling that the world was before me with many challenges and opportunities for a new life.

Leaving

I visited only three colleges prior to making a choice. Mississippi State in Starkville offered me a baseball scholarship after a visit for a tryout. It was so isolated and far from home I could not imagine going to Mississippi.

The University of Alabama in Tuscaloosa was attractive to me, and was to be my choice before the visit. However, I found its academic program not at the level I was seeking, and I finally chose Birmingham Southern College, a small school with only 1,200 students. I had won a scholarship in the statewide oratorical contest to go there and it was the best academic school in the state. When I enrolled at Birmingham Southern, my parents left me on that first morning at the entrance of the administration building, with one large suitcase. I felt really alone. My level of anxiety and being alone was never greater.

FAMILY MOTEL BUSINESS.

I learned that I was to room in an old army barracks a good distance from the central campus, and that I would have to take placement exams all through this first day. For a country boy this was a frightening experience. I quickly enrolled in my classes and discovered that my writing skills and study habits were behind many of the other students in my classes. My first written autobiographical sketch in freshman English was handed back with a letter "D." I had never received a "D" in my entire life and of course this required drastic changes in my study habits.

During that first year I found my math skills to be reasonable, my English skills to be subpar, and my language skills in German, which I was taking, to be poor. Professor Protowell said to me, "You will never master German." My pre-med advisor, Charles Blair, told me at the end of the first quarter I would either have to do much better or I could just go home now. He worked with me and became one of my strong supporters as my academic performance improved. I met with him every week during my second quarter for his advice and encouragement. Once I started the sciences chemistry, biology and physics, I found my niche and was able to make straight A's. I really enjoyed the lab exercises in chemistry, though once in organic I misread all the instructions and had a minor lab explosion.

Later I also did much better in the literature courses and finally began to develop writing skills that brought me up to at least par. By the time of my graduation I had achieved a 3.5 out of 4 grade point average, which was competitive enough for medical school. Although I was eligible for Phi Beta Kappa, there were twelve others on my campus ahead of me and twelve was the quota then. Years later I was inducted as an alumnus member because of my grade average and my accomplishment in my profession.

During college I continued to date Laura, who was now a student at Florence State Teachers' College in Florence, Alabama. Because we were going steady, I did not actively participate in Birmingham Southern's social life during my first year. Laura had worked a year as the secretary to the Hanceville High principal, and then entered Florence State Teachers' College with the encouragement of the college recruiter and me. She had limited funds and worked a forty-hour week as well as attending college; quite an accomplishment at that time.

At Birmingham Southern I joined the Sigma Alpha Epsilon (SAE) fraternity. This was quite another experience for a young country boy, especially at the end of my first year when I was 17 and was taken to a fraternity convention in Chicago. We had "manufactured" ID cards and visited lots of clubs and girly shows for adults only. Chicago was the largest city I had ever seen and the opportunity for mischief abounded. The convention was held on the campus of Northwestern University. One of the chapters from Mississippi caused quite a commotion by taking down the American flag and flying a Confederate one.

I did make a number of long-lasting friends in my college years. A roommate, Calvin Hopkins, has remained a friend. Calvin was a gaunt person with an affable personality and lots of wisdom. He was several years older but still very shy and self effacing. His calm demeanor helped to allay some of my apprehensions and anxieties. Alan Dimick was an early friend and later was also one of my classmates in medical school. He became a surgical professor at the University of Alabama at Birmingham and is one of my close friends today. Alan was more than 6 feet tall, a bit overweight, and had a receding hairline. He was from a wealthy family that owned a foundry in Birmingham. He had a great knack for teaching others. I introduced Alan to Eleanor Hamilton, one of my college classmates, whom he later married.

During my third year, I was elected to the upper division governing council of the college, and one of my responsibilities for the senior year was to be the chairman of the

> *Since at this time we did not dance because of our Baptist background, and drank only a little, these events were quite stifling for both of us.*

Sadie Hawkins Day. Laura did not come to Birmingham Southern for the event—can you imagine planning Sadie Hawkins Day and having no date? There were many fraternity parties, and on occasion Laura was able to visit to attend these. Since at this time we did not dance because of our Baptist background, and drank only a little, these events were quite stifling for both of us. Once when I invited Laura for a weekend, we went to the SAE party and when we came out it was snowing heavily, a great surprise in Birmingham. I was supposed to take her home to her parents in Garden City but we could not drive through the four-inch-deep snow. There was no phone to call her dad so I took her to her sister's in nearby West End, where we both stayed. Her dad was worried sick.

Since I was in a hurry to move on with my life, I completed the full college course in three years by going to school two summers. I also found a new sport, tennis, which was a challenge, but one I came to really enjoy. Being separated from Laura and not having telephones accessible as they are today, we wrote letters every day to each other, and saw each other either at Florence or Garden City or Birmingham about once a month. Young people today would not tolerate such separation. They have cell phones with text messaging and e-mail. One of the letters that I recently found in my collection read: *Dearest Don, I love you so much and it's so lonely here. I hope the time passes so quickly so we can be together forever. My classes are hard, especially the math which I don't understand. I think of you most nights and hope you visit soon. Your dearest Laura*

All through college I commuted home on weekends to work at my parents' restaurant and motel. I kept their financial books for the first year. I did not have a car but hitchhiked the forty miles to Garden City on Fridays after class. Hitchhiking was more accepted then, and I was frequently picked up by salespeople who knew me as "Bud's" boy. I never had any frightening experiences and always got a ride. On most occasions I had a ride back with a student who was commuting from Garden City to Birmingham.

In my final year at Birmingham Southern I took the medical aptitude test, did quite well and then interviewed for medical school at the University of Alabama, Birmingham, Emory, and the University of Pennsylvania. The trip to Pennsylvania was my first trip out of the South other than the fraternity convention in Chicago. I chose Pennsylvania because of its excellent reputation, and by this time I had become sophisticated enough to know that going to an excellent medical school would expand my future opportunities.

I was scheduled to fly, but because of bad weather I had to take the train, which took twenty-seven hours. I stayed in the SAE fraternity house at the University of Pennsylvania campus, and had a reasonable interview, but in the long run was not accepted. While I was disappointed, I really wanted to be near Laura, and the expense of tuition and living in Philadelphia would create a family financial burden. Thus, I chose the University of Alabama, Birmingham, because it was near home, near Laura, and was at that time $200 per semester for tuition. I might have been accepted at Emory but withdrew my application after learning of my acceptance at UAB.

A LIFELONG PARTNER

While Laura and I married at a young age of 21, our courtship lasted

from the time we were 16 and throughout the time we were both in college.

Some might say it really began in first grade or Sunday school.

At the end of high school, just after we had turned 17, we made a decision that we were "going steady" and we continued dating even though we were separated during our college years. Our visits were infrequent. Laura would come on the bus to Birmingham to visit me, or I would drive to Florence to visit her, which was about 150 miles away. We would eat out at the local hamburger restaurant, visit some of the state parks along the Tennessee River, Wheeler, Lake Park, and Wilson Dam Park. We became officially engaged about six months before our marriage.

On her birthday in January 1955, I visited Laura, and since it was a nice day, we took a walk near the Wilson Dam. It was at the Wilson Dam Park that I gave her an engagement ring. We soon began planning our wedding, and since we had no one in either family to do any of the planning, we did it all. After Laura's graduation in May she moved to the house of her sister, Geraldine Weber, in Birmingham, and together they made her wedding dress. We interviewed and chose the photographer, made decisions about the flowers, and planned the reception.

DON AND LAURA AT MUSCLE SHOALS GETTING ENGAGED.

The wedding took place at the Baptist Church that we had both attended, on July 24, 1955. The wedding was the most celebrated the Garden City Baptist Church had ever hosted, and I was certain that Laura McAnnally was the most beautiful bride ever to be married in that church. It was hot and there was no air conditioning, but the men wore white dinner jackets, and the women wore long dresses. After the wedding we had punch, but no champagne at our reception held in the church basement. Baptists didn't drink alcohol in the rural South. Laura's dad, Clark McAnnally, had a great smile on his face as we emerged from the church, which I read as meaning that he truly accepted me as a son-in-law. This had not always been his intention since as a strong Baptist Church leader he had objected to my parents' tavern and to their selling beer on Sunday. What neither Laura nor I knew at the time was that her dad, who had hauled sand from the Mulberry River bottom to help build my family's motel, often enjoyed alcoholic drinks with my dad after a hard day's work. This story was told to me years later by my dad and I was surprised that Clark liked a little drink now and again.

LAURA IN THE GOWN SHE MADE BY HAND.

The attendants for Laura were Joyce Campbell, a college roommate, and her sister Ruth, who was Maid of Honor. My groomsmen were college and medical school classmates. My Best Man was Alan Dimick. The evening before the wedding, we held a rehearsal party at my house. What was to have been a celebratory event for me was a sad occasion, since my mother totally opposed my marriage to Laura and refused to participate. But in spite of the gloom at the rehearsal party, the wedding was joyful. Many of our friends were there to support us, and Laura's large extended family from Garden City all came and were there to witness our vows and celebrate at the reception.

After the wedding our first honeymoon night was in Decatur, Alabama. We had dinner at the local hamburger café near the Starlight Motel. We spent two days in Nashville and visited the Hermitage, home of President Andrew Jackson, then went to Gatlinburg, Tennessee. At that time Gatlinburg was just a few motels and not the great honeymoon place it is today. I remember one of our dinners where we had fried chicken with honey, which we both thought was delicious. Our honeymoon lasted only five days since I had to rush back and we had to get an apartment ready.

Laura was to go back to work, and I wanted to be ready for my second year in medical school. Laura remembers this quite differently. She thought we could stay longer but gave in to me. It was my impatience that prompted our early return. When I finished undergraduate school, I had chosen my career mountain, medicine, and I was eager to plunge in to my second year in medical school and the next phase of our lives together.

LAURA AND DON KNEELING DURING
WEDDING CEREMONY.

I have frequently reflected back on my life up to this point and tried to understand what had molded my underlying personality and character. My mom had been a driving force to achieve in school but she was now disenchanted with my career choice. I accepted this at the time and was eager to move on. I believe all the time I spent on Mulberry River had a profound effect in molding my character. The solitude gave me time to reflect, the dangers gave me the instinct to take calculated risks, and to hunt and fish well required that I develop skills. Of course my dad had taught me perseverance and my college years had permitted me to make up for my early education deficiencies. I now felt profoundly ready to climb the mountain—my education for a medical career. I had experienced very few setbacks or disappointments and I kept my inherent optimism.

MYSTIQUE *of Medicine*

For me, a young man from Appalachia, entering medical school was a
giant step. I did feel well-prepared because of my college work, though
there was an almost palpable level of anxiety.

The boarding house where I resided was just a few blocks from the medical center, albeit in a deteriorating area of Birmingham. The house was a creaky old Victorian and I had an upstairs room at the far back of the house. The hallways were barely lighted, with open bulbs hanging on cords. The bathroom, in a very dark hallway, had fixtures that were thirty years out of date. It was cold in the winter when I frequently got up to study at 4 a.m. and I layered on extra heavy clothes. Even then I shivered until breakfast, which I usually skipped, and developed the habit of most college kids by having a Coke for that early morning "hit."

DON, LAURA, AND BROTHER-IN-LAW BUDDY WEBER
WITH LARGE CATCH IN PANAMA CITY, FLORIDA.

Medical classes ran all day and I often had dinner at a nearby cafeteria after a full day. The first year of intellectual work in a medical school class was daunting for me and still is for most freshmen. It was then and is expected that medical students operate quantitatively at a level three to four times as intense as any course I took in undergraduate school. This was not as difficult for me as for some of my classmates who went to less academically rigorous colleges. Birmingham Southern College had prepared me well.

Our medical school building was constructed of simple concrete blocks with a brick front. The classrooms and laboratories were austere, had open high ceilings, exposed pipes and electrical conduits. The halls were concrete block and all ceilings, even in the labs, were open. I was surprised, maybe even disappointed, by the surroundings in which we studied.

My first year in medical school was defined by the considerable pressure put upon us by the faculty. The first rude shock came in gross anatomy class when we were introduced to our cadaver. Few of us had had any experience with dead human bodies. The first day we were taken into the laboratory, a large, open room with twenty tables where cadavers were stored in closed cabinetry and popped up by a hinged mechanism for examination and dissection. The cadavers were not visible when not being studied. Four students were assigned to work with each cadaver. They had been preserved and disinfected in formaldehyde, and for the first six months of medical school, we all reeked from our daily dissection and anatomy classes.

We were expected to dissect each muscle, blood vessel and organ in the body and learn them in detail. About every three weeks we had exams where the faculty placed pins with tags in various anatomic structures and we were required to move from table to table throughout the twenty or so cadavers in a timed test, identifying each of the tagged structures and their function. The tests were frequent and caused a lot of anxiety. There was a one-minute time allotment for each decision and we were not allowed to put our hands on the cadaver or to move any structure. The longer we worked with the cadavers, though, the more they became like old friends. We joked about them, creating stories about what their lives might have been like.

We also attempted to determine why they died. Some of us named our cadavers—we called our female cadaver Ida the Large, for while she had a large body frame, she was gaunt, and we discovered the reason when we opened the abdomen. She had died of a large cancer. We often returned to the lab at night to work on our cadavers and study together. It would be correct to believe that it was ghoulish and a little frightening in that lab after midnight alone with all the cadavers. Alan Dimick, one of my fellow classmates at Birmingham Southern College, now in my medical school class, helped me a great deal with anatomy, so much that in the end I did better on the exams and earned the prize for being the top student in the anatomy course. I still cherish that certificate and thank him for getting me through the initial hurdles. During my junior year, I worked as a helper laboratory instructor in anatomy, where I learned even more of the structures of the body. I can still remember some of the pneumonics we used to remember names. For example to name the twelve cranial nerves we remembered "On Old Olympus thorny tops a Finn and German viewed some hops." The first letter of each word refers to a cranial nerve. I'll never forget them.

In the medical school curriculum today less time is spent teaching gross anatomy. While most medical students still dissect cadavers, much of their learning comes from computer images developed from cross sections of the body that have been developed with multi-slice imaging techniques, giving hundreds of slices across every aspect of the human body and using modern graphic techniques allowing it to be projected in many different images.

In addition to learning anatomic relationships, students learn how the body is viewed by x-ray, computer tomography, and magnetic resonance imaging, all important diagnostic tools. This leads to a better understanding of how structural elements of the body can be related to disease entities and treatment as the student progresses through his medical education. However, in my observations dealing with medical students in their advanced years and in their subsequent house staff training, I find that they know less gross anatomy; I remember more from the many hours of endeavor that I put into learning all of the structures and relationships of the human body in those labs than they learn from the new teaching techniques. I do not mean to imply that one method of teaching is better than the other. The continued evolution of newer teaching models for gross anatomy and other courses will no doubt allow more time for adding other scientific endeavors into the education of medical students.

Biochemistry was our other major course during the year's first semester. Day one brought another rude shock. Our instructor, Professor Wingo, asked us to look to our right and to our left, and told us that after a year one would be gone. It really didn't turn out this way but the scare went through the entire class. In biochemistry we learned a number of important metabolic processes, particularly the Krebs Cycle, which is how the body makes energy from sugars. Since 1955, the scientific understanding of energy metabolism has progressed extensively, but the Krebs Cycle is still the framework for understanding. We did learn a lot, in my mind, of useless information such as the composition of reindeer milk, and wondered why they would teach such trivia for something we would never use.

Finally, we studied our own body fluids. My laboratory partner was Helen Hallman, who was about ten years older than I and had been a practicing nurse for ten years. She was able to draw blood from me quite deftly, but she had poor veins and I sometimes had to attempt to stick her veins four or five times before getting blood. She winced with pain when I did this. I got better with more experience. She never complained. We also had to pass tubes through our noses down into our stomachs, and analyze the stomach fluids, a ghastly task. We were often our own guinea pigs. I'm sure that the lesson was, "Do it right the first time; you'll have less discomfort," which translates to more compassionate care for our patients.

The teaching of biochemistry to medical students has evolved even more dramatically than gross anatomy. The scientific advances in molecular biology and genetics have added immensely to the knowledge of cellular processes and organ functions. In many medical colleges these courses are no longer called biochemistry but bear titles of molecular biology, molecular genetics and integrated physiology. These courses are directed at coupling sub-cellular, cellular and organ function together in the integrated whole. It is in this area that the major advances in the teaching methods in colleges of medicine have evolved.

During the second semester, the main course was physiology. We learned the functions of all the vital organs and processes in the human body. This class was for several hours every day, five days a week, with a four-hour exam every Saturday. The lectures were very detailed and delivered in an exasperatingly fast pace for note taking. We also had extensive reading assignments in books that were five inches thick. This put tremendous pressure on all of us, and it was during this semester that I developed early morning stomach pain. Having heard about ulcers, I quickly made a self-diagnosis of ulcer disease and even convinced the student health doctor to do a GI series examination, an x-ray study where I had to drink a barium solution to outline for an x-ray the tissues of the stomach and intestines.

Today a doctor can use a gastroscope to take a direct look. The gastroscope was invented years after my test. My test was negative for an ulcer and he proclaimed that it was gastritis or inflammation of the stomach and might be related to my drinking a Coke every morning before class on an empty stomach and no breakfast. I guess he may have been right since the pain stopped after I quit drinking cokes, though I did miss the kick from the caffeine in the Cokes. This was and still is a habit of college students all over the country, to get their morning wake-up—a substitute for strong coffee. I have never taken a liking to coffee.

Another important course during the first year was neuroanatomy, a study of the structure and function of the nervous system. I attempted to master this course by reading the textbook and not attending the very boring lectures. In spite of cutting class to attend foreign movies at a nearby theater, I passed the exams. It was only later as a medical resident on a neurology service that I realized how little I really knew and wished I had attended the lectures. My neurology attending even said, "Don, I don't think you took neuroanatomy. Here is a textbook—brush up." I did and still have memories of my independent studies on the function of various parts of the brain.

Knowledge and understanding of the function of the nervous system and its relationship to bodily function has increased tremendously in the past fifty years. Neurophysiology, neuroanatomy, and neuropharmacology are now very important courses in the first year of medical school. Most of the concepts being taught in these disciplines have been developed since I was a medical student fifty years ago. New understanding of the function of the central nervous system is permitting the modern medical student to better grasp not only diseases of the brain but cognitive function, behavior and social interaction. No doubt the continuing development of concepts in this field will improve the medical profession's ability to deal with patients more effectively.

Because of the academic pressure, the entire class frequently got together on weekends for a party in the basement of a medical fraternity house. We managed to acquire alcohol from the biochemistry laboratory to spike a very potent punch. There was a great deal of binge drinking at these parties, and I have always attributed that to the intense stress of that first year in medical school. Today's medical students do not have the same level of stress that students had in my era because newer teaching models have evolved that deal more with learning than with fear of failure, which was intensely ingrained within medical students of fifty years ago. In addition, students now are somewhat older and many more of them are married; some even have families. There appears to be less weekend social interaction, and less binge drinking and irresponsible behavior than during my medical school days.

As the first year passed, I realized I was doing quite well in my classes and I finished at the top of my medical school class. During the first summer break I worked in the laboratory of Professor Wood doing organic chemistry experiments. A tall man with jet black hair, he usually did not arrive in the lab until about 11 a.m. By this time my medical school classmate and co-worker in the lab, Don Brice, and I had played eighteen holes of golf and had enough time in the lab to get it set up for the day. After Wood arrived we worked for a few hours, and then played more golf with him. Mostly we played golf.

At the start of the summer I did not have any golf clubs, so I went to a local pawn shop and found a reasonable set with a bag. It seemed a shame that a golfer had to pawn these nice clubs I bought, but I really enjoyed playing with them. We frequently played thirty-six holes a day at a local public course. Brice and I both saw great improvement in our golf games! Our National Science Foundation's sponsored research seemed a secondary matter that summer but it did ignite a desire in me to do more research. Our research that summer was to attempt to synthesize a new chemical compound, potentially useful as a drug.

Pathology was the most important course during our second year, and it lasted all year. This is a study of the diseases that occur in humankind. One of the hazards of a pathology course is imagining that you have almost every disease studied. This kept a student health physician quite busy as members of our class visited him frequently. After the first semester I was asked to be a member of a team to do postmortem exams (autopsies) for the professors who had a contract with the coroner. These were autopsies on patients whose families felt it important to determine family health tendencies, and sometimes they were from cases where the coroner had jurisdiction.

They were done at hospitals located within the region and almost all seemed to occur late at night, and I found it quite eerie to go do an autopsy on someone at one of these other, unfamiliar hospitals. Taking the bony cap off the brain with a circular saw and then removing the brain and putting it in a jar of formalin for preservation was particularly gruesome. I was never frightened, but a shudder did run down my back when someone opened a door unexpectedly during the course of an autopsy. I did a large number of these autopsies and was paid $100 for each. It was an educational experience and I learned a great deal of forensic pathology by doing the microscopic work on the tissue samples and writing the required reports, which were always overviewed and approved by a senior professor.

The second year of medical school passed quite quickly, with the second semester being devoted to an introduction to medicine as it affects patients, and an intense course in physical diagnosis. This course is the oral history taking and the art of physical diagnosis. My instructor, Ray Ledbetter, had a receding hairline and large ears. He was a postdoctoral fellow in cardiology and took me into the hospital late at night to do exams to hone my skills. His booming voice spoke comments that could be quite critical of me

After Wood arrived we worked for a few hours, and then played more golf with him. Mostly we played golf.

and of uncooperative patients. Ray was a severe taskmaster and worked me unmercifully. I was to examine patients and take their full medical history. These patients were indigent and frequently almost illiterate. I had to learn the new language and word usage of the black patients we examined.

One of the most difficult aspects of physical examination was listening to the heart, discerning the "lubs" and "dubs" of the heart sounds, particularly when they were interspersed with swishing sounds of murmurs and sometimes a series of extra sounds. Murmurs are sounds made by blood rushing through damaged heart valves, and can be detected with a stethoscope. Extra heart sounds also indicate damage to the heart muscle or a strain on it. This was quite difficult for a second-year medical student, although it seemed quite easy for Ledbetter, who was by this time a trained cardiologist. The exam of the abdomen was by palpation, or by using hands and fingers. It seemed much easier. We were also taught to do rectal and pelvic exams on these patients, and in contrast with patients' rights issues today, I feel certain that in those cases, no permission was sought from any of these patients.

The work was carried out at night in eerie exam rooms off the third floor of the Hillman

Hospital. After each of these long sessions I felt drained physically and emotionally. The poor patients must have felt the same from my long interrogation and exams. Today, models have been developed for almost all of the teaching, including recordings that a student listens to, learning to distinguish characteristics of various disease states of the heart, its sounds and murmurs. In addition, rectal and pelvic examinations are done on life-like models that resemble the body of a patient.

There are also interview techniques from recordings that have been made to simulate patients, by which the present-day medical student learns to take a history. While older physicians like me tend to denigrate these approaches, they are proving to be successful when the students are tested on their abilities. Unfortunately, as students progress through their medical school education and house staff training, they tend to rely much more on technology for imaging, sound recordings, and indirect measurement of various bodily functions, and some even tend to lose their ability to do careful histories and physical exams. I have observed this when taking morning report and teaching residents in the hospital setting.

At the end of the course, I invited Professor Ledbetter to have dinner with Laura and me at home as a thank-you for all that he had taught me. I really was grateful, and still remain so. Laura had baked a lemon meringue pie and dropped a spoon in it before he arrived, so she set about baking another one even after he arrived. This was our first dinner party for an instructor and Laura was nervous but wanted badly to please. In addition to the pie we had barbecued pork chops and mashed potatoes. Our apartment was small and our only eating area was an alcove as part of the kitchen. We huddled around a small Formica-covered table, seated on plastic-covered red chairs. To Laura's dismay, Ray and I discussed medicine. But as dinner progressed, the conversation changed to family relations and being from a large family, Ray understood Laura's and my anxieties. He praised every dish she prepared and made lovely conversation. His tutelage proved a benefit throughout my medical career, as I became very proficient at physical exams and diagnosis.

At the end of the second year, the University of Alabama teaching hospital, Hillman Hospital, did not fill its intern match group. The national intern match program is a program where each applicant lists his or her top choices and each hospital lists its top candidates. The choices are matched. Hillman Hospital was not considered a top choice nationally and did not fill its quota, which turned out to be somewhat of a benefit for some medical students.

Six of the top students finishing the second-year class were chosen to be interns, even while starting their third-year medical clerkships. I was chosen to be an intern. Hillman Hospital was the site for our clinical teaching. It had been the old Jefferson County Indigent Hospital prior to becoming the major teaching hospital for the College of Medicine.

Hillman was fourteen stories tall, built of brick, and had long, poorly lighted halls. It had 600 beds, 400 of them designated for the indigent and 200 for private patients. It had a very busy emergency room where more than 200 patients were seen daily. There were segregated wards, and my area of assignment was the black female ward in the indigent part of the hospital on the third floor. While I had experienced interaction with black females from the maids who had taken care of me in childhood, I had not been exposed to illiterate black females with a language almost their own.

Having grown up in the South, I didn't find the idea of segregated wards offensive or even strange, and around the corner on the same floor was the white female ward. Patients were treated no differently, though there were two distinct wards. I sometimes thought the attendings were spending more time on the black male ward—perhaps it was because these were frequently our sickest patients. Learning to communicate with this different culture was almost like learning another language. They would refer to "having the miseries," which I learned was their view of pain. They used the vernacular terms for all body functions and actions such as "My bowels are locked," "My heart's 'bout to jump outda my chest," and "I can't shit for a week."

The wards were made up of several units of eight-to-twelve beds with only curtains drawn around them. Many of the admissions came from the emergency room, had extremely high blood pressure, and many had had strokes. In addition to the new patients, we had to care for the patients who were quite ill. At nights we covered for each other and my responsibility was to cover both the male and female wards. The nights were quite long, with many of the admissions occurring at night, and frequently there was not even time for a catnap. We did have the supervision of a senior resident, and our duty included making rounds with an attending physician each day, when we made presentations of the case and received instructions about patient management. However, much of the management went on during the night and came from reading a textbook of medicine and the Merck Manual.

During those busy nights, I drew on experiences learned in my life around the Mulberry River, that is, to stay safe I had to keep focused on the central issues. For example, when critically ill patients were admitted, I knew to act quickly as I had learned about avoiding danger from the water moccasins on the river. While I thought I already knew a great deal of medicine, coming up with treatment plans for a wide variety of emergency problems was quite a challenge. We were allowed to do a great many things on our own, such as our own lymph node biopsies, bone marrows, and even minor surgeries. We had to do most of our own lab work, and had to draw all of our own bloods since phlebotomy technicians were not available at that time. This twelve-week rotation was really very hard work and trying for me to see so many people dying when I was so young. It was not uncommon to have more than one death each night we were on duty. On the other hand, we knew we were providing these patients the only medical care they could get.

Harrison suspected a blood vessel lesion and asked the patient if he had ever had a knife wound. The patient told of an ice pick being driven into the back of his knee.

In today's medical atmosphere, the experience I received as a third-year medical student is not possible, even for a first-year resident on an internal medicine service. The requirements placed upon attendings on such a service now require hands-on care by the attending, who must write a note each day in the chart and be on call or available to take care of such critically ill patients. In those days there were really no intensive care units and patients as ill as those we were caring for are taken care of today in intensive care units where they are administered to by a new genre of physician, a *hospitalist.* These are physicians who do not maintain an office practice but only see patients in the hospital and usually care for critically ill patients on a unit round the clock. Thus the kind of experience I received as a third-year medical student no longer exists until a trainee is at least a third-year resident in internal medicine.

Another memorable time of my medical school career was being on a surgery rotation with Champ Lyons. He was chairman of the department, and did not have an intern because of the intern shortage at Hillman. We not only operated all day but frequently operated at night too. I remember a night when we had repaired a leaking aneurysm of an aortic graft that had been done by Michael DeBakey of Houston. This occurred soon after aortic grafts became available and this patient was one of the first from Birmingham to get one. He was a tall, thin man who had a midline abdominal incision from his prior surgery. His abdomen was filled with blood when we opened. After lots of suctioning and two blood transfusions the leak of the aneuryism was found and in ten minutes repaired. We finished at 4 a.m. and Lyons called DeBakey, where it was 3 a.m. and said, "Mike, we did you a great favor tonight."

I became his acting intern because of the shortage of interns at the hospital, scrubbing with him on everything from thyroidectomies, mitral valve surgery, colon and stomach surgery and even on one occasion he pulled a tooth, demonstrating the capabilities of a well-trained general surgeon. I did well and became one of his favorites, but he was a frightening taskmaster. He gave me an A+ grade for my surgery rotation. With a name like "Champ" one could expect much expertise, and his tall, physical stature and graying hair matched his real name—"Champ." It may be hard to believe, but this was his real name.

I was very fortunate to be chosen to do research with Tinsley Harrison, the chairman of the department of medicine, and founder of the four-year school at the University of Alabama. I was often invited to see his private patients with him. He was not related to me, even though our families had come from the same area in south Alabama. From the beginning of my third year of medical school, however, he chose to mentor me and urged me to work with him on research projects. He was a small man who was balding, had big ears, and very thin, whitish hair. He smoked incessantly, and later died of emphysema. Of all the clinicians I have observed, he had the most wonderful way with patients. He sat on the bedside to talk with them, and then did an expert exam. As he instructed patients at the time of their discharge, he dictated into a dictaphone and sent them a typed copy of the instructions so there would be no misunderstanding. I learned a great deal about physician-patient interaction from him and even learned to dictate instructions to patients.

As a teacher, Harrison was at his best in a clinical conference. We had conferences with the medical and surgical staffs every Saturday morning, which is common still today in teaching hospitals. These conferences were attended by all of the faculty, the residents and the students on clinical services. The toughest cases of the week are presented and discussed. Tinsley almost always made the right diagnosis, and in a sense, put the surgeons on the defensive.

One case I remember was a patient who did not have a heart murmur but instead a blood infection thought only to occur as endocarditis on damaged heart valves. Harrison suspected a blood vessel lesion and asked the patient if he had ever had a knife wound. The patient told of an ice pick being driven into the back of his knee. Harrison found a murmur at the earlier wound site and made the diagnosis of infection in the connection between the artery and vein known as a fistula. It was a surprise to everyone.

Research and academic medicine were a passion for Tinsley. He always encouraged those whom he judged to have talent for an academic career to participate in research, and through that consider a career in academic medicine. He frequently offered research opportunities to students at the top of the class as enticement. Tinsley had just edited the most widely used medical text in the world, *Harrison's Principles of Internal Medicine.*

His research was in cardiology and we focused on recognition of coronary heart disease.

I always regarded him as my most significant medical school teacher and an individual who influenced my future career greatly. He spent hours telling me the virtues of an academic career. He often said when we were working late at night, "There is no greater calling than to be a physician; as a practitioner one can help one patient, as a researcher hundreds, but as a teacher one can train the next generation." His admonition to become an academician took place in front of the portrait of his son in the hallway of his home. This son was killed in World War II and did not become the physician that Tinsley Harrison wished. The story he was telling was almost, to me, as a son, in view of my Harrison name. This had a profound influence on me as I began to contemplate my career path.

Many years later and after his death, I was asked to be the primary speaker at a building being dedicated at the University of Alabama-Birmingham Medical Center to Tinsley Harrison. I was sorting through my reprints recently and came across the tribute I paid to him. I cherished my relationship with Tinsley Harrison who had such a profound impact on me, as I did, in fact, enter an academic career.

Another meaningful experience during my fourth year was to be an acting intern in the emergency room for a month. Every conceivable human tragedy could be seen during this rotation. Spending several hours sewing up a hundred knife slashes on an elderly grandmother inflicted by a drunken son, delivering babies of 13-year-olds on a stretcher in the emergency room, and dealing with patients with multiple gunshot wounds were all in a day's work. I remember a Sunday, trying to sew up a number of lacerations on the face of a black man who was drunk and totally uncooperative. I was afraid I would damage his eye because he was violently shaking his head. Finally, in desperation I placed a suture through each of the pinnas of his ears and tied them to the pillow so he could not move. I finished the stitches, then freed him.

By necessity, police were always stationed in the emergency room. Two men who had been brought in after a brawl were placed in the same room. When I entered to start to evaluate them they lunged at each other with me in the middle. I ran and the police entered. When I was called back they were quiet, but each had another cut on his head with a large bump. I now had to order skull films. The police reported that the two had bumped their heads in the struggle to get them into the police car. This emergency room experience helped to season me for my internship.

Present-day emergency rooms differ from my experience but still are a great melting pot for those from all stratas of life who come with their critical illnesses. Many people would not come to the emergency room if they had adequate medical coverage in another setting.

For those without physicians, this is the care of last resort. However, emergency rooms are extremely important for those suffering from critical illness and accidents.

The emergency room in a large medical center sees hundreds of patients each day and has physicians on call in almost all specialties. They are equipped to rapidly assess the need of patients for more intense care, to carry out imaging studies, and to send them directly to operating rooms when this is required. Most emergency rooms in large metropolitan centers experience times when they are overburdened and frequently rely on periods of diversion. For a defined length of time they send patients to other centers for care for critical emergencies that arrive on their doorsteps. In the emergency room setting, a doctor learns to react quickly to critical issues, and those who become emergency room physicians have the ability to do this almost unconsciously.

An indelible memory from my clinical rotations was seeing patients with polio in iron lungs, large tubular machines to help them breathe. This invention helped some patients with polio survive. Not long afterwards positive pressure respirators were invented to supplant these large machines. They have continued to be modified and now are small enough to be even transportable. These were first known as "Bird" respirators, named after the inventor.

Our social life during medical school and my clinical rotations was quite limited because of the time commitments on students. We did, however, have class parties, and I made occasional fishing trips to the Gulf of Mexico with Laura's brother-in-law, Buddy Weber. During my senior year, on one trip, we caught enough red snapper to feed my entire class at a fish cookout. Another time we had the great fortune of catching 144 king mackerel fish in a single afternoon, and to top it off, I caught an eighty-four pound barracuda. After one hour of trying to land him, I wished he would get off my line! He did not and I ended the affair by landing him, though fully exhausted.

While I studied, Laura worked days, did our laundry, and cooked for us at night. Near the end of my third year at medical school, she unexpectedly became pregnant. We had agreed to delay our family until after residency, so we were both unprepared for the consequences. She had to hide her pregnancy because if it had been recognized at work, she would have immediately had to stop working, and we certainly needed the income. It was the business custom of the time to have women stop working once they became pregnant. Even though Laura's pregnancy was unexpected, we both were thrilled to feel the fetal movements.

As the pregnancy progressed she became increasingly larger, but all evidence of fetal movement ceased. Laura had polyhydramiosis resulting from a malformed fetus. During a normal pregnancy there is the continued exchange of fluids in the uterus around the fetus. In polyhydramiosis, fluids are continually added to the pregnant uterus but are not secreted from it. This results in tremendous fluid accumulations of up to three gallons, and the woman's lower abdomen swelling to several times larger than with a normal pregnancy.

At about eight months, on her visit to her obstetrician, she received a tremendous shock. She was told in a very harsh tone that she should forget this pregnancy, that it would be best if she aborted soon or she would have to have it surgically removed. I had not accompanied her on this visit, but her niece Jane had gone with her. The harshness of the physician's tone and the message he delivered upset Laura a great deal. I felt awful about this, first for not being with her, and second hoping that I would never deal with a patient in this manner. It was difficult to console Laura, and over the next several days she broke down and sobbed off and on. After several more days she went into labor on her own and delivered a stillborn, malformed fetus. It was a relief that she did not have to have surgery to remove the fetus; however, this was a major trauma for both of us and left an emotional scar. Laura's recovery took several weeks and it was only the knowledge that we could have other children that saw us through.

Today a pregnancy would not be allowed to progress to this stage, since there is ultrasound to distinguish any abnormality in a fetus. This procedure uses sound waves, which can be sent into the body and project images of the fetus in the uterus onto a screen. There is also sophisticated technology to monitor the fetal heartbeat to determine if it is abnormal or not, and whether more frequent and higher-risk prenatal care is warranted. So the question of polyhydramiosis can be diagnosed early, and if the fetus has a lethal abnormality, the pregnancy can be terminated. As to the way such information is presented to patients, I believe there has been a major improvement over the years of my involvement with medicine and teaching. It could be that this was just one uncaring physician. He was one of my teachers, but I had little respect for the way he dealt with Laura and his other patients after this event.

Just as we were getting over the loss of Laura's pregnancy, her mother became critically ill and died during a cold December before my graduation from medical school. I had made her diagnosis of acute leukemia about six months earlier when I was asked by her to feel the lymph nodes in her neck. In the 1950s, adequate treatment for her type of leukemia had not been developed, but it can be cured today with modern chemotherapy. This was another emotional trauma for Laura and me. Laura was heartbroken and grieved for several weeks.

She was the baby of the family and was quite close to her mother. Her mom, Lillian, had always been very kind to me and supported Laura in her choice to date and marry me. I had great respect for her, knowing she had raised seven children.

During that period near the end of medical school I was assigned to the OB ward. The wards were segregated but as students we delivered babies on both the black and white wards. It seems that most babies arrive at night and one of my best teachers was the night head nurse on the black female ward. She had great sympathy for medical students and their lack of sleep, and on the midnight to 8 a.m. shift she arranged for us to sleep on a gurney that transported patients back and forth. She would keep close watch over the labor room where six patients in the later stages of labor were all together. The patients were in narrow iron stead beds separated by pulled curtains. There always seemed to be the smell of urine everyplace. The sound of constant panting moans and groans emanated from the labor room. Some called out, "Oh, Jesus, help me," and "Lord, I don't want another baby," while others yelled, "My God ---, Oh shit, oh shit."

These chants went on and on and Martha, the head nurse, seemed to know just when one of the patients should be taken to the delivery room. She would take them to the delivery room, put them up on stirrups, drape them, and then wake us from our gurneys to come in for the delivery. There was no general anesthesia being used but we did episiotomies with local anesthetics, and then either delivered the baby directly or used forceps. There was much grunting and screaming with pain as we completed the deliveries. During one such delivery I asked Martha how many babies she had helped medical students deliver. After a short pause she said, "More than 10,000." She had been the head nurse on this ward for more than ten years, and there were approximately 1,000 deliveries per year on the ward for each shift.

There have been major changes in OB services over the fifty years since my graduation from medical school. Caesarian sections were rare in my time, but they have become much more common, and in many instances in some areas of the country, more than thirty percent of deliveries have been by caesarian section. I have always been concerned that this represents the obstetrician's desire to deliver during the 8-5 p.m. hours of the day and that some women request it themselves.

Today most women have a form of anesthesia known as epidural or caudal anesthesia, where drugs are infiltrated into the nerve supplying the uterus and pelvis so that the pain that they feel is greatly reduced. Also, episiotomies are not routine anymore as they were in the days of my medical school training. Both infant and maternal mortalities have been reduced over the past fifty years quite significantly, but in the U.S. the rate of fetal mortality is still higher than many other developed countries, so there remains much more room for improvement, particularly in prenatal care of those unmarried minorities who are often very young.

———————————— ⊱ ⊰ ————————————

Near the end of medical school it was time to apply for internship and residency. Champ Lyons was pushing me for the Massachusetts General Hospital and Tinsley Harrison was pushing me for the Peter Bent Brigham Hospital, together known as the Harvard hospitals. Both were alumni of these institutions. The Harvard hospitals at that time had invited interviews on only two days in January. I flew to Boston on my first commercial flight with a fever of 102 degrees and went to the three interviews in Boston. I was on the house OB service at the time and luckily, my resident agreed to cover for me and let me go to Boston. To repay the trade I needed to work an extra weekend on OB for him and I delivered twenty-one babies in that day period, even thinking for a short time about an OB residency.

My interviews in Boston in many ways were humiliating and I wondered if it was that I was coming from what they considered to be an inferior medical college. At the end of my interview with George Thorn, chief at Peter Bent Brigham Hospital, I was told, "Son, don't feel badly when you don't get this internship. We sometimes have positions open as a post-doctoral fellow," implying that I might reapply at the Peter Bent Brigham Hospital after my internship and residency. I was crushed by this hint at rejection.

I also interviewed at the Massachusetts General Hospital, where the interview took a strange turn. It consisted of two levels. The first was with young junior faculty in a dark office with lots of bookshelves and a collection of pictures of great physicians who had served at the Massachusetts General Hospital. I was asked if I could identify any of them and tell what contributions they had made to medicine. Regrettably, I did not know a single one, but, I did manage to answer some of the questions I was asked. I was quite surprised to be invited to return for the second level of interviews with the senior staff, where we would be interviewed in groups of six. The questions in the second interview were not about medicine but about ethical issues designed to raise controversy among the six of us being interviewed as a group. One question was that old story we've all heard many times, "You are out for a boat ride in the ocean with a woman friend and a fellow doctor, neither of whom could swim. A storm comes up, the boat is capsized, and you can save only one. Which one would you save and why?"

There were many similar kinds of questions, and at the end of the interview we were asked what our thoughts were, about how we viewed the interview. Sam Barondes, the number one student from Columbia University, stated that the panel had learned nothing about us and the whole interview was a waste. Sam later told me that when he was back at Columbia the following day, he was called into the office of the chief of medicine and told that he was rude at the interview and that Massachusetts General Hospital might not consider anyone from Columbia to be an intern for several years. While I felt much like Sam did, I was too intimidated and felt the less said the better—and so responded with a simple, "I appreciate the fact that you interviewed me."

Washington University and Barnes Hospital in St. Louis were reputed to offer an excellent internship, so I took the time to also make that visit. There I was treated much more kindly and felt I made a good impression. Then it became time to fill out the card for the intern match. The top match of the candidate for internship and the hospital selection list determine one's placement. This system is still in place today, and "match day" is a celebratory event on medical school campuses. By this day I was beginning to favor staying at Alabama where I was well respected and where I was well within my comfort zone. I still felt the humiliation of the Boston interviews and at the time was working on a busy surgical service at the Hillman Hospital. On this service you lived in the hospital since you were always on call. Surgical procedures frequently went on all night.

On the evening before I was to turn in my match requests, Laura came to the hospital to have dinner with me and talk about my final decision. We discussed the choice over dinner in the hospital dining room and I told her I had already marked my card with the number one choice as Alabama. After considerable discussion, in which she pointed out that no one would ever know if I was turned down by the Harvard hospitals and Washington University, and that I should have the courage to list them first, if indeed they were a better choice for me at the time. I knew I needed to expand my medical training to broader horizons than those that would be available to me in Birmingham. She told me to mark the card to list the Brigham first, Mass General second, Barnes third and Alabama fourth.

While we both thought that I might only get the internship in Birmingham, Laura had helped me make what would turn out to be one of the most important decisions in my life. She helped me take the first calculated risk of my career. Up till then I had forgotten one of the important lessons I had learned on the Mulberry River. The river frequently became a raging torrent after heavy rains. I had to learn just when it was safe to take my flat-bottomed boat out to run trot lines or hunt for frogs. If I judged wrong, the current would take me far downriver, and without a motor I couldn't get back. I had learned to take the calculated risks, and I was doing so again.

As the date for the match announcement approached, Laura and I both instinctively felt we would be staying in Birmingham. I clearly remember the day when I heard the results. I was still working as an intern in surgery with Champ Lyons when a nurse walked into the operating room and said there was a telegram for me from the Peter Bent Brigham Hospital. It was my invitation to be an intern and the hospital wanted to know instantly if I would accept. Before I could answer Champ Lyons said, "Tell them by telegram he accepts with pleasure." From this point forward, Laura's wisdom, support, and encouragement were vital in the joint decisions we made about my medical opportunities.

After that there was considerable celebration, but in our moments alone Laura and I felt uncomfortable and nervous, since we had never lived outside of Alabama. The faculty of the college were delighted that someone from their college was accepted at a Harvard teaching hospital. Medical school ended, I graduated at the top of my class, an accomplishment I maintained for all four years, and I was now about to embark on a much bigger challenge—the medical world in the heavily academic atmosphere of Boston and a Harvard teaching hospital.

Over the past fifty years there have been tremendous changes in medical education. Many of these are the result of the advances in technology, molecular biology, genetics, bioengineering, and the ever-important sophistication in patient imaging. And as important as these things are, also important is the swing in our attitude toward patient care. Because of changes in societal values, students today do not experience the fears and anxieties that we were exposed to in our training. They have an expectation of lesser hours with books and higher quality of the presentations made to them by faculty. On the other hand, they do not gain the practical experience at the early stages that we did in our training. It is still questionable to me whether, taken in the whole, they are better equipped to be physicians at the end of their training than we were. I somehow doubt it.

Medical school had been a "growing up" experience which ignited in me a desire to be an academic physician and a willingness to take the risk to do so. Even though I had not attended a medical school with a reputation of Harvard or Johns Hopkins, I soon came to appreciate that the quality of my teachers and my training gave me the background to be competitive in any setting. In 1958 when I finished medical school, the University of Alabama Medical School was an early stage entry into medical training. There had been only eight classes since the first graduation of the Class of 1946 in 1950 and my class in 1958. In its favor, it had great leadership which continued consistently over several decades. It was beginning to grow in stature, reputation, and in the quality of its students and graduates, and over the past four decades. Today, UAB Medical School is one of the top-ranked programs. Its research funding ranks it twelfth nationally and portions of its campus now cover fifty-five square blocks in the south part of Birmingham. It is a great research and training facility and I am proud to be one of its graduates.

A *finally!* REAL DOCTOR

After graduation I took the exam for my medical license for the state of Alabama and we packed our car and a rented trailer with all of our worldly goods and even hung a mop on the back.

We drove away to the goodbyes and good wishes of our family and made our way by car to Boston, where I was about to start my internship. Laura tells a story of my anxiety and agitation, driving many miles before stopping and not allowing her to eat lunch or even dinner. She swears she thought she would starve. Though I don't remember it that way, to this day we rarely take a car trip that I am not reminded of it. Laura's been known to pack a snack bag for long trips.

PETER BENT BRIGHAM HOSPITAL IN 1959.

The second night we stopped someplace off the Pennsylvania Turnpike. Laura ate a hefty meal but I was so tired I went to sleep without eating. The next day I got lost trying to find my way through New York City to the Connecticut thruway to Boston. On arriving in Boston, we lost our way several times trying to find our apartment. We had friends in Boston that I had met during my Brigham intern interviews who found an apartment for us. Friends who lived in the same building helped us, and we got moved in. There was not much time to get settled, for I was to go to work the next morning at the Peter Bent Brigham Hospital.

We had internship orientation, then given the afternoon off before commencing patient care. On a Tuesday morning, June 23, 1958, I began my internship at the Peter Bent Brigham Hospital as a licensed medical doctor. The designation of "intern" has been eliminated today, but to me the substitution of "postgraduate year (PGY) one" is not nearly as descriptive.

The Peter Bent Brigham Hospital was built in 1912 when infectious diseases were the greatest concern. The building was only three stories tall and there were long corridors between wards, which were far apart to stop the spread of infections. Tuberculosis and typhoid fever were among the most deadly in the early 1900s but were by 1958 only rarely seen. The lobby had a bust of Peter Bent Brigham, a local Bostonian businessman, who had given the money to build the hospital. Faculty offices were on the second floor above the lobby. There was an outpatient wing where we held clinics and a below-ground emergency room. Radiology services were in the basement and intern sleeping quarters were in the attic.

There were tennis courts between the wards where we could play and take our calls. The hospital was located on the edge of Roxbury, a poor white neighborhood in Boston. At afternoon tea that first day and frequently thereafter, we were assured by the chief of medicine, George Thorn, that we were extraordinary people and had been selected from hundreds and that we would all become famous in our own rights. This was different from my experience as a candidate at the intern interviews, and appeared difficult to believe. I went through my first week of internship with a senior resident who only occasionally oversaw my patient care. I normally had a case load of about twenty very ill patients.

Life at the Brigham was not made for a married man, for we were on duty every other night, which meant we spent the night at the hospital, with very little sleep if any. Some scheduling concessions were made for us to have Monday and Wednesday night on duty, be off duty Thursday and Friday, and then on again Saturday and Sunday. The next week alternating, on Tuesday night, on Thursday and Friday night, and then off Saturday and Sunday. This seemed humane in some ways for we at least had every other weekend off. Unfortunately we had to work till noon on Saturday, and then if I'd been on duty the two previous days, I usually went home and immediately fell asleep on the floor or on the couch. Laura accepted this even though it was quite restrictive for our personal and social life. Sundays sometimes allowed us some unstructured time to readjust to the harsh schedule.

Our monthly stipend of $25 also put a crimp in our lifestyle. We could not afford many social activities. It was quite difficult for those of us who were married living out of the hospital, for we had rent to pay, a car to maintain, and other expenses. We did have free laundry and food at the hospital, and could invite our wives to have lunch with us on Sunday when we were on duty. Laura knew she needed to work to support us, and soon after I started internship, Laura began working at the Brigham Hospital as a secretary to the chief resident, Buris Boshell, and one of the junior faculty, George Cahill.

During this early period Laura and I were both homesick but we were also busy adapting to a new environment. Boston driving was hair-raising; parking at our apartment was even more difficult. I felt ambivalent about being away from my mother—both missing her and relieved that I had escaped her influence on my life. Now I was 1,500 miles away.

In the past fifty years, things have certainly changed for medical intern and residency training. Rather than $600 per year the starting pay is $32,000 to $35,000 per year, with increases as each year one becomes more senior. Most programs require the physician to be on duty and in the hospital only every fourth night and there are often one or two months of electives, with no required night duty. In many states laws have been enacted to limit the hours a resident can work to eighty hours per week. There is no longer the concept of "the iron man." This was a term used in teaching hospitals for those who could work forty-eight hours without sleep and still function.

My intern group consisted of twelve of us with quite diverse backgrounds. The person I alternated nights and weekends with was Samuel Barondes, who had been one of the students I interviewed with at Massachusetts General. He was the son of a rabbi from Brooklyn, New York. That, combined with my being a "redneck" from Alabama, made us a unique team, and over the years we became quite close. He introduced me to many good books and a good deal of culture, while I introduced him to some ways of the South.

Having come from New York City, Sam had had little exposure to southerners and he seemed to be inclined to think that we had little of the education and culture that someone who grew up in New York would have. He may have been right, and one of his missions was to introduce me to new ideas, particularly regarding segregation as one of the evils of the South. He prompted me to read more widely and frequently brought books to me from his personal library. Sam had a receding hairline with wavy black hair and walked and talked rapidly. He was a true intellectual who tolerated the lack of intellectual discussion poorly. I had some of these same traits but was less forthright with them. On the other hand, Sam never seemed to have any prejudice against me or the other two fellow interns who had also grown up in the South. He had a desire to do research, and during our second year, we worked together on a project. We spent three days at Yale University learning a new technique for measuring immunologic activity and then applied it to patients on the medical service.

As interns, we were quite competitive, yet in a friendly way. Martin Cline, who was at the top of the class at Harvard Medical School, was the most competitive. He seemed to know the names of all the obscure medical syndromes and when we made rounds as a group, he would point at patients and provide the name of some obscure medical condition in the attempt to outclass all the rest of us. We made a habit of frequently checking up on his diagnostic acumen and unusually named syndromes and found out that there were frequent mistakes.

Once Marty Cline saw one of my patients with an extremely active tremor and suggested that the patient had Huntington's chorea. I knew that the patient had no family history of this disease. Marty had taken the stance that since Huntingon's chorea was frequently seen in a population in Boston that this is what this patient had. Huntington's chorea is a progressive neurologic disease that is inherited as a dominant genetic characteristic, with other members of the family always being involved. My diagnosis was an advanced stage of paralysis agitans, known as parkinsonism. Parkinsonism also has a tremor and later may have more neurological degeneration, while Huntington's, accompanied by progressive mental deterioration and physical debility, usually leads to premature death at around age 35 or 40. We were correct, and to Marty's chagrin, we gloated over telling him. This patient improved with medications and was discharged.

In some way I felt responsible for this young man's death since I had not detected a blood clot in his leg.

Both Laura and I found it difficult to understand the dialect the Bostonians were speaking; conversely, they found it quite difficult to understand our southern accent. Over the three years in Boston our accent mellowed and we spoke some words like a Bostonian. We did not keep our slow southern twang and we stopped using the "r" and sounded like true blood Bostonians.

There were a number of things about Peter Bent Brigham Hospital that even after more than forty years stand out in my mind. Thirty patients or so would be on large wards with only curtains separating them. Open wards like this do not exist in any hospital today, even those affiliated with large city public charities. The wards were not connected above ground but there was a basement area connecting the units, and in winter that turned out to be convenient as we moved from one unit to the other to stay out of the snow.

Internship was hard work and a challenge. We drew all of our own bloods, did much of our own lab work, did all of our own procedures and attended many conferences. We were well supervised, and had as attendings many famous doctors, some of whom later won a Nobel Prize. We wore starched white uniforms, with the house staff in short coats and the attendings in long white coats.

Although my internship required a lot of hard work it provided a great opportunity for learning. Our attendings were extremely knowledgeable, our senior residents were at their peak with medical knowledge and the faculty was always encouraging us to visit the library.

The senior residents were very helpful in a crisis. I remember one tragic event which, when I recall it, keeps me now from being too optimistic about the potential outcome of a patient in the hospital. I had a young patient, a 16-year-old football star from Malden, Massachusetts, who was on my service and recovering from an episode of pneumonia. On the evening prior to discharge he was visited by about fifteen members of his family and friends from Malden. As they were leaving I gleefully told them he had made a great recovery and would be going home the next day. Less than one hour later I was called because he had collapsed in the bathroom. We made a valiant effort to resuscitate him but he died from a pulmonary embolus, a blood clot that traveled from his leg to his lung, which was revealed on the autopsy a day later.

I was so distraught that I could not call the family, who had not yet even gotten home, to tell of this tragic death. I relied on the senior resident on call that night, Saul Rosenberg, to come and comfort me, and with his help I mustered up the courage and called. This remains one of the most difficult medical calls that I have had to make in my career.

Perhaps it was only because I was young and not accustomed to such sudden tragedies, but my identification with this young man was so strong that it made this event something I will always remember. In some way I felt responsible for this young man's death since I had not detected a blood clot in his leg. However, at that time we had only the physical exam to do so. Over the past several decades, machines which use ultrasound have been developed to detect alterations in blood flow in the legs of patients who are at bed rest for a period of time as a warning sign for having a pulmonary embolus. Patients at risk for a blood clot, such as this young man was, having been in bed for a week, are given agents to thin their blood and inhibit clotting. Today, though, it is unlikely that a doctor would keep a 16-year-old in bed for a week, and not consider the possibility of a blood clot in the leg.

Another thing I also remember about several cases where death was imminent, was calling the priest to administer the last rites to the patient. At the Peter Bent Brigham Hospital, we were asked to call the priest when any of our Catholic patients were considered terminally ill. Our priest, Father Joseph, was a jolly fellow who frequently joined us in the dining room for our 11 p.m. late supper, which was available on nights we stayed in the hospital. Father Joseph loved to eat, even the high-fat, high-caloric food we were being fed, and it certainly showed since he weighed about 250 pounds, and his collar seemed to fit quite tightly around his neck.

On the other hand, he was a jolly fellow and carried on very animated conversations with us at these nightly sessions. He loved to engage us in conversation, and of course, we loved to challenge him on such questions as, "Why is the Catholic Church so opposed to birth control?"—a new and hot topic of that day. I remember one of his comments, "You young fellows shouldn't worry too much about this question. I expect in two decades they will be selling condoms with the Pope's picture on them." Of course, this hasn't happened and the Catholic Church continues to oppose any form of birth control. However, our relationship with Father Joseph continued to be quite cordial.

The first year went well, with a couple of very interesting rotations outside the Brigham. One was at the Robert Breck Brigham, a specialized hospital for patients with arthritis located on the hill overlooking Roxbury. The patients were chronically ill and did not have emergencies, so we could sleep at home and be on call. The food was quite good as compared to the awful food at the Brigham and our wives could join us for dinner in the evening.

The other unique rotation was as the medical consult to care for the medical conditions for the Boston Lying-in Hospital where we took care of many diabetics, hypertensives, and patients with heart failure who were pregnant and needed prenatal care. It was the upscale OB hospital where the Cabots and Lodges had their babies. The year went by quite quickly, or so it seemed, as we were learning to be doctors as well as being exposed to the exciting and stimulating cutting edge of medicine. I realized quickly in my internship that I was in the right place.

About three months into the year we were asked if we wanted to be considered for first-year residency at Peter Bent Brigham. I had considered moving to the Mass General Hospital for my first-year residency, but given only about a day or two to decide, I chose to remain a first-year resident at the Brigham. To this day I wonder what effect this had on my career—I wanted to be affiliated with the best of both top institutions and thought a year at the Massachusetts General Hospital would put my career on an accelerated trajectory.

We had one tragedy in our group. Bob Gilman and I played golf on the day after we completed our internship, as a way of celebration. He left that evening to drive to a wedding in Syracuse, New York, with his fiancée. He had an accident on the New York throughway and was killed quite suddenly. The car was only slightly damaged but he was thrown out and hit his head. This was before there were seat belts in cars, which surely could have prevented the tragedy. This put a real pall over any celebration we all had for the end of our internship. During that year we made new friends but missed our families, Laura more than I. We also missed the close relationships we had established during medical school. We had finally become totally independent, but I still felt ambivalent about leaving our families.

A few new people joined us during the first year of residency at the Brigham. One fellow from Birmingham, Alabama, Richard Russell, became a close friend. He had graduated from Vanderbilt, and had been a physician in the Korean War zone before coming back to become a first-year resident at the Brigham. First-year residency included a four-month rotation at the West Roxbury Veterans Hospital. Taking care of an all-male unit, some of whom had chronic illness due to their military service, provided other medical challenges. For example, some had missing limbs, as well as ulcers, kidney failure, or heart disease.

Driving the ten miles out to West Roxbury when I was on this service in winter, I learned to manipulate the car and drive in the snow for the first time in my life. At West Roxbury we were only on call every fourth night, while at the Brigham as junior residents we were on call every other night. During the junior residency year we were exposed to internationally known doctors because we managed their patients on the private service.

Some of these included John Merrill, who had done the first twin kidney transplants; George Thorn, a renowned endocrinologist and Samuel Levine, one of the outstanding cardiologists, a contemporary colleague of Paul Dudley White. During these years we also managed outpatients and had night clinics. We also staffed the emergency room for this area of Boston. On slow nights a surgery resident, Bob Goldwin, and I reviewed past medical records and collected enough data for a publication. By the end of our first year residency, we had become excellent physicians and probably knew as much about medicine as many practicing physicians.

JOY OF FAMILY

The social life and challenges in Boston related to living in a crowded city. We lived in the Back Bay area at a time when the neighborhood was deteriorating. The building was quite old and the entire area was a series of apartment buildings. Most had not been updated since the 1930s when they were built.

One of the redeeming features was a large park with the beautiful gardens, the Boston Commons, which almost surrounded the entire Back Bay area. We experienced a number of interesting and challenging episodes during our first year of living in this area, which was largely inhabited by students at the various colleges and trainees at the hospitals throughout the Boston area. Traffic was horrible, streets were narrow, and, not coming from a large city, we frequently got lost.

HAYMARKET SQUARE, OPEN MARKET, BOSTON.

Some of the stories of interest in our lives during that first year relate to people we met, how we went about surviving on such a paltry income, and how we were introduced to some new cultural activities. One of the interesting patient contacts I made was with Jimmy Ortez, which led to my introduction to a shopping market. He owned a meat market at Haymarket Square, which was an old European-style outdoor market. He encouraged me to call in orders for meat, which he would specially prepare for us and which I could pick up on Saturday. I soon found that at Haymarket Square on Saturday afternoon was where I could find many bargains. There were whole crates of strawberries, large amounts of bananas and cheese, and other things in excess because if they could not be sold on Saturday, they would be discarded. They were available at low prices if one was willing to bargain hard.

I soon acquired a large grey parka coat and coveralls and found myself going to Haymarket Square on many Saturday afternoons to buy a large quantity of vegetables and fruit and bring them back to distribute them to other house staff members living in our building. I was known to find the best bargains, and many times still do today. This activity reminded me of my days of doing the purchasing for the motel in Alabama. The effort was greatly appreciated by my neighbors, who paid me in cash. It's that "challenge thing" again, that I enjoy: the river, the woods, and here I enjoyed the challenge of finding the best bargains for all of us living well below the poverty level.

Our building was an ancient one. The laundry was in the cold and dark basement, and the building was managed by an elderly lady, Mrs. Karen, who was so thin she looked like a skeleton. Our building was heated with a coal-fired furnace. The basement was as dark as a dungeon, where there was a small laundry, but it was so eerie that Laura would frequent the local laundry at about a block and half away instead of going downstairs. Most of those living in our building were either medical students or interns or residents. We had only a sparse amount of furniture and sought to buy from anyone who happened to be moving or buy from pawn shops anything else that we could move into our apartment. Mrs. Karen bought some lumber and provided me with a handsaw, hammer, and nails to build bookshelves. Over one of my off weekends I managed to build some very nice bookshelves and side tables for our living room furniture. While we lived in this rather run-down building, we made friends with others who lived there, and they introduced us to some of the Boston culture.

DON AND LAURA'S FIRST BOSTON CHRISTMAS TREE, IN 1959.

We were introduced to live theater by several medical students on the wards with me. We could get very low-priced tickets in the second balcony, and even though we sometimes had to peer out from around posts, we saw some wonderful pre-Broadway plays, including the one I remember most, *Flower Drum Song*. Bert and Shelia Litwin, who lived in our building, introduced us to the arts and theater. The Litwins were from Alabama but had attended Ivy League schools where they gained their cultural experiences.

On weekends we drove out of Boston to the surrounding country and in the fall took trips to New Hampshire. Laura had developed a friendship with a dietitian who owned a country place there in central New Hampshire, and on occasion we went to the beach and had picnics and parties.

We soon started going to church at the Harvard Chapel. We were introduced to the Chapel by fellow house staff and we had to put behind us some of our earlier Baptist concepts. This was quite an experience, for we heard outstanding contemporary speakers. Charles Buttrick, pastor of the church, was a tall, graying man who spoke slowly in a low tone but delivered profound sermons. I still refer to one of his books, *Sermons Preached in a University Church.*

He welcomed prominent visiting ministers such as Paul Tillich and Martin Luther King to his pulpit. This church experience was in great contrast to the revival and "being saved" concepts of our Southern Baptist roots. It opened a new vista to me for the meaning of religion. It convinced me that there was more than one way to conceptualize a supreme being. In many ways it reopened some of my earlier doubts about the finality of the religious experience.

During my internship and first year residency we began our family. Laura became pregnant about one month after we arrived in Boston and in April 1959 delivered our first child, Walter Douglas Harrison. All through the pregnancy we worried about the fetus and any possible abnormality. Laura has always been a sound sleeper, seldom awakening during the night, but during this period I found her awake and unable to return to sleep on many occasions. While we knew the possibilities of another abnormal fetus, we carefully avoided the emotions of talking about it. We kept our fears and hopes bottled up in our own thoughts. The busy work at the hospital kept me from focusing on the possibilities on a daily basis, but on quiet weekends the thoughts of what we would do if the unfortunate happened again recurred in my mind.

Laura gave birth to Doug at the Boston Lying-in Hospital. I was there to be sure there were no abnormalities, and there were none. She was pampered and remained in the hospital for eight days—a far cry from the one to two days today for a hospital stay for a delivery. I could join her for breakfast, elegantly served on china with silver. For hospital food this sure beat the fat-laden food we were getting at the Brigham. Doug was a plump little fellow, weighing almost 9 pounds, and was a very good baby. Laura and I had great emotional relief when we saw he was normal. I carefully counted his fingers and toes, for at the time it was believed this was a way to detect fetal abnormalities. Soon after his birth he became a voracious nursing baby. Laura nursed all of our children for the first six months.

The joy of these first few days with Douglas soon became a challenge as my mother came to Boston to help Laura with the baby. She insisted on coming. The reality of having her in my life came again as she criticized everything we were doing, and seemed to want us to do her will. It was a terrible experience and when she left after a week we were relieved. I never knew whether she helped Laura or not. We enjoyed Doug immensely and watched every new movement, word utterances and steps taken, with fascination. He surprised us by talking at one year, and always was a happy child. To our surprise, Laura became pregnant again when Douglas was ten months old.

While Laura was pregnant with Beth, our second child, we made several camping trips to Canada and Cape Cod. During the seventh month of Laura's pregnancy, we were on a camping trip on Cape Cod and she started having cramping pains. We did not know whether this was labor or a GI upset with oncoming diarrhea, but at 2 a.m., though I was reluctant, we called her obstetrician, John F. Jewett, one of the best known obstetricians in Boston. It soon became apparent that this was a GI upset and not early labor. We packed up our tent and returned to Boston the next day, taking no further chances of being away. Beth came quickly, in fact so quickly that she was delivered in the bed rather than the delivery room. She was born November 30, 1960, and although her name is Elizabeth, we have always called her Beth. She had only a tiny tuft of hair and was a bit more quarrelsome than Doug had been. We brought her home from the hospital in early December.

LAURA BRINGING BETH HOME FROM BOSTON LYING-IN HOSPITAL, 1960.

The next day there was a major snowstorm and for the rest of the winter we had one to two feet of snow on the ground at all times. Our apartment, while warm, had twelve-foot ceilings and windows that were far from airtight. Soot came in around the sills quite readily. The heavy snow kept Laura inside with Beth but I managed on weekends to dress Doug in a snowsuit to play in the snow. He insisted on going out, and I would go through the effort of boots, snowsuit, hat for him, then bundle myself up. Out we would go, and even though we were cold, he always wanted to stay out longer. We had a small sled, and together we rode down a small embankment into a parking lot.

After we brought Beth home from the hospital, Doug experienced a bit of jealousy and began to have difficulty going to sleep at night. I spent many early evenings patting and comforting him to go to sleep. Beth required feeding at least once during the night and Laura would be up feeding Beth and go to sleep on the couch with the baby resting on her chest. Being a light sleeper, I would awaken and put them both back to bed.

One of my chores was to wash the cloth diapers we used at a launderette nearby. I usually did this around midnight when no one else would be using the launderette, and while washing and drying was going on I would read medical papers. At this time we had only cloth diapers, which required laundering. Disposable diapers, which everyone uses today, had not been invented. My job at the launderette was a quite smelly one, but it allowed me time to catch up on my medical reading.

We developed friendships with other residents and students in our building who had children. The way we were living did not differ much from the way all of our colleagues lived. We were all poorly paid and worked long hours, but felt we were doing something important. No one complained. We were able to share babysitting duties so we could have an evening out at a good restaurant or go to the theater. One family we shared with

DOUGLAS, JUST LIKE DAD, 1960.

had twins and on one occasion one of the twins bit Doug. Suffice it to say we stopped using them. Laura joined a bridge group of mothers and female residents and played once a month. We also shared books with our fellow residents when we found ones of great interest. During these Boston years I continued to ponder what my career would be.

During this year I also purchased my first Harvard tweed suit with a vest, took up smoking a pipe, collected a series of pipes, and attempted in every way possible to look like what I thought was a successful academician. We also frequented Cambridge and shopped for clothes and books at the Harvard Co-op. As I look back at this feeble attempt to demonstrate that I had acquired some Boston polish, I see how silly this was. Boston polish will not get one a job, only solid accomplishment, and in some quarters the Boston veneer can have a negative impact.

About six months after Beth's birth, I began a fellowship in cardiology. While the pace of my work continued to be very fast, I had more time for social activities and a home life with two young children. We were on-call from home but not required to stay in the hospital. This permitted time for many other family activities. On weekends we journeyed to Marblehead to watch the sailing, to Cape Cod to be on the beach, and in the fall to visit Laura's friend Ella Dow during the brilliant fall color display around the second week in October.

One place we visited frequently was the lovely park at Lexington, Massachusetts, where Doug learned to play actively in the fallen leaves. In winter we helped them make maple syrup by tapping their trees and using the sap house to boil down the sap to make delicious maple syrup. We read a great deal, attended the theater on the occasions when we could find a babysitter, and entertained other residents, fellows and interns for dinner in our tiny apartment. Our life became far more family oriented than it had been in our first two years. While I worked very hard as a postdoctoral fellow, I usually had weekends off. I was participating in a number of clinical research projects, which required a great deal of my nightly study time, but they could be done at home.

CHALLENGES

During my first year of residency, I began to consider my career path and realized that I must find a major research opportunity in order to become an academic physician with a faculty appointment.

At the Brigham, one was expected to become an academic faculty member rather than enter the practice of private medicine. Of my twelve fellow interns, nine became academic professors during the next twenty years. Many of my group chose to consider the National Institutes of Health for their research opportunity. I decided on this path, too, interviewed at the National Cancer Institute for a fellowship, and was offered a job, but since I did not wish to pursue a career in cancer I did not accept it. Finally, I chose a fellowship in cardiology with Lewis Dexter, a noted Harvard cardiology professor and one of the original developers of the techniques of cardiac catheterization. I became the clinical fellow at Harvard Medical School on this service and served as the clinical cardiologist for many of the patients of Dwight Harkin, the primary originator of closed mitral valve surgery. This position offered the opportunity for research and specialty training in cardiology that I desired.

Dexter and his wife were very sociable with the fellows. They frequently invited us to their home and always shared Thanksgiving with an old-fashioned Pilgrims' Day gathering with the cardiology fellows and their families. This was a time of joy, good food, and a sharing of family stories. I remember an incident when we visited them at Westport where they spent the summer. Several of us and our wives had been invited for a sailing trip to Chuddyhunk Island. A major windstorm blew in after we had landed on the island. I was sent to get the dingy to ferry people back to the sailboat, and once in the dingy I removed the tie to the dock before starting the motor. I flooded the motor and was soon drifting toward the open Atlantic. Dexter shouted, "Don, start the damn thing." I did after several tries, and once everyone was on board—the women, three of whom were pregnant, Laura included, were below and started to vomit and turn green. When Bob Levine, one of my associates, started smoking a cigar Dexter threatened to kill him. We made it back with several seasick passengers.

During my fellowship, I learned the techniques of cardiac catheterization, although we had ancient x-ray equipment, which provided a very limited view during studies. Catheterization is an important way to learn what kind of heart disease a patient has. Fifty years ago, most patients considered for catheterization had rheumatic heart disease with heart valvular lesions. Today rheumatic heart disease in the U.S. has almost disappeared. Patients are brought to the laboratory on a hospital bed, or gurney. They are placed on a special x-ray table, and at the time, we were doing this in a dark room to enhance the ability to view the images.

A catheter is a long tube that is passed through a blood vessel up into the heart to measure pressures, oxygen content, and the pumping function. This procedure is done without anesthesia but the patient doesn't feel the passage of a catheter up either an artery or a vein because there are no pain fibers inside the arteries and veins. The only pain is from where the catheter enters the artery or vein, and that is anesthetized with a local anesthetic. At the time we were doing these studies, there was a screen for viewing, which extended over the patient. This is an ancient setup when compared to today. We were able to view the catheter, about the size of a small pencil, being passed up the arteries and veins into the heart. Dye was injected to give even higher contrasting images and to demonstrate whether there were problems with valves, obstructions in arteries, or the presence of some kind of congenital heart defect.

Over the past several decades there have been major improvements in the process of catheterization. The procedure is now carried out in a lighted room. There are machines to record electrical signals and pressures from multiple sites. The monitors are overhead on a large television screen and can be viewed by the operator. Images can be taken in several dimensions and computer processing allows for digital reconstruction of the images. At the time we were doing the catheterizations at the Peter Bent Brigham Hospital there was only a moderate number of sites in the country where the procedures could be carried out. Today there are several thousand institutions where catheterizations are performed, and probably a million and a half procedures carried out each year. Because we had primitive equipment, we learned the techniques with a high level of skill.

Research was always emphasized in the laboratory—both animal experiments and human trials. In the Dexter laboratory everyone carried out a research project, and near the end of the year it was my turn to make the presentation of my research at the New England Cardiovascular Society meeting. My presentation went well. It was on the effects of digitalis, a stimulating drug for heart function in patients with valvular heart disease. Then the renowned Paul Dudley-White stood to ask me several questions, one of which was, "What are the side effects of digitalis glycosides in patients with valvular heart disease?"

I answered, "There are few if the proper dose is given." That was the correct answer at the time. Today, we have the ability to measure the amount of the drug in the patient's blood and determine the correct dose. I gave my answer before we had the technology to make this measurement and it was based on clinical judgment. Though we were not doing basic laboratory work, we were carrying out major transitional and clinical research with most of the postdoctoral fellows writing and being accepted for publication, thus making themselves attractive as academicians at other institutions.

———————————

During my fellowship year it was becoming uncomfortably clear that the army was a possibility for me since there was a doctors' draft at this time. If drafted into the army I would likely be separated from my family and possibly sent overseas for two years. For that reason, I set out again to try to find a position at the National Institutes of Health (NIH), which was more acceptable to me, even though I had already rejected the Cancer Institute. Two years at the NIH would satisfy my military obligation, since I would be in the Public Health Service.

At this time all physicians had an obligation for two years of military service. This was a holdover from the Korean War, when we had received deferment to continue college. I learned from a colleague that there had been a reorganization at the National Heart Institute and that a very young and talented physician, Eugene Braunwald, had just become branch chief of the cardiology unit. He was to have one opening for an associate. Dexter, my mentor, placed a call to Braunwald, after two weeks of prodding by me. By this time I was feeling left behind since most of my intern group had been accepted at the NIH and were already there. However, I was willing to take the risk and badger Dexter to call, even though he seemed hesitant. During the call he summoned me to his office and said that Braunwald would interview me if I would come the next day and he would make his choice by the weekend.

While I was making arrangements with Braunwald, Dexter called and purchased the ticket for me to fly to Washington. I left the next morning and spent the entire day with Braunwald. During this day I became aware of what a driving intellect Braunwald was. He discussed his plans for building the best research program in cardiology in the world, and of the virtues of a career at the NIH. I was totally convinced and desired an appointment. At the end of the interview, I spent the night with Bruce Bower and his wife Betsy, one of my former intern mates who was now at the NIH, and we visited about Washington the next morning. I returned to Boston after being assured by Braunwald that I would hear something on Friday. Knowing that he had interviewed about thirty people for this position, when I received no call or mail on Friday I assumed that I was out of the running and set about considering my next moves.

When I went to the mailbox at the Peter Bent Brigham the following Monday morning, I found, to my great surprise a one-line note saying, "I have selected you as my clinical and research associate. I will arrange to get you in the Public Health Service." I was elated—I knew this would help me begin an active research assignment for an important career in cardiology, but also knew that this would mean a much disciplined several-year stint at the NIH. Being in the Public Health Service would also satisfy my military obligation. I was soon instructed by Braunwald to learn new catheterization techniques from another cath lab group at the Brigham. I found a receptive Richard Gorlin to teach me catheterization of the coronary sinus of the heart. This is the great vein in the heart through which blood that had nourishes the heart muscle drains. This was a difficult technique but allowed one to monitor the metabolism of the heart. This would become one of the skills I took to the NIH. It was a new technique to the staff there and I was able to teach it, and also used it in my research.

During my fellowship at Harvard, my support came from a grant from the American Heart Association and with a supplement from the Dexter lab. My salary was around $6,000 per year, just enough for our growing family to live on. In addition, I had an opportunity to take courses in statistics and laboratory techniques at the Harvard Medical School, which would help my career later. I was also exposed to many other areas of clinical cardiology and became competent as a cardiology postdoctoral fellow.

Near the end of the year I made another trip to Washington to find a house for us and was aided by the wife of one of my former interns from the Brigham. I found a house in Bethesda about two miles from the NIH. Since it was available and might be taken by someone else, I made an instant decision to rent it. This instant decision was contrary to my usual cautious approach, and as I reflect on it, I believe I must have been in a manic phase because of the anticipation of being at the NIH. I returned jubilantly to Boston to tell Laura that we would have our first house with a backyard, basement, and three bedrooms. She was overjoyed to get out of the cramped and soot-filled apartments in which we had lived all our six years of marriage—three years in Alabama and three years in Boston. We had always envisioned living in a real house and when I rented this one, it was a great start, for we knew we would be there for at least two years.

What a wonderful feeling this was when coupled with my elation to be working with the most productive cardiology investigator in the world at that time. By this time Braunwald was recognized as one of the best mentors for someone seeking an academic career. He was short with curly hair and a bit of a midline paunch. He gesticulated with his hands when he talked, and he was all business in his demeanor.

With the move from Boston my career at Harvard came to an end. The Harvard Medical School and residencies at its teaching hospitals were at that time and still are important stepping-stones to academic careers. It is clear, however, that the best opportunities were when one left that system to be recruited elsewhere. Although this was true, many remained at the Harvard teaching hospitals for years. I recognized that the pastures would be greener for me elsewhere but I secretly believed that Laura and I would eventually return to our roots in Alabama.

A CAREER STEPPING-STONE

The NIH was the best place for a young person to begin to build a research career and find a good academic position. I was delighted with my prospects. And so at the end of my third year in Boston we moved to Bethesda where I began my research career at the NIH in June 1961.

We moved in a single day with two babies on the back seat of our 1954 Chevy, long before the days of seat belts. Fortunately the Public Health Service paid for the move of our household things. They packed our belongings in Boston, and moved us. Laura and I, with the babies, Doug and Beth, moved as a family into our "new to us" house.

There were really only two phases of life at the NIH: My work phase and my social life. The social life was compacted primarily into weekends because of my sixteen-to-eighteen-hour work day through most of the week. Laura and I tried to set aside time on the weekends for both the family and for us to have time for ourselves. We frequently prepared a late dinner on Saturday night after we had tucked Doug and Beth into bed. Most of our social life in Bethesda was family oriented, and our children were fortunate to have two 12-year-olds, Mary and Amanda, who lived across the street and came to play with them frequently.

DON WITH THE BIKE HE RODE DAILY TO THE NIH.

As a research and clinical associate I was a member of the Public Health Service, but required to wear a military uniform for travel. We borrowed them from the uniform room, so I never bought one, and whatever I used was usually too large. I was immediately recognized as one of those "dodging the draft by being at the NIH" by others traveling with military documents. I rode the three miles to the NIH by bicycle since we had only one car, which Laura needed. I even rode when there was light snow on the street.

At the time I was stationed at the NIH it had just become the epicenter of life science research in the United States. The NIH was founded after World War II to support research, life science, and medical application of that research. There were two major programs. The first was the internal research program, which funded the activities carried out on its Bethesda campus for its nine institutes at the time. The second, and equally important program, was to fund sponsored research at academic institutions throughout the country.

Predetermination of what research is to be funded is based on evaluation of its likely success by an appointed group of peer researchers. Many major medical centers were building their future counting on this support for their research programs. At this time, however, most of the residents and postdoctoral fellows aspiring to an academic career wanted to go to the NIH. There were at least fifteen candidates for every position that was available. Once at the NIH one had access to resources that were unparalleled in any institution throughout the country, and the opportunity to work with mentors who were at the leading edge of their own research fields. If you worked diligently and had brilliant ideas, you could have great success at the NIH.

My early work agenda at the NIH became evident the first day when Braunwald took me to the surgical service, and introduced me to the head of cardiac surgery, Glenn Morrow. He told Morrow that I was to be his consultant in cardiology, and that whatever I did with him in the way of research could be my own. He also coupled me with his group of investigators working in pharmacology with a major interest in the mechanisms of heart failure. They were studying the autonomic nervous system, which has nerve connections to the heart that can increase its force of contraction. I was accepted as a member of the group. We wished to prove its effects by studying the autonomic nervous system of the heart as it responded to exercise. We were measuring hormone levels in the blood draining from the heart as markers of increased nerve activity. This is where the coronary sinus catheterization technique I had learned was vital.

———————————— ✥ ✥ ————————————

A day in my life went like this: I arrived at 7 a.m. to make rounds with the cardiac surgeons and take care of any of the medical problems that had arisen overnight, assuming that I had not been called during the night to come in to the hospital for a problem. I next went to the animal lab where I sacrificed twenty-four rats, removed their hearts quickly, and put them in liquid nitrogen to be taken to the lab to measure the concentrations of norepinephrine, which is the hormone that controls heart rate and the force of contraction.

I then went to another building where the technicians had prepared two or more dogs for heart study. Dogs were the animal of choice because the pound supplied them and they had been the model for human studies for years. We now know the pig is a better model for the human heart studies. Though dogs are much easier to work on, the circulation to the pig's heart more closely resembles that of humans and for studies on the heart, the pig is now the model of choice.

At the NIH I used the new technique of coronary sinus catheterization that I had learned in Boston. The chief laboratory technician did not believe that anyone could put a catheter in the coronary sinus of a dog under an x-ray fluoroscope. For the first several dogs where I managed to do this, he cut the dogs open at the end of the experiment to check on my accuracy. His comment was, "Doc, you did it; you are real good!"

Our aim was to measure the release of norepinephrine from the heart in dogs, like we had in rats. This is the neurotransmitter of autonomic nerve action. I collected large numbers of blood samples, iced and took them back to the lab for analysis of norepinephrine levels. This was usually followed in the afternoon by a research conference, then rounds with the cardiac surgeons at the end of the long day.

Some days I met the surgeons and went to the operating room where we put electrodes on the human heart and made electrophysiologic measurements. Electrodes are tiny needles placed in the heart to measure the electrical activity that causes the heart to beat. The operating rooms at the NIH were quite large. The patients were anesthetized and placed on the operating table under an intense light. They were attached to monitors for the oxygen content of their blood, their blood pressure, and their electrocardiogram. Their chests were opened and their heart exposed. The procedure was often for heart valve replacement or the correction of congenital heart defects. Our research was for secondary purposes. Once the chest was opened and the hearts exposed, we placed several electrodes on the heart. These were specialized wires with the tips modified to record the electrical signals and to be able to stimulate the heart simultaneously.

We had a sixteen-channel recorder so that we could record many areas of the heart. Our initial task was to make measurements of the electrical potentials on the heart in a controlled time and then to give drugs at repeated doses and make measurements over a series of times. We were able to determine exactly how these drugs work and how long they acted. We were also able to simulate abnormal rhythms of the heart and to determine if the drugs worked to stop those abnormal rhythms.

This was one of the first times drugs controlling the rhythm of the heart were studied in humans with the kinds of electrical equipment we had. We studied the action of lidocaine, a prominent local anesthetic, and procainamide, a widely used drug to stop abnormal rhythms. We demonstrated that lidocaine produced major electrophysiologic actions that had antiarrhythmic effects clinically, which lead to a new use for this drug. The electrophysiologic effects are the drug's action on heart cells that produce the electric signal to the muscle causing contraction. When these cells are injured there is an abnormal rhythm. We discovered that drugs such as lidocaine, which was widely used as a local anesthetic, could correct the abnormal heart rhythm. This was the first time the observation had been made in humans. Our research with lidocaine led to its widespread use to combat major ventricular arrhythmias when coronary care units were built several years later. It was the subject of some of my most important work after I moved to Stanford, where I authored a paper showing its effects in patients who had heart attacks. That paper was published in the *New England Journal of Medicine*, and helped me obtain my NIH grants at Stanford.

My early NIH research work to demonstrate the electrophysiologic effects of antiarrhythmic drugs in the beating human heart would be difficult to do today. Such research in patients can no longer be done easily because of federal regulations relating to research in human subjects. The regulations, which have been developed over the past several years, are to protect patients undergoing research interventions without full, informed consent. It seems unlikely we could have gotten such consent.

The hospital for the clinical research at the NIH was called the National Center and was a magnet for drawing patients into new research protocols that could only be carried out at the NIH. While many of the top medical institutions around the country had clinical research centers, none were as large or as comprehensive as the NIH. The funding for the 450-bed Center in Bethesda far exceeded that of any four or five institutions taken together. All beds were used for research subjects, even though many were also being treated for a rare disease. During this period the NIH was the most progressive center translating basic research into clinical application, and we were able to recruit volunteers for our clinical trials. Again, I knew I made the right decision to seek a position here, and that prodding Dexter to make a contact in my behalf was the right thing.

Some days I worked in the cardiac catheterization laboratory doing coronary sinus catheterization and learning a new technique called transseptal left heart catheterization which I would later take to Stanford. This technique revolutionized the study of patients with valvular heart disease. For the first time it was possible to study the structures and function of the left chamber and valves of the heart. The technique required great skill in manipulating a long needle to puncture a dividing structure (septum) in the heart and then passing a catheter through it to the left chamber of the heart.

In our laboratory work we had every instrument and tool available. We also had the most up-to-date library and staff. I'll never forget seeing my first photocopy machine. It was amazing that a machine could copy a page of a journal in about one second. Photocopying technology had just been commercialized and we were allowed several hundred pages of reproductions a week and a technician to do the copying. What a way to build a personal library of research papers for reference! To provide us with knowledge about the advances in chemistry, physics and statistics that would apply to medical research, there were night courses we could take two to three nights per week. This was just like going back to graduate school.

The primary goal of all clinical research is to make new treatments and diagnostic techniques available for patients. This, of course, was the primary objective at the NIH. The plan for my research was to learn more about heart disease and to develop new treatments, then to publish the results and make them available for other physicians to utilize. It was also to help build a foundation for my academic career. In order to build a respected research career, one had to publish in peer-reviewed journals, and the NIH provided a unique opportunity for those willing to work long hours. We were constantly made aware that the only way our work would be known at institutions that might be willing to hire us on as faculty would be to publish high-quality work as frequently as possible. Nowhere has this idea been more pronounced than in the cardiology unit where I worked.

We worked long hours at research and usually wrote up our findings on the weekends and nights. I wrote a number of papers with Glenn Morrow, the chief of cardiac surgery. My job was to assemble the data and meet him on a Saturday morning with twenty-four sharpened pencils. He clearly had an obsessive-compulsive personality. We used a dictionary to look up many words and we drank ten or fifteen cups of coffee before the day ended at 5 p.m. at which time we usually had a completed manuscript that never needed any rewriting—only the figures or charts prepared for the manuscript to be typed and it would be ready to go off to a journal. After a long and tedious Saturday, I would need several glasses of wine to loosen up and be tolerable with Laura and the children.

Braunwald helped me write research papers for the work I did with him. He was an exciting scientific researcher and excellent writer. I was fortunate to have him as a mentor. I often wrote with Braunwald on Sunday nights at his house. Braunwald's wife was a cardiac surgeon who thought us "nuts" to work on Sunday night, and would burst in and tell us so in no uncertain terms. She would often "shoo" me out of their house.

The second phase of our Bethesda life was the social side with our growing family. We bought a wading pool, which Doug and Beth enjoyed immensely in the hot, humid summer.

We were always purchasing new toys for them to play with in the basement. We did take the children and go into downtown Washington to see the monuments, libraries and galleries. As one might guess, they were too young for this, but seemed to enjoy the outing anyway.

Laura and I had an annual subscription to attend the Arena Stage, a premier resident theatrical group, and with some of our friends, we shared weekend dinners. Wine, which had just become something of interest to me in Boston, became a serious interest now, and on the weekend we always had wine with our meals, far different from our background experience at Garden City. "Plain Old Pearson's" was a great wine store in Washington where I went frequently for tastings and presentations. I also found a small wine store in Chevy Chase with a salesperson who knew a great deal about wine. He'd sell me a case of quite good Côtes du Rhone wines for $10 or $.88 per bottle.

She still had great periods of moodiness and temper outbursts which resulted in many hostile comments, such as, "Why don't you get your ass back to Alabama where you belong? You are only pretending that you have had that Boston training. It doesn't mean a thing to me."

Several families of our relatives from Alabama visited us in Washington, and we soon developed our own unique tour of the city. Over our two-year period, we had visits from my family and Laura's family. Laura's brother Red and his wife visited with us, as did her sister Blanche and three children, staying in our house with us and visiting the sites of Washington.

On two occasions my mother and father came to see us. As I remember the visits, they were not cheerful or pleasant. My mom was still critical of my work as a physician and vocally opposed how we were raising our children. She was reasonably pleasant dealing with Laura, but almost stridently hostile with me over my medical pursuits and the fact that I was continuing to progress as a physician.

Some of this resulted from my mother having made an incomplete recovery from a major depression. She still had great periods of moodiness and temper outbursts that resulted in many hostile comments, such as, "Why don't you get your ass back to Alabama where you belong? You are only pretending that you have had that Boston training. It doesn't mean a thing to me." By this time I had been away from Alabama and my mom's constant nagging for a number of years, so I could more easily ignore her comments, though I still longed for her recognition of my accomplishments. On the other hand, she seemed quite interested in Washington, D.C., and had a good memory of her high school studies of the

U.S. government. She was particularly impressed with the Smithsonian Institution. Our family tours included the Capitol, the White House, the Washington, Jefferson, and Lincoln monuments, and Arlington National Cemetery.

Laura began to work part time and the children were put in nursery school. She worked for an accountant, a job that was never very satisfying. He had a practice of small businesses and individuals, was quite disorganized, and Laura experienced tremendous frustration in trying to help him organize his practice. It was also a stressful experience for her because she placed the children in the care of the nursery. They had initial difficulties in adapting, but in time came to accept this as an interesting time to play. Doug made an acquaintance with another toddler named Cindy Welland, who became a lifelong friend. Cindy's family moved from Bethesda to California after we moved and they became one of our best family friends. Laura worked for almost one year but always found it frustrating and stressful.

I wanted to present my research work to my medical colleagues, and traveled to a number of meetings, including the American Heart Association meetings in Miami and Cleveland. I also began going to basic science, pharmacology and physiology meetings, both for my own education and to present my research findings.

In the fall of 1961, the Cuban Missile Crisis was developing and we were living in Washington, a potential target city. It was a scary time for us. We tried to protect the children, who were quite young, from any concept of fear, but we watched the television, waiting for news, and probably on a more regular basis than at any time before, hoping against hope that there would be no escalation of the crisis. I have always been an optimist about the balanced deterrent concept, which was prevalent at this time, and believed that neither side would have the temerity to launch a first-strike nuclear missile.

It was for that reason that I was skeptical that any attack would occur but wanted to remain vigilant. We were advised to stockpile food and other necessary supplies. Our basement turned out to be ideal to stockpile food, water, and other supplies in case there was an attack. The whole Washington area was on alert, since this would be the center of any strike against the United States. We were not reassured when we saw Nikita Khrushchev on television banging on the lectern at the United Nations with his shoe and making dastardly threats against the United States. As time went by we waited for the Russian missiles to fall but they never came. It was only thirty years later when the Kennedy papers were released that we learned how serious the crisis really was.

During the autumn of my second year at the NIH, it came time to make a decision about finishing my house staff training and continuing my career. I needed another year of residency to be qualified to take my board exams in internal medicine. I talked to Saul Rosenberg, who had been one of my senior residents in Boston, but he had now migrated to the new Stanford Medical Center in Palo Alto, California. His desire was to have me do my chief residency in medicine there. However, I had no real thought of going since I had never been west of the Mississippi River.

One day I received a letter from the Brigham inviting me to come back as a senior resident, and wanting an answer within two weeks. At that point I called Saul, since he wanted to introduce the Brigham system for resident training at Stanford and wanted me to come there to be the first chief medical resident with the new system. He asked if I could come for an interview soon, and I went that very day, flying on a new jet plane from Baltimore to San Francisco. Transcontinental jets were just coming into use, and while I was apprehensive, I found this was the most time-efficient way to travel.

I saw Saul and spent the entire day being interviewed by Hal Holman, the chief of medicine, and being shown around the area. It was beautiful and very enticing, but the hospital was small and was on a college campus, surrounded by eucalyptus trees. It was quite different from Boston. The next day I was taken to San Francisco and spent the day touring the city. It was a clear day, but fog was coming in over the Bay and the Golden Gate Bridge looked immense. I was very impressed, and on the following day took the plane home, making a decision on the plane that I really could not turn down Boston, since in my memory no one had ever said no to a senior residency at the Brigham.

BETH, DONNA, AND DOUGLAS IN BETHESDA, MAY 1963.

On arrival at home, Laura announced that she was pregnant again with our third child. This came as quite a shock to both of us. I wavered in my decision over the weekend and made a call to the Brigham to tell them I would come back. The chief of medicine, George Thorn, was away at the time I called, and I had to call back at a later time. This was another time of crisis in my career. I was quite emotional and equivocated. Should I say yes to Boston as I had decided, or no? I wavered. I wanted to say yes to Stanford, but I needed more reassurance. Laura stepped in and encouraged me to call my past mentor, Lewis Dexter.

I called Dexter and he encouraged me to go to Stanford. He said, "Harvard is too crowded with bright people unwilling to go elsewhere where there is also great opportunity. If you come here, they'll give you a bathroom-sized laboratory and expect five to six years of work before receiving an academic appointment." At that point, I made up my mind, and probably became the first person to decline an opportunity to come back to the Brigham as a senior resident. Laura had again helped me make another crucial career choice.

Time passed swiftly after the decision. Laura went through the stages of her pregnancy, my work progressed well, and we made our plans to go to Stanford. We bought a new station wagon, made another visit to Alabama to see our parents, and twelve weeks before we were to leave, Laura gave birth to Donna, our second daughter, at the Bethesda Naval Hospital. This was quite a different experience from the Boston Lying-in where our first two children had been born. The chief of OB came in to deliver Laura even though it was late at night. Military medicine was effective although not necessarily patient friendly. Here the mothers were summoned from their beds to pick up their babies and take care of them, not the coddling that mothers received in Boston. To make matters worse, I left the day after Donna's birth for a two-day medical meeting. Neighbors took care of Doug and Beth and when I returned I took over until Laura was discharged. One can certainly appreciate that medical care in the military was cheap. Our bill was $11.45. Laura's food was our only charge.

The last few weeks of my time at the NIH were a frantic rush to complete work and to get as many papers finished as I possibly could. As I was leaving, Braunwald urged me to go to Stanford for a year and come back and join him as a senior associate. Perhaps I had that in mind, but for now the excitement and allure of the West Coast held sway.

While my life at the NIH was quite intense and competitive I accomplished a great deal that would aid me in establishing myself in academic medicine. By the time my two years were up, I had published or had in press thirty manuscripts in high-quality journals. It was the most productive time in my life as a first-line author and investigator carrying out high-quality work. This gave me the potential for a productive academic career and an academic appointment at a major medical center. During the decades after I left the NIH, I depended on it for research support that came to the external sponsored programs at Stanford, and later, in Cincinnati. Over the next thirty years, the NIH budgets and research programs grew tremendously. Then and now research productivity seems to be the primary basis for a successful major medical university academic appointment.

Faculty members are selected for appointment at major research institutions based on their success in carrying out and publishing high quality research. This success generally leads to significant financial support for research from outside sources, the NIH being the largest source. Universities generally support only a modicum of faculty research through their budgetary process. Having a strong publication record is important in recruiting the highest quality postgraduate fellows and graduate students from the available candidate pool. Today, even more than in the 1970s, it is important to gain prominence and recognition by publishing the results of high-quality research in the most respected academic journals. The adage to "publish or perish" applies in the strongest sense to medical sciences today. That I was able to publish a large number of papers from successful research while I was at the NIH became the cornerstone for my future academic career.

UNBRIDLED ENTHUSIASM

Our trip across the country in 1963 introduced us to long-distance driving with three children under age four, at a time when car seats were rudimentary, not very safe, and there were no seat belts.

We placed the two older children in the back of a station wagon where we had built play space. Donna, who was just twelve weeks old, was in a portable bassinet and was held

EASTER MORNING, DON AND THE CHILDREN
AT MOUNTAIN VIEW RENTAL HOUSE.

to be fed, even when we were driving. We arranged a gift of playthings each day for Douglas and Beth, and the new toys seemed to keep them occupied for several hours. We usually started out about 5 a.m., stopped by the roadside for breakfast that we heated on a gas-fired camp stove, and ended our travels by 2 p.m. to let the children play.

Our first night on the road, we stayed in South Bend, Indiana, in Notre Dame's Campus Hotel, since the motels were already full. On entering, Doug, our four-year-old, announced in a loud voice, "The Harrisons are here!" Everyone looked amused and commented, "What cute kids." We prayed that after a week in the car we could say the same thing.

Our next stop was Iowa, and it was a very hot day. The motel owner directed us to the local town pool and a nice motherly woman asked if she could look after Donna, while we played in the pool with the other two children. We let her mind Donna for thirty minutes. Today, no one would allow a stranger to do such a thoughtful favor.

We stopped for the third night at Ogallala, Nebraska, where the outside temperature was 106 degrees. Fortunately there was air conditioning, so I made a trip to the grocery store and we made sandwiches and had a picnic supper in our room. We drove on to Green River, Wyoming, to spend a day and two nights with Laura's Uncle. He was in his 70s at the time and ultimately lived to be 103, which was surprising in that he had moved from Alabama for health reasons. The common practice in medicine for patients with asthma in the 1940s was to recommend moving to a dry climate away from pollen and mold. Uncle Bud Shaver chose Wyoming, where he could get a job. Surprisingly, his asthma cleared and he thrived in a new job as a dispatcher on the Union Pacific Railroad. Today, while the prevalence of asthma has increased markedly, drugs are used to control it and patients are not moved from their families to dry climates. He showed us the Wyoming countryside and the children were fascinated by a fossil collection he had accumulated over a forty-year period.

We were particularly awed by the sheer size of the Sierras, having never seen mountains like them.

Winnemucca, Nevada, was our next destination. After finding a motel we participated in the town's Fourth of July celebration and the children observed their first fireworks. Doug was gleefully jumping up and down, while Beth was frightened by the big explosive noises. Donna slept peacefully in her tote bassinet. Compared to our rural background in Alabama, Winnemucca seemed like the end of the world. It was isolated and surrounded by miles of desert, and the dusty streets and shoddy houses spoke of poverty. From there it was on to California, the beautiful Sierra Nevada Mountains, the great San Joaquin Valley, and San Francisco. We were particularly awed by the sheer size of the Sierras, having never seen mountains like them.

Our arrival after the long drive across country was quite auspicious. We had pre-rented an efficiency apartment at the Stanford Arms in Menlo Park. The apartment had been converted from a motel of a long-ago vintage, and it was ill suited for cooking. It was near a main street, the El Camino Real, which made it extremely noisy at night. However, our young children were ready for the outdoor pool and some time to exert their energy, having been cooped up in the car for six days. We settled in at the Stanford Arms and went about our first task of finding a house to rent. We found a house in Mountain View, working with a local real estate agent who owned the house and rented it to us. The house was flat roofed, had many glass doors to the outside, and was quite spacious with four bedrooms and a nice floor plan to provide space for our growing family. We celebrated our holidays there for more than a year and I was able to spend considerable time with the children. It was in a quiet neighborhood, and only ten minutes from the Stanford Hospital.

We moved in as soon as our furniture arrived from Bethesda. By that time we were becoming accustomed to the California climate—quite warm during the day, in fact, hot, but the evenings were cold as the fog came in over the coastal mountains. The white fog over the green mountains was quite beautiful but seemed almost ethereal. We had never observed anything like this fog, and in the morning overcast we were concerned about rain. But we soon learned it never rained in July or August. We also found that the fog was the "air conditioning" for the area, the main reason our house had none. Laura missed our Bethesda house but enjoyed the openness and the easy access to the outside.

During our first few days at Stanford we met Saul Rosenberg, who was responsible for my appointment, and his family, who brought us a tasty dinner casserole and red California strawberries while we lived in the Stanford Arms. The Rosenbergs had a large home at the top of one of the local hills, and planned a gathering for us with the families of several of the senior residents with whom I would be working. I was most grateful for this opportunity that helped me to get to know my future Stanford colleagues. There was also a welcoming party at the home of Thomas Fiene, one of my senior residents, where our children got to meet and play with their children of the same age. We, along with all the children, have for years been close friends.

One day after our arrival I began my tenure as the chief medical resident at the Stanford University Hospital. The hospital was a beautiful building and was designed by Edward Durrell Stone. It had many courtyards and fountains. The hospital was completed in 1959 and was a combination hospital for the city of Palo Alto and Stanford University. It also accommodated the move of the clinical portions of Stanford Medical School from San Francisco to the main campus. The medical school was also designed by Stone and was directly attached to the hospital. The sharing arrangement of the hospital with Palo Alto proved difficult at the management level and the city was unwilling to accommodate the residency training requirements of the University. After about ten years, this resulted in Stanford buying out the Palo Alto City interest and the hospital becoming the entire Stanford University Hospital and Medical Center.

In spite of its beauty, the hospital had three floors and wings that were widely separated. This was a somewhat dysfunctional layout since patient transport took considerable amounts of time. Apparently Stone had not done any time/motion studies for efficiencies of a working hospital. The hospital was also not air conditioned, except for operating rooms and intensive care units, but with the stucco and concrete design and appropriate shielding of the courtyards, this was not required. On each wing of the hospital there were private patient rooms, shared twin rooms, and at least one five-bed ward. This concept for at least some private rooms was moving toward modern hospital design; and this certainly was an improvement over the large twenty or more bed wards at the Peter Bent Brigham Hospital in Boston. As hospitals have

evolved over the past forty years, private rooms have almost become universal. The hospital was in a picturesque part of the campus and was surrounded by eucalyptus trees, very nice lawns, and had several fountains in the entrance area.

STANFORD MEDICAL CENTER.

I had four senior residents and twelve interns as my tutelage as chief resident. There was a level of jealousy due to my being from elsewhere and recruited to be chief resident, when several of the residents in the program could have graduated to be chief resident that year. This was an unusual situation in that I had never known anyone to become chief resident at an institution where they had not previously served as a resident. This occurred because Stanford was making the switch to the junior-senior resident type approach similar to the Brigham residency where I had trained earlier. This approach to residency training was not the norm at other medical centers.

The senior residents directed interns rather than junior residents who in this system were assigned to the private patients or to subspecialty consulting. In spite of some petty jealousies, several of the residents invited us to their homes for dinner and to meet their families. Everyone on the faculty accepted me with gusto. I found my job to be one of great delight to be dealing with a wide variety of patient illnesses.

This was quite different from my NIH experience when I dealt solely with patients with heart disease, and I liked the variety. I was also fully engrossed in the delivery of high-quality health care, as compared to research, which was the primary mission at NIH. I was also teaching, which I loved. There were six or eight senior-year medical students on the ward at all times. I was responsible for seeing that they had a good educational experience, and took them to see the most interesting patients after I had received permission. We met at the bedside and I had the students elicit the most important physical findings. I also sent the students to search medical literature on the latest treatment for each patient. Every day I had a patient presentation by the interns and residents where I prodded them on the diagnosis and treatment plans. We worked in a communal way to deliver the best care to all patients, while at the same time to provide the best education for interns and students.

The Stanford Department of Medicine philosophy was one that I had never experienced before. It was a "socialistic society" in which no one was viewed to be higher than anyone else. All interns, residents, and faculty were considered students. Thus, I had direct opportunities to be with the chief of medicine on a daily and sometimes almost hourly basis. The clinical atmosphere in the Stanford University Hospital was far less formal than I had experienced earlier in my residency training at the Peter Bent Brigham Hospital; however, the house staff did wear short white coats, and the faculty long white coats similar to what was worn in Boston. We had very carefully lettered name tags so patients could identify us.

As contrasted to Boston, most of our attendings were full-time faculty and heavily engaged in research while in Boston many attendings were full time practicing clinicians. The Stanford attendings were frequently relatively young, and attempted to create a more relaxed atmosphere rather than the formal presentation atmosphere to which I had been subjected in Boston.

I was called out of grand rounds and told to announce that President John Kennedy had been shot and was dead.

Hal Holman, the chairman of medicine, made rounds with me and with the resident staff twice a week, and although he was a moderately good clinician he had wonderful insights into people and how to build a prominent department of medicine. He was very young to be a chair of medicine, blond, good looking, a marvelous speaker who could speak extemporaneously on many social subjects. To help build the faculty, I came to Stanford with two other recruits from the NIH, Tom Merigan and Peter Rowley, whom Holman had recruited because of their research expertise. We were new faculty, each hoping to find our niche on the West Coast.

The faculty of the department of medicine was largely new to Stanford, since the original clinical departments had been in San Francisco. When the clinical programs moved to Palo Alto, most of the clinical faculty remained in San Francisco where the clinical program had been for almost fifty years. They had long-established practices in San Francisco and did not choose to move. My class of new recruits from the NIH and the Brigham represented the core of what would become a nationally recognized department of medicine over the next 15 years.

At this time, the Department of Medicine at Stanford was rather small, and did not have faculty consultants covering all aspects of internal medicine. There were very few consultants in some of the medical subspecialties. Consultants have had two or more years of extra medical training in a sub-specialty field and limit their practice to that subspecialty, e.g., cardiology, gastroenterology, etc. I soon found that I was expected to be the consultant in many clinical cases where specialty experts were not available. Our residency program called for me to be the chief resident at the Stanford University Hospital for six months, and the second six months I was to be at the Palo Alto Veterans Hospital located about three miles away. It was part of the Stanford University house staff training program.

During both of these experiences, I began to serve as a consultant to my senior residents, as a specialist in a wide range of areas. It was easy in cardiology but less so in gastroenterology, urology, and other areas. Even though I had been doing research and largely focused on cardiology for two years at the NIH, I soon found that my training from the Brigham Hospital in Boston gave me an advantage of being competent in many subjects within medicine. I also spent considerable time in the medical library reading the most up-to-date literature in areas where I had too little expertise. Soon after my chief residency year, I found myself being consulted by some of the private physicians on their complicated patients to help them with the diagnosis and treatment plan. They had observed my clinical acumen while I was chief resident. This was quite rewarding for me, though quite eye-opening for someone so young. I was fortunate to make a diagnosis in some difficult cases, and was soon respected as an excellent clinician by the community physicians practicing in the hospital.

As chief resident, my plan was to work with the residents and the interns to establish the highest quality program. I organized special teaching meetings, and journal reviews, and for the first six months examined every patient admitted to the medical service in an attempt to "pick up" findings missed by others, which I was frequently to do. This elevated the quality of care for all of the patients on our service. My intent in examining every patient was to instill in the house staff the discipline for physical diagnosis that had been taught to me by Ray Ledbetter at the University of Alabama. I was also wanting to create a new sense of pride for the house staff so they would be more challenging to the medical students who were now part of the first five-year class; they were reaching their last year and finishing their clinical training. Stanford had established a five-year medical school experience to provide students with a year to do research.

The faculty at Stanford had decided to choose very bright students and provide them a path to become academic leaders by giving them both clinical and research experience as medical students. This was in contrast to most schools' four-year programs, which were oriented only to clinical practice. I was also attempting to introduce a greater research orientation into the house staff thinking patterns based on my NIH experience. Our plan was to learn together. I made explicit assignments to medical students to look up and bring back facts about particular subjects.

With the blessing of Hal Holman, I was able to take over the management and updating of medical grand rounds, quite different from the past, and to bring in speakers from other services. I was trying to create the med-surg type conferences that I had observed at Alabama. Hal Holman was not the clinician that Tinsley Harrison had been, but David Rytand, the emeritus chairman of medicine who was an excellent clinician, was on the faculty, and I frequently called on him to challenge the surgeons in these redesigned grand rounds.

I have memory of one particular grand rounds because of the tragic event that occurred on that Friday in November 1963. I was called out of grand rounds and told to announce that President John Kennedy had been shot and was dead. With a quiver in my voice, I did so. There was total shock in the audience and I was then asked to announce that the Stanford vs. California-Berkeley football game on Saturday was to be delayed. Everyone left in silence. The next few days were sad ones for the country, and those of us on the Stanford house staff covered for each other for part of the time so we could be with our families to view the history-making events in Washington on TV, and comfort and talk with our children.

We had interesting patients with diseases that I had not seen at Harvard or NIH, such as something known as "Valley Fever." This was caused by coccidioidmycosis, a fungal organism found only in the San Joaquin Valley of central California. There were few options to treat this disease because of the toxicity of drug used. The disease inordinately affected emigrants from Southeast Asia working in the San Joaquin Valley. The treatments that have been developed in the past thirty years are far more effective and less toxic.

During my senior residency year there was a rash of mushroom poisonings in patients admitted to our service, several of whom died. I made a special point of following and doing special laboratory tests on some of the patients. I also found that Stanford had an outstanding mycology specialist in the botany department with whom I consulted. In spite of his expertise, no clinician had ever approached him. He was delighted to help me identify the mushrooms that the patients had collected and eaten.

Before the year was over I wrote a paper on mushroom poisoning in which I described the clinical phases of the disease process of mushroom poisoning which had not previously been understood. This paper was published in the prestigious journal, *The American Journal of Medicine*. The poisoning's clinical presentation occurs in three phases. Initially there occurs a severe diarrhea with cramping. The patient then enters a quiescent period and is discharged. However, during this period severe liver and kidney damage occurs. The third phase starts about the fourth day with liver and kidney failure, frequently leading to death.

It has become one of my most quoted and requested papers. In the years following, I was invited to speak on mushroom poisoning at many medical centers up and down the West Coast. Every year when the rains came in October and November mushrooms sprouted and were picked and eaten without recognizing the poison *Amanita* varieties. We admitted patients every year with poisonings. In my opinion, no one should pick and eat wild mushrooms. Even experts can't always distinguish the poison ones. In France, where the harvesting of wild mushrooms is common, there are several hundred reported poisonings each year. To this day I always worry when I see dishes in restaurants listing wild mushrooms on their menu, and I usually avoid these choices.

My first year was definitely challenging and time consuming. I did find most of my interns and residents to be highly intelligent and extremely dedicated, and many of them today are on the faculty of other medical institutions around the country. We developed great camaraderie, and I soon felt at home with the faculty and house staff. We invited the resident group for outdoor cookouts at our home, a nice gesture to bring the families together as our guests when the stress levels were high. I also made a point of inviting two or three house staff members to have lunch with me each day. My working schedule was intense. Although I tried to be with the family for dinner, I frequently had to go back to the hospital at night and work to well past midnight.

It was an exhilarating year, one in which I knew I had to make a momentous decision about my future career, whether to remain at this institution, which was planning to become the premier center on the West Coast and rivaling the Boston Harvard program, or return to the East. This decision weighed heavily on my mind every single day.

CRITICAL DECISION

When I came to Stanford I had already been invited to return to the NIH in Bethesda to become a Senior Investigator. Thus, during that first year at Stanford, I thought a lot about what my next position would be, as anyone would at this stage in their career.

The possibilities were a bit frightening and caused me a great deal of anxiety. However, by this time I had had more than thirty papers published in high-quality journals and considered myself to be an excellent junior faculty member. This understanding did not fully allay my insecurity.

LAURA AND DONNA.

About six months into the year I was offered an opportunity to remain at Stanford in the cardiology division and to be appointed instructor in medicine, the highest level of appointment for someone just graduating from the house staff. The faculty of the medical college at Stanford was quite small, compared to the much larger faculty at Harvard. There were only a few openings and the budget to hire new faculty was limited. Hal Holman wanted me to stay but had little to offer. He was also confronted with the rule of the university that postdoctoral fellows and house staff are graduate students, joining the faculty from a position within the university, and you could only be appointed at the instructor level.

There were no employment benefits to being an instructor, and in fact, one had to wait to be included in the retirement plan for two years after becoming an assistant professor. Holman had to face the reality of promising me more in the future. So, at this time he was only able to provide an appointment as an instructor, but with many promises for the future.

In a way I thought this offer was an insult for someone who had published so many papers and in my view had such a great potential as an academic faculty member. It was also clear that the senior two people in cardiology had not been consulted about my coming to Stanford as a chief resident, or being offered a position on the faculty in their division. I agonized over my decision. Finally, in January 1964, I came to the conclusion that I should stay at Stanford and begin to build my career there.

There was no local funding available to start my laboratory program at Stanford. However, grant funds from the NIH were much easier to acquire at that time, and I set about preparing a grant application for a substantial amount of funding even while I was still chief resident. I was able to have my application reviewed by my former mentor, Eugene Braunwald, who made many helpful suggestions. My application was to open a new field of investigation around the nervous control of cardiac function. This was an area in which I had worked at the NIH. I also planned to focus on the mechanisms of abnormal heart rhythms, another area in which I had done some early work at the NIH. I worked on writing the application for almost three months. The application was quite extensive and it was for $300,000 a year for five years, at that time an enormous amount. In today's terms it would be about $1.5 million for each year. It seemed a bit audacious that someone so young would apply for this kind of money. However, I was fortunate and had good research foundations. I was awarded most of the money to begin my career.

After some negotiation, I was paid the gross sum of $13,000 per year, which was barely a livable wage for the area for someone with three children.

Stanford had very limited laboratory facilities and I was given a laboratory that I shared with the hematology faculty. The only problem was that in this laboratory the hematologists were studying the blood from chickens, and throughout several of my experiments using dogs or rabbits I was showered with chicken feathers. While this did not interfere with my experiments it did provide a jocular exchange with the hematologists. The laboratory was rather small compared to the present day, but after I received my grant I was able to equip it very well.

I was also given an office in the cardiology department. It turned out to be one of the rooms that had previously been used for recording EKGs. It was small, with no window, and was in an obscure location. I was able to hire a secretary, the wife of one of the junior residents, who also served as a lab technician since she had worked in that capacity in Salt

> *The only problem was that in this laboratory the hematologists were studying the blood from chickens and throughout several of my experiments using dogs or rabbits I was showered with chicken feathers.*

Lake City. My first offer of compensation was $11,000 per year. This seemed inadequate to buy a house and sustain my family. After some negotiation, I was paid the gross sum of $13,000 per year, which was barely a livable wage for the area for someone with three children.

My work was well known nationally, and during my first year on the faculty I was recruited by the University of Washington to head the cardiology division at the Veterans Hospital in Seattle. However, after a visit to the university I decided it was best for me to keep my activities focused at Stanford.

Then in my second year on the faculty, I was recruited to become a junior faculty member at Washington University in St. Louis. I gave a scientific presentation, made rounds with house staff, and had active interchange with several faculty. My overall impression was favorable. The chairman of medicine, Carl Moore, interviewed me. He was an imposing figure with a shock of grey hair and broad shoulders. He spoke with authority and was one of the giants of academic medicine. After a few pleasantries, when we sat down in his office he glared at me and said, "For a young man you have published far too many papers." At the time, I took this as an insult. At first I thought he was challenging the quality of my work, but it seemed that he resented the fact that someone so young could have published so many papers.

I was able to do so because of the resources provided to me for research at the NIH. He had an old-fashioned view that was quite prevalent in medical schools around the country: one should work in a very junior capacity for at least ten years before achieving any status as a faculty member. This older generation of chairmen of departments of medicine had grown up in that atmosphere for many years and resented young upstarts such as myself for having been quite successful in research activities. I recovered from the feeling of being insulted after giving it some thought and wondered how long such old-fashioned chairmen could remain in control of academic medicine. This attitude was so vastly different from what I was experiencing at Stanford. In the end, I did not give serious consideration to the job in St. Louis. With all that was developing at Stanford with a new faculty and a dynamic leader in Holman, I saw that my career had great opportunity at Stanford and I set about building it.

FAMILY ACTIVITIES

We quickly began to adapt to the California lifestyle and found our family niche. Initially, Laura was extremely tied down with three children under the age of four and getting us settled into our rental house.

For that reason, I did the grocery shopping, usually for a full week, on Friday evenings. I usually took Doug and Beth, our two eldest children, with me. Since our finances were quite limited, I shopped at stores where we could get the greatest discounts and best bargains. Beth usually was sitting in the shopping cart and Douglas was walking alongside.

LAURA AND THE CHILDREN IN FRONT OF THE PEPTO-BISMOL COLORED HOUSE IN LOS ALTOS.

Shopping with toddlers, we'd spend an hour or two at the grocery. The array of vegetables and fruits was far greater than I had ever envisioned; this gave me an opportunity to let the children pick out the ones that they liked, and to point to their favorite breakfast cereals. They also cherished buying ice cream for $1.50 a half gallon. Chocolate was their favorite.

During our first year in California our children were growing, and once I made a decision to remain on the faculty, we began to look for a house to buy. After visiting about fifty houses from Palo Alto to Saratoga, we made a bid on a house in Los Altos. Saratoga was too far away, although the houses were newer and larger. Our bid was accepted for $38,000. This was our first large purchase and we had few assets. We both were anxious; we had stomach cramps and tight muscles and a great deal of anxiety. Driving by the house that had just become ours, I turned to Laura and said, "This house is ugly. What have we done?"

The house, Pepto-Bismol pink stucco, was even smaller than our rental, but the lot was slightly more than a half acre and considered large for the area and backed up to a creek. I was quickly reminded of the wonderful times I had at the creek when I was growing up.

The house also had a basement, unusual for a California house, which gave added space, and with this it was considerably larger than our rental house. The basement space was in need of finishing. Laura engaged a retired carpenter, Mr. Cleveland, who had expertise in turning unfinished spaces into top-quality rooms.

In the basement he created a large family room and an office for me, and a large work room for Laura's sewing and the children's projects. Across the creek there was a fourteen-acre farm. This farm was active, with several crops of vegetables planted each year. Several years of watching a farmer plow with a mule proved entertainment for the children and reminded us of Laura's dad's farm. Later when the farm was sold it became the site of forty-two new houses.

Since we had little money to pay for a house, we took the cash value from my only insurance policy and a loan from my dad for the down payment. We moved ourselves, using a rental truck and the help of three of the residents from the hospital. In some ways, our first year was one of adapting to the California climate and lifestyle, and we came to love all of the possibilities for family activities outdoors and far different venue to raise our children than back in the East and this new house seemed to provide a way to enjoy the California lifestyle.

After we purchased the house in my second year at Stanford, we moved to Los Altos where we lived for twenty-two years. When we moved to our Los Altos house we had a large outdoor patio with a party room and garage, with considerable storage space attached. I was known as the chef for weekend pancake breakfasts, as well as for many dinners cooked on this patio. On some weekend mornings I cooked breakfast for visiting children and on some occasions we shared these breakfast gatherings with our newly arriving postdocs. There were many outdoor activities available in the surrounding area. We spent considerable time exploring the outdoors and the California coastline at Santa Cruz.

I was known as the chef for weekend pancake breakfasts, as well as for many dinners cooked on this patio.

Even though I continued to have my doubts about religion, a carryover from Alabama days, we did need to find a church to attend with our children. Both Laura and I wanted our children to attend Sunday school and learn about organized religion so they could make their own choices when mature enough to do so. We chose the Stanford Chapel, which was recommended to us by several colleagues. However, we found the religious services to be lackluster and the church programs were not well prepared to accept young children. We only attended for our first two years. One of the exceptions to the dull services was a magnificent candlelight service on Christmas Eve, which was quite inspiring. Even after we moved on to other churches we still attended this service. The Stanford Church is a magnificent structure. It resembles old European cathedrals with lots of stained-glass windows, a great organ, and a beautiful tile fresco over the entrance. It is a landmark on the campus tours at Stanford.

THE STANFORD CAMPUS
WITH HOOVER TOWER.

After two years at the Stanford Chapel as our church, we attended the Los Altos Methodist Church, where there was a large congregation and an active Sunday School. I was extremely busy during these years and drifted away from church, although Laura and the children continued to attend for several more years. However, we all sought a church with a small congregation and we found that with the Foothill Congregational Church, where we started attending in about 1972. The congregation was about 200 families and the minister, Chuck Besdick, was a very good minister. We shared many church activities with friends there. Our favorites were the Pilgrims' Thanksgiving where we all dressed accordingly, the Maundy Thursday services, supper groups, and the educational programs. I chaired the education committee that invited speakers and program facilitators, and called on several of my patients. Edward Teller and Milton Friedman were among the favorites. This church gave our children the foundation for making their own choices for their religious lives.

Another thing we recognized about California life when we arrived in 1963 was the need for a second car, which we really couldn't afford. Driving was necessary to get almost anyplace and there was no public transportation. We were driving the station wagon we had purchased just a few months before leaving Bethesda, and I set out to find an inexpensive used car. I bought a 1951 Ford with 100,000 miles on it for only $135 from the son of a friend. This car served us well, and I drove it at least another 60,000 miles over four years. It was battered and had clearly been subjected to poor care. The body of the car had large areas of rust and the green paint was faded. However, its engine and brakes functioned very well and I drove it all around the San Francisco Bay area. If I needed to drive the children to school or to any of their activities, however, they refused to be seen in my old car. They said, "Dad, your car is gross." After driving it for about four years, I sold the car for $135, about the amount I paid when I bought it. In fact, I had never changed the oil, only adding it when it when needed, which was often!

A weekend excursion Laura and I often enjoyed was to go on winery tours in the Sonoma and Napa valleys. Even on weekends there was little traffic and the winery staffs were friendly and welcoming. This is no longer true. There are traffic jams and the staffs at the wineries seem always harassed. The Napa Valley has become commercialized but the Sonoma Valley and the Russian River wineries are still pleasant to visit. Our three youngsters enjoyed the scenery but complained of having to wait for us while we were wine tasting.

We were also able to go to Carmel on occasions. I remembered one particular event when I went to be interviewed at the Pebble Beach Lodge for a competition for a Giannini Fellowship for junior faculty. The lodge had a magnificent lobby with a high ceiling and windows overlooking one of the most famous golf courses in the world and was across from the Carmel Beach. That beach was one we walked on and watched the Pacific waves crash against on many occasions. I was very anxious about the interview, and as I suspected, there were many difficult questions about my plans for an academic career. Because of my Boston internship and NIH interview experience, I responded with well-structured answers. I was awarded the fellowship, which would support my salary, and I was delighted. We stayed

PILGRIM THANKSGIVING AT CHURCH WITH THE FAMILY.

for the evening to have dinner at the French Poodle Restaurant in Carmel, which quickly became a favorite of ours. It was small and the intimate atmosphere was complemented with food prepared by an excellent French chef.

After a few glasses of Chardonnay I relaxed and we enjoyed pecan-crusted lamb and our favorite dessert, "Isle Flotant." We eagerly anticipated other trips to Carmel when we were able to have someone stay with the children, and we could find some quiet time together and refresh our energies. On these later trips we would stay at the Highland Inn—a series of small cottages with fireplaces and beds that sunk in the middle, but being young and full of energy, this could not displace the feeling of romance we experienced. There was also a large heated pool that overlooked the Pacific Ocean, and a great restaurant. The costs of such an outing were reasonable and the American Plan covered not only our room but all meals. The woods around the cottages and the water in the pool were extremely relaxing. These trips were just the beginning of our many Carmel experiences.

LAURA AND DON SKIING.

Laura and I were invited to go to Lake Tahoe and the Sierra Mountains. One of my junior residents had a house at Alpine Meadows, a well-known ski area, and in our third summer in California we had a week to spend at Tahoe. The weather was a bit unsettled and it actually snowed several inches in August. That was quite a shock for us, having come from the East where August was hot and humid, rather than snowy. A few years later the kids wanted to learn to ski and when they were about eight or nine years old they learned to use a rope tow rather than chair lifts, which was the way skiing was taught at some of the smaller resorts. After several years, all of our children became excellent on the ski slopes and we went to the Sierras several times each winter. Laura and I decided that we were too old to learn to ski, but after about five years, our minds were changed and we both took up the sport. It was a bit humiliating to me to start with lessons at age 35, and I had more than my share of falls. In my first week of lessons I was doing so poorly that I considered giving up, but my dad's lesson of perseverance kept me going. My most humiliating event during that week of lessons was falling on my face on the test run after all five women in the group had done so well before me on the run. I lived down my humiliations, however, and over the years became a reasonably competent skier. I am still skiing at age 73, but have tempered my style to reduce the risks.

Making sure our children received the best educational opportunities was of the highest priority for us. The two eldest children, Doug and Beth, attended preschool at the Wooden

Shoe prior to being kindergartners at the Almond School in Los Altos. This was a small private one with an excellent program. Donna attended preschool at the Thorneycroft School in Los Altos Hills. This was more upscale and was one where children from more affluent homes attended. Later she joined the others at Almond School.

It was an excellent school with small classes and dedicated teachers, quite typical for California public schools at that time. Laura and I were the head of the Parent Teacher Association in 1970 at Almond School. She did most of the work and had to coax me not to be too dictatorial when I was running the meetings and to remember that PTAs could not be run like my research lab. I mellowed a little, and tried to be kind to those who asked what seemed to me stupid questions or inane remarks. While I have learned a lot over the ensuing years, I still have to "bite my tongue" when people ask stupid questions. In any case, I was a figurehead president who only ran the formal meeting and Laura did all the organization.

We also made a trip to Alabama on a plane sometime during our first two years in California to visit with family and have our children meet their cousins. It was also an opportunity for them to see how we had grown up in Appalachia. We visited with several of Laura's relatives, some of whom still lived on a farm. Appalachia had changed in the years since we left. Now everyone had phones, TVs, and new cars. One part of

BACK TO ALABAMA WITH THE CHILDREN.

the trip was to go to Las Vegas where I was being offered a job as head of cardiology at the largest hospital. It offered almost twenty times the compensation I was receiving at Stanford and there was no board-certified cardiologist in Las Vegas at the time. After careful consideration and a veto by Laura, I turned it down and stayed at Stanford in academic medicine.

It is interesting to note the increase in numbers of specialists available in urban areas. Las Vegas has gone from no cardiology specialists in 1967 to thirty-two today. One of the reasons for Laura's veto was the observation that the casino in our hotel was still crowded at 5 a.m. on Sunday morning. She did not consider Las Vegas a proper place to raise our

A FASCHING CELEBRATION AS POPE AND WENCH.

children. But because the offer was so lucrative I told Laura she could live in Hawaii and I would come on weekends. She said vehemently, "I did not marry you to live apart and raise these children without a father." She was in the process of also instituting a rebellion by the children if I chose Las Vegas.

Our family life was much like that of others living in the Bay Area, focusing largely on raising a family. However, Stanford offered many additional social opportunities. We attended family movies at Memorial Auditorium on the campus on Sunday nights. All of our children have reminded me that the best movie we viewed in the auditorium was *Lawrence of Arabia*. We frequently had dinners at the Student Center on campus, and later enjoyed many sporting events of the Stanford teams. Football was our most favored viewing sport and we all enjoyed activities at the new and beautiful Faculty Club, built in 1975. Sunday brunch was a particular favorite. The spread of food contained varieties from many cultures. There were many opportunities to party with other families.

THE QUEEN AND I.

I have fond memories of a Fasching Party where we dressed as the Pope and his wench, and of a very dressy Valentine's Day Party where we dressed in royal costumes that Laura had made for us.

After the children finished Almond Elementary School they attended the middle school about three miles from our house, and on most days they rode bikes to school. They attended Los Altos High School where they had excellent teachers who were wonderful influences on each of them. Los Altos High competed most favorably with the private schools in the area. This was before Proposition 13, the Gramm-Rudman Act, which markedly reduced the property tax and gravely damaged the quality of California schools. It was a California referendum to roll back property taxes and limit their increase. Advanced placement courses and opportunities for extracurricular activities were abundant. Our children all did well in high school and both of the girls were class speakers at their graduation exercises.

On the other hand, social life in the Bay Area was tough for our children. Drugs were prevalent, marijuana was easily available, and binge drinking occurred on the weekends. Doug and Donna had minor involvement but were never part of the "druggie" crowd. For much of the year, their lives away from school revolved around the home. Our pool was an attraction not only for our children but also for others in the neighborhood. We had a redwood hot tub, the first in the neighborhood. It was situated beside the pool and we used it in winter too, even when the pool was too cold for swimming. Even in winter, we frequently heated the pool, since natural gas was inexpensive and heated our pool in a few hours.

A MARATHON WITH BETH.

There were frequent trips to Tahoe, for now the whole family was skiing. Everyone participated in jogging, and I trained for a marathon with both Beth and Donna. In 1978, Beth and I ran the Avenue of the Giants Marathon, held in the Redwoods National Park in Northwestern California. We trained for six months, getting up as early as five in the morning and running anywhere from six to twenty miles a day.

We had trained for a cool day, as the weather normally was at that time of year, but marathon day turned out to be hot at nearly 100 degrees, and Beth almost collapsed at nineteen miles. I left her behind with tears in my eyes. We had previously agreed that if either had to "drop out" the other would continue. I finished the marathon, but my spirits were dampened because Beth was not with me. I watched other runners come across the finish line, and about five minutes later, there came Beth. She had recovered to finish and then fall into my arms, exhausted.

This was a wonderful experience, so almost two years later I trained with Donna for the San Francisco Marathon, but a few weeks before the marathon she had to drop out because of mononucleosis. I was attempting to qualify for the Boston Marathon, but they decreased the time required for qualification just a few weeks before, and even though I tried vainly to reach their level to qualify, I found it impossible to do so. At the end of the San Francisco Marathon, which I did in three hours and twenty-two minutes, I was having severe leg cramps and collapsed on the ground. Laura took photographs of me and had them enlarged, and from viewing those pictures I decided on no further marathons. The photos made me look as if I were about to die.

THE SAN FRANCISCO MARATHON.

The children did occasionally get into mischief. Doug and one of his classmates, Mike Sanservino, placed smoke bombs in a telephone booth in a nearby town while on a bike trip. It was reported they were caught by the local police, and of course, threatened with jail. The boys were rescued by Don Sanservino, Mike's father, and were quite shaken, promising never to do it again. They did, however, pay a price for their mischief. They were grounded to their home for several weekends that summer, which seemed a high enough price to them.

Because of their high school records, all of the children wanted to go to top-ranked colleges. I took a college trip to the Northeast with each of them. These college trips were a great time for me to interact with the children. We had a week together and all of our meals. We also visited the birthplaces of Douglas and Beth. We discussed their career plans and what they really wanted from a college. They did not get their first choice, but each was selected by their second choice. Douglas went to Dartmouth, Beth and Donna to Stanford. I was pleased with their choices and valued the time I had spent with them on these trips.

As I remember my years at Stanford, it was difficult for me to have enough time with the children, being very busy with my career. I have questioned each of them about these years, and while they say they missed me, the quality of my time with them seemed more important to them than the quantity, and the quality seemed to work out favorably. When I look back, though, I do wish I could have spent more time with Laura and the children.

CHALLENGES

One of the prerequisites for succeeding in academic medicine is to have

appropriate space to carry out one's research. Space was especially important

for me, for I wanted to expand the group of postdocs in the cardiology program.

After other medical schools tried to recruit me, Stanford gave me additional laboratories beyond the one I shared with hematology. I was given two smaller labs, so I had a dog laboratory and two laboratories for biochemistry and physiology.

Since I had just completed my stint as chief resident, I thought I could recruit postdocs to my cardiology division from the house staff who had served with me as chief resident. In addition to recruiting talented postdocs I was relentless in

POSTDOCTORAL FELLOWSHIP GROUP WITH DON.

my pursuit of work space. I soon found I had no funding for fellowships and stipends, but I was able to recruit four outstanding medical students for experimental work. They were in the Stanford five-year program and were eager for a research opportunity as part of their program. These students came to work with me because they heard I had grant support and that I was a young talented investigator.

All four had great knowledge about physiology and pharmacology from their medical school program, and several had prior research experience. Walter Henry, the first student I recruited, developed our computer programs for cardiac studies in the catheterization laboratory. Denver Nelson, who considered himself a real ladies' man, did isolated heart studies because of his prior work in this area as a college student in Iowa. Brian Paaso, a big football player in college, had some dog lab experience, and Bob Griffith, a biochemist by training, set up all of our biochemistry laboratory studies. They were a great team with their research experience and a desire to be fully engaged in our research. They were willing to work long hours, and because of their experience, could work independently.

When doing dog experiments, though, I soon noted they had great fear of barking and snarling dogs. I frequently found my student researchers cornered by barking dogs when they were sent to the kennels to anesthetize them for lab studies. The dog was the chosen animal for studying cardiac function then, but after 1984, the pig became the best model. Its circulatory system more resembled the human system. For the dog experiments, I would march in, muzzle the dog, and administer the anesthesia.

I learned at the NIH that dogs could detect fear but if one had none they were submissive. Over time I was able to teach the students to have no fear. Once the dog was anesthetized, it was taken to the dog physiology laboratory, which was equipped like an operating room. We had monitors for all their heart and respiratory functions and we had temperature controls for maintaining steady body temperatures. We were quite careful to continue to administer anesthesia as we operated on a dog.

We were attempting to create models of human disease in the laboratory...

We put catheters or tubes in the arteries and veins and attached electrodes to the heart after we opened its chest. It was necessary to have the animal on a breathing machine, which required us to monitor the oxygen in the blood on a continuous basis.

We were attempting to create models of human disease in the laboratory and then determine the action of some very new drugs being considered for clinical trial. One of our machines recorded multiple levels of blood pressure and its electrical signals were transmitted onto a paper output to be studied at a later time. We made a series of control measurements, then administered the drugs and measured their activities over a period of time. This allowed us to predict how the drugs might act in a human.

We were also working with rabbits and attempting to use their isolated hearts for experiments. Denver Nelson had experience with isolated heart preparation as a senior in college and brought this expertise to our laboratories. Hearts could be removed and placed in a water bath and attached to a tube resembling the circulatory system, where we could study heart functions. Before we had grant money I provided a personal check to buy platinum for electrodes to stimulate the heart, and we borrowed the water baths and recording equipment from the student physiology laboratories. This was the way young investigators succeeded in their research efforts before grant money became available. I quickly learned that it was mandatory to become an academic entrepreneur, which enabled one to pursue one's investigations.

Concurrently with dog and rabbit studies, I attempted to work with the pharmacology department to use some of their expertise and their space. Even though I had become a member of the Society for Pharmacology and Experimental Therapeutics, the most prestigious basic science society for faculty in pharmacology, I was snubbed by the department and not even asked to present a seminar on some of the work I was doing. The pharmacology faculty was very insular, purposely isolating itself from other departments in the school. The department head did not consider any of our clinical research to be worthwhile, and told me so. I was infuriated. Later, when he wanted to be included in the proposal for a new center developed with gift funds, the pharmacology faculty was not welcome. I had my academic revenge.

In order to continue to be successful, however, I needed to be able to recruit top-level postdocs, in addition to my medical students. They do much of the hands-on research for senior investigators. Postdocs are trainees who generally have completed their residencies and are receiving additional experience in a specialty. They are permitted and encouraged to do research as part of the program. To support these individuals I needed to receive an NIH training grant in addition to my research grant.

I was fortunate to meet the head of the training grant division from the NIH, Lee Langley, when he visited the physiology department at Stanford. Eugene Yates was the head of Stanford physiology, and he was quite different from pharmacology, as he helped me with my fellowship application and on many occasions with my research programs. When I showed the NIH director around our labs, he was quite impressed with the activities I had ongoing with my students and believed that we could successfully recruit postdocs. He helped me write a successful training grant application to support six postdocs and their research. It was awarded after my second year on the faculty. Several of the house staff from the Harvard hospitals who knew me from my residency training applied, and along with applications from the Stanford house staff I had a large pool from which to select.

So, after my second year on the faculty, I was able to recruit excellent postdocs and fellows who shared my ambition for academic medicine. Many of them had excellent research experience in their earlier training and were eager to continue research. As was the haircut style in this period, we all had crew cuts, and as I look back seemed exceptionally young to be physicians.

In addition to my research program, I carried a large clinical load for patient care. Most of the patients we were seeing at Stanford had rheumatic heart disease or valvular disease of some other origin. Many also had advanced heart failure and presented with extreme shortness of breath. The Stanford University Hospital had long maintained a contract with the Kaiser Health System of Northern California to do cardiac catheterization and cardiac surgery for their patients when the clinical program was in San Francisco. When the Stanford faculty moved to Palo Alto they were able to keep the contract. Kaiser had no cath labs and no cardiac surgeons, so this was mutually beneficial. After a decade, Kaiser developed its own cardiovascular programs as their enrollment increased and we no longer saw their patients. For several years, however, this made up almost half of our volume of patients and gave us a steady patient flow.

Over the years, as I have observed the many changes in health care delivery, I often reflect back on the Kaiser Health System in California. This system was one of the first attempts to create an integrated health care system involving prevention, diagnosis, treatment and rehabilitation.

Created by Henry Kaiser for his workers in the steel mills and shipyards of California and Hawaii during World War II, it was a fully prepaid plan with both the company and employees contributing. The system was set up so that each individual had either a family physician or an internist as their primary care doctor. Referrals were controlled through this mechanism and an integrated data system was established, although in the early period it was paper based. Charts and paper records had to be transported around to different departments within the system. With each referral to our cardiology unit we received an excellent summary of the patient's medical history and treatment. The Kaiser system also had fully employed doctors and owned their clinics and hospitals. The profit motivation was not part of this ethos and patients generally were pleased with their care.

The $150 teaching fee I was paid helped our budget at home.

Kaiser also maintained a strong educational program for its physicians and I was engaged to make teaching rounds once a month with physicians and residents at the Oakland Kaiser Hospital, the largest Kaiser facility in northern California. The rounds were generally held from 4 until 6 p.m. on a Friday afternoon. On these occasions Laura could accompany me to Oakland and then we could drive into San Francisco for dinner at a nice restaurant. Jack's and Ernie's and Blue Fox were among our favorites. They were then the top French restaurants in San Francisco but have not survived.

After a long week of clinical and research responsibilities and a grueling teaching lesson, I was always ready for a quiet evening with Laura and the great San Francisco food. The $150 teaching fee I was paid helped our budget at home. While my reflections back on the

Kaiser system might seem irrelevant in the fast-paced, changing medical world today, I truly believe it was far more integrated and successful than most of our current delivery programs.

During my first five years, for our clinical work we were working in a cardiac catheterization lab that was of the 1950s vintage—at least ten years behind modern labs of any type at that time. The x-ray equipment was so outdated that seeing the catheter in the heart was difficult in extremely obese people. The hospital was very apathetic about upgrading this laboratory until we developed the volume of patients necessary to compensate for the cost. I was teaching new trainees to do transseptal catheterizations to study the left-sided chambers of the heart. This was the newest procedure for studying patients with valvular disease. The antiquated x-ray system made this difficult. However, after I became chief of the division we modernized these labs, as the hospital administration recognized our potential to attract more patients. We added the most up-to-date equipment to our catheterization laboratories that was in some ways ahead of the best available.

At that time, calculations from doing a cardiac catheterization were tedious, requiring several hours of manual calculations. One of my medical student researchers, Walter Henry, had worked with computers in a business environment in his job prior to medical school, and wanted to develop a method for doing all of the calculations on-line with a computer. Small computers could not handle the task, so we enlisted support from Dr. Joshua Lederberg, a Nobel Prize Laureate, who had convinced the National Aeronautics and Space Administration to provide a large IBM 370 computer for the university to help us. He provided us free access to this state of the art computer.

It was housed in a huge glassed-in room, and to use it for calculations on-line, while a catheterization was in progress, required that everyone else be taken off the computer. For fifteen or twenty minutes we had full use of the computer. We managed to take full control of the system, which annoyed other users. After a number of trial and error efforts we managed to develop programs which calculated all pressures, flows and the status of the heart's work. Several years later we were able to compact this program into a smaller computer by establishing a relationship with the Hewlett-Packard Medical Division, where a series of small computers had been developed. Working with Stanford's technology transfer office, we licensed the system to Hewlett-Packard. It was distributed worldwide as the *Stanford System* and it gave our cardiology program international recognition for being one of the first to use computer technology in cardiology.

Another advance in cardiology in the 1960s was a new way of treating patients who had suffered heart attacks. And we considered that computers could be useful here, too. Coronary care units were just beginning to be developed in the late 1960s. These units had specialized equipment and well-trained personnel to take care of patients with heart attacks. In 1971, Stanford University Hospital invested in a six-bed coronary care unit and we worked diligently to make this a top-of-the-line unit for both clinical activities and clinical research. The concept of a coronary care unit was developed in Edinburgh, Scotland, by Desmond Julian. I had visited this site on several occasions and was able to help with the design of the unit at Stanford University Hospital.

The concept was to create a specialized unit for continuously monitoring the electrocardiograms of patients who had heart attacks. They could be monitored on a real time basis by a nurse watching these recordings on a TV monitor. Monitors were also designed to sound alarms when the heart rates became either too slow or too fast, or an abnormal rhythm occurred. These units were generally created around the central nursing station with glass observation windows into each of the patients' rooms from the central nursing station. It had been observed that most of the deaths occurred when abnormal heart rhythms developed in the first three or four days after a heart attack. For that reason, patients were to remain in the coronary care unit in the specialized monitored beds for that three- or four-day period.

Over the next ten years, coronary care units provided a level of care that reduced early deaths from heart attacks from about thirty percent to around twelve percent. Patients could be given specialized drugs for abnormal rhythms, and also treated with electrical shock from a defibrillator unit to restore normal rhythm. If they had total arrest of their heart they often could be resuscitated. While these coronary units were first developed at university hospitals throughout the country, they were soon widely adopted by almost all hospitals of more than a hundred beds. The sophistication of such equipment and monitoring techniques has continued to evolve and improve.

The care of patients with heart attacks has undergone dramatic changes since the time I was an intern at the Peter Bent Brigham Hospital. Even at the Brigham Hospital our care of patients with heart attacks was considered radical and maybe dangerous. Most institutions at that time kept a patient with a heart attack in bed for six weeks, and in fact, lifted them up to carry out their bodily functions in bedpans. They were to remain totally inactive to avoid any stress on a heart with an area that had been damaged and that could potentially rupture. Sam Levine at the Brigham Hospital had designed a bedside chair and a bedside commode, and after the first few days of being in bed with a heart attack, the patients were lifted into the chairs or to the bedside commode to carry out their bodily functions. After a few more days of this, the patients were allowed to get themselves into the special chair on their own.

This early ambulation was considered extremely radical by many cardiologists. It was thought that it took six weeks for the damaged heart to heal. The Levine program, as this came to be known, kept patients in the hospital for only three weeks and the patients became ambulatory during this period of time. By the time I was at Stanford, patients were still hospitalized for three weeks, and with the development of the coronary care unit, were kept in that unit for three or four days before being plced in the open ward. Patients were allowed to become ambulatory after the first week and generally went home after about two weeks.

By the 1980s, patients with heart attacks were rushed to the emergency room and given thrombolytic agents that would break up the blood clot in the coronary arteries, and then be hospitalized for several days in a monitored unit before being allowed to become ambulatory. They were generally discharged after a week. Now patients with heart attacks either receive thrombolytic agents that dissolve blood clots, or in many cases, undergo catheterization and balloon angioplasty followed by placement of a stent in the coronary artery during the acute phase of the heart attack. This allows rapid recirculation of blood to the damaged area of muscle. For balloon angioplasty, the catheters are inserted into the heart under x-ray. A balloon, which is on the outside of the catheter, is inflated to dilate the artery, and on this balloon is a stent that stays inflated and expanded to hold the artery open after the balloon is deflated and the catheter removed. Patients are then maintained on agents to prevent or reduce blood clotting for several months thereafter. They are generally discharged from the hospital in four to five days. These dramatic changes in the management of heart attacks have resulted in the marked reduction in deaths from acute heart attacks, as well as earlier rehabilitation and return to work.

We used the coronary care unit at Stanford as a major clinical research site. Our focus was to determine effective blood levels of various antiarrhythmic drugs that prevent life-threatening arrhythmias in patients experiencing myocardial infarction. These abnormal rhythms were the leading cause of death after a heart attack and if they could be prevented more patients would survive. We were studying the same drugs I had studied in patients at the NIH. Jopst Von Groben, a computer scientist from the anesthesia department, worked with us. He had developed computer algorhythms for quantifying arrhythmias in patients. While we could not do this on-line, we were able to put the data on tape and later do the analysis. Subsequently, we made modifications in our computer algorithms to work in real time when the capacity of computers increased to accommodate our large program.

Our initial programs were developed without a great deal of input from the nursing staff.

This program was developed in association with the Hewlett-Packard Medical Products Group. Our initial programs missed many easily detected abnormal rhythms that were easily called by the nurses, and our system sounded many false alarms. The nurses in the coronary care unit were so disturbed that they turned off the computer and draped the monitors with black crepe paper. This was their method of telling us our programs did not work. However, we used their expertise to continue to improve the system after co-opting them to become part of the development team.

After improving the programs, we needed a second site for a beta test of the equipment. To be close to the Boston Hewlett-Packard (HP) Medical Equipment Plant, the company chose a Providence, Rhode Island, hospital. A beta site had not been exposed to the various modifications and early failures and would judge the final system on its merit. Just before Christmas 1972, I was summoned to meet with Lewis Platt, the engineering director of HP Medical, to spend a night observing the unit working in the hospital's CCU. On the day before Christmas Eve I remember saying, "Lew, we are crazy being here when we should be with our families." We agreed that this problem could wait until the beginning of the year, and I returned to California and my family. Back in Los Altos, I was called the "Grinch who almost stole Christmas" by my family.

After major modification, over a period of six months, our detection of arrhythmias by a computer became very accurate and the nursing staff readily accepted our systems as helpful. We licensed the programs to HP and thousands of units were sold worldwide with the label "Developed by The Stanford Cardiology Program." This again gave us international recognition.

We also developed methods for determining blood levels and the effectiveness of several antiarrhythmic drugs administered to our patients. We used the computer programs to give quantitative measures of the abnormal rhythms and related that to quantitative blood levels of specific drugs. This work lead to our protocols being widely adopted in coronary care units around the world. One of my seminal publications appeared in the *New England Journal of Medicine,* relating the blood concentration to the effect on arrhythmias. This was also one of the earliest papers demonstrating that plasma levels of drugs could be closely correlated with some physiologic or pharmacologic action. Until this time it was generally assumed that if a patient was given a medication, they received enough of it to have a specific desired action on either the heart or some other organ in the body. It was not widely understood that some patients absorbed the drug in their intestines more slowly than others; some excreted more of the drug through their kidneys; others had the drug metabolized in the liver. Some of the drugs were bound more than others to proteins in the blood.

Thus, the idea of developing a standard level of a drug in the blood by which one could assess its direct effect was new, providing a way to more precisely quantify the action of a drug when studied in a group of patients. The study of how a drug is distributed in the body, how it is absorbed, and how it is excreted through the kidneys is known as pharmacokinetics. We were using these pharmacokinetic concepts in our study of drug levels in blood for treating patients with heart attacks and/or heart failure. We were some of the early pioneers in this type of work and this important research led to my being invited to participate in research programs both in the United States and in Europe. Our clinical research utilizing some of the newer analytical and computer techniques became the focus of work for many of our postdocs and permitted them to appear on programs for their presentations at the American Heart Association and the American College of Cardiology annual meetings. This provided a platform for beginning their academic careers.

For me, these early days at Stanford were also a period of learning other diagnostic methodology in the field of cardiology. I had only limited experience in electrocardiographic interpretation, but I was required to read the hospital electrocardiograms (EKGs) for one-third of the year. EKGs are electrical recordings of the heart's activity and are used to diagnose heart attacks and arrhythmias. While at the Peter Bent Brigham as a resident I had a one-month rotation reading EKGs under the supervision of Harold Levine, who was the author of a widely used textbook on EKG interpretation. At the NIH I was the backup EKG reader when Joe Greenfield, the primary reader, was on vacation. So I had some experience, but it was somewhat limited. Together with my postdocs I learned the newest EKG diagnostic categorizations and applied them later to help develop computer interpretation. This work was directed by William Hancock, one of my fellow faculty members in cardiology who was a well-known expert in EKG interpretation. He helped me to learn as well.

We also hosted many nationally recognized cardiologists who had retired from their academic posts. Howard Burchell, who had been chief of cardiology at the Mayo Clinic and the University of Minnesota was one of our favorites. He and his wife spent a month with us on several occasions. He was an excellent mentor for our eager postdoctoral fellows.

In addition to clinical and research activities, I was expected, as were other members of the faculty, to take teaching responsibilities for the medical students. Because of my strong research background, I was recruited to teach the sections on heart function and its control by the nervous system. Some of my students became my first recruits to work with me in the laboratory. For the first two years I presented one or two clinical correlation sessions with the department of physiology for the first-year medical students. A clinical correlation session is used to relate the physiology of heart action to the clinical symptoms and course in a patient. These are used to expose medical students to practical knowledge early in their education.

Starting in my fourth year, we were asked by the physiology department to teach the section on the heart and vascular function by giving a series of fifteen or so lectures. Together, Mark Perlroth and I, along with several members of the cardiology division, developed a core curriculum and a syllabus for teaching the first-year medical students. We gave approximately fifteen lectures and demonstrations. Each year I was responsible for several of these during the first several years of this teaching assignment. My teaching assignments were closely linked to the research I was engaged with relating to the nervous system control of heart function.

This was also at a time when students were given the opportunity to evaluate the quality of the teaching. At the end of each lecture they gave grades for the faculty performance. I was quite pleased, having

DON AND LAURA WITH DR. HOWARD BURCHELL.

always received an average of approximately 4.5 on a scale of 5, or an A for my teaching effort. Teaching was an important function for the faculty. We took it quite seriously, even though we had other major responsibilities as faculty members in a clinical department. Faculty members with large clinical responsibilities or large research efforts are frequently faulted for not doing enough teaching. This has not been my experience.

———

Despite cardiology's quick advances in research and technology, this period in the late '60s and early '70s was a very difficult time for Stanford. There were numerous demonstrations across the campus, largely protesting the Vietnam War. Faculty and student protests were almost a daily occurrence. A sit-in in the president's office lasted for days, and the unrest lead to the president of Stanford University's resignation. The undergraduate students at Stanford were among the most vocal and outspoken. They frequently led demonstrations throughout the San Francisco Bay area and a number of them, including the president of the student body, were imprisoned for refusing to be drafted into service for the war.

The medical students did not participate in these demonstrations to any great extent. When I discussed this with my students who were doing research and my students on the wards, they stated they were too busy getting their medical education to be involved. They were more interested in the five-year curriculum of the medical school, which was unique in this country. The Stanford five-year program was a success in creating doctors for academic leadership; however, it was abandoned after sixteen years because of societal pressure to shorten the requirements for a medical degree and also because of the rising cost of medical education. The five-year curriculum met its goal, as was documented by the large number of students from these sixteen years of classes who entered careers in academic medicine.

While I did not participate in any of the Vietnam demonstrations, I became philosophically opposed to the war, as was most of the faculty at Stanford University. Some of the more active protestors participated in destructive tactics; one faculty member attempted to destroy the computer center and was later dismissed from the faculty because of this behavior. The country, especially the West Coast, was in emotional turmoil over the Vietnam War. My emotional response was triggered by reading the reports of the destruction of the entire country of Vietnam and the fact that rather than reaching an endpoint, the war was dragging on, with a much greater loss of life for American servicemen.

I also began to see veterans returning, as I made rounds at the VA hospital where they were being treated for either injuries they received or for psychiatric rehabilitation from the destruction of human life that they had observed. We were concerned that these traumatic experiences could accelerate heart disease, and worked with patients to develop preventive measures, such as blood pressure control, regular exercise, and a healthy diet.

A YOUNG CHIEF

In early 1967, after three years of being on the faculty at Stanford, I was being recruited to the Southwestern Medical Complex of the University of Texas, Dallas, as director of cardiology.

I had done much to promote further clinical activities by the cardiology division and I had numerous research projects, which were now well funded with NIH grants. The question was, "What could Stanford do to keep me?" Hal Holman, the chairman of medicine, approached me about becoming the chief of the division of cardiology and the chief of cardiology for Stanford University Hospital. He made the bold move of asking the then chief, Herb Hultgren, to go on sabbatical and then come back and be head of cardiology at our Veterans Administration Hospital, but still part of the division that would report to me.

However, the medical school had just recruited from Harvard a new dean for Stanford's College of Medicine, and it was determined that I should meet him and gain his approval before I could be appointed to this position as head of cardiology, since it was such an important appointment. Dr. Robert Glaser was a leading administrator of academic centers, having been at St. Louis, Colorado, and Harvard. I met with him at the Academic Medical meeting in Atlantic City, the site for the major academic medicine societies meetings from 1937 to the 1980s. It was a recruiting site for medical department chairpersons from almost all colleges of medicine. In the 1980s the specialty meeting became prominent and attendance dwindled, chairpersons no longer attended, and the meeting site changed to Washington, then finally to Chicago. He questioned me about my career plans and how I planned to build cardiology programs at Stanford. He heartily approved of my appointment and was always supportive. Norm Shumway, the head of cardiovascular surgery, was also asked for an opinion, and he strongly supported me because we had begun to work closely with his unit.

Hal Holman's decision to make me chief of cardiology when he could have recruited a much older and established cardiologist from elsewhere was a calculated risk on his part. While I do not know the exact reason he made this decision, I always speculated that he understood the success in research that I had attained at the NIH and was impressed that I had been able to attract talented students and postdoctoral fellows to work with me in the Stanford environment. He must have appreciated the fact that I had been able to secure excellent funding for my work from the NIH, and even with a heavy research program I had been able to develop a major cardiology practice.

I had also worked with Holman on changing medical grand rounds and had shown an interest in being fully engaged in departmental activities. I was one of three members of a committee that interviewed candidates for the house staff. This required about ninety or a hundred interview sessions per year. He must have thought I had the energy, enthusiasm, and the risk-taking capability to create an internationally known cardiology unit. He was also concerned that he did not have the financial resources or space to attract a well-established figure from another institution.

With this major appointment, I thought I should at least become an associate professor, but after discussion by the executive committee, representing the chairmen of all the departments, it was decided that I had been an assistant professor for only a year and a half and therefore was not eligible for promotion to associate professor by university rules. I would have to wait a year, but was promised the promotion. I was also disappointed in the fact that they made no big compensation increase, only to $17,000 per year. Stanford was well known nationally for low compensation for faculty in the medical school.

On the night before the boards were to be given in Los Angeles, I took a Textbook of Cardiology and set out for Los Angeles by plane...

While I was honored to be the chief of cardiology at a major center at age 32, it seemed this was occurring with a lower-level faculty appointment and less-than-fair compensation in my opinion. I was quite angry about this and it took several years for me to quiet the anger. However, I took the job and stayed. Despite the low salary and academic rank, I knew that it was a great opportunity to build a major program and few would get such an opportunity at such a young age. I was confident that when I proved my ability I would be justly rewarded. It was also significant that Herb Hultgren, the former chief who had been asked to move to the VA Hospital, never showed any malice toward me. I believe Hultgren realized that there were so many newly developing technologies in cardiology and he was eager for the talented young leadership to step in. Because of his loyalty to "his" university where he had spent his entire career, he was willing to step aside for new leadership.

To my surprise, Hultgren became one of my major supporters. He was quite helpful in promoting my membership in the Association of University Cardiologists organization, which had a very select policy for membership, accepting only those who were leaders in academic cardiology. He also encouraged me to take my subspecialty board examinations in cardiovascular medicine. I had not considered this important because of my training in Boston. In the Harvard system people did not usually take subspecialty boards. Most of the clinical faculty at Harvard regarded themselves as excellent physicians covering the full range of medical conditions. They did take boards in internal medicine, but shunned the subspecialty boards. Even though I had passed my boards in internal medicine, I had waited for several years to take my subspecialty boards in cardiovascular medicine because it would be devastating to fail when I was already the hospital chief of cardiology.

Hultgren was about to become chair of the committee administering boards in cardiovascular medicine, which at that time had less than 1,000 certified specialists nationwide. Today there are over 21,000. He urged me to take the boards before he became the chairman, because of the question of conflict for him if I either passed or failed. We agreed, but with all of my other activities, I had little time to study. On the night before the boards were to be given in Los Angeles, I took a *Textbook of Cardiology* and set out for Los Angeles by plane, planning to study the entire evening. On that same trip there were three members of the examining board, who were also on their way to Los Angeles. They invited me to go to dinner with them. It turned out that I knew every member of the examining board at that time—further study seemed out of the question so I joined them for dinner.

The next day I took the boards and was given two very difficult patients with congenital heart disease to examine, then I had to meet with the examiners. I diagnosed one very easily; the second one I missed the diagnosis but gave a rational discussion. The six subspecialty areas in which I was questioned, including EKG, cardiac surgery, pathology, physiology and others, proved quite difficult. I remember vividly the pathology exam. I entered a room and met the pathology examiner, who was a slightly built young female pathologist with a quiet voice. She instructed me to put on gloves and approach a large metal table on which there were about forty hearts from autopsies. I saw in an instant that there were tiny, small hearts, no bigger than chicken hearts at one end of the table, and large, adult hearts at the other. Knowing that I had little understanding of the congenital heart disease probably present in the small hearts, I approached the end of the table with the large adult hearts.

She said quite forcefully to me, "Dr. Harrison, go to the other end of the table. I want you to explain the blood flow through the first of those four hearts on the left side of the table."

They were very tiny; I recognized instantly that each of them was from a child with congenital heart disease. They had been opened so one could view the chambers and connection of the various vessels, but this only made it more confusing for me. After some period of time I was able to trace the flow of blood that would have occurred through several of these hearts.

Then I had to move to the other end of the table. For the adult hearts I delivered a much more competent explanation. Throughout the rest of the day, all the questions for me by each of the examiners focused on congenital heart disease. This was particularly true for the x-ray imaging studies and the treatment programs.

Afterwards, when I talked to the other twelve people taking boards with me that day, none of them had any patients with congenital heart disease, nor had they discussed congenital heart disease with the subspecialty inquisitors. It seemed that they had given me an extremely difficult test, and that I was probably selected to be given a difficult time. In spite of a difficult test I did well on all the six subspecialty areas because of my broad clinical care practice.

Upon returning to Stanford I was told that I had passed, and was quite pleased to have this hurdle behind me. Since I had been examined by Noble Fowler, the chairman, and missed the diagnosis with his patient, I sent him a letter saying, "You are a gentleman and a scholar. Thanks!" He was on the faculty of the College of Medicine in Cincinnati, and later when I moved there, we laughed about our memories of these events. Today the cardiovascular board has adapted to a larger number of applicants by requiring only a written test that is graded by a computer. There are no patient exams. There are far too many applicants for the personal patient exams such as I went through.

She said quite forcefully to me, "Dr. Harrison, go to the other end of the table. I want you to explain the blood flow through the first of those four hearts on the left side of the table."

Upon becoming chief of cardiology, I recognized that I needed some mentoring. I needed the advice from leaders at successful institutions. I returned to Boston and spent several days at the Massachusetts General Hospital and then at Johns Hopkins visiting with the chiefs of cardiology of those institutions. I chose these two because I knew the chiefs: Ed Haber at Massachusetts General and Richard Ross at Johns Hopkins.

Each institution had a premier program and both chiefs welcomed me and provided helpful insights for a new program. From them I learned that I must apply for more grants to get more pos-doctoral fellows and to begin to build a talented young faculty, while at the same time keeping a strong clinical program. These were then and still are the prerequisites for building successful academic programs. By the time I was appointed chief, several of my postdocs had been successful with their research, and I observed those who had creative ideas and worked diligently in their pursuits, and chose them to join my faculty at junior levels. These included John Schroeder and Edwin Alderman, later adding Richard Popp, Jay Mason, Roger Winkle and David Cannon.

I also began to participate in American Heart Association (AHA) activities in the San Francisco Bay Area, where we were trying to reorganize the research committees of nine counties into a single Bay Area research committee. This required many nights of activity but proved to be rewarding in that several of my junior faculty and my postdoctoral fellows received support from the AHA through the Bay Area Heart Committee. This became the first American Heart Consortium, rather than an individual chapter to award competitive grants for research.

As the new chief I found I had to juggle multiple tasks, and I was so exhilarated that I could hardly sleep beyond 5 a.m. I was fortunate to have a wife with well-honed organizational skills. Laura willingly took over the management of the house, the children's schooling and our finances. I sought every opportunity to tell others about Stanford's programs and I honestly believed we could be one of the top programs in the country. I told myself, "We can out-gun those old Harvard programs at the Mass General and Brigham. We have the talent and the excitement." My tasks included recruiting good people, applying for increasing grant funds, building a stronger clinical program, and working out mechanisms for additional referrals of patients to Stanford.

CARDIOLOGY

Restructuring

In 1969, the department of medicine was acquiring space in a newly constructed wing of the medical school building. I was given laboratory space there and also space to share with the new head of infectious disease, Thomas Merigan, who, like me, had been recruited from NIH to Stanford around the same time. Merigan was a molecular biologist and he taught me how to grow embryonic heart cells in tissue culture.

I had learned that tissue-cultured cells were a good model to screen drug activity. These cells would develop contractile patterns responsive to drugs when we grew the cells in Petri dishes. The bottom of the dish would soon be covered with a mass of rapidly dividing embryonic heart cells that were starting to pulsate like a beating heart.

In carrying out these types of experiments one must use early embryonic heart cells. We chose chick heart cells, since it was easy to isolate their hearts from a developing embryo in a chicken egg. Embryonic heart cells continue to divide and will completely cover the bottom of a Petri dish. One cell among the hundreds will develop pacemaker function. It will be the cell that causes all of the others to be electrically stimulated and to contract or move rhythmically, since all of these cells are connected electrically. There may be several such sites within one Petri dish but there is usually a dominant rhythm for the entire cell population. Once a pattern is established the whole cell mass pulsates at a fixed and regular rate.

It is possible to focus a beam of light through a microscope on the borders of some of the heart cells and record their movement and contraction. More recently, laser pulses have been used to make such recordings. Heart cells of this type can be used to screen the effectiveness of drugs with activity in heart muscle, and for that reason considerable interest was developed in our work. We continued this work and published extensively on the heart cell model for preclinical drug testing. While I had only a limited laboratory, I managed to squeeze in experimental work with these cells in five or six areas, with the students and postdocs working with me.

Once I made a presentation at a major national medical meeting (the American Society for Clinical Investigators), showing a movie on a large projection screen of heart cells photographed with a scanning microscope. It showed them contracting and responding to drugs, which demonstrated that they had receptors for those drugs. Other scientists were amazed that heart cells grown in Petri dishes could contract and respond to drugs. I received many requests to describe our methods to others. We used this model to study the effects of many cardiac drugs, and several of my former postdocs have used this type of work to build academic careers. The most successful was William Barry, who improved on the techniques, moved his research program to Harvard, and later to the University of Utah.

I was strongly supported in my research by the chairman of medicine, Hal Holman, and I had a cordial relationship with Joshua Lederberg, the Nobel Prize winner at Stanford who was working closely with the National Aeronautics and Space Administration. He helped me to gain work and research support at the Ames Research Center, the major West Coast NASA research center. The Ames Center was located about eight miles from Stanford and was focused on determining the astronauts' cardiac response to the weightless environment occurring in space.

NASA contracted for us to develop studies to understand the weightless condition on the heart and circulation. We could never convince a "real" astronaut to be a guinea pig for our studies, although they frequently visited the Ames center. We had a clinical research center at the Stanford Hospital and we did many collaborative experiments using bed rest to simulate the weightless environment. We used

...became an adjunct faculty member in my division and helped gain NASA support for our research programs.

paid volunteers for these studies, which required the subjects to be at bed rest for seven weeks. We studied their response to the bed rest and to exercise, and then to becoming upright after the long periods of inactivity.

Harold Sandler, director of human research at the Ames Center, became an adjunct faculty member in my division and helped gain NASA support for our research programs. In the mid-1970s I was also appointed as a member of the National Academy of Sciences Advisory Committee for a five-year term to develop plans for the American Space Station. My introduction to botanists, physicists, engineers, and others opened other investigative vistas. I learned that plants that would be on a space station would grow upside down because the pull of gravity was from below. Plant growth is gravity sensitive.

During the five years we consulted with many experts and met regularly three or four times each year. To write the final report we were sequestered in a motel in Santa Fe. It was not all work, as we were able to enjoy the Summer Arts Festival. Sam Their, chief of medicine at Yale, was the only other M.D. on the panel. We tried to estimate the effects of long-term weightlessness and how to prevent its effects, while others were concerned with food development for long-term space travel, and safety from atmospheric radiation. These proposed studies proved to be the basis for NASA launching the space station. Many of the medical and biologic experiments performed in space in the past decade were designed to assess the questions of man's survival in space.

As many of my programs were developing in the late 1960s and early 1970s, the space crunch at Stanford became limiting. We had too little space for the size of our developing programs. Universities had not built enough laboratories to support the expansion of funding from the NIH at that time. However, the NIH funding bonanza convinced some universities to build many new research buildings and to acquire complex equipment, but I was impatient and knew it would take years to build what I needed at Stanford.

I began pursuing funds to build our units by seeking private donations and in the intervening time rented 20,000 square feet of space in a nearby office building. We were able to transfer several of our clinical and research programs to this off-campus site. Our research and clinical programs were becoming more successful and my young faculty appointees were beginning to build their own programs. We were now attracting highly talented postdocs into our program at every level, many of them coming from overseas.

When I became chief of the division of cardiology in 1967, it was clear that we needed to restructure and build a stronger division for our clinical care programs. At that time each faculty member was admitting patients with cardiac disease to the general medical service, supervising cardiac catheterizations, directing one or two outpatient clinics per week and reading the electrocardiograms for the hospital. All of these activities were necessary for fellowship training but still required each of the physicians in the department to be full-time in clinical service delivery.

In order to provide time for scholarly work and research, we restructured into divisional responsibilities where one person would be responsible for the inpatient services, one for electrocardiograms, and one for cardiac catheterization. As we added several faculty members, these duties were rotated so that each person had time off for research and scholarly work at least for a few months during the year. Each of us on the faculty had been building referral patterns with general practitioners and internists throughout the region. This increase in our practices brought more patients into the hospital and more opportunities for clinical research. In addition, we continued to maintain the contract for the Kaiser Health Systems consultative cardiology. This was important for us since it still represented one-third of our patients and good for Kaiser since they had no specialty cardiology and cardiovascular surgery programs. Their own program was still a few years away.

To improve our relationships with the referring physicians, we organized a once-a-week educational cardiologic conference where patients from the service who were referred by physicians from the community could be discussed. We made a special effort to bring our referring doctors from a hundred miles around to attend and had special sessions of postgraduate education for them. I personally tried to get to know each of them by name and permitted them to call me directly when they had a difficult patient needing care.

It was important to have a steady patient flow into our cardiology program to allow the development of new and better treatments and techniques. In addition, we depended on the income derived from patient fees to pay our faculty, and the financial success of the hospital depended on patient volume. We also needed patients for our clinical research. Thus we provided state-of-the-art cardiac care and communicated frequently with our referring physicians. These conferences combined the efforts of radiology, cardiac surgery, and cardiology. The conferences consisted of patient case presentation, and frequently sparked controversy about the best method of management.

Some of the surgeons frequently went to sleep in the conferences, and I remember once when a difficult case was presented that Tom Fogarty, a junior cardiac surgeon, who has subsequently become famous for his skills in developing successful medical commercial companies, was suddenly awakened at the end of a presentation. He uttered, "Ah shit, we will operate." He had not heard the presentation but took the view that surgery could cure any problem.

Nonetheless, these conferences did much to improve the esprit de corps between the surgical group and the medical cardiologists. This resulted in improved patient care, since each of the major complicated cases could be discussed in detail and rational decisions could be made about care.

As the technologies for caring for patients with heart disease became more sophisticated, the cardiology faculty and I believed that a specialty cardiology service as opposed to a general medical service would provide the highest quality and most efficient care for our patients. While we had hospitalized our patients on the general medical service, where the attending might be from gastroenterology or infectious disease, the newly developed technologies were not well understood by them. However, there was major opposition from the other medical specialties for creating a specialty cardiology inpatient service. The argument was that "cardiology was becoming too powerful and Don would soon want his own department."

This was, in fact, true. I did want my own department, which might have created a nationwide trend because of the prominence of our programs. It took five years of battles to get acquiescence from the department of medicine leadership for a trial program of a specialty service. However, after a year, almost everyone agreed it was best for patient care, and the house staff would receive better education. It was a major victory, but it created animosity with other divisions that lasted for years.

Coronary angiography was becoming the prominent diagnostic procedure in the early 1970s, and many newly trained cardiologists wanted to do what was then and up until 1972 considered a radiologic procedure. There was major competition between radiology and cardiology for the control of coronary angiographic procedures at Stanford. Initially, the catheterization laboratory did not possess the necessary equipment for angiography. However, with the construction of new laboratories and the developing need in the early 1970s for direct coronary arteriography, there was an even greater competition.

Over a period of about six years, cardiology managed to convince the radiologists doing cardiovascular procedures to be affiliated members of the cardiology division and to provide training for the cardiac fellows in these procedures. While this was an uneasy compromise, it worked effectively for a few years. However, over a period of a decade, I worked with others on my staff to wrestle control of angiography in our cardiac patients from the radiology department.

It always seemed that we had the major responsibility for patient care, since the patients were on our ward and had been referred to us. If complications occurred we were the ones who had to discuss it with patients and their families; therefore, we felt it should be our responsibility to carry out the procedures. The members of the radiology department resented this encroachment and were upset because of the loss of clinical income for their department. They acquiesced after a stiff fight when the dean and hospital director supported cardiology. It was one of those internal battles in a medical center that in the business world makes little sense. It is always said that "academicians battle over such trivial things," though at times some of the battles are for survival of a discipline and economic mobility.

These battles for turf still occur among specialty groups in medicine, and to my mind, do not serve the patients well. In many ways this is the result of the misalignment of reimbursement for medical services. One is paid more for doing procedures than for thinking and doing diagnostics and preventive care. Over the past four decades the control of reimbursement for medical care has been dominated by surgical specialists and interventionalists, i.e., radiologists, orthopedists, and the like.

Naturally, the reimbursement for their procedures was elevated to high levels while the fees for family doctors, pediatricians, and internists were maintained at lower levels. Medicare accentuated this with its DRG (Diagnostic Related Groups) reimbursement schedules. Cardiologists have benefitted by developing many interventional procedures and in the last decade have become among the highest paid physicians. However, I still believe a major realignment of reimbursement is needed.

A new diagnostic technology called echocardiography utilizing ultrasound to study the beating heart was developing in the late 1960s. It had been used in World War II to detect submarines as a major scientific application of principles of the physics of sound. New modifications of the technology had been made so that ultrasound could now be used to detect heart functions. In early June 1969, I received a call from John Hickam, professor of medicine at Indiana University, who had observed that I had just been given a large new training grant for cardiac fellows. He wanted to send me a first-year postdoctoral fellow at Indiana, Richard Popp, who had completed his first-year fellowship but who was not interested in remaining in the Indiana program. This was just a few days before a new group of postdocs were to begin their program on July 1. Popp wanted to apply what he had learned at the foremost center for echocardiography, located at Indiana University.

I interviewed Popp and agreed to accept him. He informed me that we needed to buy an echocardiographic machine, and it would be the third one in any cardiology department in the country. I approached the hospital with a well-organized plan to move into this new diagnostic technology, but was rejected. I then discovered that I could spend up to $900 from several of my NIH grants without getting it pre-approved; thus I was able to buy an echocardiograph machine piece by piece, and assembled it into an operational machine. This machine permitted Popp and me to institute a new research program. We soon discovered this new technology would permit us to not only study the structural abnormalities of the diseased heart but to make functional assessments too.

Over the next twenty years, the cardiology division maintained control of the echocardiology laboratory. It was one of the most productive in the world for the development of new echocardiographic diagnostic procedures. This also proved to be a very profitable laboratory and allowed a great margin of financial return to support programs in the cardiology division. While we were mindful that the large medical reimbursement was unfair, we thrived on it as one of our highly specialized procedures.

On numerous occasions the hospital proposed to take the laboratory back, but since I had totally funded it and operated it as an independent laboratory I always refused. This resulted in a yearly battle with hospital administrators when we presented our cardiology unit budget without including the income from this lab. After I left Stanford, the lab was taken back by the hospital, where it runs today as still one of the important diagnostic laboratories in the country.

My expanding postdoctoral fellowship program also produced an inordinate number of applicants, sometimes up to 200 per year for six to eight positions. Initially, I reviewed every candidate and did all of the selecting myself. Later, as the division grew and added faculty, we became a bit more democratic. We worked out a review system and a grading system to evaluate potential postdoctoral fellows. However, I always retained one slot that I could fill with someone who did not exactly appear to be from a top-ranked school but who, on an interview or on recommendation, had great potential. I did this because of the way I had been selected when I entered the Harvard system as an intern, as someone who was not from a top-ranked medical school. I always looked for someone who had shown ability to succeed by taking risk—perhaps someone who had overcome a disadvantaged educational background.

These individuals frequently turned out to be among our best fellows, and confirmed my belief that excellent talent could be recognized, and that it should be nurtured. Ed Alderman, one of our trainees who joined the faculty to become head of our cath lab, came from a modest medical school performance but was very productive. Bob Ginsburg was from a third-tier medical school, but brought a new research focus in drugs controlling blood pressure. This selection method also permitted me to bring more women and minorities into the program. At one time we had six women postdocs—the most of any program in the country.

The women in the program provided an opportunity for some misunderstanding too. As an example, I was a member of a prestigious organization, the California Academy of Medicine. The members could bring other male physicians to the meetings, but no females. Prior to 1972 this was a male-only organization. We had renowned speakers, we dressed formally in tuxedos, we maintained our own wine cellar, and had three major dinners each year. After a two-year battle that I helped promote, we agreed to admit women physicians as members and guests.

I invited Sharon Hunt, one of my attractive postdoc women, to accompany me on the first night this was possible. With her red hair and physical beauty, she stood out in a crowd. We had a great time and I introduced her to many members of the Academy, but for several weeks a rumor circulated around San Francisco and Palo Alto that I had left my wife for a voluptuous redhead. Laura was not amused! We had a great tradition with our fellows to have a farewell party at the end of the year. They chose to do a "roast" of the faculty as a skit each year and they proved to be very talented, but not so good with costumes.

By 1970, the coronary care unit that was developed in the mid-1960s had become an important place not only for improving patient care but for clinical research. It needed a new, energetic leader interested in clinical research. John Schroeder, who had been one of my early postdocs had gone into practice in the Carmel area but was very interested in coronary care work. I distinctly remember visiting him where he lived on seventeen-mile drive near Carmel, and walking on the beach with him one Sunday afternoon, making him an offer to come back and join the division. After considerable thought, and over-ruling his wife's objections, he did, and became the director of the coronary care unit and its research programs. It still amazes me that I could recruit anyone away from the beauty and peace of the Monterey Peninsula.

FELLOWS ROAST AT THE ANNUAL PARTY.

It was not only important to attract faculty to our institution, but to retain them. Endowed professorships were a real "plum" with which to do this. An endowed professorship at Stanford was a coveted position, and having an endowment created for and awarded to a specific faculty member gave them a certain level of independence.

One of the most successful ways to convince donors to establish endowed chairs is to provide them an excellent service at their institution or for them to be alumni of that institution. Early in my tenure as chief of cardiology, I took care of several very prominent alumni. Two such individuals discussed with me their desire to create endowed professorships and I worked with the University's development staff to see that that occurred. Neither of them went to cardiology. One went into law and one went into business.

In 1972, however, I was taking care of Dr. Gunther Nagel, who was an emeritus professor of surgery from Stanford University. During a routine operation he experienced a heart attack and I admitted him to our coronary care unit and took care of him over a period of several weeks. He was a member of the board of directors of the William G. Irwin Charity

Foundation in San Francisco. After that event, he proposed an endowed professorship for the University to be awarded to me. I was promoted from associate professor to professor and assumed the William G. Irwin Endowed Professorship of Cardiology, which I held until I moved from Stanford. Being awarded this honor helped keep me at Stanford. While some of my colleagues might have been jealous, they never expressed this openly.

The cardiology division was seeing many wealthy patients from the community, so it seemed prudent to begin a program to increase the philanthropic funding for the division. In late 1976, together with the development staff, we created the "Friends of Cardiology," which consisted of leading business and social leaders in the Bay Area. We had social events coupled with educational programs, and other events at which we requested the advice of this group on how to improve our services to the community. They were encouraged to fund specific programs and individuals within the cardiology division. When we needed $500,000 for a new program that was too immature for NIH funding, I would meet with the group and generally obtain support for part of the new program.

HEART TRANSPLANT

During my fifty years as a cardiologist, one of the defining advances

in which I participated was the first heart transplant at Stanford, then

watching how this advance developed over the next three decades.

THE "HONORARIUM POOL" IN LOS ALTOS.

The person leading the way for this was Norman Shumway, head of cardiovascular surgery at Stanford and my colleague during the twenty years I was chief of cardiology. Cardiologists and cardiovascular surgeons must work together for a patient's benefit, but in academic settings they frequently find themselves in competition. Norm and I had very little of this competition and we worked well together over that twenty- year period.

Shumway was renowned not only for his pioneering work with heart transplantation but for the unique training program he developed for cardiovascular surgeons, many of whom now head their own units throughout the world.

My early encounters with him before I became head of cardiology were positive, and he supported the chairman of the department of medicine's decision to make me chief of cardiology at age 32, even when there was a possibility of recruiting a well-known cardiologist from someplace else in the country. Once I assumed the role of chief of cardiology I worked with not only Shumway but his other faculty members and residents. The aim of our cardiology and cardiovascular surgery programs was to build Stanford's program into one of the top units in the world.

The research in cardiovascular surgery was heavily weighted toward heart transplantation. Starting in the mid-1960s, animal models were developed and basic work was done with immunosuppressive programs, all with the goal of developing a human cardiac transplant program once the feasibility was established.

In cardiology we were at the same time developing protocols for patient selection, patients who could not survive their heart disease without undergoing heart transplantation. Cardiologists also were working to help develop immunosuppressive therapy. Since the heart transplanted would be from another individual, the recipient's body would develop an immune mechanism to reject it; therefore, therapy to suppress the immune response was required. Shumway and his colleagues had developed an innovative surgical technique for transplanting a donor heart into animal models, with long term survival.

Thus, by 1967 we had developed a program at Stanford that included all the necessary planning for a human heart transplant. After much consideration, the Institutional Review Board for the Protection of Human Research Subjects considered the matter and approved. It took

...would the assailant be charged with murder or would the murder charge be relegated to the cardiovascular surgeon who removed the heart...

almost a year for a committee to develop the legal and ethical criteria for certifying brain death for a donor. After this had been established, the major consideration was, for example, how to handle a donor who had been shot in the head by an assailant, who had then been apprehended.

If the donor was still alive, and the heart was harvested, would the assailant be charged with murder or would the murder charge be relegated to the cardiovascular surgeon who removed the heart for transplantation? Potential donors, who expressed their wishes in writing to be donors, might not choose to do so if they knew initially that their donation might be connected in some way to a crime. During that era in California before there were laws requiring the use of helmets, people suffering major head trauma (usually resulting from motorcycle accidents), were considered the most likely candidates for being donors. This proved to be true in that many of the early donors were from brain dead motorcycle riders.

When everything was all set in July of 1967, I consulted with a patient dying of advanced heart failure and recommended the first heart transplantation. This patient had received radiation to cure a mediastinal cancer, which had damaged his heart and lungs. After reviewing the case, the surgeons wisely turned down this patient as a candidate, and in an autopsy a few days later discovered their decision was justified, by evidence of the fibrosis in the chest of this patient from radiation. A successful transplant could not have been done.

Later that year in December of 1967, Christian Barnard in Cape Town, South Africa, performed the first successful human heart transplant. Barnard had never done any research work on transplantation and had only spent one month observing one of Shumway's trainees who had moved to Richmond, Virginia, and was doing transplants in animals. After this event received such worldwide press coverage and attention it became urgent that we try to move our program ahead at Stanford. There was urgency to do transplants at Stanford because most of the basic work had been done there.

On January 5, 1968, I was caring for a very ill patient with heart failure, Mike Kaperian. When we utilized our protocol to evaluate and decide who might not live for a long period of time without heart transplantation, this patient met all of the requirements. On a Saturday night, with a great deal of security, an acceptable donor was identified for this patient, and the transplantation accomplished. In the operating room that night, it was marvelous to watch the dexterity of the surgeons as the donor heart was removed and was transplanted into my patient. Once the donor heart was attached and the patient warmed to normal temperatures, the donor heart started to beat strongly. We were all elated.

Afterwards, I stayed up all night making measurements of cardiac output and the pumping action of the heart, and monitoring this patient's cardiac function in the intensive care unit. All of these studies were to determine how well the new heart was working. We were making almost hourly measurements to be sure that the heart was pumping blood effectively. Everything seemed to be going quite well and a press release was issued by the PR department at Stanford Hospital.

The next day, January 6, a Sunday, was designated for a national press conference to discuss the successful heart transplant. There was tremendous press interest and more than 200 reporters were on the scene and showed up for the press conference. This was covered by a one-hour live national television program. Norm Shumway and I were the only participants in this press conference and some have said that I stole the show showing diagrams and measurements of cardiac functions that I had been making throughout the night. This is not true. I did everything to make sure that Shumway had the limelight. Recently, I had an opportunity to review some of the photographs from that press conference and am now shocked at how young I looked. I had a crew cut and was dressed in green scrub clothes.

For Stanford this was a momentous day and the press coverage for the medical center was extremely positive and certainly put cardiovascular surgery and cardiology programs on the map worldwide. Unfortunately, this patient died thirty days later because of other organ failure, even though his heart continued to function well. Over the next several months, we were able to identify a series of other patients who required transplantation, since now many patients with late-stage heart failure were being referred to us for consideration. The next four patients who were referred by cardiology to the Shumway team for transplantation did quite well.

One of these early patients lived twenty-one years after his transplantation and became an outspoken proponent for the procedure, speaking at Rotary Clubs throughout the country. He traveled the country on a powerful Harley-Davidson motorcycle, even though in his prior life he had been a cautious man who had never been on a motorcycle. He attributed this new development in his life to the fact that his donor heart had come from a patient killed in a motorcycle accident, and felt this was influencing his behavior.

In the operating room that night, it was marvelous to watch the dexterity of the surgeons as the donor heart was removed and was transplanted into my patient.

Following these procedures at Stanford, a number of other places throughout the country began heart transplantation programs, generally without any basic research or knowledge of the immunological and medical care needed for these patients. Many of these programs received initial enthusiastic press coverage, but over the period of the next two years, many of these patients who underwent heart transplantation at other medical centers did not do well, and many of them died of immunological rejection.

Stanford became the only center doing transplantation on a regular basis starting in the early 1970s and up until more research by the Shumway group proved that his program could provide long-term survival of patients. Heart transplant programs have grown around the country and today about 3,000 patients each year receive transplanted hearts. The only limiting factor is the number of donors that are available.

Following several heart transplantations at Stanford, it became the focus for presentations at national and international meetings throughout the world. In the spring of 1969 the American College of Cardiology was meeting in San Francisco and Chris Barnard and Norm Shumway were asked to be on a panel to discuss their work. Barnard wanted to visit Stanford to see the success of the program but Shumway refused to see him. I spent most of my time keeping them apart and showing Barnard around. The panel discussion at the meeting did take place but Shumway never forgave Chris Barnard for preempting him.

Following the success of cardiac transplantation at Stanford, I was invited all over the world to speak on heart transplantation and I traveled to France, Argentina, Japan, and Canada to speak on the subject. I was also invited frequently to speak in Los Angeles and other cities on transplantation and on the other research activities of our cardiology program.

I was generally paid an honorarium of $250 to $500 for these speaking engagements and consultations, and over the course of about a year, I saved all of this money and in 1969 was able to build a swimming pool at our home in Los Altos. The children and I frequently referred to this as the "heart transplant honorarium pool."

On another occasion I was asked to speak on heart transplantation and brain death for donors to the National Convention of district attorneys at their annual meeting in San Francisco. They were concerned with the definition of brain death, especially in criminal cases where hearts might be donated. I gave my prepared speech, and during the question-and-answer session I was asked questions about the artificial heart, which was also being widely discussed at this period. I had served on a national panel that was evaluating the concept for an artificial heart program. I made the comment that there would be several hundred thousand patients who could benefit from an artificial heart, if it existed.

Later, a second question was asked about how much it would cost to have an artificial heart, and for the full operative procedure. Without any real facts, I gave an estimated figure of $100,000. After the meeting ended, I went to dinner with my wife, and upon arriving home in the evening, my phone was ringing. It was the *San Francisco Chronicle*, San Francisco's largest newspaper, calling to tell me that on the AP wire service, a story was out that I was projecting the artificial heart business to be the second largest business in the United States within a decade. It was front-page news all over the country. There had been a reporter in the audience, although I was assured this was not to be. He took the number of potential cases I mentioned, multiplied it by the $100,000 and came up with a multibillion-dollar business. My phone was ringing continuously.

I was being asked for interviews by New York television stations and newspapers calling from all over the world. I finally developed an approach of telling everyone that Dr. Harrison had gone on vacation and that I was only the house servant answering the phone. The next morning I issued a correction statement from Stanford and went on vacation for a week. When I came back, I was being summoned by a congressional committee to testify on this large business opportunity, which I was able to dodge by telling the true story. I was appalled that a reporter was allowed to be at the meeting when I assumed this would not be the case. I was now convinced that the press was capable of distorting facts to get an exciting story.

At the annual American Heart Association meeting that year I was chastised by the association's president in his presidential address for issuing spectacular cardiovascular news. Of course, none of this was true; it was an extrapolation by a reporter. This demonstrates the way one can be misquoted by an overzealous press and that one must be extremely careful when talking with reporters.

After the success of the heart transplant program, our patient volume in the cardiovascular surgery and cardiology expanded, and we found every reason to cooperate even more fully. Being one of the leading cardiovascular centers on the West Coast we were frequently seeing patients who had very prominent positions in the business and academic world. Shumway and I made a point of being very objective in dealing with these patients and handling them in the same way that we handled all patients. It is too easy to be impressed with someone's status and thereby try to give preference to their care. In general this has been shown in many instances not to work in the patient's best interest because certain shortcuts may be taken. We attempted to always be objective in the management of these patients and while we understood some of their special status we handled them with the same objective protocol for their diagnosis and treatment as all other patients.

I finally developed an approach of telling everyone that Dr. Harrison had gone on vacation and that I was only the house servant answering the phone.

The lessons I learned and the acclaim that developed around the Stanford cardiac transplant program proved to be valuable to me as I continued my career. When I arrived as senior vice president and provost for health affairs at the University of Cincinnati, consideration was being given to starting a heart transplant program. With my background and experience I strongly endorsed this concept and I worked with both cardiology and cardiovascular surgery to help establish a program. In just a few years this program became quite effective, and just as it had at Stanford University, attracted considerable attention and resulted in the referral of many patients to be considered as candidates.

It also helped boost the community understanding of the importance of a University Hospital, which in Cincinnati had not yet quite been totally accepted. My experience with the transplant program, a very seminal event, also turned out to be very useful in helping me achieve my goals at the University. Heart transplantation is now a widely accepted method for treating advanced heart failure. Since there are literally hundreds of thousands of patients with advanced heart failure, only a small fraction of them received a donor heart due to the limitation of the number of quality donor hearts available; however, the survival rate of patients who do receive the quality donor hearts is now more than ninety percent for one year, and outwards of seventy-five and eighty percent percent for five years. The longest surviving patient has lived more than twenty-five years beyond the procedure and is still surviving. Our early experience at Stanford has expanded the scope of cardiology and cardiovascular surgery worldwide.

Shumway and I became colleagues with a vision of a cardiovascular center with a greater mission of excellence in research and clinical care. We did not always agree but we managed to move the whole cardiovascular program forward. Shumway had a habit of "shooting from the hip" with his comments and getting into trouble with other department chairmen. I was able to ameliorate some of these problems, but when we were seeking permission to build the Falk Cardiovascular Center in 1980, I had to ask Shumway not to come to the meeting where I was making the presentation to gain approval to build a separate center with its own facility. It was clear to me that his comments would cause a negative vote. After approval we did work together to raise the funds by soliciting our patients to build the building and to make the program successful.

Even after I left Stanford, we remained friends. In 2000 Shumway, who had retired, but was still at Stanford, called me to say that he had been asked to mediate a nasty dispute going on in the department of psychiatry. We laughed as I remembered how abrasive he was in dealing with everyone and said to him, "Norm, this is hard for me to believe."

He has been in Cincinnati on two occasions, and we had an opportunity to renew our friendship and discussions. Ours was a symbiotic relationship that made the Stanford Heart Program one of the world's best. Shumway died of cancer in 2006. In September 2005, while on a trip to Palo Alto, Laura and I had an opportunity to visit with him in his home. Although he was extremely ill, he still had a sparkle in his eye and had maintained his iconoclastic sense of humor. We remembered some of our earlier experiences together and had hearty laughs about some of the more trying moments we had shared. It was very sad for me to know that a treasured colleague of mine was about to die. He died about five months later and there was a memorial service for him at the medical center.

Chapter Twenty-one

THE FLAG

After we restructured the cardiology division, the faculty and staff

began to focus on research and publishing. By 1970, the program at Stanford

was beginning to be recognized internationally.

I was invited to be a keynote speaker and to participate in the international conference on arrhythmia in Edinburgh, Scotland. The Edinburgh conference was organized by

DON WITH NORM AND MARY LOU SHUMWAY.

Desmond Julian, the physician who developed the concept of a coronary care unit. The most important research work being performed in a coronary care unit relating to the management of abnormal heart rhythms that frequently develop in patients with heart attacks was to be presented.

By this time, the Stanford cardiology division had completed major research demonstrating that lidocaine was an important agent that could be administered in the coronary care unit for preventing and treating the abnormal rhythms in the heart attack patients. Lidocaine was well known for its local anesthetic effects, but until my work at the NIH, its action in preventing abnormal heart rhythms was not appreciated. We had been the first to study the pharmacokinetics of lidocaine, demonstrating what level of the drug was necessary in the blood to result in the desired clinical effects. We studied its distribution within the body, its metabolism, and its excretion by the kidneys or liver.

The conference brought together specialists in arrhythmia management from throughout the world. At this time there really were few clinical electrophysiologists other than those whose studies dealt with standard electrocardiograms. The conference was sponsored by the Astra Pharmaceutical Company and was held at the University of Edinburgh.

This was to be the first trip to Europe for Laura and me as a couple and her first trip out of North America. In addition to the scientific meeting, we attended the Edinburgh Festival, held annually in August, and I remember a cold September evening—while we snuggled under a blanket—the wonderful music of the Military Tattoo. The weather in Edinburgh was unusually cold that year, even chillier than San Francisco in the summer.

At the conference we would start our scientific work at breakfast meetings and complete the scientific presentations by noon. Afternoons were devoted to social activities such as visiting castles and seeing the countryside. The wives had separate social programs, and this gave Laura an opportunity to meet wives of my colleagues, as well as do some sightseeing. I was thrilled with our acceptance by the world scientific community and their appreciation of our pioneer work.

The World Congress of Cardiology followed the Edinburgh meeting, and is only held every four years, alternating between Europe, Asia, South America and North America. The congress brings together the academic cardiology leadership from eight to a hundred countries. It occurs over a period of a week and focuses not only on the latest advances in scientific progress in cardiology, but also on epidemiology and prevention of heart disease.

Sangria was brightly lighted, had a series of fountains, and we enjoyed its music and dancing.

Following the Edinburgh conference we traveled by train to London to participate in the World Congress of Cardiology. There were delegations from many countries around the world. I presented several papers at the conference and highlighted the research of our Stanford program which was well received. There were major presentations on heart transplantation, and on new treatments for heart failure at both of these meetings. I was invited to be a keynote speaker at both of these major international meetings. I was quite excited and prepared for several weeks for my presentations. But what I remember most about the London trip was attending the opera in the Royal Opera House on the bank of the Thames and taking a walking tour of London with Norm and Mary Lou Shumway. The four of us were determined to see all of the sights in London in one day and we all ended up with aching feet and blisters.

Following the attendance at the World Congress of Cardiology in London, Laura and I vacationed in Paris, where we were able to experience the delightful art and architecture of the city while sharing some of the outstanding food for which France is so well known. We then took a packaged tour to Switzerland, visiting a number of sites as eager tourists. We had made plans to travel to Lyon, France, to visit with John Carraz, head of immunology at the

Pasteur Institute, so we boarded a train in Geneva to travel to Lyon. We had previously met Carraz in Argentina at a special international meeting on heart transplantation when we were both speakers.

We arrived in Lyon, were met at the train station, and were immediately taken out to the Sangria Restaurant, which was located in the suburbs. Sangria was brightly lighted, had a series of fountains, and we enjoyed its music and dancing. The restaurant was filled with cigarette smoke to a choking level and everyone seemed to be smoking. It was Nouveau Beaujolais time in Lyon and we had a very long dinner with many pitchers of Beaujolais. This was our first introduction to the tradition of Nouveau Beaujolais.

The next day I made presentations at the Pasteur Institute of Lyon, the major center in France doing immunology relating to heart transplantation. By this time in the saga of heart transplantation, Stanford and the Pasteur Institute at Lyon were the major institutions studying methods to prevent the rejection of the implanted heart. Rejection occurs because the body recognizes the transplanted heart as being a foreign object. In this early phase of heart transplantation an immunoglobulin had been developed as a substance injected into the blood that prevented the rejection of the heart. The Pasteur Institute was one of the outstanding institutions carrying out such work.

The institute was associated with a 500-bed hospital serving the entire area around Lyon. It was a very modern hospital, having been built after World War II, and it had the most modern technology for cardiac care.

I was impressed with the scientific work and I felt quite honored to be making a presentation. My presentation went well. There were many questions about the Stanford experience. I met and visited with not only the basic scientists but also the clinical immunologists and the heart surgeons. During lunch with the surgeons, I was amazed that they had wine with their lunch before returning to the operating rooms. The next evening we were taken to the home of our hosts, the Carrazes, and after opening seven locks to get into their apartment, we were rudely shocked to see six stuffed German shepherds sitting around the fireplace. They explained to us they had had six German shepherds and that they had been killed by a leak in the gas system, and that they loved the dogs so much, they had them prepared by taxidermy to sit in their living room. This observation should have alerted us to the unusual nature of this couple. They also explained the reason for the seven locks — that there were lots of thieves in the area. With such observations, we began to suspect these people lived a weird life.

That evening we were again taken to a very famous Lyon restaurant, Leon of Lyon, but we were rushed through our dinner to attend a disco show. The food and wine were outstanding but the rush did not allow us to savor it fully. Our hosts were apparently big disco fans. The disco was brightly lighted, the music was deafening, and everyone was dancing the twist. The room was also filled with smoke and everyone was drinking a great deal of wine. It was unfortunate that we had to "wolf down" our dinner, for the food of Leon of Lyon is famous. We returned by train to Geneva and for the first time encountered concerns about terrorism. Our luggage was examined by men with guns before entering the country, something I would never have expected in Switzerland.

After our experience in Lyon, Madrid, Spain, became our next stop as tourists. Our visit to the Prado was quite memorable; the dark mood of the Goya paintings was offset by the greatness of the work. We were also introduced to Flamenco dancing at a local night club. Then we flew on to Portugal where I had to step back into my physician-cardiology researcher role. We had previously made arrangements to interview a potential postdoctoral fellow in Lisbon for our Stanford program. The interview with Mario Lopes had been arranged by the director of cardiology at the University of Portugal. Mario and his wife entertained us royally in Portugal. We were taken to visit Sentra and Estoril, coastal towns in the environs of Lisbon.

The casinos on the Estoril Coast were quite amazing to us, very similar to Las Vegas, though we were surprised to see so many people participating in gambling on a weekday. With the Lopeses as our hosts, we sampled some tasty Portuguese food and Mario introduced me to a hundred-year-old port in a tasting at a local bar.

We flew home from Portugal to find that our children had thrived and had been well taken care of by one of our postdocs, Doug Ridges, and his wife. This was at least the interpretation given to us by the adults, but our daughter Beth remembers it differently. She missed her mother desperately and claimed she cried herself to sleep at night. I think this story has been embellished over the years and their experience was really a good one.

Chapter Twenty-two

PARENTS *Surrogate*

As chief of cardiology at Stanford, the opportunity to travel and present our research came frequently. In many instances there was also the opportunity for Laura to accompany me on these trips.

For the overseas trips I was frequently offered first-class fare for me or two coach-class tickets so that I could bring Laura along to the meetings and to the interesting places to which I was invited. This posed quite a problem for us, with young children, since we were not living near relatives and had no ready mechanism for child care while we were away on a three- to four-week trip. By this time I had a number of married postdoctoral fellows and we had intimate knowledge of their stability and capability for taking care of our children. This appeared to be a ready solution for our problem. We chose to call them "surrogate parents" rather than babysitters. We decided that they could do an excellent job if they were given the details of the children's schedule, permission to act in the case of medical emergency, detailed knowledge of how things worked at our house, and how we could be reached. Most seemed eager to move temporarily to our house, with a pool and a nice yard and patio.

THEY GOT ME THIS TIME. FELLOWS DAVE CLARK AND ANTHONY GRAHAM.

We developed a series of selection criteria for these surrogate parents; namely, that they were married, they were stable and trustworthy, that they were known to be flexible, that they knew the area around Stanford University, and that they were well-connected with the other postdoctoral fellows in case they needed help. It was by these criteria that we chose at least seven sets of surrogate parents for our children, with some caring for our children during many trips. Many became close friends with the children, and a number of them have kept in touch with our children, their careers, families, and activities. Dave Clark in particular has remained a close friend of ours and of my son Doug, who water-skis with him summers at Lake Tahoe.

Dave penned a letter to us while staying with our children for an extended time in 1971 to show the humor that they could express while staying with our children. He mailed it to us while we were on the trip. He wrote:

Dear Harrisons,

Everything is going well. Beth was a little glum for a few days but was easily distracted from her sadness by conversations or activity. Doug has been a great help and has had no trouble sleeping. By the way, I think his ghost came from the Bill Cosby record—the bit about old weird Harold and the wino on 9th Street is scary. So, to make him forget, I let him get another Bill Cosby record. (Bet you can't wait to hear it!) Now he worries about the giant chicken heart that ate the Empire State Building. Seriously, he is fine. And as for Donna, Carol, Dave's wife, said, 'We are just going to put her in our suit case and take her home with us when you get back.' None of the kids have SOB, DOE, PND, or orthopnea—whoops, I forgot I wasn't writing a medical history. See you soon.

One could see the Clarks were having a fine time with our children.

Looking back at our use of our surrogate parents, it seems to us that no one would probably do this today. People have become too suspicious of others and would be concerned for the well-being of their children. We did not pay these individuals except for the expenses they incurred while living in our house. They seemed to enjoy being there— our house and the pool, and even the children. Of note, however, four of the six of them have subsequently divorced. Did this come from observing what kids can be like with our children? I have asked several of them that question, and have been assured that was not the reason for the divorce.

Whatever the effects on the couples, our children were exposed to other people's views and habits, which gave them a broader, more flexible outlook. In turn, being able to trust others to take care of the children permitted us an opportunity to travel worldwide to many interesting places. This arrangement permitted Laura to travel with me—to become acquainted with my colleagues and to view my world. We also coupled each trip with a vacation or an opportunity to learn about another world culture. It also was of value to the cardiology program at Stanford in that in most places I traveled to we were able to project the high quality of the work we were carrying out at Stanford. This also helped us recruit very bright postdocs from many countries.

Chapter Twenty-three

KNIGHTING party

In 1972, I received an invitation to join a five-person team of cardiologists and cardiovascular surgeons from the U.S. to attend the ceremony and celebration knighting Professor Barrett Boyes in New Zealand. Boyes was the most famous cardiovascular surgeon in New Zealand and Australia. This invitation came from John Kirkland, who had been the mentor for Barrett Boyes when he had his training at the Mayo Clinic. This program was to be for more than a four-week period.

Since at the time I was also consulting for Hewlett-Packard and Astra Pharmaceutical, arrangements were made for me to participate in activities in Australia for both companies. Our trip began with a planned stopover in Tahiti. We were seated very far back in the full coach section of a Pan Am 747 from San Francisco to Tahiti. Laura had a friend who was a Pan Am cabin attendant who knew we were on this flight where she was the chief attendant in the first class section. Soon after we were airborne, she brought us a bottle of French champagne, two glasses, and a rose, and we settled in for a long evening in flight to Tahiti. She said, "Champagne is good for the soul and for sleep on these long flights." Everyone around us looked on with envy. The champagne eased the crowded conditions and we slept like babies.

On arriving in Tahiti we immediately were transferred to the island of Moorea to a small resort of twelve thatched-roof huts directly over the beautiful, clear water and the reef surrounding the island. We were able to plunge into the water right out of our hut and see thousands of beautiful swimming fish by snorkeling around over the reef. Our food was served in an open-air dining room in a thatched-roof hut as well, and was excellent seafood. For us this seemed to be a heavenly adventure. After a few days we transferred to the island of Tahiti where we had a drink at Harry's Bar, one of Hemingway's drinking sites when in this area.

From Tahiti we flew to Sydney. I was treated like a celebrity by the Astra Pharmaceutical representatives and they arranged for me to speak to a group of cardiologists on my recent work with antiarrhythmic drugs, and the coronary care unit. Fabulous Australian wines were poured for us and we were served great food. The Astra president for Australia shipped two cases of wine to me at home. Unfortunately, it had to go through Los Angeles and disappeared while in transport to San Francisco, probably drunk by the ship's crew. There was also a dinner for a large group of cardiologists sponsored by Hewlett-Packard, to present the latest cardiologic equipment. We were taken on a day trip to Canberra, a planned city, which had become the capital of Australia and which as a small town seemed out of place for a country capital. I also visited the University of Sydney and spoke at one of their research conferences.

From Sydney we moved on to Melbourne. One of my postdocs practicing cardiology in Melbourne, Bernard Treister, arranged for my visit to the university and for a presentation at a research conference. The university hospital was as well equipped as any U.S. hospital and had a twelve-bed coronary care unit. The research there was first-rate and was focused on developing new pacemakers for patients with heart block and excessively slow heart rates.

We also had an opportunity to go spearfishing off the south coast and for the first time I was learning to use a Hawaiian sling to spear fish.

We also had an opportunity to go spear-fishing off the south coast and for the first time I was learning to use a Hawaiian sling to spear- fish. Unfortunately I did not quite understand the principle, and my first shot resulted in the loss of the harpoon to the bottom of the water, about thirty feet down. We managed to rescue it and I did finally learn to shoot some small fish.

From Melbourne we traveled to New Zealand. We had arranged to stop in Wellington, where we spent an interesting Sunday afternoon relaxing in a local park since everything in Wellington closed on Sunday. We did not understand why we could not find a restaurant for dinner. Wellington had some resemblance to San Francisco but was ten times smaller, and quite a dull place on Sunday.

The next day we were to fly to Rotorua to visit the Maori native villages. Unfortunately, because of fog, all flights were cancelled so we planned to rent a car. Laura asked another couple if they would like to drive with us. They readily agreed and said that since they had been driving on the left side of the road for a week or so they would drive. This man was a maniac on the road and on several occasions over the first fifty miles he almost got us killed. He passed in the face of oncoming cars and veered all over the road. At one stop I volunteered to drive and never let him behind the wheel again. We attended a Maori ceremony in Rotorua and there our so-called friends departed. We took the car and drove to the Waitomo Caves where we took a boat tour through the caves and saw the colorful fireflies. We got lost in the back country, and finally were rescued by a passing farmer who let us follow his truck to the main road. We arrived in Auckland with a car that was so covered with mud someone wrote on the side of it, "Plant on me rather than wash me."

The official ceremony knighting Barrett Boyes took place in Auckland in a large auditorium. It was a very formal ceremony with all of the dignitaries from the university and the city participating. Everyone participating in the ceremony wore academic robes and had colorful headpieces representing the universities where they had graduated. A delegation had arrived from London with a representative of the queen for this affair. There were speeches highlighting the career of Barrett Boyes. John Kirkland, who had organized our trip, spoke to highlight the medical career of Barrett Boyes and to present a special award from the Mayo Clinic, recognizing the honor that Barrett Boyes was receiving. There was a formal reception after the ceremony, followed by a very nice dinner. Following all the formalities, we then proceeded to the most fun part of the event, and what turned out to be the highlight of our trip. We had three days of celebration on Barrett Boyes's ranch, where we had a haggie (cooking a pig in the ground with all of the root vegetables and fruits with it.) We drank a great deal of New Zealand wine which, compared to now, wasn't very good. New Zealand wines have improved tremendously since then, and their Sauvignon blancs are among the best in the world. The food and drink continued way into the night with much jovial celebration. It was a party befitting New Zealand's first Knight.

On our homeward trip we stopped in the Fiji Islands for three days. These were reported to be the most romantic islands and we did stay at a beautiful resort. One of my memories is that several of the native boys invited me to go spearfishing with them if I would rent a power spear gun. I thought I was a pretty good swimmer but found that they, even without fins, were much better swimmers. We went off the edge of the reef spearfishing, where the water was extremely rough. Though I had a snorkel and mask and fins, I would not dive down into the caves and under the edge of the reef to shoot fish, but they did. They were quite successful and speared enough fish for several weeks. It was really scary and the waves were huge.

In retrospect, going out with them and their outrigger canoe was risking my life, and when I returned Laura had been quite frightened for my return. She said to me, "I'm happy you are back alive and I never want you to take such a risk of making me a widow again." During a little over four weeks of wonderful times we made many new friends with whom we have since communicated and visited in their countries on several occasions.

Chapter Twenty-four

ESCAPADE

In the summer of 1972 we planned a big family trip to visit many of the U.S. western national parks and western Canada as a reward for the children after Laura and I were away so long in Australia and New Zealand.

We bought a large Chrysler station wagon, which in today's terms was a gas guzzler, but would accommodate us on our trip. The wagon was the longest I could find, and had a large and very powerful V-8 engine. We were able to pack all our supplies for camping into a roof carrier, and on the first day we drove to Lake Tahoe and spent the night with the Clarks, former surrogate parents of our children.

Our reunion with them was joyful and exciting for our children, who then seemed to remember and divulge more stories of their times with the Clarks while we were away. The next day we drove across the state of Nevada to Salt Lake, where we stayed with another of the children's surrogate parents, the Ridges. The desert drive was hot and very boring and we were amazed at the size of the Great Salt Lake. After a day in Salt Lake City, we went to the Wasatch Mountains with the Ridges to their summer cabin. Fishing in a small creek, Doug, caught his first trout, and he was quite excited as together we cleaned it for dinner.

From Salt Lake, we drove into Wyoming and to the Grand Teton National Park. We had made advance reservations at the Jackson Lodge on beautiful Jackson Lake. One of the highlights here was a family horseback ride. None of us were accustomed to horseback riding and the children fared far better than Laura and I, who found some new sore muscles. We had dinner at Jenny Lake Lodge, a meal that would do well at a three-star *Michelin Guide* restaurant. The food was outstanding and the surrounding scenery made for a memorable evening. After three days we packed up and moved on.

Our next destination was north to Yellowstone Park, where we stayed in cabins near Old Faithful. The spectacle of Old Faithful erupting was one of the highlights. The weather in the Yellowstone area was rainy and cool but we explored the park for several days, finding everything overrun with tourists. For that reason we decided to move on to Glacier Park in Montana. The interstate roads had just been completed across Montana and on an early Sunday morning I drove 120 miles in eighty minutes on our way to Glacier National Park. There was no speed limit, the roads were straight, and we saw no state patrol cars.

We were amazed to see large herds of buffalo on a federal land preserve in north central Montana. At Glacier, we luckily found, without reservations, a vacant cabin on McDonald

Lake where we could swim, hike and ride up the "Going to the Sun" road. Our stay here was quite restful after all the driving. We then drove across the mountain section of Glacier to a remote area, and camped on a stream for two days in the far eastern reaches of the park. There, moose wandered down the stream near the camp, and we found a spot to fish for rainbow trout, which we prepared for dinner each evening. From there we went north to Banff and Lake Louise. We had never seen such emerald water as was in the streams and lakes due to the sediment from the Mountains. The Canadian Rocky Mountains were far more covered with spruce forests than their U.S. counterparts.

From Banff we drove north through the Columbia Ice Fields to Jasper. We were quite amazed at the thickness of the glaciers in the Columbia Ice Field, and managed to walk on the glaciers and to see the numerous ice caves. The area around Jasper was very dry and there were severe forest fires, with sparks flying across the roadway. Driving from Jasper on our way to Vancouver, we were detoured several times by major forest fires. It was a shame that the beauty of this area was ruined by the smoke and destruction. We had never seen such forest fires burning in the tall trees, and it took away the thrill of being in the area.

For a one-day trip this was a long and tiring drive and all I can say is we visited the lodge and looked down on beautiful Crater Lake, but little else.

In Vancouver we visited beautiful English gardens and rode on double-decker English-style buses to explore the city. Our next move was to take the ferry across to Vancouver Island and the city of Victoria, which was very English-like, and we wished we had stayed more than one day as the flowers were exquisite. We then took a long ferry ride to the Olympic Peninsula where we visited Olympia National Park, and after a camping sojourn we took the ferry across to Seattle to visit with Eric Feigl and his family. Eric was a physiologist at the University of Washington and a friend of mine who lived on Mercer Island. Mercer Island was then pretty isolated and from the living room of their house they had a scenic view of Mt. Rainier.

From Seattle we drove south along the Oregon coast, staying at a motel on the beach for a day and then making a sudden decision that we wanted to visit another national park at Crater Lake. For a one-day trip this was a long and tiring drive, and all I can say is we visited the lodge and looked down on beautiful Crater Lake, but little else. As the driver, I was exhausted, and I had a car full of ornery kids.

From there we drove down to the coast and down the California coast to the newly created Redwood National Park, which was now just being established. The trees are larger than we could even imagine. As we rolled into California we were greeted at the border by the statue of two golden bears, very symbolic of the great state. Once in California we were eager to be home after thirty-one days and driving over 6,000 miles. It had been a great trip to introduce our children to the wonderful west of the United States. Such adventures still exist, but places are now far more crowded and the roads more congested.

Chapter Twenty-five

BAHRAIN *connection*

The Middle East has become much more important for the United States over the past five decades because of our dependence on the region for a source of oil. In addition, Bahrain and other friendly Arab countries have been major bases for our military in the region.

My connection to Bahrain began when I was asked to see a member of the Al Khalifa family. The Al Khalifa family has for generations been the ruling family of Bahrain. They

IN BAHRAIN WITH THE EMIR.

have frequently sought medical care in Great Britain and the United States. My introduction to the Al Khalifa family, with whom I have maintained a longstanding relationship, took place in early 1973 when I was asked to come to Los Angeles to be a cardiology consultant for the son of the prime minister.

Mohammed was a student at the University of Southern California and was hospitalized with a severe fever and an undiagnosed illness with major heart failure problems. One of the physicians at the University of Southern California had suggested an international group of experts meet and discuss his particular case. Attending were a famous cardiologist from Great Britain, one from Australia, two from the United States, and me—I was about twenty-five years younger than any of the others and quite surprised to be invited. I expected to go for one evening and therefore took no luggage. When I arrived in Los Angeles I was met at the airport by the prime minister's executive assistant, Jamil Wafa, who escorted me to a long limousine and stated that he had made hotel reservations for me. I protested, saying I had no clothes or toiletries and had not planned to stay overnight. He informed me that I would be staying and that he would arrange to get those items I needed, and asked me my shirt size.

This began a long association with Jamil that continues even today, and he is still a "take-charge person." We went to the hospital that evening and we reviewed all of the records, examined Mohammed and had an extensive conference. The following day I did return to Stanford and began reading about the types of heart disease that might be present in someone from Middle Eastern Gulf States. It was almost by accident that I discovered what was a classic syndrome in this young man and recommended a course of therapy. I was the only one to make the diagnosis and develop a treatment program.

Mohammed improved and was out of the hospital for a few months but soon had a relapse and became much more severely ill. When the situation became desperate arrangements were made for him to be transferred to Stanford with the idea that if he improved he might be a candidate for heart transplantation. He was in our intensive care unit for several days. This was 1974 and the time of the Middle East oil crisis. The prime minister, his father, came to Palo Alto, and was living in one of the hotels. He was accompanied by a large contingent of the U.S. Secret Service to assure his safety, because of the U.S. interest in Bahrain.

She filled as many as twenty to thirty pieces of luggage with gifts for her more than thirty grandchildren.

I spent a great deal of time with the father, and came to know him well, and of course, interacted on a daily basis with the secret service men. They milled about the hospital, blending in carefully with the physician staff by putting tongue blades in the pockets of their borrowed white coats. They could only be recognized because they had small earpieces for communication. I was amazed at how inconspicuous they were, but fully protective of Mohammed and the prime minister. Mohammed did not improve enough to become a candidate for heart transplantation, and died about ten days after coming to Stanford. This was a real tragedy and almost an international incident.

Following this, several years passed before I had another encounter with the Al Khalifa family. This occurred when Jamil Wafa called me to say that Sheikha Hesa, the wife of the emir of Bahrain, who was the older brother of the prime minister, would like to come to Stanford and have me be her physician for an evaluation and recommendations for treatment for her high blood pressure. I readily agreed and she arrived with approximately twenty people accompanying her. They occupied almost one whole wing of a local hotel. She was accompanied by Jamil Wafa, who was her spokesperson, and some of her staff.

The evaluation went well and we placed her on a successful program of therapy. During this visit she went on a shopping expedition in the Palo Alto area and in San Francisco, filling as many as twenty or thirty pieces of luggage with gifts for her more than thirty grandchildren. She was a real fan of all the department stores in the Stanford Shopping Center. Since this visit was quite successful, she returned on a yearly basis for the entire time I remained at Stanford until 1986. Her visits were always like the first. She came with a contingent of individuals, though the number had diminished to five or six. We did the medical workup and she always had an opportunity to do lots of shopping for gifts, clothes, and jewelry. It became customary for us to have dinners with her at outstanding San Francisco or Palo Alto restaurants.

We usually hosted tea and a reception in our home where we invited prominent people from the community. These were memorable occasions. I remember once when I was working with her directly on her medical exam and the limousine driver did not arrive on time to pick her up to meet her daughter who was shopping elsewhere. On that day I was driving my four-wheel drive Blazer with large tires and a very high entrance to the cab. She was a very short woman and had been accustomed to riding in limousines, but needed to move quickly to join her daughter. The only way I could get her into the cab was to get behind her, lift her with my hands and push her into the cab. She laughed about this and we both considered it quite amusing at a later time. I'm certain that in Bahrain this might be regarded as a major break in royal etiquette.

After a few years seeing Sheikha Hesa, I was invited by her to come to Bahrain and to bring my wife. Knowing the customs about the role of women, we were somewhat concerned but agreed to travel there. Upon arrival we were greeted by Jamil Wafa and placed in an upscale hotel with a large suite, which we learned was owned by Sheikha Hesa. The hotel was in Manama, the capital and major city in Bahrain. The island of Bahrain is rather small but it has been a very important crossroad for travel in the Middle East for centuries and is the site for Bahraini pearls, found by divers who free dive deep into the gulf to pick up oysters and extract the pearls.

We had an opportunity to visit a number of historic places, including the first oil well in the Middle East, even though Bahrain did not have a large amount of oil reserves at this time compared to Saudi Arabia or the Emirates. This small well was still pumping oil with an old-fashioned rig.

As we had suspected, Laura was not able to visit the public buildings of the government but the emir invited us to one of his beachside palaces for lunch, where he hosted Queen Elizabeth several years later. We were not certain how we would be treated or what we would be served. Since we had a limousine and driver for our entire visit, we were picked up and taken to the beach palace, which was quite palatial. The other guests were the French ambassador and his wife, the U.S. ambassador and his wife, and Jamil Wafa and his wife.

To our surprise, we were greeted at the door by an attendant with French champagne. We were then allowed to visit about the palace and to enter a sitting room with the emir. We had a wider-ranging discussion about the relationship of America to the Middle East. We then moved to an intimate dining room. I had imagined that we would be served lamb and that I would be offered the eyes, which I had heard was one of the offerings to honored guests. To our great surprise, however, we had a multi-course French dining experience with wonderful French wines, and we participated in very animated and interesting personal conversation. Upon returning to our limousine we found the back seat loaded with expensive gifts for ourselves and our children, without any explanation or notification. The next day I asked Jamil Wafa how they knew they would not be stolen by the driver or someone else. He said that was easy. If anyone found out that we had not received the gift, the thief's hands would be chopped off. This must work for them to prevent theft.

During this trip I visited the hospital that was being constructed as one of the showplace hospitals of the Middle East. It clearly had been planned quite well and was to be equipped with the latest technology available. I met the physician who was in charge of medical affairs for the Baharaini oil company. He was Australian and frequently cared for members of the royal family and referred them to London or the U.S. I examined a number of the members of the royal family and some of their staff during this trip and made medical recommendations. I was invited to a majlis with the emir, which was for men only.

Laura was invited to one for the women hosted by Sheikha Hesa. These are strange affairs if considered in Western ethos. I was assigned to sit on the couch at the front of the large auditorium-like room room, by the side of the emir. There were four men kneeling in front of him with falcons on their arms, and those making requests for special favors sat on French Provincial couches lined around the wall. They came forth individually to make requests, for instance, a wife was ill and needed to go to London for care, which the emir granted, or a son had been accepted at some American university and needed funds to go, and he granted this too. One thing I did not know was that pointing the sole of one's foot to the emir was a sign of disrespect, as it was to any Arab person. As I crossed my legs, the sole of my shoe was exposed, and later I was informed that this was rude. I learned quickly, and when invited to attend majlis on other occasions, I did not break this rule again.

Upon returning to Stanford, I received frequent requests to send specialists to see various individuals and important patients in Bahrain. I sent orthopedists, rehabilitation specialists, dermatologists, neurologists, and surgeons. On one occasion, the emir's sister had a significant heart rhythm problem and I was summoned to evaluate her. I flew to Frankfurt, and since my plane was late and I had a good deal of medical equipment in the luggage compartment I was concerned about making my connection to Bahrain. In fact, the Bahraini air carrier, Gulf Air, whose plane was to fly me to Bahrain, was informed about my being late, and an attendant rushed to meet me and arranged to have my luggage quickly transferred. They delayed the Gulf Air flight and I made the connection.

The medical consultation was successful, with a new diagnosis and a comprehensive treatment plan. After three days I flew to Hong Kong and back to San Francisco. This was my first time to make an around-the-world consultation, but twenty-eight hours on a plane in four days is not a picnic. On each of my visits to Bahrain, I was given impressive gifts. The visits by Sheikha Hesa continued on a frequent basis during the remainder of my time at Stanford. During this several-year period, two of my children, Doug and Donna, were invited to visit Bahrain and were treated royally. It was an enlightening experience for them.

JAMIL WAFA WITH DON AND THE BAHRAIN MINISTER OF FINANCE.

When I moved to Cincinnati, Jamil Wafa transferred the medical care for the Bahrain royal family to Cincinnati, and allowing me to continue as the medical physician for Sheikha Hesa. She came for visits to Cincinnati, usually bringing several people with her. We followed the same pattern with her examinations and treatment schedules. She did extensive shopping, and the individuals at Saks and Lazarus became her admirers because of all that she bought. That pattern continued and I kept close contact with the Al Khalifa family and was visited by Sheikha Hesa and one of her sons on several occasions.

In 1991, just prior to the Gulf War with Iraq, I received a call at 4 a.m. that the emir had had a heart attack and they wanted me to fly to Bahrain to evaluate and treat him. I was also called by the Bahrain Embassy in Washington and urged to go. The Gulf War appeared imminent, and of course my family was appalled that I would go, but I did, and arrived about thirty hours after the emir's heart attack. Working with the emir's son, who later became the emir and king of Bahrain after his father's death, we managed to get the large number of doctors who were attempting all sorts of treatments for the emir off the case and set up a standard treatment regimen, as any cardiologist would do in the United States.

Although he was quite ill, we had things under good control. During this time, I was visited by the American ambassador, who informed me that there were hospital ships in the Gulf and they could carry out almost any procedure if needed and required. I asked about coronary bypass surgery and was informed no—not that procedure—but they could fly him to the United States. Of course, the Americans had tremendous interest in being certain that the emir survived since Bahrain was the home of our naval base for the Middle East for the Gulf. It was agreed that after the emir recovered from this episode he would come to the United States for coronary angiography and consideration for coronary surgery. The standard medical facility for high-level individuals from the Gulf States was the Cleveland Clinic.

About three months later he came to the United States, and the Cleveland Clinic graciously allowed me practice privileges so that I could be his cardiologist. I flew to Cleveland every other day to see him. He was accompanied by Sheikha Hesa, underwent coronary bypass surgery, and made a fine recovery. He returned to Bahrain and remained the emir until his death in 2000, almost ten years later. I continued to see Sheikha Hesa up until 1999.

Throughout all of this I have also continued to be the physician for Jamil Wafa and his family and have maintained their friendship, helping with medical problems for several members of his family. We have also traveled with Jamil Wafa and his wife, Haya. One memorable trip was to northern India with the couple and one of his employees and his wife, who were high-caste Indians. This was a marvelous trip and a wonderful opportunity to travel with them, which gave us a great introduction to India. Our visits were to Delhi, Agra, Rogistan, and the Taj Mahal.

Dealing with the royal family gave me new insights into the culture of the Middle East Gulf States and also made me aware of their graciousness and generosity. On several occasions we dressed in typical Middle Eastern garb together with Jamil's friends who were members of the government. These medical experiences provided me with a good understanding of the high regard in which U.S. medicine was held in other countries. During my years of involvement with Bahrain I observed a marked improvement in the quality of care for its people. Western-trained physicians traveled there and the latest medical facilities and equipment were acquired. The royalty, however, continue to seek American or British medical care. In my visits to Bahrain I never encountered any anti-American activity. However, recently there has been considerable turmoil in the country because of the ruler being Sunni in a country with an equal population of Shias.

Chapter Twenty-six

HAWAII'S PARADISE

When one lives on the West Coast, it is always one's dream and desire to go to the Hawaiian Islands. The history of these islands is also quite remarkable and we have enjoyed visiting some of the historic sites.

The islands were explored by Captain Cook, and after he encountered the natives and King Kamehameha he was killed on the Island of Hawaii. Unfortunately, these explorers brought scourges to the natives of the islands such as smallpox and syphilis, which decimated much of the population. Later the New England Protestants came as missionaries, but soon turned to land grabbing and subjugating the natives in the name of religion. The native Hawaiians have survived, however, and their culture

RICH AND JANICE POPP WITH LAURA AND DON IN HAWAII.

is now thriving, particularly on the big island of Hawaii. Hawaii is advertised as a lush, tropical paradise where the language is English and the people are extremely friendly, and we have found it to be so.

When our children were 12, 10, and 8 we decided that our annual family vacation would be to go to Hawaii. There are many nonstop flights to Hawaii from San Francisco, so travel to the islands is convenient. We rented a small VW camper with a small kitchen and a pop-up top, where there was sleeping room for all of us, although we were quite tightly packed together, one above the other, for sleeping. We had read extensively about the islands, anticipating visits to state and national parks on Oahu, Hawaii, and Kauai. Hawaii had extremely nice parks and great beaches readily accessible to campers, and the children looked forward to visiting that island.

I recollect two interesting stories about this trip. The first, while we were camping at

Simpson's Beach, on the west side of the Island of Hawaii, I was teaching the children to snorkel and reached out and grabbed a sea urchin by mistake. My hand was immediately filled with sharp spines that were very painful. The spines could not be extracted because they were barbed like fishhooks, but on reading my first aid book I found that they could be dissolved with an acid solution. It recommended either vinegar or urine. Not wanting to use urine, I went to my neighbor's camper and found that they had vinegar, and for the next two hours I soaked my hand that had the sea urchin spines in the vinegar. They dissolved, and I never had any more trouble.

While camping at the same beach, we decided to visit the Mauna Kea Beach Hotel, which at that time was the premier hotel in all of Hawaii. It had been built by the Rockefeller organization as part of a string of luxury hotels. It had several million dollars' worth of Asian art distributed throughout. Having camped for several days, we were a bit bedraggled but went for their fancy buffet lunch. We knew they had the most beautiful beaches in the area, and being quite brazen, after we finished lunch, we asked

I found that they could be dissolved with an acid solution. It recommended either vinegar or urine.

if we could use the restrooms to dress and spent the afternoon enjoying beaches at the most luxurious hotel on the island. Very few people would be as outgoing as this but we were treated well by all of the staff. We also spent time on Kauai and visited Honolulu. This was a great trip and quite wonderful for the children.

Our next trip to the Hawaiian Islands occurred after I had started to see Wendel Carlsmith, who was a graduate and longtime supporter of Stanford and a native Hawaiian, as a patient. He was a member of the board of trustees of a chain of island hotels, the Surfs, and the chain also owned a car rental service. After several patient visits to me during which I successfully treated his heart problem, he invited us to come to the islands, bring our children, and he would arrange hotel accommodations and cars on all of the islands as a thank-you to me. Much of the activity was to take place on the Island of Hawaii, where the Carlsmiths owned a private beach home.

On this trip we flew to Hilo and stayed in a beautiful Surf hotel that was sparsely occupied but had lush tropical plants all around. We next moved to Kona, where the hotel was even more beautiful. The children experienced a great time ordering room service, used the pools, and participated in all of the activities on the waterfront. The Carlsmiths invited us to their beach home for a day of boating and fishing, and an afternoon cookout. Donna, our youngest, had never caught a fish, and while several of us had fished through much of the morning without catching anything, Donna and I got to go out fishing again in the afternoon. We immediately saw hundreds of gulls diving into the water, obviously catching small fish. The small fish are driven to the surface by large fish feeding on them from below. The Carlsmiths' son, who was driving the boat, knew that we would be able to catch fish if we followed the gulls and fished in the area where they were diving. We were trolling and as we swept through the areas where the gulls were feeding, we could catch four approximately ten-pound tunas with each sweep. We caught about sixty and Donna, who had never caught a fish, was extremely excited. We took the fish back and cleaned some of them for dinner, which we cooked on an outdoor grill.

THE PIG ROAST IN HAWAII.

While also on the big Island of Hawaii, we were taken to a private wilderness area on the North Coast, where the kids could swim in a lagoon out to a small island. While they were out at the island, we saw fins coming through the water, which made us believe they were sharks. This gave us a great scare and we immediately got the children to swim back to shore. In retrospect these were probably not sharks but manta rays with their fins out of the water. We later came to see many of these on our other Hawaiian trips.

Our next Hawaiian adventure started in 1975, when the postgraduate education department at Stanford organized an annual cardiology postgraduate conference at the Mauna Kea Hotel. For ten years we participated in this conference, which usually amounted to giving lectures in the morning and having afternoons for exploring the island for fishing, golfing, tennis, and snorkeling. The conferences were well attended by about sixty cardiologists, and it was a profitable venture for the postgraduate education department.

On several of these trips I hired a guide and a boat to fish. On one trip I caught two large ono, one weighing forty-four pounds. These are fish native to the costal waters of Hawaii.

We brought the fish back to the hotel, had them cleaned, and there was enough to feed the entire group of a hundred for dinner on one of the evenings. On another trip I caught a fifty-two pound shortbill spear fish. The record was eighty-eight pounds so I consider it a prize and had the fish mounted by a taxidermist. Laura hated the fish and relegated it to the basement and discarded it when we moved to Cincinnati. These postgraduate conferences were attended by people from all over the country, and we made many friends of cardiologists from all sections of the country which resulted in patient referrals to our cardiology program at Stanford.

After we moved to Cincinnati, we did not return to Hawaii for many years. However, in 1998, we noted that the Vermont Bicycle Tours was sponsoring a ten-day bike trip on the big island with accommodations and the opportunity to bike around the whole island. We decided to do this, and with seventeen individuals we biked around the island, visiting the black sand beaches, the volcano, Hilo, and the Kona Coast. Some of the riding was quite difficult, but on the hilliest part, the bikes were taken to the top of the hill by van and we were able to ride as much as twenty miles down. There was time for hiking, swimming, and snorkeling as part of this trip. We were delighted to return to the paradise of the island and enjoyed the trip and the new company of our fellow bikers.

To my mind, Hawaii represents the best of the island vacation venues in the world. People are extremely friendly, the climate is almost perfect, the scenery beautiful, the beaches among the best in the world, the accommodations are inviting, and the variety of climate and vegetation from one side of each island to the other is quite remarkable. Over the almost thirty years that we have been going to Hawaii, we have observed tremendous growth, particularly in Honolulu but also on the Kona Coast, and in many ways the great flood of tourists may well denigrate the wonders of these islands.

Chapter Twenty-seven

ADVENTURES
South American

Some of my early travels abroad were to South America where I was invited to travel for medical conferences as a speaker. As with almost all of my trips abroad, Laura and I always attempted to combine the medical conferences with some sightseeing and some tourist activities.

Perhaps my most memorable trip to South America occurred even before I had been to Europe. It was in 1969, when I was invited to participate in the InterAmerican Congress of Cardiology that was to occur in Buenos Aires, Argentina. I was also invited to visit Rio de Janeiro and to speak on heart transplantation. Our first stop was Rio, where we stayed in the Oro Verde Hotel with a view out across Copacabana Beach. It also had a great view of the Corcovado, and of Cristo Rev, the Christ statue overlooking all of Rio. During the trip we were invited by the U.S. ambassador, whose son was a graduate student at Stanford, to speak at his home, where he held a reception for us. For native Appalachians, this was a major event! At this time Rio was quite safe, and one night after we had met some locals at dinner at a restaurant, we were invited to go dancing at a club on Ipanema Beach. We found Rio to be an exciting and adventurous place. The people we met from Brazil were friendly and took us to many sites, restaurants, and activities over the five days we visited their country.

Our next visit was to Iguacu Falls on the borders of Paraguay, Argentina, and Brazil. We stayed at the only hotel there that was suitable for American tourists, the Cataratas, which was aptly named. At that time the falls represented the largest-perimeter falls in the world and in retrospect, the hand-rowed boat trip that we took out over the top of the falls to an island to look down seems like a great risk. We had planned several days there but decided to leave early and go on to Ascension, Paraguay. We had no hotel reservations and the one hotel, known as Guarani, was filled with members of an IBM conference. We went to an agency and a room was finally located for us over the train station, but the country was so poor that the trains did not run frequently. Our room was so small that we could not open our luggage without putting it on the bed and closing them before sleeping and stowing them under the bed.

The water came on only from 7 to 8 p.m. at night, and only in the men's bathroom. I had to stand and guard the door while Laura took a shower. Ascension was a very poor place, and we were quite surprised when our guide, who had important government connections took us into the palace of the dictator, Stroessner, who remained dictator of Paraguay for many years. We had a chance to see him but not meet him. Our guide also arranged for us to go to a special party where the guests were in tuxedos and there was a dinner dance. To us, this seemed highly extravagant in what was a very poor country.

From Ascension we flew to Buenos Aires, and as we checked into our hotel, The Plaza, which was the most plush European-type hotel we had ever seen, we asked about a dinner reservation for eight o'clock. I was told, "No respectable restaurant opens before 10 p.m." They recommended La Cabana and made reservations for us. We took a nap and then went to dinner, wanting to celebate since in the past few nights we had not been blessed with the best of food. We had a fish course of a local fish with quite tasty Argentine Rose wine. For the next course I asked if we could share a Chateaubriand. I was told, "Not even the poorest in Argentina shares a Chateaubriand, and you shall have one each." We shared a ten-year-old bottle of a Malbec Argentine wine that was outstanding. This was followed by a flaming cherries jubilee dessert and a glass of port after dinner. The U.S. dollar was very strong, and the total cost for this extravagant meal, with a nice tip, was $12.60.

The U.S. dollar was very strong and the total cost for this extravagant meal, with a nice tip, was $12.60.

The next morning when we left the hotel there was a man on each side of the door holding a machine gun and dressed in military uniform. We had never seen this type of security and scurried back into the hotel. I went to the desk and asked, "Is there some disaster?" I was told that these were security guards and that they would never shoot tourists. I responded, "How can they recognize us as tourists?" Over the next few days we participated in the InterAmerican Congress of Cardiology, went to a lot of very dressy dinners and affairs, and could see that Buenos Aires was very much like Paris, to which it was oftentimes compared. Because of the great value of the dollar we did a lot of shopping and bought, in particular, a lot of leather goods. We returned home with a new appreciation of the culture of South America and had made many new friendships.

Five years later in 1974, our next trip to South America was to attend the World Congress of Cardiology in Buenos Aires. While the meeting was a great success, the city had become almost an armed camp because of political unrest. In a car ride on the way to attend a horse show in a suburban area, we were passed by a car with machines guns pointing out the window. We quickly ducked down below the windows and the car sped away. This was a period in which citizens of Argentina were disappearing, never to be heard of again.

One instance I remember happened when I was crossing a main street, accompanying Lou Platt, the head of Hewlett-Packard Medical. He grabbed me by the arm and pulled me from in front of a double-decker bus, where I had inadvertently stepped. I have always been appreciative of his friendship and thankful for his saving my life. From Buenos Aires we went to Peru and visited Lima and Machu Picchu. At Machu Picchu we were one of the lucky couples to stay overnight at a twelve-room hotel on the grounds of the ruins. Our group had a whole evening and early morning without any other tourists visiting the ruins, meeting natives, and climbing Wayna Picchu to look down on the whole mountain city.

One year later I was invited to Colombia to participate in a cardiology meeting in Medellin. Laura had other plans so I went alone. I wanted to jog and the only place that I was allowed to jog was in a military guarded golf course surrounded by barbed wire. This was the time that the Colombian drug lords were well in control of the city which became much more violent in later years. This was one trip in which I was frightened because of the political unrest. The organization did not have the money to pay my expenses and instead traded me emeralds and emerald jewelry. Once back in the states, I had the emeralds mounted in jewelry for Laura.

Three years later in 1980, I was invited by the Syntex Corporation's subsidiary, Syva, to make a South American tour to promote one of their diagnostic products. We began by landing in Bogotá, arriving late at night. Early the next morning I went for a six-mile jog that could have turned out to be a horror story. When I told my hosts, they were quite surprised that I came back alive. I promised never to go out alone again.

The lectures I gave at the university were well attended and we had educational tours of the city. Our most gracious hosts were the two Professors Roone and their beautiful wives, Rita and Sofia. Laura was accompanied by Rita and Sofia on numerous tours while I gave two or three lectures each day. The evenings were filled with luxurious dining experiences in top restaurants where outstanding food and wine was accompanied by local entertainment.

We then proceeded to Santiago, Chile, where we made presentations at the university and had an opportunity to tour for only one day to see the beautiful countryside around Santiago. We went on to Buenos Aires and took a trip into the South American Alps, where we visited the village of Bariloche. It was a Swiss-style ski area, but we were there during the summer, when it was much like the Lake Tahoe area. We met and dined with the elite doctors of Buenos Aires, Rene Favaloro and his wife, who were our hosts for several occasions. After the meetings in Buenos Aires, we flew to Sao Paolo, Brazil. It was a bustling city where we made presentations at two universities, and were able to view what was the most industrial city in all of Brazil. We found this city to be very vibrant, resembling Chicago.

In 1981, I was again invited to Buenos Aires to present a series of lectures on the modern use of drugs in cardiovascular disease. Laura did not accompany me. The meeting was sponsored by Rene Favaloro, who invented coronary bypass grafting while he was a surgeon at the Cleveland Clinic. He had returned to his home country of Buenos Aires and had established a foundation and research organization, which was sponsoring my five days of lectures. He was a local hero and was considered to be a candidate for the presidency of the country.

He did not consider politics should take precedence over his medical work and never agreed. Tragically, his institute had financial difficulties and he committed suicide over these problems in 2000. While there were many social events, I was required to give two-hour lectures each day, for which I was paid a handsome sum. The food and entertainment was as lavish as it had been on our other visits to Buenos Aires. During this visit I made friends with many Argentine physicians, whom I continue to visit with at national and international meetings.

My last trip to South America was in 1995 when one of my former trainees, Milton Godoy, invited me back to Rio to participate in the InterAmerican Cardiology Conference. This trip proved to be quite different from my first trip to Rio. The city was extremely unsafe, robberies were occurring every day, and my hosts would not let me leave the hotel unless I was in their presence. One of the participants in the meeting was robbed at knifepoint twenty-five feet from the door to our hotel. Rio was as beautiful as ever but because of the unsafe conditions, I had little opportunity to visit the sites that we had seen on our first trip twenty-five years before. The meeting was a success, though it made me sad to be back in a country where it was impossible for anyone to walk on the streets or to feel safe even in their home.

Chapter Twenty-eight

A HAPPY CONSULTANT

Prior to my appointment at Stanford I had no experience with the medical device or pharmaceutical industry. A year after I arrived, however, an engineer from the Becton, Dickinson and Company, which was developing a noninvasive blood pressure-measuring technology, visited and asked me to be a consultant. The company had its laboratory in Mountain View, about ten miles from the campus.

Since I was making ony $13,000 per year, their offer of $400 per month for a four-hour period one afternoon a month was enticing, as an addition to my meager salary, and I found consulting with engineers of the company intellectually stimulating. They asked excellent questions about the accuracy of their equipment and its clinical usefulness. They also helped me with new recording equipment for heart measures for my Stanford labs. We worked diligently on the project, but did not succeed in developing the Holy Grail of a noninvasive blood pressure methodology, which was their major objective. This work continued for about twenty-four months.

After two years in my Stanford faculty role, I was introduced to an Indian physicist named Narinder Kapany, who had worked with Professor Schalow, a Nobel laureate in Physics. Kapany had developed medical applications for fiber optic techniques. These techniques would provide the opportunity for looking inside the beating heart, and for determining oxygen saturation in a flowing blood stream. These fiber optic bundles could be put into catheters and inserted directly into the heart for oxygen measurements.

Kapany was tall, dark skinned, and wore a large turban. He was convincing in his presentations, and with his equipment, we were successful with measuring oxygen in the heart. The fiber optic bundles provided for looking inside the heart and we even took photographs inside, using a balloon to avoid the image being obscured by the blood cells. However, the blood obstructed extensive views in the arteries supplying oxygen to the heart.

Kapany's company was successful, became public in 1969, and for the first time I had options for stock and an opportunity to sell, making a grand total of probably $25,000. I almost missed making the conversion before the options expired because I did not understand their worth or the concept of stock options. Options were not as widely given in those days as they are today.

In 1968 I was asked to visit the Sanborn Division of Hewlett-Packard in the Boston area. Bill Hewlett, one of the Hewlett-Packard founders, had purchased Sanborn, a medical equipment company, but had no idea exactly how it would fit into the Hewlett-Packard product line or how it could advance medical technology. He had spoken to Bob Glaser, the dean of our medical school, and asked for a consultant to visit the plant in Waltham, Massachusetts. I was chosen to make this visit and meet their chief engineer, Dean Morton.

While I did not know exactly how Sanborn would develop into a successful part of Hewlett-Packard, I offered some suggestions for clinical focus. It was never possible for me to determine if my suggestions had any impact. However, several years later I became a collaborator and clinical consultant for Hewlett-Packard. Our cardiology unit developed many software solutions, which Hewlett-Packard licensed from Stanford and sold. These were based on computers with specialized programs

This was my first step in developing a consulting relationship with Hewlett-Packard, which lasted more than twenty years.

for making cardiology measurements. They became best sellers. These technologies are still used today for many of the calculations for cardiac catheterization and for monitoring in intensive care units.

This was my first step in developing a consulting relationship with Hewlett-Packard, which lasted more than twenty years. The technology transfer unit at Stanford was in its infancy and was just learning to deal with industry. The negotiations were a learning process for all and were valuable to Stanford. When the volume of tech transfer increased dramatically, we all began to learn how university-developed technology could be transferred to a commercial company. Our initial computer programs for heart measurements became a test case for the university in negotiations with Hewlett-Packard.

Because of my early success with clinical research and blood level determinations of pharmaceuticals, I was approached by the American Home Products pharmaceutical company and offered an opportunity to consult with the company on studies with propranolol, the first clinically available beta-adrenergic blocker.

Previously I had done a study with propranolol which appeared in *The New England Journal of Medicine* as a lead article. I was delighted to now have an opportunity to use this drug for an extensive series of investigations. I wrote numerous papers, and in 1968 published a book on research with propranolol. This also led to my becoming a consultant to American Home Products when they filed with the FDA to get approval to market propranolol to treat angina pectoris and arrhythmias. This was a very contentious meeting, as were many with the FDA, but in the long run the drug was approved. Both sides had their lawyers participate and there were angry shouts back and forth. There were accusations that the FDA was not interested in helping patients. I remember a company official saying, "This product is effective, it's safe, and you won't let us get it to those suffering patients." The FDA approval process was far less sophisticated but more contentious than today, and far more volatile.

I had a similar experience when the Astra Pharmaceutical Company also approached me for studies with lidocaine. Lidocaine was a drug we were studying in the coronary unit with blood levels to determine its effect on abnormal heart rhythms. We succeeded in our research and had numerous publications from our lidocaine work. My experience with lidocaine at the NIH was helpful for the continuance of this work on arrhythmias and its electrophysiologic effects in new patient groups. This work led to my first trip abroad to participate in a milestone conference in Denmark on arrhythmia treatment.

I had a terrible cold on my arrival and developed a plugged tube from my ears to my throat. The Danes assured me that being in the sauna twice daily would clear my sinuses and the tube to my throat. It did not, and on a painful flight home I perforated my eardrum. I remember this as very painful and disruptive for two weeks.

The Denmark conference, where my work was among the highlights, proved to be a great success and was featured with several articles in the book that was published as a summary of the conference. All of this early stage research was setting the stage for a much broader development of clinical research by my associates in the division and my postdoctoral fellows. We were becoming known as an institution on the "cutting edge" of clinical research.

In order for medical technologies conceived in the laboratories or academic settings to become applicable, collaborative work with drug and/or equipment companies is required to make medical advances commercially available. The research required to take the basic concepts from the laboratory to a product that could ultimately be used is frequently called "translational" research. For there to be successful transfers of this information, it is generally necessary for faculty to become consultants who work with the developer company. In some instances the faculty members become chairpersons for a scientific board to direct the continuing research in the company.

In other cases the faculty may take a sabbatical and continue their work in the laboratories of the company. In my earliest experience, these approaches were both financially rewarding and intellectually stimulating for me to develop new ideas. Frequently the companies provided equipment to carry out the work within the university laboratories, and worked with our staff in the development of high-quality laboratory equipment.

The amount of money involved in such transactions in my early consultative experience was relatively small. More recently, the compensation for academic physicians involved with companies has increased to significant amounts, and frequently involves the ownership of stock and stock options in companies. There have been many publications to suggest that translational and clinical research bias in favor of the company's product can occur when researchers have financial linkage to a company. For that reason, several institutions developed rules to limit compensation that a faculty member can receive from a company and also to limit an investigator from working specifically with a product from a company from which he receives financial compensation. This has led to considerable controversy among academic physicians and their institutions, and in some cases to researchers leaving institutions for ones less strict.

In my view, some institutions have gone too far in their limitations of the relationships their faculty may have with companies. The results are that they impede the movement of basic research to clinical application and commercialization. On the other hand, some reporting and regulation of a faculty member's relationship to companies is necessary, and if the question of bias is raised, a noninvolved group should review the process. I always believed that a transparent reporting mechanism was necessary and that this included reporting financial arrangements to the journal where our publications appeared. Universities should set up independent review mechanisms to monitor faculty conflict-of-interest questions.

Faculty members should be required to report their involvement with commercial entities on a regular schedule. In addition, companies should establish policies to guide their involvement with physicians and institutions. Responsive adherence to these policies and the regular reporting of the relationship should always promote the patient's and society's best interests.

Chapter Twenty-nine

FOR A CHINESE LEADER

Being on the West Coast at Stanford and near San Francisco, the home of many Chinese people, provided me with many medical referrals from the Chinese communities in the Bay Area and from Asia.

By the mid-1970s, I had begun to see many Chinese patients from Hong Kong in my role as chief of cardiology at Stanford. And I had also started to travel extensively in the Far East, and was invited by several universities and international meeting sponsors to participate in programs throughout the Far East. This raised my profile with Chinese nationals from Hong Kong, Indonesia and Taiwan.

An example of how I made further contact with Chinese patients followed a 1978 trip to Thailand. I had been to Thailand for the Asian-Pacific Cardiology Meeting, and on my last night had dinner with my host outside of Bangkok on one of the klongs until late at night. The next morning I awoke, severely ill with vomiting, diarrhea, and dehydration. Dinner on a klong requires a strong stomach to eat the boiled fish and shrimp and a toleration of terrible smells from the decaying weeds and fish. There is also a risk of infection of the gastrointestinal tract, which I now had in spades. I was scheduled for a flight to Hong Kong, and I only made the flight with the help of medication. To stay healthy, one should never eat the food from those ponds or klongs—a lesson I learned the hard way.

I arrived in Hong Kong and was staying in a suite in the Peninsula Hotel. It was difficult, being ill and being gracious to the hotel staff, when they brought me a tray of sweet smelling soap, a small tray of food for my selection, and a tray of fragrances and cologne to choose for myself, which was a special custom for this great hotel. The odors almost caused me to become ill all over again. The Peninsula Hotel at this time was considered the best hotel in the world because of the many amenities.

I did manage to improve, and later in the day received a phone call asking me to meet with a Stanford business school graduate named Johnson Cha and his father, Cha Chi Ming, whose goal was to talk me into going to Beijing for medical consultation with one of the most important men in the Chinese government. Cha Chi Ming was a thin elderly man who spoke exceptionally good English and was a major industrialist in Hong Kong. His son, Johnson, had a round face, and also spoke exceptionally good English. They arrived at 4 p.m., gave me the information they had available, and after considerable persuasion and conversation I agreed to go to Beijing the next day.

I had only summer clothes, having come from Bangkok near the equator and it was

December in Beijing. I also had no cardiac medications and was concerned that I might not be able to get what I needed in Beijing. I made contact with one of the local cardiologists who often referred patients from Hong Kong to me, and he collected a large package of pharmaceuticals for me to take. I bought a pair of trousers and top coat at an open air stand. I tried on the trousers behind the curtain and they were hemmed on the spot. I also bought a camera and long underwear. The next day at noon Johnson Cha and I left by train from Hong Kong to go to the Chinese border because it was not possible at that time to fly directly into China. I informed the U.S. Consulate in Hong Kong and my wife that I was making this journey. It was only after we crossed the border into China that I began to think, "What if things go poorly on this trip and I am sent away to Outer Mongolia or some other obscure place in China, never to be heard from again? The State Department of the United States could deny that I had entered the country, and only my wife would be available to protest."

On the third post-op day his wife decided to take him from the hospital, got him into a wheel chair and out to the street...

After crossing the border and being given documents we were taken to Guangzhou by train and then flown to Beijing, where the weather was even colder than I expected, minus 5 degrees centigrade. For the next four days, I visited with the patient, Liao Zheng Zi. He was a brilliant man who was number five in the hierarchy of the Chinese government, being in charge of all overseas Chinese development. Liao was elderly, slightly obese, had a kind face, and welcomed me warmly. He spoke seven languages, had been on the long march with Mao, and had for many years been a prisoner of the Japanese. Liao's father was even more famous and had been one of the five men who had overthrown the emperor and was a close confidant of the "Father of the Chinese Republic," Sun Yat-Tsen.

Liao had a serious cardiac problem and I did not have the specialized equipment to make a definitive diagnosis. However, my physical diagnosis acumen came in quite handy and I was able to make the correct diagnosis using only the physical exam. I wanted to explain my findings and recommendations to the patient but was told I could not do so. This was "an official government matter," was the answer, but although I insisted, I was initially restricted from telling the patient that he could not be treated effectively in China and that he should come to the United States for his treatment. I was told by the physicians caring for him that this could never happen. I was now learning how politics could influence medical care in China.

To entertain me between hospital visits while in Beijing, I was taken to the summer palace, even though it was the dead of winter, and to the Great Wall, which was covered with snow. They showed me the Beijing subway and a number of the museums. I was amazed that there were no tall buildings and millions of bicycles. There was only one hotel in the center of town, the Beijing Hotel, where I had a suite, but little heat. There were no private cars but I had a government car and a driver. On our last Saturday night, Johnson Cha, who had accompanied me to Beijing, and walked with me to the Forbidden City, where a Democracy Wall had been created for people to protest treatment by the government. This was one of the first steps of the government to address the evils of the Mao era and the Cultural Revolution. This was the last night for the Democracy Wall to be maintained in the center of Beijing since it had become a source of embarrassment to the government.

Most of the protest writings were against the Gang of Four. It was moved to a distant suburb the next day and soon thereafter was shut down. It was an extremely cold evening and we returned to the Beijing Hotel and had a brandy or two. Johnson Cha explained to me that he flushed in the face and got a rapid heartbeat, and thought it was due to the brandy. I did not understand this but upon returning home discovered that many Chinese men have an enzyme defect for metabolizing alcohol. When I tried this experiment on Johnson Cha at Stanford, I recorded his heart rate increase with an ambulatory recording device and detected the flushing and secondary tachycardia after he ingested alcohol. Later this was confirmed as a genetic defect in almost fifty percent of Chinese males.

My medical judgment was being questioned and I did not like it. So, just before I was to leave Beijing I talked with Liao about his prognosis and told him that he needed to come to the United States for treatment. This was against the advice of his Chinese physicians. He advised me to go home and make preparations for him to come in a month, and that he would be there. Again I was told by other officials that there was no chance of this happening. I returned to Guangzhou and then went by hover ferry to Hong Kong.

Back at Stanford I received a telegram stating that he would be coming in a month, we rented a house in Atherton which could accommodate the large retinue of people who would be coming with him, which proved to be approximately thirty, including his wife. He was evaluated by my cardiology group and seen by the cardiac surgeons. None of our junior staff wanted to operate on him for fear he would not survive surgery, since he had such a difficult problem and was in moderate heart failure. Norm Shumway, the head of cardiac surgery, and I, knowing that he had survived six years in a Japanese concentration camp and that he was a rugged and tough individual, were convinced his surgery could be accomplished. He readily agreed to have surgery and came through the operation beautifully and did quite well.

On the third postop day his wife decided to take him from the hospital and got him into a wheelchair and out to the street, rolling him towards their temporary home, before she was caught. We brought him back to the hospital where he recuperated for a week, and after six weeks of rehabilitation, he returned to China. After his return, I was invited to visit him yearly to check up on him and to travel throughout China if I wished, because he had major connections in nearly every city and province.

On one trip in 1982, I took my whole family and we spent five weeks traveling around the country. From 1978 until 1985 Liao did well, but while I was at a meeting in Dallas in 1985 I received a call that he was gravely ill and that I should come to China as his physician as quickly as possible. Upon arriving at the airport in San Francisco I was informed that he had died. A later postmortem exam showed that he died of a pulmonary embolus, a blood clot that had migrated from the legs to the heart and shut down blood flow, and not of his heart problem, which we had corrected.

During all of the adventures with Liao I was befriended by his chief of staff, Lu Ping who took over his position in the government after Liao died. Lu Ping accompanied me on trips throughout China during my several visits. I continued to communicate with him over the years, and as he rose in prominence, I had an inside view of what was happening in China. In the 1990s, he became head of the Chinese delegation to transfer Hong Kong from the British back to China. During this time he spent much of his time in Hong Kong and became the real nemesis of the British leader Sir Kenneth Patton. I visited with him in Hong Kong on one occasion when there were many protests, with tire burnings in the streets.

He was living in a very protected compound, where I had breakfast and an opportunity to talk with him. He was adamant about the transfer and the date for it. He was in no mood to accept any change in the agreement although he stated, "Hong Kong will be governed separately and they will like being returned to China." In the past five years he has stepped down from that job and Liao's son has taken it but the position has been reduced considerably in scope with the developments that have taken place in China since that time.

My friendship with Lu Ping has been extremely helpful on several occasions when I needed access in China. On one occasion, our daughter Beth, her husband, and her two children were living in China at the time of the unfortunate bombing of the Yugoslav Embassy. They were in Beijing for my son-in-law's job with Cummins Engines Company. I made contact with Lu Ping and was assured that he was looking after Beth, and he managed to call her every day and make sure she was safe. Beth's husband, Peter, was in the United States, and she was alone with two of our granddaughters. She was also teaching at the college where those killed in Yugoslavia had attended.

Laura and I were planning to go to China one week later. He assured us we should take our trip and come on to Beijing. We did and had an insightful visit including a banquet arranged by him, which was the usual custom with Chinese government officials. As things have developed, his grand niece, Wei, became a graduate student at the University of Cincinnati and has now completed her Ph.D. in the College of Pharmacy, one of the colleges under my direction. She now works for a pharmaceutical company in Philadelphia. These connections have provided a continuing link with Lu Ping, whom I last saw in 2001 in Shanghai when he introduced me to the hospital directors and medical school deans of all of the colleges in the Shanghai area. He arranged a sumptuous banquet in my honor to which he invited the well-known Chinese academicians. We spent the evening discussing the system of medical education and medical care.

The progress which has been made over the past twenty years in their hospitals and medical education is tremendous. The long waiting lists for surgery have been reduced and the quality of equipment in the top hospitals has greatly improved. However, many are very old, and much new construction is needed to provide for an adequate medical system.

I believe I was the first non-Chinese cardiology specialist to be invited to China to take care of a high official in their government. I also had a trainee from Beijing Hospital work with us at Stanford after my visits and she remains a cardiologist there. On numerous trips to China I have visited many of the major cardiology centers throughout the country. I also examined several of the high officials and generals on those trips. From a personal standpoint, my relationship with the Chinese leadership has encouraged me to believe that people-to-people interaction can overcome difficulties that governments are having with each other. China's development has occurred at a pace which is hard to believe even though in my ten trips to Beijing over the past twenty-three years I have observed the rapid change firsthand.

A FULL YEAR OF MY LIFE

The American Heart Association (AHA) is nationally known
for its support of heart research, public education, and national meetings
where the latest science and clinical applications are presented. I have had
a long and harmonious relationship with the association.

My initial experience, in 1960, was as an AHA research fellow at Harvard Medical School. I did my first clinical research and really commenced my career in cardiology with its support. After two years of starvation wages of $25 and $100 per month, the $500 per month that I was paid as an AHA fellow seemed like a fortune and allowed us to live at a higher standard in Boston, but not very high for someone with a wife and two children.

My next experience with the association was when the Santa Clara County Chapter in California supported my early research at Stanford. I became very active on its research committee and was one of the leading figures who attempted to bring the nine-county

AMERICAN HEART ASSOCIATION LEADERSHIP—
BOB CRUICKSHANK AND JOHN FITZPATRICK.

programs in the Bay Area under a single research committee. There was considerable local pride and jealousy about San Francisco becoming the predominant chapter, so the name Bay Area was selected to represent nine counties. Over a period of two years we were able to break down resistance and established one of the earliest mergers of the research allocations of county chapters in the country. The Bay Area allocations to heart research programs have supported major cardiovascular research over the years.

After becoming chief of cardiology at Stanford, I was invited to join the AHA's national scientific session planning committee as a member at large. This committee develops the program for the annual national scientific meeting and is extremely active. At that time, the headquarters for the AHA was in New York City, and for a country boy, traveling to New York City several times a year and participating in meetings was an eye-opener. The executives managing the scientific sessions were dyed-in-the-wool New Yorkers, and I had an opportunity to dine with them in wonderful restaurants, stay over an extra night, and attend the theater. I remember one particular night, leaving the theater with one of them in a snowstorm, and walking miles in New York to find a restaurant open after midnight. After three years on the committee, I was chosen to chair it for a three-year period.

In 1974, the headquarters of the AHA moved from New York to Dallas, and this occurred while I was chairman of the Scientific Sessions Committee. During my three-year tenure, there was an increase in the number of submitted abstracts from 3,000 to about 8,000 for the national meeting and the national meeting

...John Fitzpatrick, an Irishman from Connecticut who could do a wonderful imitation of "Casey at the Bat."

attendance doubled during the time I was chair of the committee. One of the responsibilities of the chair of the committee was to participate in the science writers' forum, which was organized to provide up-to-date information to news reporters about heart disease and heart research. We met in picturesque locations such as Marco Island in Florida, and at the Westward Look Resort in Tucson. It was during these meetings that I became acquainted with many of the scientific writers for the national press.

At the end of my three-year term as chair, I was asked to be on the research committee that would judge research submissions for funding from the American Heart Association. I served for one year, when there was an opening for the chairmanship of the publications committee of the AHA. I was chosen to be chair for a four-year period rather than remain on the research committee. During my time as chair, we initiated two new cardiology journals, *Hypertension* and *Atherosclerosis*. This again proved to be a delicate job of managing people through major change. During my last year on the committee I was chosen to become president-elect of the AHA.

The association has a president who is a physician and a leader in cardiology and a board chair who is a major lay leader after working through the association at either the local or state level. As president-elect my counterpart chairman was John Fitzpatrick, an Irishman from Connecticut who could do a wonderful imitation of "Casey at the Bat." He was a devoted family man and we visited his home in New Hampshire for an association retreat, and enjoyed a real dose of New England hospitality. It is difficult to describe New England hospitality, but it includes lots of tasty fish, clams and lobster, pumpkin pie, and lots of wine.

During my years as president-elect, I was chosen to be part of a group to restructure the heart association in its national headquarters and to consolidate many of the local community chapters into statewide chapters. These moves were being made to improve the efficiency of the AHA. We had a large committee, met frequently over the subject with a great deal of controversy, but did accomplish our job quite successfully. The AHA has this structure even today.

During this year I also became acquainted with the board chair, Robert Cruickshank, head of Deloitte & Touche in Houston. He had a great love for wine and had invested in a winery in Napa Valley. On many nights we sampled multiple wines from California and throughout the world, to the point of having difficulty remembering the names of some of them. The next morning frequently required treating headaches. Cruickshank was my major collaborator in the heart association for the time I was president and past-president. We shared social activities, and in 1982, I invited all of the officers of the heart association to Lake Tahoe for an officers' retreat. The meetings took place in our living room with glass doors onto our deck with a view overlooking Lake Tahoe, and we had spectacular dinners at one of the finest restaurants, Le Petit Pier at Lake Tahoe. We also had a number of other social adventures with Cruickshank.

One of the memorable ones was to celebrate Laura's and my anniversary at Chez Louis, an outstanding French restaurant in the Watergate Hotel in Washington, D.C. Bob Cruickshank wanted to have something special and ordered a bottle of Chateau Lafite wine from 1945, which was purported to be the greatest vintage of the century and it has been so characterized by numerous wine experts. Cruickshank graciously spoke of this as a reward for Laura's allowing me to devote so much time to the heart association. I was amazed that this bottle of wine cost $1,800 and had to be brought from a dusty cellar, and allowed to breathe for forty-five minutes, but it had a wonderful bouquet and was smooth and memorable. I have had that wine only one time subsequently, and I can still remember the taste and bouquet. To my mind it may be the best vintage of the century.

I became president of the American Heart Association in 1982 and during that year I visited more than thirty states and spoke at heart association meetings throughout the country. During my year of presidency, the World Congress of Cardiology was held in Moscow. I led a delegation attending that program. Our delegation visited Leningrad before going on to Moscow. It was our second visit to Leningrad and we enjoyed another visit to the Hermitage. Most of all we enjoyed visiting the history museum, which celebrated the fact that Leningrad held out for 1,000 days against the invading Germans in World War II.

When we landed in Moscow the plane on which we had flown stopped in the middle of the tarmac and a stairway was brought out. A Russian official came on the plane and asked for me and my wife. We were escorted off and into a limousine which was embarrassing to us. We were taken to our hotel, which had been built by the French and the Getty Oil Company from Los Angeles, and was brand new. It was off limits to ordinary Russians but had an extensive commissary with French products, including good French wines selling for as little as $3 or $4 a bottle. We were to attend a formal affair and we were rushed to our room. While taking a shower I noted that the drain seemed to be occluded and commented loudly to Laura about that. Without our making any comment to anyone else this was corrected the next day. That seemed a bit suspicious, but on another occasion Laura wanted to go to Zagriff, a preserved Jewish settlement outside of Moscow, but did not have a ticket.

One of the Jewish representatives from Tel Aviv had to attend a meeting with me and gave Laura his ticket, but told no one. Later, when we called the front desk, they inquired as to why Laura was going to Zagriff. We had discussed this privately in our room but had let no one else know. These two events led us to determine that our room was bugged and our conversations were being monitored. We searched widely but could not find the monitoring device.

On one evening we were taken to a party at a dacha owned by Chezov, the director of health of the Soviet Union, about fifty km outside of Moscow. The trip was hair-raising in that we were driven at about seventy miles an hour down the middle of Moscow's wide boulevards in a limousine with drawn curtains, the horn blowing loudly. All other traffic stopped for our passage. The party turned out to be a wild one. This was an unusual experience, with lots of vodka, Russian wines, and large amount of excellent food, in what was said to be a totally equal society. Laura and I each had an interpreter, and they became intoxicated and very vocal. The two French delegates were particularly critical of the Russians because they showed a cartoon in the movie theater in the dacha. So much for our view about a level of equality in the Soviet Union.

When the meeting was over, we traveled on to

THE RUSSIAN HEALTH MINISTER CHEZOV.

Czechoslovakia, Austria, and Germany, where we visited with other cardiology delegations as representatives of the American Heart Association before returning home. We celebrated July 4 in a beer hall in Munich—with lots of beer and singing of American songs. Most of us did the polka after filling ourselves with large steins of excellent German beer.

One of the other duties of the president of the American Heart Association is to testify before a congressional committee on health-related proposed legislation. During my tenure the Senate was considering requiring cigarette makers to put health warnings on every pack of cigarettes. When I testified, the subcommittee room was packed and all members of the subcommittee were present because this hearing was being covered by national TV; otherwise, only the chairperson and staff would have been present. I presented a rational position for health warning labels and concluded with a large poster showing the Virginia Slims cigarette ad and asked, "Senators, how do you like having your young adult and teenage daughters bombarded with this kind of misleading advertisement?"

After a number of clarifying questions, Senator Wendell Ford of Kentucky spoke and pulled up a large poster showing Ronald Reagan as a major Hollywood star in 1937 promoting Chesterfields. Ford said, "If smoking is good enough for our president to have been advertising for it, we should not be trying to limit advertising—it is free speech!" I was followed to the podium by the chairman of R.J. Reynolds, who testified against the labeling. He was questioned severely by the other senators and when he stated cigarettes were not the health hazard noted in the proposed label, he was chastised by several senators. He lost his temper and responded angrily. The TV folks were having a field day recording these hearings for the national evening news, which showed my exchange with Ford. Suffice it to say, later that year the labeling legislation was approved. I may have had little impact at the hearing but was delighted with the labeling approval.

The following year when I was past president of the heart association, I shared the speaking activities with Mary Jane Jesse, the president. She did not like to travel a great deal, and I did many of the presentations for her in the western part of the United States, since she at that time was living in Miami, Florida.

Every year the AMA has a banquet in which they present the Gold Heart Award to someone who has made contributions. I received that award in 1984. These dinners frequently honored movie stars and we had the opportunity to meet several of these, including Walter Matthau. We sat with him at dinner and he was knowledgeable and vocally supportive of the AHA's activities in promoting healthy hearts.

Another activity of the association was to develop a national business advisory committee during the time I was president. We had many well-known, high-level business individuals as members of this advisory committee. The two I have the most vivid memory of were T. Boone Pickens and Ewing Kauffman. These individuals tried to outdo each other by flying in their own private planes for the meetings and dominating the meetings with some absurd suggestions. I remember one time being invited to Amarillo, Texas, the headquarters for the Boone Pickens company. He had become a diet and exercise enthusiast. We were gotten up at five in the morning to go for a jog and then fed a breakfast of fruit, cereal, and skim milk. "The American Heart Association started me on this healthy lifestyle approach, and by God, I think all the officers and staff should live it," Pickens quipped. Amarillo, Texas, seemed like the end of the world at that time.

The American Heart Association was chosen to host the World Congress of Cardiology in 1986 in Washington. I was chosen to be program chair for the meeting. This turned out to be a great deal of work, and I traveled extensively throughout the world to promote this congress and to be certain that we had international representation for the presentations. This turned out to be far more traveling and far more work than I had anticipated; however, the travel was made easier because Pan Am had given the American Heart Association free travel, first class, on all of the flights throughout the world. The meeting in Washington came off with a far larger attendance than any of the other previously held World Congresses of Cardiology. We had excellent representation and for the first time had a delegation from mainland China.

My activities with the AHA continued when I moved to Cincinnati. As national past president, I was appointed as a lifetime member of the board of the local heart association. I was also chosen to be the first recipient of the Kaplan award for scientific achievement. This had been established to honor Sam Kaplan, a leading pediatric cardiologist at Cincinnati Children's Hospital Medical Center. I continue to serve on this board, though I have not been active recently.

As I have calculated the time I have devoted to the American Heart Association it adds up to almost one year of my life. I am proud of the contributions I have made to its scientific programs and publications. I am also proud of the research I did while being supported by the organization. One of the memorable activities was the restructuring of the national organization, which continues even today.

Of course, being a participant in the American Heart Association gave me name recognition throughout the United States, and my participation as president in the World Congress and as program chair for the U.S. site of the World Congress gave me international recognition. I have never regretted the time I spent working for the Heart Association and the resulting friendships. I believe the association, through its research and community programs, has been a major contributor to the improvement of care for patients with heart disease and stroke.

Chapter Thirty-one

FACE OF NATIONAL MEETINGS

Over the past forty years of my involvement in national medical meetings, there have been major changes in attendance, scope of presentations, and venues. These changes in cardiology's national meetings are almost unbelievable and to the lay public probably appear unreasonable.

My first national meeting was the American Heart Association meeting in 1961 held in Miami Beach. It was here that I presented my first paper—from work which had been completed in the cardiology unit at the Harvard Medical School—at a national meeting. The meeting was held in a single hotel and there were approximately 450 attendees. There was only one general session and the only exhibitors were a few book publishers.

Attendance at this meeting of the American Heart Association contrasts with meetings today of the newer association, the American College of Cardiology, where the maximum attendance is up to 40,000. There are there simultaneous sessions, making it almost impossible to judge which session you want to attend. The exhibits now cover the area of three or four football fields, and for this reason only a few cities in the United States can host the meetings. These are New Orleans, Chicago, Anaheim, Orlando, and Atlanta.

The astronomical growth did not take place in a single year or decade, but was progressive over forty years. For example, from 1974–1977, I was the program chair for the American Heart Association annual meeting. We were receiving approximately 3,600-8,000 abstracts for consideration for presentation, increasing progressively from a few hundred in 1961. Today, there are more than 12,000 abstracts submitted for presentation and publication and yet the acceptance rate is pretty much the same as it has always been, between 25-30 percent for the program. The programs have been expanded from only oral presentations to many poster presentations, where a large area of the venue is set aside with poster boards where abstracts are posted and the presenter explains his research to strolling doctors who are interested.

This change took place at the time I was program chair for the American Heart Association. I had an opportunity to observe and participate in much of the growth. The present abstract number of 12,000 requires enormous work by the staff of the American Heart Association and the American College of Cardiology. There are over 500 reviewers involved, and the chairperson is now far busier than I was when I was chair, where we used about 250 reviewers.

Another major change is that these meetings have become international in scope. Almost half of the abstracts submitted are from overseas, and at least one-fourth of the attendees are from overseas. The meetings have become a melting pot for ideas from all over the world.

Cities and their convention bureaus vie for the meetings. For many years the American Heart Association meeting was held in October or November in Atlantic City. The year I was to become program chair, gambling had become a major industry in Atlantic City for the first time and crime was on the rise. Many of the attendees had also experienced lousy hotels and poor food. It became my responsibility to talk to the mayor and the convention bureau, to tell them we would not be coming back to Atlantic City in view of the crime rate and what was going on with hotels. I had some fear of winding up in the bay, face down.

...board certified in cardiology in 1972, there were fewer than 1,000 board certified cardiologists—today there are over 20,000.

However, we moved from Atlantic City to a rotation between Miami, Dallas, and Anaheim, which over the years worked very well, until Miami was replaced with Atlanta, New Orleans, or Chicago. It is worth examining what actors have driven the massive increase in attendance and participation at these meetings. The major one is profits—profits by pharmaceutical companies, device and instrument manufacturers, and of course, the associations that profit from these large meetings. The large increase in research funding, the larger numbers of investigators and postdocs, and the frantic drive for individual recognition have all contributed to the rise in attendance. There has also been a major increase in the number of practicing cardiovascular physicians.

When I became board certified in cardiology in 1972, there were fewer than 1,000 board-certified cardiologists—today there are over 20,000. In addition, the meetings have become international. The major sponsors are big pharmaceutical and device companies and big imaging companies. At one point the meetings were checkered by many give-aways, and early in my career I did attend an event one evening sponsored by a pacemaker company. Besides gifts and food, there was entertainment consisting of a large cake being brought out, from which emerged a scantily clad young woman. These kinds of abuses have been tempered, and the associations now have rules to enforce good behavior.

Pharmaceutical and device companies now frequently sponsor symposia in the evening or a day or two before the meeting, to highlight their specific products. The exhibitors are forbidden to distribute any gifts except pens and info booklets to attendees. There are several groups that plan their activities for just before the primary meeting. This means some attendees are at the meetings for a whole week.

In addition to the logistic details involved with abstract selection, and putting on the meeting itself, there is the problem of housing, and housing bureaus are created to handle the many hotels involved. There is also the problem of transportation with chartered bus systems moving all around the city to all of the hotels that house the working personnel from the associations for registration, as well as the registrants and guests. Instructions to delegates must be handled appropriately, and of course, the airlines also are very strong sponsors to the meetings, since this increases their revenue as well.

There are both good and bad outcomes that have resulted from the changes in these meetings. The good is that much more educational information is presented. Frequently basic concepts are brought to the forefront for clinicians, and there is promotion of research that is both basic and translational. There is also a major effort for the development and presentation of guidelines for the management of various cardiovascular diseases. These are then presented to a large group of cardiologists, and this helps to standardize care throughout the country.

On the down side, it is clear that the tremendous expenses involved in these meetings drives up pharmaceutical and device costs. There is considerable "me too-ism" in the presentations at the meetings, and in many instances these presentations deliver a false sense of progress. In addition, it is difficult to choose the sessions one wishes to attend and to maneuver around the meeting. My view, however, is that there will be no going back to smaller meetings; but I have detected that a plateau has been reached and it seems unlikely that further increases in the number of attendees or programs will occur.

Chapter Thirty-two

ADVENTURES

I have always been interested in the game parks of the African subcontinent as a place to visit. In 1975 I was offered an opportunity to attend a major medical conference in South Africa and to visit game parks. I accepted eagerly, and we planned our trip over several months.

Since it was a two-day trip by plane to get there, we decided to stop over in Rio de Janeiro where, in 1969, we had spent several memorable days. The beaches in Rio were now populated with beautiful women wearing the latest craze—string bathing suits. One couldn't help but ogle, as they had not yet appeared in the United States.

We revisited a Portuguese restaurant on the north end of Copacabana Beach that served about the best seafood that I have ever eaten. This overnight gave us some rest before another overnight flight to Johannesburg. We arrived in Johannesburg for the meeting and on the first night were taken to a play, *Equis*, where, to our surprise, we were able to mingle with people of color. One of the black doctors informed us that this was the first time they had been able to attend any program of this type with the white Africans. He responded to my question about this, "I doubt that South Africa can sustain this apartheid policy for very long."

IT COST $5 TO GET OFF THIS ANIMAL IN EGYPT.

I also visited Baragwanath Hospital, where I made rounds to dozens of patients with rheumatic heart disease in a 3,200-bed hospital, one of the largest in the world. The hospital was in the heart of Soweto, a black ghetto of Johannesburg, where major riots would take place just one year later. At one of the dinner parties, an Afrikaner family with strong feelings about white supremacy stated riots would never occur. I predicted that in a decade that riots would occur, and white rule would end. This prediction was very upsetting to this group. To my surprise, major riots did occur one year later in Soweto. This was the beginning of the downfall of Afrikaner rule in the country. On this trip, we were also taken on a two-day tour of Kruger National Park, where we viewed in large numbers many of the animals that could be seen only in zoos in the United States. This only whetted my appetite for more game park visits and viewing.

From Johannesburg we traveled to Cape Town, one of the most beautiful harbor cities in the world, even when compared to San Francisco, Sydney, and Stockholm. We visited Cape Town's hospitals, and gave lectures to medical students and residents. Hewlett-Packard had arranged for me to meet with a number of physicians to give a dinner presentation. The HP managers took us to Stellenbosch, the quality wine-producing area, to visit the wineries and to sample and choose wine for the dinner. The high quality of the wine in the area surprised me, and the ones we chose for dinner were excellent. The vineyards were beautiful and the winery technology appeared to be very modern.

...settled by the Indian population and once was the site of Gandhi's residence while living in South Africa.

My lectures were given at the famous Groot Schuur Hospital and were attended by many faculty members of the University of Cape Town Medical School. From Cape Town we journeyed on to Durban on the east coast of Africa, which had been heavily settled by the Indian population and once was the site of Gandhi's residence while he was living in South Africa. We visited a large teaching hospital, and in one afternoon I think I examined about fifty patients with mitral stenosis, something that had almost disappeared from the medical scene in the United States. (The disappearance of rheumatic heart disease has been attributed to antibiotic treatment of sore throats caused by beta streptococcus. Another explanation is that the beta streptococcus organism that causes it has become less virulent.) We also visited an Indian spice market and purchased dozens of kinds of spice, some of which we are using thirty years later. Durban was an international city with populations from other parts of Africa, Asia, Europe and the Americas. It was a seacoast town with a wide beachfront.

After completing my invitational activities in South Africa, our next stop was in East Africa, where we stayed for two days at the Thorntree Hotel in Nairobi, Kenya, before setting out on a tour of the game parks of Kenya and Tanzania. We visited Tsavo, Mt. Kilimanjaro, Arusha (which was at one time planned to be the capital of Tanzania), and to

Uganda and Kenya at a time when they were planning to come together as a single nation. This never occurred, but Arusha still was a very interesting marketplace, with people and products from all three countries.

In Tanzania, we also visited Ngorongoro, where we saw huge numbers of almost all of the animals of the region. We visited an old German fort , Fort Ikoma, which had been turned into a game park lodge, then moved on to the picturesque lodge at Keekorok. Before reaching Keekorok, we visited the Olduvai Gorge and the site of the Leakey excavations, famous at the time for the discovery of Lili, the skeleton of the oldest homonid. The Leakeys were away but we explored the site with graduate students. The excavations were taking place in an old creek bed and we were amazed at the simplicity of the tools being used.

Each day we went on long game drives every morning and afternoon, and on returning to the lodge we were greeted with a beer while sitting on the veranda in rocking chairs. The food was exquisite, contrary to our expectations, consisting of locally grown vegetables and fruits, and guinea hens for meat. The numbers and types of game that we saw running across the plains of the Serengeti were almost unbelievable. There were large populations of giraffes, zebras, elephants, gazelles, lions, cheetahs and wildebeests.

After this ten-day safari, we returned to Nairobi and continued our trip by plane. (This was the time when Idi Amin, president of Uganda, was holding Jane Goodall hostage for two years. Jane is a well-known Stanford professor who has studied chimpanzees for years.) Unbeknownst to us, the plane stopped in Uganda on our way from Nairobi to Cairo. Because I had listed Stanford as my address, and knowing Jane was there, I refused to get off the plane, even though they urged everyone to get off for a rest.

We arrived in Cairo, where we had arranged a private tour, and were surprised to find few tourists. Our tour company was prompt in meeting us and in planning our visits throughout the country. The Russians, after years of domination of Egypt, had withdrawn from the country just two months before we arrived, and we found no other American tourists. During the Russian domination, Americans had been discouraged from visiting. There were a few Italians and some French tourists. Our guides were very adept and also extremely friendly, even taking us to their homes for dinner.

In Cairo we visited the souk which, outside of Istanbul's souk, is said to be the largest in the world. A souk is a large market combining the concept of a large shopping mall, a flea market and a farmer's market. One can buy just about anything there. We also visited Giza, the great pyramids, and the Sphinx. As tourists we were offered a camel ride, and once we reached our destination near the great pyramid, my camel kneeled and let me off, but according to the guide the camel with Laura on it would not kneel.

After $5 was passed into the hand of the camel owner, the camel kneeled gracefully and allowed Laura to dismount. We still laugh about that today. We departed Cairo to visit the Valley of the Kings and Queens at Luxor and many of the other excavated sites. We were impressed by the Karnak temple complex and by how well preserved many of the burial sites were. Aswan and the giant dam on the Nile was our next stop. The lake was still filling and would later cover some of the ancient sites. However, Abu Simbel was relocated to preserve it, and we flew up to do a day visit. This site was as amazing to us as the Great Pyramids.

Upon returning to Cairo we stayed at the Cairo Hilton, one of the city's premier hotels. We visited the Cairo Museum and were almost the only visitors. Our guides obtained permission for us to examine hands-on many of the items that later toured the United States in the King Tut exhibit. In Cairo, we were horrified at the traffic and were almost afraid to cross the street. We were careful to avoid any food that might be contaminated. Laura was drinking only bottled water, while I chose to drink only beer, even using it to brush my teeth. She developed explosive vomiting and diarrhea, and I told her the water was bottled directly from the Nile River, where we had seen humans bathing, as well as oxen and donkeys. Since that day, she always drinks beer when we are in developing countries and avoids the consequences of contaminated water.

We returned via New York to San Francisco. Our African experience left us marveling at the wonderful game parks and animals, but we were highly disturbed by the Afrikaners and segregationist policies of South Africa. We realized we had visited one of the sites of the beginning of the human species at the Olduvai Gorge. We were amazed at the ruins of the great ancient civilization in the Nile River Valley and throughout Egypt. This was the civilization that preceded the Greek and western European civilizations, and was little known to us before our visit.

Chapter Thirty-three

PATIENTS AND FRIENDS

During my position as chief of cardiology at Stanford Hospital many famous patients were referred to me. My relationships with them had a great impact on my life and my career.

In the early 1970s, a patient named Gene Fife, who at that time was head of Goldman Sachs in San Francisco, was referred to me. After an extensive diagnostic work-up we decided that medical treatment and followup for his heart disease was the choice approach. Thus began my long and cordial association with Gene. He was not only under the stress of the Goldman Sachs operation but at this time his wife had terminal breast cancer, and passed away soon thereafter. I continued to see him as a patient, and he also became a close friend of our family.

GOLDMAN SACHS' GENE FIFE WITH DON.

About a year and a half after his first wife's death, Gene married Anne and we attended his wedding and came to know his two children, David and Amy. During the next few years I saw Gene as a patient on a regular basis and he did well. Laura and I were invited to participate in a number of Goldman Sachs activities with him in San Francisco. His firm hosted meetings with internationally known speakers meeting the business leaders of San Francisco. One of the most memorable ones he hosted featured Henry Kissinger. We were also guests at this meeting and Gene introduced me with great fanfare and accolades as his physician before introducing Henry Kissinger, who surely must have been miffed at being upstaged.

Just prior to my moving to Cincinnati, Gene moved to London to become the head of Goldman Sachs International. He had become symptomatic and near the end of my Stanford time he had undergone coronary bypass surgery that was quite successful. He required continuing follow-up care by a cardiologist. He wanted to keep me as his physician. After our move to Cincinnati and within a couple of months he came for his first visit. Over the next twelve years, he came from London to Cincinnati twice a year, staying with us at our home, and undergoing medical tests each time. We each made a special effort to visit back and forth with our families.

In London, Gene was a very seminal figure in European banking as well as in financial circles throughout the world. He was responsible for building a new Goldman Sachs building on Fleet Street, and at the opening ceremonies, to which he invited us, we had dinner with Margaret Thatcher and had an opportunity to talk with her.

Another renowned individual came to me in 1978. Edward Teller, who was considered the father of the hydrogen bomb...

He did much to make Goldman Sachs a major international organization. When he decided to step down from Goldman Sachs he moved to Charlottesville, Virginia, where he had purchased 546 acres of land and has since restored a large home that was built in the 1920s on the outskirts of town. He is the only person who attended all of our children's weddings and receptions, and so far we have also managed to attend the weddings of his children. One of the highlights was to attend the wedding of his daughter Amy, who had always considered Laura a surrogate grandmother. In recent times, Gene and his youngest son with his second wife, Doug, and I had a father-son trip together in the Charlottesville area. He was a principal speaker at my stepping-down ceremony from the senior vice president and provost for health affairs position at the University of Cincinnati, and was most complimentary about my leadership there since he had viewed first hand the transformation of the medical center.

Another renowned individual came to me as a patient in 1978. Edward Teller, who was known as the father of the hydrogen bomb, was then a fellow at the Hoover Institute on the Stanford campus. He was referred for his heart disease, which I was managing medically over a period of several years after he had undergone a study in our cardiac catheterization laboratory. At that time he had only obstructions in his coronary arteries that did not require surgery. I saw him on a regular basis several times a year.

In 1983, while sitting in my office one morning, I received a call from the White House. The physician calling had been informed by Teller that I was his physician at Stanford. I was told, "Dr. Teller is here making a presentation on his proposal for a protection system against incoming foreign warheads, but in the last hour he has used his nitroglycerin four times and keeps clutching his chest. I wanted to call you and have you speak with Dr. Teller." I agreed to do so and Teller came to the phone. "I have had more chest pain and those little white nitroglycerin tablets are not giving me full relief. What do you think?"

I queried him a bit more about his activities and finally said, "Edward, I think you should quickly return to California and I will schedule an appointment to see you as soon as you arrive."

He replied, "I vill not, I still have to make a presentation in Boston and stop in Chicago on my return. I vill see you next week."

I pondered this response and said, "Edward this is a warning sign. You may die if you continue the trip."

He replied heartily, "Everyone must die sometime, I have my work to complete and vill see you upon my return," and he hung up.

About an hour later I received a call from our cardiac catheterization lab asking, "Did you authorize Dr. Teller to call and schedule a coronary arteriogram?" I replied that I did not, and would have to see Dr. Teller before this procedure was carried out. I called back to the White House, was able to reach Teller, and told him, "Edward, you cannot take over management of your own medical care. You must see me first, and I have scheduled an appointment in my office with you on next Monday morning at 8:30 a.m."

He said, "I vill be there."

Teller completed his trip to Boston and Chicago and showed up in my office. After taking a full history, I authorized a catheterization procedure that was carried out later that day. This time the blockages in his arteries were such that he needed to have open heart surgery. I presented the proposition to him, and he was somewhat reluctant to consider surgery. He then said, "My friend Henry Kissinger has just undergone that procedure a few months ago; let's call him and see what he has to say." I was surprised at this and doubted that we would be able to talk to Henry Kissinger but gave the telephone to Teller. He apparently had Kissinger's private number, and soon we had him on the speaker phone. Teller queried him about his operation, which was carried out at the Massachusetts General Hospital, and I remember Kissinger saying, "Edward, don't be a fool. Quit trying to be your doctor. Do what the doctor suggested. Yes, it was painful for a few days, but I have made a good recovery in three months." Teller acquiesced, underwent the procedure, and did quite well.

There is another story of something that occurred because of a famous patient at our center, though he was not my patient. A major medical news story during the 1980s was the proposal that Vitamin C would prevent and treat the common cold and other maladies. Linus Pauling was the principal proponent of Vitamin C. He was convinced that Vitamin C had a role in heart disease too. I remember a day when he wandered into my office. He was disheveled and had a jacket pocket filled with articles from journals.

He said to me, "I am told you are the chief here and I wanted to tell you about my heart test." He explained that he had just had a twenty-four-hour Holter monitor test, which recorded his heartbeats for a full day. He said, "They tell me I have lots of extra beats and they are dangerous and that I should have an angiogram. Instead, I'm going to take more Vitamin C since I believe it can reverse heart disease."

I was puzzled and disbelieving. He said "Young man, I don't think you believe me. I will be back next week to convince you." True to his word, he returned with lots of papers from medical journals and began outlining his ideas on my blackboard.

BIG SALMON FISHING WITH THE VRHS.

He reviewed the process of atherosclerosis, the cause of heart attacks by the obstruction of arteries with cholesterol. He believed this process could be reversed by Vitamin C. After all, he had won two Nobel prizes and how could I doubt him? He was so convinced that he established an Institute in Palo Alto to study heart disease. Unfortunately, it ran out of funding before he completed his work, but he lived for more than fifteen years and had no known heart disease. Vitamin C does act as an antioxidant and there may be a relationship that prevents the breakdown of fatty substances and cholesterol plaque formation, but this has not been proven. However, taking antioxidants to prevent a number of maladies has recently become a popular vogue. He may have been right—just ahead of his time.

Two patients, Irv and Bessie Vrh, who were from Turlock, California, had heart disease and my care really enhanced the quality of their lives. They were not famous, but became caring friends. They shared some adventures with me, which they were able to return to after a pacemaker for Bessie and control of blood pressure for Irv. The most enjoyable of these was to join them at their Canadian retreat at Quathiaski Cove, on Quadra Island in British Columbia. For ten years, we joined them in September for salmon fishing, crab catching and exploring the wild parts of the island. We caught large numbers of salmon, and used the heads and insides of the fish to bait crab traps.

On one occasion I pulled up a trap with twenty-three large Dungeness crabs. Irv fished by the *Farmer's Almanac*, which projected times when fish would bite and we were far more successful than the privately paid fishing parties. Bessie made the best raspberry jam and Irv brewed his own beer that was like champagne. We usually transported approximately a hundred pounds of salmon and crab back with us to our home in Los Altos. We have fond memories of these trips and the friendship and generosity of the Vrhs.

I was the physician for many famous and greatly successful men and women, and when

FISHING WITH VRHS. AN EXCEPTIONAL DAY.

they became friends, I assured them that I could still be the physician in charge of their health issues, and we would handle their medical problems totally objectively. While I would not force them into any procedure or treatment, I could give them my reasoned opinion and rationale, and I expected them to respond positively. It is difficult to be a friend and a physician to such people, but I found this to be a most rewarding experience and I believe I successfully served the dual role.

In addition to caring for famous patients, I was still involved with making medical recommendations for my father and regulating his medications. My parents were still involved with our lives, even though my mother was quite withdrawn from our daily activities. I wrote to my mother on a weekly basis beginning when I was in Boston. This continued after we moved to Bethesda, and then to California, and about every third or fourth year I was able to convince my parents to visit us.

After we had settled in California, they would drive across the country, taking four or five days to do so. My dad liked very much to visit Las Vegas, and while he was not what I would call a gambler, he loved the action, and frequently won a few dollars. Our children wanted my mom's full attention on her visits to us in California. She did make an attempt to spend time with them and was civil with them, but she was still very critical of what I was doing as a physician, and refused to accept the fact that I was succeeding. These visits were not very pleasant for me.

In addition to writing letters, I tried to call weekly to find out how my parents were doing and to share some of the children's activities. My dad usually took these calls and kept me posted about what was going on at the home front. My mother did not answer any of my letters and when I visited Alabama, which I combined with some of my business travels on occasions, she was functional but still quite withdrawn. Dad's health after his prostatectomy was quite good. For a retired man, he had become a champion golfer, playing six days a week at a local course near home. He sold his nursing home, which was a conversion of the motel and now had time for golf. In fact, he was so interested in golf that he was letting the home place deteriorate. He was very happy to be away from my mother and with his friends on the golf course. On my visits I was always trying to help my parents with house repairs as well as assessing their medical problems and needs.

Chapter Thirty-four

SCARE *of our lives*

In 1979, I was invited to the Philippines to participate in an

international cardiology meeting for the opening of the Philippine Heart

Center. This was scheduled for a few days after we returned from a cruise

that was an eleven-day postgraduate conference for physicians with Denton

Cooley and his associates, on the Golden Odyssey.

On the final three days of the cruise, it was so rough on the ship that we became experts at holding onto our wine bottles during our dinner. We were delayed a day in returning so there was only time for a twelve-hour stopover at home to collect clothes for the Philippines trip.

We flew to Manila on Pan Am and participated in the conference. After the first day of the meeting, we had a day to visit Corregidor, where the Japanese had held American prisoners during World War II. This brought back memories of the suffering of our servicemen in World War II. The final event of the conference was a formal dinner hosted by Imelda Marcos. As we were doing our formal dressing in Philippine costumes, Laura asked me to feel a small lump in the axilla under her arm. Upon feeling it I tried to reassure her, though I recognized instantly that it was firm and fixed, the characteristics of a likely cancerous lymph node. She observed my anxious face and knew it was a real concern. We went on to the dinner, and even though I did not tell Laura the full magnitude of the finding, she sensed my great anxiety. When we returned to the hotel, I shared with her my concerns, and we began to make plans to return home immediately, although we had been scheduled to

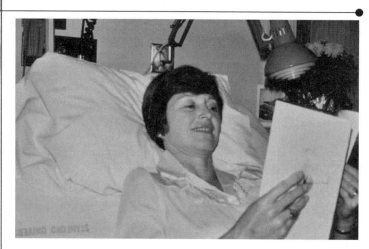

LAURA AT STANFORD UNIVERSITY HOSPITAL BEFORE BREAST CANCER SURGERY.

go on to Hong Kong to celebrate the Chinese New Year with the T. F. Kwok family, whose patriarch was one of my very favorite patients.

We had a two-day wait before we could get a plane home and were taken to a resort about seventy-five miles from Manila for relaxation, a beautiful place on the China Sea, but of course we did not enjoy it at all knowing what was ahead for us. On the return trip, our plane stopped in Hawaii and I called Saul Rosenberg, the head of oncology at Stanford, and asked him to see us immediately upon our arrival. We arrived, and upon examination he confirmed my suspicion. Laura then had a series of tests to determine whether or not there might be metastatic disease someplace else in the body. The lymph node was biopsied, revealing undifferentiated carcinoma, likely breast, even though no exact nodule had been found in the breast.

A bone scan showed a suspicious lesion in the pelvis, and though a mastectomy had been scheduled it was cancelled. Gloom set in on all of us, as we were thinking this was a distant metastasis. Donald Nagel, chief of orthopedics and a friend and colleague, looked at the scan and said the lesion did not appear to him to be cancerous, and he wanted to biopsy it. He did, and twenty-four hours later it turned out that he was correct, it was not cancer and the mastectomy was planned the following Monday and carried out. The surgery was a modified mastectomy with a lymph node dissection in the axilla. No primary tumor was found but there were twelve lymph nodes positive for cancer in the axilla. This gave Laura a terrible prognosis,

A bone scan showed a suspicious lesion in the pelvis and although a mastectomy had been scheduled, it was cancelled.

probably only a predicted 10 percent survival for five years. However, her oncologist proposed radical chemotherapy and Tamoxifen to suppress ovarian function.

CMF was a chemotherapy regimen that had just been shown to be helpful in an Italian study. CMF is an abbreviation for Cytoxan, Methoytrexate and 5-Fluorouracil. The studies in Milan, Italy, showed prolongation of life after CMF therapy, but Tamoxifen had not yet been shown to be helpful. She was to have this triple therapy monthly for one year, and daily Tamoxifen. Frequently during the year her white cell count was depressed, she had a number of upper-respiratory infections, and had to delay that month's therapy, so the entire course took fifteen months.

While this therapy is still used for breast cancer today, there are powerful drugs to combat nausea and drugs to stimulate the production of white blood cells, and the course of treatment has been shortened to six months. The side effects are greatly reduced. During the year we traveled extensively to meetings in Switzerland and Russia that had been previously arranged. I always took a medical kit with me on these trips to care for Laura if anything bad occurred. She was always extremely positive, even though she lost her hair, had ulcers in her mouth, and obviously felt bad much of the time.

The experience with breast cancer led Laura to start to work with a support group for breast cancer victims, and in this support group she met Gladys Nogoya. Gladys became one of our best friends and someone who stayed in our house for many of our trips from 1980 to 1986. She was Japanese American and was one of the many who were interred in camps during World War II. She harbored no ill feelings toward the U.S. government but always felt this had been unnecessary. Her brother had been an officer in a group of Japanese soldiers who fought in World War II in Europe, and had been decorated many times as a hero. Gladys was a great friend to Laura and to me. She did house sitting for us on many occasions. Her cancer was not cured, and she succumbed to her breast cancer after a few years.

Laura's experience with the support group led her to become a participant in the Reach for Recovery Program, which she continued for several years. She has had no recurrence and has fully recovered from her chemotherapy. In fact, she grew a full head of hair that has turned an attractive white as she has aged. However, any symptoms that occur are frequently examined by me to determine whether they could mean recurrent breast cancer. After twenty-eight years, we have to believe that she was totally cured by what was to us a miracle. It was our good fortune that this chemotherapy that could completely cure metastatic breast cancer was discovered at that time.

We are thankful for Don Nagel, the orthopedist whose findings allowed the operation to go forward, and for the scientifically rigorous oncologist who put her through chemotherapy that was not yet approved by the FDA. We are forever grateful to all these caring medical professionals. Medicine involving breast cancer therapy has advanced greatly since the death of my grandmother from breast cancer in 1955. She had a radical mastectomy which left her with a muscle disability in her arm. She did not receive post-op chemotherapy or radiation. After three years there was a recurrence and she died. Hopefully, there will continue to be progress in treating this terrible disease.

Chapter Thirty-five

TAHOE RETREAT

In the fall of 1979, after Laura had received eight months of chemotherapy for her cancer, we recognized how tenuous our lives are. We had always enjoyed great vacations at Lake Tahoe, and for years had visited and used various houses that we could rent or borrow.

We backpacked and participated in water activities at the lake in the summer. During several winter vacations there, all of us had become avid skiers, so we decided to purchase a condominium for our family near Lake Tahoe. Aggie Bennett was the real estate agent we chose, and we drove up to Lake Tahoe where we had made reservations in a Tahoe City bed and breakfast named the McDowell House.

THE LAKE TAHOE RETREAT.

On Saturday, our first day of searching, we viewed condos all around the north lake, not finding anything we liked. Late in the afternoon we were at the Kingswood Estates near Kings Beach and did see condos we might want to purchase. Unfortunately there were no three-bedroom units, and none would be available for at least a year. Aggie pointed out that a house had just been built one block up from the condos and was likely to be for sale. It had been built by a builder to be his home after his marriage. The wedding did not take place, and he was now ready to sell what she thought was a beautiful house. We agreed to take a look, and on walking into the house, seeing all of the glass in the front and a deck with a full view of Lake Tahoe, we were quite impressed, but tried not to show it by being too eager.

We saw other houses on Sunday morning, but none quite measured up to the one we had seen on Canterbury Drive above Kings Beach. We had lunch on Sunday with our agent at Sunnyside, one of the Tahoe hangouts, and after some deliberation, decided to make an offer on the house. We returned to Los Altos, and the next morning we received a counteroffer, which we accepted. The real estate agent came that evening to sign the papers, since we were leaving on the following morning for a two-week trip to Finland and Russia. We signed the deal not knowing how or when we could get a loan, but on our return from Russia we easily obtained a desirable loan for the house.

Now we had a house but no furniture and said, "We'll figure that out when we have a chance." Later that week I saw my patients Irv and Bessie Vrh, from Turlock, California. On telling them our good news they said, "Why don't you come to our furniture store and we will help you choose the furnishings, take them to your house at Tahoe, and put them in." Their store was one of the largest in the central valley of California. And so the following week we visited their store and chose furnishings. They kept discounting things, fifty, sixty, eighty percent, until we purchased everything we needed for the house for about $5,000.

The master bedroom furniture included a heavy headboard that Laura said she did not want, but when all the furniture was taken to the house, the headboard was included since the Vrhs thought it would be ideal for our place. On delivery day, Laura and Louise McFarland, one of her close friends, went to Tahoe to get it all assembled. Our intent was to have the house ready for our first Christmas in the mountains, which was the first of many family Christmas celebrations at Lake Tahoe. One of our Christmas rituals was to visit the Innis Free Club that had a twenty-eight foot Jacuzzi near the lake and heat ourselves in 104-degree water before wading through the snow to jump into 45-degree Lake Tahoe. It is a wonder we did not kill some of our older house guests.

It is a wonder we did not kill some of our older house guests with this routine.

The house has been a wonderful retreat, and even though we moved to Cincinnati, we still spend the month of August at Tahoe. Our children vacation at Tahoe several times a year, and I try to get several ski trips in during the winter, and at least one father-son outing with Doug. The house has much of the furniture that we bought twenty-five years ago, though we have replaced the carpets and bought new living room furniture. When we moved to Cincinnati I wanted to sell the Tahoe house, but all three of the children were ready to disown me if I did so. Therefore we have kept it, updated it, and still find it a place we can greatly enjoy and escape from the burdens of my career. It is a great retreat and still enjoyed by all the Harrisons and their guests. We generally spend most of August there every year.

EDUCATION & CONSULTATION

As Laura was recovering from her chemotherapy in 1979, we were

pondering possible new ventures we could undertake that might be profitable

for us, our future retirement, and the educational funding for our children.

We looked for opportunities for a business.

During this time I was participating in a growing number of medical meetings directed by a small New York public relations firm. These meetings were always a disappointment to me. They were not well organized, and at the end of any presentation the organizers required that a paper be submitted for publication. All of this occurred without prior notice, and the sponsors' payment to presenters was usually only a few hundred dollars for preparing a presentation, participating in the meeting, and for submitting the manuscript.

Almost all of the clinicians and investigators we knew were disappointed and unhappy with this arrangement. Laura and I decided we could do a much better job planning the meetings, and that we could gain acceptance of the clinical presentations as accredited postgraduate education conferences, now required for continued medical licensure. Most of the meetings were pre-launch presentations for their new drugs by pharmaceutical companies, to acquaint a group of leadership doctors with information about a new agent before it was available for patient administration.

We formed a corporation, Medical Education and Consultation (MEC). The idea actually sprouted when we were doing estate planning with Alan Moo, our insurance agent. Alan was a family friend who had numerous ideas on how to create businesses and ways to use the profits in support of an investment and retirement program. Our aim was to contract to do conferences, initially planning to do only one or two per year. Our plan was to be able to reach more physicians by hand writing the invitations to participate rather than having them sent out bulk-mail style with printed labels. Most physicians get tons of mail and discard printed label invitations.

For this we hired Stanford students on a piecework basis. We would also pay $2,000 to each physician or scientist participating, with the prior understanding that they would provide a manuscript prior to coming to the meeting. Their compensation would be paid when the manuscript was in acceptable form. Laura and I then acted as editors of a special edition or supplement of the journal that had been chosen for its publication. We could arrange for publication within a number of weeks. Since I was on the editorial board of several journals, I usually was able to precontract to be a special editor of the supplement of the journal where these symposia were published. This seemed like a winning combination, and in fact it was, and rather than one or two meetings a year we found that we were asked to do four or five in some years.

We contracted with Merck Pharmaceutical, Astra Pharmaceutical, Stuart Pharmaceutical, Bristol-Myers, Meade-Johnson, Hewlett-Packard, Syntex, and others. We held meetings in inviting places—New Orleans, Tucson and Carmel—sometimes in association with large national cardiology meetings. I remember one instance at a large national meeting in New Orleans, where we planned for several hundred participants and wished to have an announcement poster in the lobby of one of the larger hotels to advertise the symposium. When I asked the bellman about putting up the poster he informed me that this was not possible. I handed him two $20 bills. H went away instantly and brought back an easel for the poster, and it stayed up not only for the meeting that was to occur the next day, but for the entire American Heart Association meeting, even two days after our successful evening meeting.

We had enormous support from the editors of the *American Journal of Cardiology,* where most of the symposium issues were published. Laura and I quickly became editors for manuscripts and once we received the manuscripts, we made suggestions for editing them, sent them back to the authors, and rapidly assembled them in a package for publication. This satisfied our partners, and MEC became a highly profitable corporation. We created a pension plan for MEC, and it has been an excellent vehicle for growth over the past two decades. Alan Moo again came into our lives by directing us to other lawyers and business consultants for our business and personal life.

This satisfied our partners and MEC became a highly profitable corporation.

In addition to a meeting and planning function, MEC served as a vehicle for my consultative efforts with Hewlett-Packard, as I made yearly trips to Europe and to HP's research and production facilities in Oregon and in Massachusetts. I also consulted for divisions of Syntex and made trips to Europe, South America, and throughout the United States. Even after I moved to Cincinnati, my consulting activities continued to grow. This work provided not only income for MEC, but since Laura was the manager of MEC, and was responsible for dealing with the pharmaceutical companies, she could travel with me and attend these meetings throughout the world.

One of the largest international conferences that we sponsored was held at Stanford University and resulted in our publication of a book of the compiled papers. It is entitled *Cardiac Arrhythmias, a Decade of Progress*, and I was the editor. This was a followup to a meeting that I had attended in 1969 in Denmark, and it brought together almost all of the experts on arrhythmia throughout the world. We had contracted with Astra Pharmaceutical to develop the book, and once the forty manuscripts were in hand, Laura and I retreated to our house at Lake Tahoe for a month, where we edited several manuscripts and papers each day, and sent them back to authors for modification. It was our first experience in using Federal Express from the then remote Tahoe region, and it worked like a charm. We usually spent four hours editing, and the rest of the time was spent enjoying the wonders of Lake Tahoe from our newly acquired house. The book has turned out to be a classic for understanding the etiology and treatment of arrhythmia, and it was widely distributed by Astra pharmaceutical company. It is still a classic today.

MEC continues to exist today, and has helped to provide us with the funds for a comfortable lifestyle, and will no doubt provide us with the necessary funds for a successful retirement even beyond our imagination. Even today, Laura continues to spend fve to ten hours per week managing the MEC activities. Thus for more than twenty years, it has been an integral part of our business directions. We have always had an entrepreneurial spirit and have taken advantage of the opportunity MEC has permitted us to exercise this spirit of "can do"—the same spirit that allowed us to move from Appalachia to much broader horizons.

Chapter Thirty-seven

CARDIOVASCULAR CENTER

During my early years at Stanford, I had dreamed of creating a Center of Excellence in Cardiology with its own facility for collaborative efforts from the departments of physiology, pharmacology, cardiac surgery, radiology, and pediatric cardiology.

In 1978, with the approval of the senior administration of the medical school, I organized a planning effort to create such a center. In order for us to develop such a center, we had to overcome the reluctance of the Stanford Medical School department chairs, who were like warlords, to share control of each of their own cardiovascular programs in their department in a center. Thirteen attempts to create centers or institutes in other disciplines had failed at Stanford because of this reluctance. This seemed unfair since the idea for cancer centers nationally was proposed at Stanford by Henry Kaplan, the department chair for radiology, but he was never able to get one approved at his home institution.

LAURA'S SISTERS VISITING THE FALK CENTER.

For cardiology, we had to find the appropriate space to expand the faculties and to develop the cross-disciplinary programs. The planning effort for a cardiology center took almost a year and ended with a well-designed, written document that called for raising funds to build a separate cardiovascular building. This had to be approved by the development office of the university and by the board of trustees as one of the top-priority items of the medical college. After considerable discussion, the development office approved the project and I was assigned a young development officer, John Ford, who later became Stanford's director of development for the first billion-dollar campaign for any college in the country. He was relatively inexperienced at the time, but I had already had experience meeting with alumni and knew we had great fund-raising possibilities. I had spoken to the university alumni in Phoenix, where Sandra Day O'Connor was the president, and I had attended and spoken at a Portland Stanford alumni group. I attended with Jing Lyman, the wife of the president of the university, and we were well received. Based on the Stanford fund-raising experience, John and I mapped an extensive plan to raise funds to build the cardiovascular center building.

During this time I was the physician taking care of three patients who were trustees of a major foundation in Reno, Nevada, the Fleischman Foundation, which had been founded with money from a Cincinnati family. We met on several occasions with the three members of the foundation and ultimately secured our anchor gift from them, since the foundation was in the final stages of distribution of the corpus of its funds. Norm Shumway obtained a $4 million pledge from the Falk Foundation in Chicago, which had been created from money from the Falk Enterprises when it was sold to Baxter, a large medical supply organization. This gift led to the naming of the center, The Falk Cardiovascular Center. With these two anchor gifts we then went about raising money from several of our patients, ultimately raising $17 million from just fifty-one individuals.

NBBJ, a well-known architectural firm, was selected to develop the building plans. We spent many hours in consultation with the firm. My aim was to get as many laboratories, offices, and conference rooms as we could into the building. In the end they proposed a large atrium with ficus trees in the center of the building. I was opposed to this because it took the space of eight laboratories. They ultimately convinced me that I would be in the building for a few years

Laura's sisters from Alabama toured the Center on a visit to be with us.

but that the building would be there for fifty years, and that some of the esthetics of the building should be preserved for the future.

We created labs for animal research, for artificial heart research, for computer work, and space for conference rooms, faculty offices, and fellow training areas. One of my patients, Lowell Dillingham, patriarch of a prominent Hawaiian family and president of one of the largest construction firms on the West Coast, made a $1 million gift and agreed on a fixed price to construct the building, even though he knew it would cost more than his bid. This was a wonderful gift and allowed us to break ground and to start building in 1981. The building had a great deal of glass and looked out across picturesque areas of the campus. We had frequent visitors to the new center. Laura's sisters from Alabama toured the center on a visit with us. The desks and all of the filing cabinets had cherry wood as their facings. I had a large office and a personal conference room on one end of the building, and Norm Shumway had an office and conference room on the top floor of the other end of this three-story building. It was completed in 1984, and after having spent so much time in raising funds, working with the architects, and getting the building constructed, I remained in the building for only two years. The building continues to be a major attraction for recruits considering cardiovascular research at Stanford. Getting this project from a dream to completion was one of the highlights of my career at Stanford.

In addition to raising the funds to build the facility, we needed to get support to designate it as the Falk Cardiovascular Research Center. This required a presentation to the medical school department chairs. That meeting was very contentious following my extensive presentation, and initially it looked as if the proposal would fail. It was rescued when Don Kennedy, the university provost, who was attending the meeting, asked that it be approved. The opposition melted and approval was unanimous. We had succeeded in getting a cardiovascular building and in naming the program as a research center.

Chapter Thirty-eight

TO CHINA

After my medical care for Liao, the Chinese government in 1982

invited my family and me to visit and asked me to review the medical training

and services in a number of their provinces. This provided the opportunity

to see the last fading vision of old China.

My patient Liao sponsored our invitation to come for this four-week visit to China. We were scheduled to visit hospitals, universities, and factories, as well as many of the

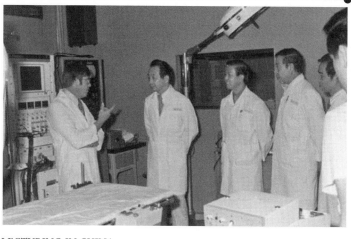

LECTURING IN CHINA.

wonders of the great country. Johnson Cha, who had accompanied me on my first trip to China, and six other members of the Cha family, joined us for the visit.

We flew from San Francisco to Shanghai, where our trip was to begin. Unfortunately, we missed a connection in Tokyo and had to spend a night near Narita

Airport in Japan. I had warned my children in a personal memo on travel in China to carry on at least a one-day supply of toiletries and underwear. With great embarrassment, I found that I had forgotten to do so. The children found this very amusing and tease me still today about this oversight.

The next day we arrived in Shanghai, a bustling city of thirteen million people. We stayed at the Jin Jiang Hotel in the old French section of town. Prior to World War II, Shanghai was divided into different districts controlled by European countries—the French, British, and Germans. Our hotel was an old luxury hotel, reminiscent of Shanghai in the 1920s, before the revolution. In the sixth-floor dining room we had sumptuous Chinese banquets of fifteen and sixteen courses every day while meeting with some of the leading figures from the government in Shanghai.

My medical visits were to Shanghai University and its two medical schools. I was impressed with the welcome and open discussion with the faculty. The buildings were old and the laboratories were antiquated but busy. The approach to medical education was to incorporate western medicine yet maintain a bit of Chinese-style traditional medicine, herbal treatments, acupuncture, and massage therapy. I also visited the Shanghai Thoracic Hospital, which was relatively modern and had reasonable cardiac equipment. The patient load was very large.

I examined about twenty patients with a congenital heart lesion, tetralogy of Fallot. This condition is characterized by an abnormal connection between two chambers of the heart and a narrowing of the artery to the lungs. It results in patients not getting fully oxygenated blood to their body. There were as many with this diagnosis as I had seen in my whole career. When I asked what the waiting list was for surgery for tetralogy of Fallot, I was told 4,000 patients and only ten patients could be operated on per week. It would take more than eight years to do all of these—and many would not live that long. Patients came here from several provinces, and the need for all cardiac services was overwhelming. I made clinical rounds with the staff and trainees and gave a scientific presentation.

The Bund in Shanghai, or the old waterfront area with its preserved buildings, was bustling.

Highlights of the rest of our visit in Shanghai included seeing factories producing many Chinese products for export. We also visited the performing arts center, known as the Children's Palace, where talented children from all over China were brought to have training in musical arts and theatrical performance. Many prominent Chinese who compete throughout the world are graduates of this center. After our move to Cincinnati, we noted that the College-Conservatory of Music attracted numerous graduates of the Children's Palace program. We had an opportunity to see some of the training in action and were greatly impressed.

The Bund in Shanghai, or the old waterfront area with its preserved buildings, was bustling. Many new buildings were under construction. We had an opportunity to visit the headquarters of the founding of the Communist Party. This site is not open to the general public. We were very fortunate to see the room where Mao and his associates met to establish the Communist Party before they went to western China, from which the famous Great March commenced. It was a simple, small conference room facing out over a lake. It contained a few books and a plaque commemorating the founding. We were amazed that such a movement, encompassing over one billion people, could have commenced in such an inauspicious place.

Our next stop was Beijing. We were again put up at the Beijing Hotel. There had been some moderate development in China since my earlier visits there in 1978 and in 1980. Now there were a few hotels in central Beijing and some private cars. Still, most people moved about on bicycles. We spent considerable time visiting hospitals and meeting the medical faculty of Beijing's colleges. I was taken back to visit the Beijing Hospital, which was only for high party members, and was where I had attended to Mr. Liao. The hospital had only a hundred rooms. Each was a large suite with a waiting room, a dining area, a large living room with a fireplace, and a hospital bed area. There were many nurses but no monitoring equipment. I wondered whether this was a facility to provide a restful environment for government officials or to function as a real hospital.

I examined Liao there again and found him very well. I visited the premier heart hospital for Beijing, the Fu Wei Hospital, which was the equivalent of the Thoracic Hospital in Shanghai. It was old but had all modern medical equipment from both Europe and America. Several hundred attended a conference I presented, after which I made hospital ward rounds with the medical staff, with whom I was very impressed. The hospital lacked air conditioning except in the operating rooms and intensive care units, so the wards were hot and there was a faint smell of urine and alcohol everywhere.

My family and I did the tourist rounds, spending a day at the Forbidden City, going to the Summer Palace, and taking an excursion on the Great Wall. One of the highlights for us was having dinner at the Great Hall of the People on Tiananmen Square. This was specially arranged for government officials and special guests. *The New York Times* correspondent, James Reston, was present. He had just undergone an appendectomy in Beijing, but by now had fully recovered.

During this trip we spent hours with Liao and his staff. We had not known where we would be going in China before we arrived, and were informed after arriving in Beijing that we would be going to Xinjiang Province. This was a hallmark of all my sponsored Chinese trips. I did not know my itinerary until I arrived. Our trip began with a flight to Urumqi, the capital of the province. Xinjiang, located at the center of the Taklamakan Desert, is one of the autonomous provinces of China, populated largely by Turkic Uyghur and Kazakh people. Though the desert is not well known, it is large and far dryer than even the Sahara. The province borders on Afghanistan.

At the time the Afghan war with Russia was in full swing. Urumqi was an interesting city, as was their medical school, where acupuncture was widely used. Douglas had finished his first year in medical school and was allowed to see many of these procedures. My hosts did not believe that I would have an interest, or that I would believe in its effectiveness, so they shielded me from it.

We visited a pharmaceutical manufacturing facility in Urumqi and had a chance to see their manual for drug manufacturing, which was almost 400 years old and had been transported from Turkey. It was a very worn book written in an earlier Arabic script. Their equipment was antiquated; much of the work was done by hand. A large black pill for treating vitiligo, a condition of depigmenting of the skin, which is common in the population of this area of China, was one of their products. I noticed there were variations of more than 100 percent in size among different lots. When I questioned what kind of quality control they had, they pointed out that when a person had to take forty-eight of these in a day, the size did not much matter. This was a very interesting comment to me, which represented the practical Chinese approach.

DONNA JOHNSON AND LAURA CHA, SOMEWHAT LIKE THE PIED PIPER IN XINJIANG.

The Urumqi medical facilities were primitive, and must have resembled those in the rural United States in the early 1900s. The hospitals had large, open wards with dozens of patients in each. The units were hot, and the smell of sweat and blood permeated the air. Patients were gaunt and appeared to be quite ill in both of the hospitals I visited. Many had large goiters due to the lack of iodine in their salt.

The plan was for us to visit throughout Xinjiang, using Urumqi as our base city. Our first stop was Hoten. Hoten had been the first stop on the Silk Road in China when traveling from Europe. Hoten had no hotels, so we were housed in a camp with the Chinese army. There were only five flush toilets in town; we had three of these in our quarters. On one occasion we sneaked away from our Chinese host to visit a medical clinic in town. We soon found ourselves followed like the Pied Piper by a host of people just observing us. It turns out that we were the first Caucasian visitors to the area since 1947. We went exploring one day without informing our host, and visited an ambulatory medical center caring for the local residents. It was a dusty old adobe building with a donkey cart out front for delivering patients. This was their version of an ambulance. The staff members of the hospital were "barefoot doctors," who were trained in a practical way to practice Chinese-based medicine. They had few medications and almost no equipment. They focused on public health measures to improve life in China, which included clean water, elimination of tuberculosis, and avoiding deadly diarrhea in infancy. Our military hosts were not amused by our foray, but did not reprimand us.

On Saturday, there was a large open-air market in town. Donkeys and ox carts brought in wood from the hills, and all types of vegetables, meats, and other things were being sold. We were driven through the area and our cars and jeeps were stopped by crowds of people staring at us, just like we were animals in the zoo. We were obviously a curiosity.

From Hoten we went to Kashi, another Chinese town that was the crossroads of this whole area in terms of marketing between Russia, China, Xinjiang, India to the South, and Afghanistan to the West. The market was very large, covering several acres, and had a huge variety of spices, drugs, meat, vegetables, jewelry, clothing products, and contraband. It could be described as the largest flea market I had ever seen. The meat, which was almost always mutton, was hung outside the stalls; it frequently included the head of the sheep attached to its meaty parts, which were covered with flies.

VISITING WITH THE COSSACKS AT A YURT IN XINGCHANG.

On another day we were taken into the hills to visit with the Kossacks, migrants who usually come from the Soviet Union. We drank their sheep's milk, which was curdled, and had our meals in yurts, their animal-skin tents.

In this era, the Chinese were forcing families from the coastal area of central China to move to Xinjiang in order to assume Chinese domination over the Uyghurs by becoming the majority. They had established a model city of Sheheiz where we were taken for two days to observe how modern it might be and how the native people might improve their lot if they adopted the Chinese way. There was a modern hospital, or one at least equivalent to Beijing standards. The housing was quite new, and much improved over what we saw elsewhere in Xinjiang. Even so, it was hard to believe that Chinese families from Beijing and Shanghai would volunteer to move there. We assumed that they had been either enticed or forced.

We then proceeded along what was the Old Silk Road to visit Turpan, which is below sea level and is supposed to be one of the hottest places on earth. It was over 110 degrees the day we were there. We could understand why heatstroke was so commonly seen in the health clinic we visited. We stayed two nights, and since it was so extremely dry, we learned to drink Chinese beer spiked with lemonade known as shandies, a term from Ireland. There was an excavation nearby of old burial grounds from a city that had once had 50,000 people more than 2,000 years ago.

We were taken to underground grave sites and caves being excavated, and we found that mummified bodies there were quite well preserved. We were able to put our hands on these bodies and move the still-mobile joints. Ancient drawings and paintings lined the walls of these cave grave sites.

As I talked through our interpreter with the leaders about maintaining the sites, I learned that there were few significant attempts being made to preserve them for posterity. This distressed me, for it represented a truly ancient civilization from 1,000 years or so before the Silk Road was opened. When we returned to Beijing I mentioned my concerns to Liao's staff. I have subsequently learned that Chinese archeologists have instituted preservation measures as they continue excavation in the area.

At one point in our travels across Xinjiang we crossed the desert in army jeeps. There were frequent sandstorms, making visibility poor. We stopped at several oases and had lunches, dinners, and banquets with Chinese generals, for all of the oases were occupied by the army. All of them seemed to know about my medical expertise and the fact that I had taken care of Liao. Some wanted a medical examination. At one such military complex where we were staying I examined one of the generals, who then asked for an electrocardiogram. They brought out a machine that had been developed prior to WWII. I couldn't make it work. I happened to look at the way it was wired, and found that the plug was wired in the wrong way. I was able to rewire it and get a reasonable EKG on the general. I felt a sense of pride at being recognized as an eminent cardiologist.

A personal medical event of note happened to our daughter Beth in Urumqi. While out jogging, she fell on a pathway where there was donkey dung and a great deal of the dung ground into the tissue of her knee. Even though Doug scrubbed it vigorously, I was concerned that she had not had a recent tetanus shot. We took her to the Urumqi Hospital, which was one of the dirtiest that I had ever observed in my life. The smell of human excrement made one nauseous and the courtyard was littered with bottles, paper, and all sorts of medical waste.

They insisted on skin testing her before giving her a tetanus shot. I objected, since this was not the way we worked in the United States. In the U.S., we had absorbed tetanus toxoid. Their tetanus toxoid still contained egg protein from the medicines in which it was prepared, since it was not absorbed out. She reacted violently to the skin test. In order to get the appropriate nontoxic tetanus shot I spent three hours calling Hong Kong, arranging to have it sent in two days by way of Beijing. It was fortunate that I knew a doctor in Hong Kong who could supply this for me, since there was none anywhere in China. Once I had a supply, I gave a tetanus shot to everyone on the trip, since no one could tell me when they had last received one.

We attended many banquets during our two weeks in Xinjiang. Some of them had at least twenty courses of a great variety of Chinese delicacies. Some of these contained insects, snakes, and dog meat. We frequently had many toasts with Maotai, the Chinese version of vodka, and a sweet red wine. It turned out that many of the Chinese generals had served in Vietnam and spoke a little French. My children and wife all speak a little French and could communicate a little in French, but what was most hilarious was my son, who had been a Dartmouth student, doing "gam beis" (equivalent to "bottoms up") with the Chinese generals. He was able to drink almost all of them under the table, since most Chinese men lack the enzyme in the liver that metabolizes alcohol. As I had realized in 1978, this is a defect that seems to be transmitted genetically and is sex-linked, found predominately in males.

One of our most interesting purchases in Xinjiang occurred when visiting a carpet factory. We saw one square meter of a carpet under construction that we liked and wished to buy. We were told that it would take six more months for it to be completed, since it took two people that long to hand weave a single carpet. Nonetheless, we purchased the unfinished carpet and it was later shipped to us in California. It is still our favorite.

On this trip we came to realize that China would be a rising economic power when we compared it with what we had observed in 1978. The people by 1982 were still poor but industrious, and seemingly welcoming to outsiders. The zeal to improve their lives and their willingness to work long hours was apparent almost everywhere we visited.

Following our two weeks in Xinjiang, we returned to Beijing. My understanding of the enormous task that China faced in bringing its health care up to modern standards increased after our visit. On the other hand, we marveled at the effects of their "barefoot doctor" program. The Communist Party had recruited thousands of young people, given them a few months of education about the rudiments of public health, and sent them into the small villages to practice. They had been successful in reducing infant mortality, deaths from diarrhea, and tuberculosis cases, which had been very prevalent. As a result, improved life expectancy was increasing. While this was not modern western medical care, it had certainly improved the health of a population of over one billion people.

Next, we journeyed to Hong Kong. Laura and I parted from the Cha family in Hong Kong and sent our children home to San Francisco. The Cha family had accompanied us on the whole trip inside China. Mrs. Cha was recognized by many people we encountered, since she had visited many of the factories with her father, who was a major industry owner before the communist takeover. We were delighted we could share these experiences with our young adult children. We had been able to see a whole civilization in transition and realized that few people have an opportunity to be the guests of the Chinese government to observe the many changes.

Laura and I left Hong Kong on the next leg of the planned trip that was to continue in South Africa. I was scheduled to present a series of lectures for Pfizer Pharmaceuticals and to visit with their medical professionals. In South Africa we visited all of the provinces, their medical schools, and the academic medical groups. Perhaps one of the most impressive places we visited in South Africa was the Orange Free State and its capital, Bloemfontein. This was the home of the most fervent Afrikaners, and in the center of town there was a large monument celebrating the Afrikaner victories in the Boer War.

Cape Town was as beautiful a city as I remembered. The views of the ocean and mountains, its gardens, and the older buildings were eye-catching. There were also many excellent restaurants. We visited Stellenbosch again, and sampled the top quality wines of the region, their Sauvignon Blanc being outstanding, as it still is today. The South African health system was organized on a provincial basis, with each having a medical school. Large regional hospitals were new and well equipped. The physician staff was well trained and had modern drugs and technology. The contrast at each of the medical schools was apparently related to the emphasis on Afrikaans versus English. My presentations were well-received at each center. We also had social gatherings with the faculty and had interesting discussions about the future, both medical and political, of South Africa. At the end of our time in South Africa, we returned home to California via New York.

Chapter Thirty-nine

MY FEMALE GUIDES

Early in my career I found that sometimes patients became friends, and those friendships would continue over many years. The true test of one's professionalism is to remain objective in medical judgment and care when this occurs. There are two examples in my career where two women patients were also friends and confidantes and played important roles in my life.

A woman who was a patient and friend, and who influenced my life and career, was Mary Wiley. She was the director of physical education at San Jose State College when she came to me with a heart problem. She had been one of the first fifty patients to undergo finger fracture mitral valve surgery in Philadelphia when she was a young woman. This was a procedure to open a stenotic, or narrowed, heart valve. It preceded the development of assisted cardiopulmonary circulatory devices and had to be done with a beating

MARY WILEY AND DON AT CARMEL.

heart. This was the dawn of open heart surgery in the 1950s. There was no cardiopulmonary bypass machine to take over the circulation while the surgeon corrected the heart problem, and there were no substitute heart valves. She was a pioneer patient for the development of heart surgery; finger fracture of the mitral valve was dangerous, for if any leaking of the valve resulted there was no way to correct it. Even after the successful surgery, she was told that she might not survive to the age of 30, and therefore she chose not to marry.

After the surgery, Mary was a member of the USO during World War II and served in South America and England before she settled in California. She became not only a patient but a great friend, and was almost a surrogate grandmother to all of our children. She took an early retirement from San Jose State and in 1974 moved to Carmel, where she was successful in selling real estate. She owned an apartment as well as a house, and she always invited us to use her apartment anytime we wanted to come to Carmel. We used it frequently, often several times in a year, almost always coordinating our visits to be with Mary. We met with her friends, and came to know people such as Clint Eastwood, who was then the mayor of Carmel.

In 1984, when I was clinically depressed, I went several times to Carmel to spend time being cheered up by Mary. I had become depressed after making a decision not to move to a new major opportunity. I was also under tremendous stress to get more grants. I was traveling excessively, and did not recognize the importance of some relaxation and downtime interspersed with my very busy schedule.

Mary had the touch of a good psychiatrist, and a walk with her on the beach at Carmel would cheer up almost anyone. She understood my dilemma, and helped me to see that there was a brighter future. Mary would always say, "There has to be a brighter side coming soon." She gave me a meaningful leaded-glass desk plaque with the words known as the mantra for Alcoholics Anonymous, "God grant us the serenity to accept the things we cannot change, courage to change the things we can, and the wisdom to know the difference." Mary helped me put my depression behind me after about nine months.

She was a stimulus to me in many ways, and was a great help to my career.

After we moved to Cincinnati, she came to visit with us at our home and became a great friend to Beth, who was in Cincinnati with us a good deal of the time. Mary was here for parties and weddings, and added to the joyous atmosphere. As she continued to age, she asked me to help her look after her personal affairs, and together we chose a retirement community in Monterey, California, to which she then moved. I helped her with this big decision as she had previously helped me. She became a legend for working with other people, especially the men in the retirement community. Playing pool was a big sport, and she could outshoot the men living there. In 1996, she died a sudden death in a very peaceful way while in bed watching TV. I always treasured her happy company, and still remember her frequently. Our family thinks of her often.

Another woman of importance in my life was Mary Jane Jesse. She was a stimulus to me in many ways, and was a great help to my career. She was a colleague, and later, a patient. Mary Jane was a pediatric cardiologist and vice chairman of the department of pediatrics at the University of Miami. She had been an advertising executive in New York, and at age 40 wanted to become a nurse. When she went to Columbia University and asked to apply to nursing school they told her she was too old, but that she should try for medical school, as they were now accepting women. The office for medical applications was across the hall. She applied, and to her surprise, she was accepted on condition that she meet the requirements. She took summer courses in organic chemistry, qualified for medical school, and graduated from Columbia at the top of her medical school class.

I first encountered her when she was at the National Institutes of Health serving as head of the Heart and Vascular Program. We had developed a grant application to create a new center for cardiac rehabilitation focusing on research in addition to high-quality clinical service. None of us in my division of cardiology had experience working in the area, but thought we brought a number of innovative concepts to advance rehabilitation because of our extensive clinical research expertise. She happened to visit with me at Stanford and had a chance to review our program. She understood that we had no experience and no track record and in a regular review could not be funded. However, she helped us put together a quality program for one of my associates, Bob DeBusk, who still runs it today. By carefully choosing the individuals who were to review the program, we managed to get funding to create a cardiac rehabilitation research program that is still ongoing as one of the most innovative in the country.

My next encounter with Mary Jane was at the American Heart Association, where she was president-elect when I was president. We formed the East Coast-West Coast team to support the American Heart Association, visiting almost every state and speaking on its behalf. She hated to travel long distances, and since she lived in Miami, the West Coast was far away. I made appearances throughout the West and she returned the favor by doing many of the visits to the East Coast sites. In November 1982, when I was president, we were together at the annual meeting in Dallas, and there came an unusually early freezing cold snap. The temperature in all the buildings was extremely low, since neither the hotels nor office buildings had reached the set date to turn on heat. I had to be involved in meetings and receptions all day. Mary Jane, Laura, and Mary Jane's sister piled up in our suite with heavy blankets over them to stay warm. I captured food from one of the receptions, including a cheese tray, vegetables, bread, and hot hors d'oeuvres with Sterno cans to heat them, and lots of wine. There was more than enough food and drink for all of us, and we have great memories of this evening that we spent almost freezing to death in Dallas.

After I moved to Cincinnati, Mary Jane showed up at my office in 1989, saying she was now living with her sister here in Cincinnati and would like to have some part time-work in medical administration. I recognized how she could be of great help to me, and made her the associate provost. She assumed this role enthusiastically and helped me immensely. She executed many searches for deans and department heads, worked with Earl Gilreath and me in rebuilding the Drake Hospital, a rehabilitation hospital owned by the county, and making it highly functional. She also was always available to handle difficult interpersonal relationships when jagged feelings frequently caused major problems in the academic medical center.

We had a great working relationship and she had great impact on my career. She always told me her view of my plans and activities honestly, even when they were critical. We worked together for over ten years. She became a great friend of the family, our children, and almost everyone in the medical center. Later in her life she developed coronary heart disease and I became her physician. She demanded that I shield her from overzealous specialists who wanted to do all sorts of interventions. Her other physicians advised against alcohol, but I permitted her two glasses of Jack Daniel's every evening at home. I did not wish to create a conflict, and at that time it was clear she would have done it anyway.

She became increasingly disabled, and in 2001, died of heart disease. I spent considerable time with Mary Jane in the hospital during this terminal stage.

Women have been of great importance in my life and careers. Some of them came into my life as patients and brought a lasting friendship. I have great admiration for them, and had a real emotional attachment to some of them. At times I have wondered if these attachments were the result of my seeking to overcome feelings of regret at being rejected by my mother.

East TRIPS WITH FRANK JONES

Living on the West Coast gave me many opportunities to participate

on several occasions in the Asian Pacific Conference of Cardiology

that was held every four years, and to be invited on a regular basis to visit

throughout the region.

An interesting trip I made to speak for a pharmaceutical company in Japan took me to a number of cities and meetings that were well attended by many Japanese cardiologists.

LAURA IN OUR SOMERSET MAUGHAM SUITE IN BANGKOK.

I was constantly being photographed and filmed at each site. The drivers for our party would even drive the car around to give the movie cameras time to be set up before I would exit the car at a hotel entrance. I found it highly unusual that the conference sponsors wished to pay me in one-hundred-dollar bills, and I had to insist that I be paid by check at home. While I was lavishly entertained and academically well-received in Japan, I always felt there was a distance in personal relationships.

There were at least two trips to the Philippines, where we stayed in a beautiful Manila hotel and participated in the Philippine Heart Institute's programs. Our formal evening wear for the various social events was lacy cotton shirts, a style popular in the Philippines.

One of my early trips to Asia took me to Malaysia, the first stop being Kuala Lumpur, where the leading cardiologist of the country, Joe Aravelli, had invited me. We participated in a cardiovascular conference at the medical college and made teaching rounds at the university hospital. We toured the city and arrangements were made for recreation. As crazy as it might sound, we took a helicopter ride to a gambling casino in the Genting Highlands, a mountainous area in the center of the country. As I look back at this, having left three small children at home, it seems almost insane for the two of us to have taken this risk.

We also were taken to an island resort, Pinang, near Thailand, where there were beautiful beaches. This area was known for its monsoon floods and they soon came. We were to take a flight to Kota Baharu on Malasia's east coast. The flight was so rough in the monsoon weather that we were not able to land at a designated stop on the route. I noticed that the only cabin attendant was sitting down, green and vomiting, and I knew that we were on a very rough flight. It was quite scary, and when we asked the cabin attendants when we landed in Kota Baharu if this roughness was unusual, they said that they always carried their passports with them because they never knew which country they would be landing in.

Though the hospitals we visited in Kota Baharu were very primitive, the doctors were very interested in all of the clinical comments we shared with them. We were driven along the east coast of Malaysia, which had beautiful beaches but very rough unpaved roads. The ones that the Japanese had landed on in WWII were called the Beaches of Brotherly Love. The Japanese had marched down these beaches along the east coast of Malasia to conquer Singapore. I didn't see much love in this designation.

We were taken to Kaula Terengganu, a city along the coast, where we stayed in a very primitive hotel, and had dinner in a Chinese

Perched high on a large hill, we had a view overlooking the rather depressed town of Taipei.

restaurant that was nothing more than a tin roof over an alley. The chef prepared some of the best Chinese food that I can ever remember. We were awakened at 3 a.m. and taken to the beach to watch large sea turtles as large as VW Beetles lay eggs on the beach. These giant turtles came all the way from South America to lay their eggs. Poachers were taking the eggs and threatening the giant turtles' survival. The naturalists were salvaging the eggs and hatching them in a protected area. We returned in the early morning to the fish market for the town, where all types of seafood was brought in and sold openly. The remainder of this trip took us to Singapore, which was much less pristine then than now. We were taken to Bugis Street, which was the home of transvestites from throughout Asia. We were shocked and amazed at the openness of this lifestyle. We ate food from wayside stalls but stayed healthy for the entire trip.

On several of these trips we stopped in Taiwan. Many of the cardiologists in Taiwan had trained in the United States and were always happy to invite us. The cardiology practice was quite sophisticated, and we gave lectures and participated in teaching rounds at the hospitals. We stayed at the Grand Hotel, which was built by Madame Chiang Kai-shek and was quite impressive. From its perch high on a large hill, we had a view overlooking the rather depressed town of Taipei.

We found it safe to get up early in the morning and jog with the Chinese troops, who were always training near the hotel. The Chinese Art and Archeological Museum in Taiwan was one of the best in the world, but our earliest trip there occurred after a long flight from the United States, and we were almost walking in our sleep. Later on another trip several years later we were fully awake and able to appreciate all of the artifacts that had been brought from the mainland of China before the communist takeover in 1947.

One of the most memorable characters that I met from the Far East was Frank Jones, a representative of Rhone-Poulenc, a French pharmaceutical company. He had seen me on several of my trips to Asia and had heard my medical presentations. Because of this, Frank called and made an appointment to see me at Stanford in 1979. He presented a plan for me to lead delegations of speakers to visit various countries in the Far East, to speak at medical schools and medical societies. These were to occur yearly, and I had the discretion, together with him, to select the speakers. I was reluctant to accept his offer. I was in quite a hurry to leave for a trip to the East Coast, and at the end of our conversation, I presented what I thought to be a ridiculously high consultation fee, fully expecting him to reject it. He instantly said yes, and that he would start setting up the trips.

For me, these trips were made under the auspices of MEC, our newly formed company. For four years we made trips with him, which included Korea, the Philippines, Hong Kong, Thailand, Indonesia, Malaysia, Singapore, and Australia. One of the memorable trips covered a period of ten days, visiting several of the major islands in the Indonesian Archipelago, giving medical presentations at each stop.

On that trip I vividly remember being driven to the monument at Borobudur, which was one of the Seven Wonders of the Ancient World, and it was raining so hard that I did not understand how the driver could keep us on the road. When we arrived at the monument the rain stopped and we viewed a truly wondrous site. This large archeological site held many ruins that were well-preserved, and I can understand why it was one of the wonders of the early world civilizations.

In several trips to Indonesia we stayed in guarded compounds at the Hilton Hotel or InterContinental in Jakarta. They had their own gardens, their own walkways, and their golf courses are all enclosed in a protective fence. Jakarta was large, but in terms of sanitation it was rather backward. Many people still had outdoor toilets that opened over the rivers and canals. It was some sight to go about early in the morning and see people sitting in them, open to public view, carrying out their bodily functions.

We enjoyed remarkably good food as we traveled about these countries, but Frank Jones, a Brit who had lived in the area for fifteen years, had a steady diet of one thing: steak cooked well-done, and four boiled potatoes. He was resolute in getting this everyplace we went to avoid the G.I. upset, since in his early Asian experience he had many illnesses from food. Another remarkable memory is that in Bangkok we stayed at the Oriental Hotel, which at that time was rated the best hotel in the world. Some of the suites had authors' names, and we stayed in the Somerset Maugham suite with our own private butler twenty-four hours a day.

We visited many of the great temples in Bangkok, and at each stop I shopped for jewelry in the Chinese section and bought many pieces of jewelry for Laura, after some hard bargaining on my part, reminiscent of my earlier days shopping at the Haymarket in Boston. I paid prices that are now five percent of the current value of the jewelry. Since Frank Jones was from Singapore, we spent considerable amounts of time there at the famous hotel Raffles, and had meals at the British Club where he was a member. It was a stuffy place that reminded us that the British had established their rule over Singapore in the 18th century.

I recruited many renowned cardiologists to accompany us on these trips, which also included bringing their wives. We were welcomed with lavish parties everyplace we went, and shared social events with the inviting cardiologists. Bill Roberts, who with his wife Cary accompanied us on two trips, remembers and often tells of my ordering four brown suits in Hong Kong. It became my custom to always go to my same tailor in Hong Kong and have suits, shirts, and sport clothes made. I continued this until 2001. The good suits that I could have made in Hong Kong for $200 to $300 equaled in quality those that one could have made at the top tailoring places in New York and London for $2,000 or more. These trips helped keep me well-dressed in tailor-made suits, sportcoats, trousers, and shirts.

I learned a great deal on these trips to the Far East about medicine and the economic development of the region. I also recruited a number of trainees from these countries. Over the last thirty years, it has been impressive to watch the growth and development of countries that were somewhat primitive when I first visited, and are now important economic and social institutions. The developments of South East Asia over the twenty years I have been visiting are remarkable, both for economic growth as well as for the quality of its citizens' lives.

Chapter Forty-one

MISTAKE IN MICHIGAN

By 1983, I was becoming restless at Stanford. Even though I had been a candidate for the chair of medicine at many institutions in the late 1970s, I had visited only two of them with serious intent. I rejected an offer at Rochester after the dean could not come up with a package that convinced me to believe I could develop an outstanding department.

Meanwhile, my hard-charging approach as chief of cardiology had not won me internal support for advancement at Stanford. Even though I was restless, I still believed that I would stay at Stanford for my entire career. However, my name had been submitted to a search firm that was responsible for recruiting a new senior vice president for the University of Michigan. I was invited as a candidate to visit Ann Arbor and to try to understand the job, which would be to head the university hospital and the college of medicine. The new hospital was being constructed at a cost of more than $250 million, and was reported to be one of the most technologically advanced hospitals in the world.

I would be senior vice president and would have the dean of the college of medicine and the hospital director reporting to me. Needless to say, I was impressed with the faculty and with the facilities being built there. I also had a strong and good impression of the provost, Professor Billy Fry, who was doing the recruiting. I had friends in the department of medicine and one of my postdoc trainees, Andy Buda, was a faculty member in the medical college's cardiology division. I must have made a favorable impression and was invited back with Laura for a second visit just two weeks later, which meant they were obviously serious about considering me. I met many people from the other colleges at the university and spent time with the department heads in the College of Medicine as well as the director of the hospital. The visit seemed to go well, but for the next several weeks I heard nothing from them.

At this time, Laura and I were planning a three-week trip to Europe to participate in a series of meetings and then return to New York and Philadelphia for cardiology meetings in the United States. On the eve of this trip, I was invited to stop over in Ann Arbor to meet with Harold Shapiro, the president of the University of Michigan, for further discussion. I was not anticipating that I would be offered the job and Laura did not go with me, but we planned to meet in New York to continue on our trip to Europe.

I arrived in Ann Arbor on a Saturday morning and spent all day with the senior officials of the university. On Sunday morning, before leaving for New York, I had breakfast at the home of President Shapiro, with whom I was greatly impressed. He made an offer for me to accept the job as senior vice president for the hospital and medical college, and also promised me that the senior vice president would soon also be responsible for the dental school, the nursing college, the optometry school, and the public health college. He told me that this could not occur at this time but over the year after my arrival it could be accomplished.

I asked for time to consider his offer on my trip to Europe, and notified people at Stanford that this was a possibility. I heard nothing of a counteroffer from Stanford, and after completing my trip to Europe I was back in a New York City hotel when Harold Shapiro called me and asked for my decision. Having heard nothing from Stanford, I accepted the Michigan position, and in the ensuing two days an announcement was made and my appointment was reported in the *Detroit Free Press*. I completed my East Coast visit in Philadelphia and returned to Stanford, and for the next two weeks there was intense pressure on me to remain at Stanford to complete what I had started in building the Falk Cardiovascular Center. Pressure to stay came from Stanford's president, but negotiation was primarily with the senior vice president, Larry Crowley; the dean of the medical college, Dominic Purpura; the chairman of medicine, Ken Melmon; and the head of cardiovascular surgery, Norm

While I do not know what would have happened had I taken that position, ...

Shumway. After much agonizing, I withdrew from the Michigan position and decided to remain at Stanford and complete the work for the Falk Center, becoming co-director with Norm Shumway. I recognized that I had burned my bridges with Michigan, and that I had probably also prevented any possibility of being recruited into a senior academic position at any other institution. Once one reneges on such a position, his reputation is poisoned for another offer.

What happened next is a horror story in my life. Within six months, Stanford's senior vice president stepped down because of health reasons. The dean of the college of medicine was fired, and the chair of medicine was accused of plagiarism and was ultimately removed from his position. Norm Shumway, the head of cardiovascular surgery, had never really been much in favor of the co-directorship, and I found myself isolated and clearly unable to advance my career at Stanford.

The new hospital at Michigan was completed and was a great success, and the college of medicine at the university there moved into national prominence, as did the entire university during the decade. While I do not know what would have happened had I taken that position, I believe I could have been a leader participating in its ongoing development. Of course, it might have worked out differently, since Billy Fry left Michigan to become provost at Emory within one year, and four years later Harold Shapiro moved from Michigan to become president at Princeton.

I have always thought that I could have had a major impact on the institution with national prominence, such as Michigan was, and thus believe this was a mistaken choice in my career. I have a nagging habit of looking back at decisions, but Laura correctly reminds me that while I looked back at the Michigan decision for a few months, it was these events coupled with the changing environment at Stanford over which I had no input or control that lead to my severe depression, which lasted for nine months. I was successfully treated with antidepressants and lots of friends offering a helping hand. The most important healing factor was Laura, and I eventually took her admonitions and sought other opportunities. It is important not to look back, but to look forward to other challenges and opportunities.

Chapter Forty-two

DAYS AT STANFORD

Not long after my decision to remain at Stanford and not to move to the University of Michigan, I became co-director of the Falk Cardiovascular Center, as was promised when I decided to remain at Stanford.

At the same time, the position of dean of the medical school became open. The chair of pathology, David Korn, and I were the two logical internal candidates. He got the job and then asked me to take his position as head of the group practice plan, which he had held. I agreed. The practice plan is the administrative and billing entity for the doctors who have clinical duties, and it also determines compensation plans.

It was the year that the practice plan needed to be totally overhauled, and I spent one difficult year trying to get people to work together to create an equitable plan. Practice plans represent a way to equate the earnings from practice with meeting the roles of faculty members. It is a mechanism to collect fees for services of physicians from all departments. This allows the organization to redistribute clinical income to support new programs and then fund needed programs for which reimbursement does not meet the costs. Reimbursement is on a fixed schedule by payors, so therefore not balanced among all clinical departments.

It also became clear during that year that the department of medicine was having budgetary difficulties and was taking more of the money earned by the cardiology faculty to keep the department afloat. This resulted in my not being able to pay my cardiology faculty enough to stay competitive with other places in the country. Over the ensuing two years, several senior faculty members left the division. One group of three moved to the University of Utah, and several left to go into private practice in the community.

Stanford was also imposing far more controls over our entrepreneurial activities. During this time there was an interim chair for medicine and no one was really in charge. In spite of this, a ten-year review of the division of cardiology was ordered. After three months, it came back with a decidedly negative tone, and was critical of some of my decisions. I responded quite angrily to this and issued a major rebuttal. Since I had created the division and had given it national and international prominence, I was offended by what I considered to be an unfair review. During this time I was becoming extremely unhappy, feeling trapped, and unable to continue to advance the programs that I had begun and to keep my productive faculty.

The problems in this period of time had a negative impact on my health. In 1984, I suffered a major depression, already mentioned, and my work ethic suffered since I spent days not being able to work effectively. I retreated from responsibility. I was irritable and frequently unable to sleep. I also had stomach cramps, ate poorly, lost weight, and was miserable to be around. I consulted my general physician and was placed on antidepressants, in addition to reinstituting a major exercise program. I also visited Mary Wiley in Carmel for those walks on the beach and a lay person's psychiatric help and counsel. There were many ups and downs in my mood and because of these, even Laura lost patience with me. However, my general physician was insightful, understanding, and helpful, and after nine months I recovered fully.

It was also during this time that I had begun to advise a number of venture capital firms on investment opportunities. My children were now all away from home and in college, and it began to dawn on me that my future at Stanford was going to be quite limited. Perhaps it was time to consider other opportunities, so I would not again fall into the depths of depression.

In 1985, I needed to think all this through. I decided to take my first sabbatical to consider what I should do for the remainder of my career and what challenges might lay ahead. In the past, I had always found reasons to put off taking a sabbatical, even though I was awarded one every seven years. Sabbaticals of one year are generally granted to academic faculty every seven years. I received my compensation during that year,

With these findings, I planned to write a book on the emerging changes in the medical system...

and was expected to engage in research or scholarship to enhance my academic career and the reputation of Stanford. My plan was to spend six months in the Bay Area working with venture capital companies and being in charge of a start-up for which I had recommended funding, and I was asked to be the acting CEO.

After six months, I planned to study health care delivery systems throughout the world. Managed care was becoming the predominant way in which medicine was now being reimbursed in the United States and I thought lessons could be learned from others' experiences. With these findings, I planned to write a book on emerging changes in the medical system that were being brought about by changes in the financing of medical care. As background experience for my plans, I had previously organized a conference sponsored by Merck and Hewlett-Packard and hosted by MEC on the rapidly developing managed care programs. We brought together many university cardiology directors throughout the country at a meeting in Tucson. The speakers were leaders of managed care throughout the country, and included Uwe Reinhardt, a Princeton economist and a major guru on the medical economy; David Jones, the founder of the Humana Health System; and many other prominent individuals in the field. Managed care was just becoming a reality in California for all services and would spread rapidly to all parts of the country.

At the end of six months, I had organized the venture-backed firm securely in place. We then chose to spend six months out of the country, with the first two weeks to be spent in Israel, then to settle in Zug, Switzerland, in the villa of my Chinese patients, the Chas, to study the Swiss health system. We left Stanford to journey to Israel, and while en route, the Libya confrontation with the United States government occurred. We arrived in Jerusalem at a time of heightened tension, just before Easter 1986. One of my postdocs had previously settled in Jerusalem and was the host for a meeting on "ambulatory cardiology," to which he invited me. This is the mechanism for continuously recording the rhythm of the heart over twenty-four hours onto a tape recorder. The tapes are analyzed by a computer to quantify any abnormal rhythms. The meeting was well-attended and for two days we gave lectures, participated in discussion groups, and visited hospitals at the teaching institutions.

While in Israel, we also spent much time in Jerusalem, seeing the sites of origin for the three great religions. We also visited the Dead Sea, Bethlehem, the Masada, the Sea of Galilee, and Nazareth. On Good Friday, we walked the Via Della Rosa, stopping at all the historic religious sites. On Thursday evening before Good Friday, we attended a service at the Christ Episcopal Church of Jerusalem and walked to the upper room where the Last Supper is believed to have occurred. There were readings in Aramaic, the original language of Jesus. Because of the darkness of the night we did not join the group to walk to Gethsemane. We have always regretted that. This service and the walk to the upper room were emotionally moving experiences, as we reflected that we were experiencing something similar to the events that were at the heart of Christianity.

On Easter morning, we visited both of the sites where it is thought Jesus was crucified— one outside the wall of Jerusalem and one inside at the Church of the Holy Sepulchre. Both are considered the sites of Golgotha, and we wanted to be sure we covered all possibilities. It was raining on Easter morning when I awoke, and Laura had to convince me to go to the sites. At the site outside the wall, we were under umbrellas for the sermon—but just as the minister said, "He is risen," the sun appeared, shining brightly through the clouds. It was almost as if the heavens opened up as an omen. This scene brought my thoughts of Christianity to the highest level they had been in many years. We returned to the city via the Damascus Gate, where there were Israeli soldiers with guns, checking entry. We visited the second site designated as Golgotha, inside the Church of the Holy Sepulchre. This church has been maintained in the state in which it was built several centuries ago. It was less impressive to me than the site outside the wall.

The following, Monday, we transferred to Tel Aviv and were taken to give a presentation at the Weitzmann Institute, one of the premier sites of basic research in Israel. We dined with friends at a reception held in my honor that evening, and made our plans to depart. At the airport on Tuesday, we were delighted to learn we had been rerouted directly to Zurich rather than via Paris to Zurich. Security was the most thorough I had ever seen—we were body searched—even in 1986. We spent our first ten days in Israel as we had planned, and then flew to Switzerland to settle in at the villa in Zug.

Although we had expected warm weather in Switzerland, since it was now April, the weather for most of the time was quite cool. All three of our children were able to visit us during this early spring in 1986, and we did much sightseeing around Switzerland. We observed the celebration for the end of winter at Zurich, which was highlighted by a guild parade and a large bonfire for the burning of winter in effigy. The villa was near Lucerne, and on Sunday nights we found ourselves going back to the same small hotel for dinner, where we became well-known.

Although we had wonderful accommodations in Zug, we felt a little isolated because of our inability to speak German, which is the language of the region. The weather was also cold, and it prevented us from some of the outdoor activities which we normally enjoy. The days passed slowly, and I was agitated at having so little to do—not a good thing for someone who is trying to decide on his next career.

Chapter Forty-three

CAREER MOVE

As the days of my sabbatical went by, I grew more restless and agitated. I knew I would be returning to Stanford, albeit reluctantly. After about six weeks in Switzerland, I received a call from Cincinnati, asking about my interest in the position of senior vice president responsible for the medical center.

I was about to begin a trip back to New York to participate in the Worldwide Advisory Committee for Bristol-Myers, on which I served for six years, returning to Zug for the remaining weeks of my sabbatical. The call was from William Schubert, head of Cincinnati Children's Hospital Medical Center and chair of the search committee for a senior vice president and provost for health affairs at the University of Cincinnati. The position intrigued me, and after thinking about it for several days, I agreed to come to Cincinnati for a first visit. At the time, I hardly knew how to spell Cincinnati, let alone think that I might leave Stanford and come to the medical center there. However, I felt desperate, and that I should not pass up the chance to look at this opportunity.

On arrival I was met by Vic Warner, the dean of pharmacy, and over the next two days I had extensive interviews with many people whom I found receptive to new ideas and supportive of someone coming from outside to head the medical center. The position that was being offered was one that was quite new and unique, in that it was a provost role as well as that of a senior vice president who would provide control over the health colleges and University Hospital.

Generally in medical centers, the vice president had responsibility for the academic programs in the health colleges. The hospital director and health system operated independently. Those whom I met clearly wanted to change the image and direction of the medical center from a purely local one to a national one. I had the firm belief that a single leader with responsibility for the health colleges, hospitals, health system, and the physician organization was the best model, and one that was likely to become more prevalent in the future. This newly created position had great appeal for me. I was also particularly intrigued with the president of the university, Joe Steger. Upon returning to Switzerland, I was soon invited back for another visit with Laura accompanying me to gain her view of Cincinnati.

We decided to terminate our time in Switzerland rather abruptly, even though it was originally scheduled to last eight more weeks. We visited Cincinnati, and then returned to California. Soon after my visit there with Laura, we received an invitation to return to Cincinnati a third time. In retrospect, as Laura sees it, we never really enjoyed a complete sabbatical during my whole career. This is because I spent the first six months organizing companies and then spent only three months of the remaining scheduled sabbatical before moving on to a new career choice.

Laura and I were quite impressed with Cincinnati and its many cultural activities, and with the beauty of several of its residential areas. I became convinced that there was a possibility to remake the medical center in the image of an institution with much higher national visibility. Not knowing whether I would be offered the job, I planned a trip to China in August 1986, which was part of the venture capital work for which I had continued to be a consultant. Before leaving on that trip, I had a mountain of work to complete. It was then that an opportunity was presented to me.

It was a cool and bright summer morning on the Stanford campus, and I was sitting at my cluttered desk in the corner office at the Falk cardiovascular building, quietly contemplating my career possibilities. As I looked across the campus through the live oaks, past the Hoover Tower, to the fog hovering over the coastal mountains, I was ruminating on my three visits to the University of Cincinnati as a candidate for the newly defined senior vice president's position. Numerous thoughts were going through my head. I felt attracted to the Cincinnati job, but the shock of learning the day before that a leading Cincinnati university researcher had fabricated his scientific data for years gave me pause. The institutional

They probably won't offer me the position anyway, since I had made that career mistake...

trauma resulting from this kind of scandal was well known to me from recently observing a committee that dismissed a senior professor at Stanford for plagiarism.

My inner conversation continued: *They probably won't offer me the position anyway, since I had made that career mistake of accepting the vice president's job at the University of Michigan, and then reneging even after the announcement was published in the Detroit Free Press.*

That morning, I was struggling to finish an overdue manuscript before leaving that night for the fourteen-day trip to China. Erin, my faithful secretary, broke the silence: "President Steger from the University of Cincinnati is on the phone."

I said, "Put him on, I'll take the call," not knowing what might be in the cards for my career.

After a few pleasantries he said, "Don, after your three visits here, the search committee has unanimously recommended you to become the first senior vice president and provost for health affairs for the university. Since you will be my closest associate, I wanted to make sure you would accept before I sent you a formal letter. Do you have any questions?"

I hesitated to answer because I thought I did want the job. But because of the impending scandal, I wanted time to consider its impact. After several moments I replied, "President Steger, I am honored with the offer. I'd like to visit again to assess the impact of the current research scandal before giving you a final answer, and since I leave tonight for China, that can't happen for a few weeks. I assure you I am quite interested."

Steger did not even pause with his answer. "If you are going to let a little event like that keep you from making a decision, you are not ready for a job of this magnitude. There will be plenty more challenges just as great. If I do not hear from you by 4 p.m. today, the offer is off." He hung up.

Over the next hour I was agitated, and paced the floor of my office. The sky suddenly did not seem so blue, nor the sun so bright. My inner self was continuing to struggle, and was saying, *I want the job and the exciting possibilities, but that first few months in dealing with the fallout from the scandal will be hell. Is Joe Steger right about there being more challenges?*

In my heart I knew if I turned this job down, as I had done in Michigan, there would be no possibility of this type of career move for me. My inner feelings were saying, *You are at a career turning point, you are the right age, this is a challenge, and you can do it.*

It was now noon, and I had Erin get President Steger back on the phone. I blurted out, "President Steger, I accept your offer, and assure you I can meet any challenge that will occur at your institution." He accepted gleefully, and that evening I left on a trip to China, feeling I had made a great move for my future career. While I was apprehensive, I felt that I had found a challenge that I could meet.

When I came back from China, I knew that everything at Stanford would be quite hectic before I could move on. Upon returning, I found that two major individuals in Cincinnati had made contact with my office and had already set up a mechanism for me to communicate with the university via e-mail. These two individuals, the head of finance for the University of Cincinnati Medical Center, Cyril Kupferberg, and the head of the medical center information technology section, Nancy Lorenzi, were on the phone with me almost constantly after that. They both became important associates and friends in my career at U.C., and remain so even now.

How quickly I became a "lame duck" after announcing my decision to leave Stanford amazed me, and while I tried to make decisions and move decisions forward, this was just not possible, and I spent most of the next two months, collecting my affairs, finishing as much of my research as I could, and trying to create the best situation possible for my Stanford colleagues. It is amazing how one's influence fades when a decision is made to move on.

Upon making the decision to leave California and move to Cincinnati in 1986, the question that was asked of me most frequently (and sometimes multiple times in a single day) was, "Why would anyone leave California and move to Cincinnati?" This was a difficult question for me, but in retrospect, I think it was for both the opportunity and the need for a new challenge. The question burned in my mind and kept me sleepless many nights. I finally reconciled it as "taking advantage of a career change." Even now, twenty years later, that question is still frequently asked of me. Now I usually answer, with tongue in cheek, "I moved for better weather." Everyone reacts with surprise to this, wonders what I mean, and moves on. Of course, it is only a way of turning aside the question. The real reason I left was for an opportunity to grow and an opportunity to build a new component of my career. My medical career had always been dedicated to achieving excellence and doing all I could to promote academic medicine. I wanted to be able to develop a new area of competence. I believed I could bring what I had learned at Stanford to successful fruition in another institution.

Thus, my rationale for why I chose to leave Stanford can be summed up as the presence of both a negative push from Stanford and a powerful, positive pull from Cincinnati. Stanford is a difficult place in which to continuously succeed and grow. At Stanford, one must continuously succeed. The years of struggle and competition began to put me in a corral and fenced me in where further growth was limited. As I struggled in this environment, I unavoidably made enemies who began to block the way for further career advancement. My visits in Cincinnati and all of the individuals I met led me to believe that there was the need for a leader to stimulate major change and improve the quality of the medical center. This was a very positive attraction.

Everyone seemed to express the need for new leadership, and there seemed to be no overwhelming financial hurdles to overcome. Most times, when one is offered a job like this, the first task is to dig the place out of a major financial difficulty. That did not seem to be the case, and the desire to be an agent for change, and to understand what that might mean, was reasonably clear in my mind. I knew the difficulties I would likely encounter, and understood that I could fail.

On the other hand, I had acquired a great deal of experience in a top-flight academic medical center, and was at a stage in my career where I could make a change. I thought this might take seven to eight years, bringing me to age 60, at which time I had said I would retire. Since I stayed for seventeen years, my daughter Donna once observed that I "was a slow learner." To me it always seemed that there were new challenges, and each of those challenges offered me the opportunity to further the reputation and quality of work going on at the medical center. Thus, I answered the question quite honestly, "I came for a career change and for a new opportunity where I could make a much larger contribution to academic medicine."

Chapter Forty-four

L E G A C Y

I have attempted to evaluate my legacy at Stanford, even though this is difficult to do without bias. I have always considered my most important legacy at Stanford to be the careers of the 156 postdoctoral fellows who trained in my program.

Of course, I was proud of the worldwide recognition of my research, the quality of the faculty I recruited and developed, and the Falk Cardiovascular Center, but my pride was the postdocs. The past twenty years of my career at Cincinnati have provided time for these individuals to mature in their own careers, to become more important physicians in academic cardiology. While it is difficult to summarize the impact that they have made in cardiology over the last three decades, many have and are making important contributions to medicine and the academics.

Graduates of our program have become professors in twenty-one institutions, including Yale, Massachusetts General Hospital, Beth Israel Hospital, Brigham and Women's Hospital, the University of Colorado, the University of Utah, the University of Pennsylvania, the University of Iowa, the University of Kentucky, the University of Massachusetts, the University of California at San Francisco, Tulane University, Stanford University, Vanderbilt University, Cleveland Clinic, Mayo Clinic, Scripps Clinic, the University of Southern California, and The Ohio State University. One has become a chair of medicine, six are directors of their cardiology divisions, and four have become co-directors of the cardiology units at their institution.

In Canada there have been twelve of the postdoctoral fellows who have become professors at several institutions, and four have become heads of cardiology at Canadian schools. Almost all of these individuals in the United States and in Canada have made contributions to cardiovascular research, and they have served on editorial boards. One has been president of the American College of Cardiology, and several have served as program chairs of the scientific sessions of the American Heart Association or of the American College of Cardiology. Of the overseas postdocs, one is the equivalent of the director of the FDA in France; six are editors of their cardiology journals in their home countries of France, Portugal, Italy, and England, and one has been chair of medicine in Singapore.

In addition to their educational and research activities, the postdoctoral graduates of the Stanford program have made important contributions to interventional and noninvasive cardiovascular commercial products, and in rhythm changes and corrections. Twelve successful commercial companies have been formed by my postdoctoral fellows, and one has founded a large health management company involving over 250,000 patients in Nevada and the Southwest of the United States.

Laura and I have managed to keep in contact with many of our postdocs and their spouses, and had a reunion in 1990 with a two-day scientific symposium and a reenactment of the "roast" and awards ceremony that we used to have as each group graduated from the program at Stanford. In addition, when we visit cities where there are postdocs, Laura and I almost always make contact with groups of them, to have dinner with them and their spouses.

A recent get-together was in San Diego, where we had dinner on Fat Tuesday to celebrate the coming of Lent with five of the postdocs who are in that area and their wives. Paul Teirstein of the Scripps Clinic organized the group, and we had a lovely evening with Dave Reberson, Mark Efron, Maurice Buchbinder, Mark Yaeger, and their wives. They made reservations at a restaurant that was having a great Fat Tuesday celebration. We had beads, balloons, great food, and Mardi Gras music. It was a wonderful celebration and an opportunity to see the growth and development of these five very successful postdocs from the Stanford program.

In reviewing the accomplishments of my postdocs, I am pleased that more than half went into academic cardiology, and that many have made important research and clinical contributions to the field. Perhaps the few years that they spent with us at Stanford ignited a spark of innovation and creativity within them that carried forward into their careers. As time marches on, I hope to keep in contact with them as their careers continue to mature and to grow. As I look back over the Stanford years, I recognize that we consider these postdocs almost as family and as "developing children" who at a later stage of development went forth to make the world a better place by their contributions to cardiology.

Chapter Forty-five

CHALLENGES

During my recruitment in 1986, I evaluated the Cincinnati medical community environment, but soon after my arrival it became clear that I did not fully understand the history and background of the medical center, and I had only gleaned superficial knowledge of the recent direction of the center.

I recognized that there were major voids in leadership in the colleges and hospitals. University of Cincinnati Medical Center, sometimes referred to as the Academic Health Center, included the colleges of medicine, nursing and pharmacy, and University and Children's hospitals, the Shriners Burns Hospital for Children, as well as the Hoxworth Blood Center, and the physician practice organization.

The University Hospital did not have a full-time director, had no strategic direction, and had difficult financial problems. The chair or dean at the college of medicine was vacant, and there were no appointees for the chair of medicine, chair of psychiatry, or chair of obstetrics. The college was drifting, needing new inspiration and focus. The magnitude of these leadership voids had not been made clear to me during my recruitment, but immediately I knew I had major recruitment challenges that would occupy me fully for the next year or two.

To learn more about the medical center's needs, I established a four-member advisory committee with which I met every week for the first six months, usually for 6:30 a.m. breakfast at Children's Hospital. The committee consisted of Bill Schubert, who had recruited me and was director of the Children's Hospital and head of pediatrics at the college of medicine; John Tew, chair of neurosurgery; Jerry Wiot, former chair of radiology and interim senior vice president and provost for health affairs; and Bob Hummel, a well-known and respected general surgeon in the college and community. This group, individually and collectively, had knowledge of the problems in the hospital and the college of medicine. They also had relationships in the community that could be helpful to me. I wanted to understand fully how the departments practiced medicine and used their revenue as I had some new ideas I wanted to bring to the table. This advisory committee gave me good advice about what was possible and how to proceed, especially focusing on University Hospital.

Some of the advice related to the clinical department's long-standing practice of medicine. One of the first needs they outlined was for a new practice building to supplant the sixty-year old clinic buildings where both private and charity patients were being seen.

They pointed out that this need had been well documented for years, but awaited a leader who could propose a new mechanism for funding a new building. By the end of my first year, with the help of David Fine, whom I hired as director of University Hospital, we were able to put together a plan to build the Medical Arts Building, which would house the medical practices and get them moved from the antiquated space to which they had been assigned. The clinical practices were located in various pavilions which had been built in 1912, and were scattered around the medical campus.

Next, my advisory team pointed out the need for being able to bill for services under the Ohio Medicaid Plan, which had just instituted a policy that required that all of the specialties come together and have a single corporate billing number and mechanism. It was on the basis of this advice that we created our own health maintenance organization, known as the University Health Plan (UHP). This was the brainchild of David Fine, and it allowed us to bill the state under a single entity for our many Ohio Medicaid patients. We enrolled private patients in UHP and developed a health care plan for university faculty and employees.

This was a successful venture, and our plan grew to 40,000 covered lives. However, as managed care consolidation grew in the area, we could not compete with the larger national companies, and sold our unit to Blue Cross of Ohio in 1994. The proceeds from this sale were $4 million, which we then used to create the Health Policy and Health Research Institute, for the University of Cincinnati. There was intense debate and considerable controversy over this allocation of funds, which the clinical practice departments thought should revert to them. However, I withstood the heat and was able to prevail, and appointed Al Tuchfarber, a well-known professor with a background in health care polling, to direct the institute. Al is a self-assured, well-spoken individual who co-opted the department directors to allow some of their faculty to become appointed as fellows of the institute. He was a long-time member of the political science department of the university, and possessed the finesse to work with the clinicians. The institute became successful and had a major impact on evaluating indigent health care and in negotiating contracts with Hamilton County for services provided by University Hospital. Al also advised me and the director of University Hospital on the political approaches to pass the Hamilton County tax levy. This supported patient care for the indigent of the county.

My advisory group also told me of the need to convince the Children's Hospital board

This was a successful venture and our plan grew to 40,000 covered lives.

of directors that their relationship with the college of medicine and the medical center was important, and that the future of the Children's Hospital Medical Center depended on a strong university relationship. This had not always been the case. Bill Schubert, head of Children's Hospital clinical programs and administration, proved to be the leader who would make this a reality over the next five years.

I established a search committee for dean of the college of medicine, and to everyone's surprise, I chaired the committee myself. At Cincinnati, the usual practice was for the leader of the medical center to choose another dean or department director to chair a search committee. To me, this represented the most significant appointment I would make in my tenure, and I wanted full charge. My past experience at Stanford convinced me that a collaborative partner as dean of the college was essential.

I knew a number of national figures whom we might attract, and I wanted to move rapidly. But after almost a year of searching, visits by many candidates who were introduced to the medical center—and a lot of wining and dining—I was unable to recruit any of them. None of the national candidates were willing to buy completely into my belief that the University of Cincinnati could be converted into a national player. They were not persuaded to take the risk. Disappointed, I began to consider internal candidates. While everything else seemed to be going well at the University Hospital, the recruiting of new clinical leadership was in limbo until a new dean was recruited.

On one of my low days, there was a knock on my door and John Hutton appeared. He was head of research at Children's Hospital and he said he wanted to be a candidate for dean of the college. Hutton said, "I like my research, but my career has been directed to helping medical students and basic researchers. I think I'm ready to be a dean." He had a background very similar to mine and had much of his training in Boston, though his research was in oncology while mine was cardiology. I checked his references, met with him on numerous occasions, and decided we could work well together. We were a solid team for fifteen years. Hutton is tall, with a receding hairline. His refusal to wear the starched white shirt and suit of the Cincinnati business community did not deter his colleagues from a regard for his authority. John still has that "signature" floppy hat that he always wears to keep off the sun, and one could tell it is John from quite a distance. He was somewhat of an introvert who spoke bluntly, but always with knowledge to back up his pronouncements. Hutton was devoted to the needs of students, and mentored many of the good ones to encourage them to consider academic careers. We were a good match for our two jobs—with my background in cardiology and his in cancer—as we were able to promote and strengthen the programs in these areas.

Aside from hiring a new dean of the college, another early effort was to recruit a director of the hospital and someone to establish a health system, which I believed was the wave of the future. I had learned much about the oncoming managed-care revolution when I was head of the practice plan at Stanford. During my first six weeks in Cincinnati I recruited David Fine, a very young man who had been serving as a consultant at the University Hospital and who had successfully privatized a state-owned hospital in West Virginia. Fine drove a very hard bargain but finally was recruited. His favorite saying was, "To get high-quality people, you must be willing to pay the financial price at least equal to the compensation rate on the East Coast." We spent hours pouring over the language in a contract and over his compensation.

Fine was unusually energetic, and he spoke quickly and with authority. He engendered confidence and was persuasive with the clinical chairs. He had boundless energy and was a real risktaker. Sometimes I had to moderate this creative energy and focus it on our goals. He had considerable experience with the University Hospital Consortium, which was renamed University Health Systems, a national health organization for academic medical centers that also had a purchasing division that could negotiate better prices for group purchasing. In addition to directing University Hospital, he was well aware of the idea of creating health systems, and over a period of six months, we developed a plan for creating the Health, Education and Research Corporation (HERC).

HERC was to be an integrated health care system centered in the university. It was to provide tertiary care and access to services offered by no one else. It was a model for a regional health care system, which was a popular concept at the time. I believed strongly in such a system and lent my full support to the idea. We employed a legal firm to set up the program in business terms and involved many of the internal leaders in the medical center, but did not involve the board of trustees of the university in the early plans because we did not know exactly when or what to tell them.

Once the planning started, other hospitals in the community and medical practitioners learned of our plans, and brought considerable pressure on the board of trustees of the university to reject our proposals since they made us more competitive than we were under the managed care environment that was developing in Cincinnati. Fine and I did not understand the magnitude of the community medical leaders' influence on the board, and when we made our presentation to the University of Cincinnati board it was clear that some did not support our plan for HERC. The major opposition from UC board members included some who were beholden to organized labor, which in this city also opposed the idea.

The University Hospital at the time was fully represented by seven different unions.

I remember a particularly controversial board meeting where we were accused of "empire building" by the board. They ultimately voted no confidence in the plan and undermined David Fine's belief that he could develop the ideal health care system for Cincinnati. Eventually this setback forced Fine to leave UC, although his actual departure did not occur until two years later. In retrospect, it was clearly a plan for the future and would have been a great benefit to the university and the community. The plan was to make the university the control hub of a regional health care system by buying or aligning the other hospitals into the university system of care. This would have truly created the regional medical system that I had envisioned. It was the model we had proposed years earlier in the San Francisco Bay Area as part of the regional medical planning.

This experience and others early on taught me the importance of avoiding the appearance of coming in from California "riding a white horse." I had to "shake the Stanford dust" from my feet, although it was that model that I wanted to emulate for the major changes. The most vivid display of opposition by the department directors to my continually putting Stanford plans in front of them came during a meeting with the chairman of the department of surgery.

I was discussing the practice plan at Stanford and saying I wanted to impose a similar plan in Cincinnati. Practice plans are the organizations under which the academic departments do their clinical work. They usually involve a "tax" to support the infrastructure of the college as well as support compensation for clinical faculty. His reply to me was, "If you think Stanford is so great, why don't you go back there?" From this rebuke I realized that though I could quote experiences and comparisons with Hopkins or Duke, if I ever mentioned how matters were done at Stanford, I would meet with resistance.

In order to promote change of strategic direction, I needed a well-conceived plan for action. Soon after I arrived I appointed a planning group that worked for almost a year drawing up a plan we called "Reaching for the 21st Century." I worked with the group day-by-day on this plan, which was to be for a ten-to-twelve-year period. That seemed to be the title for everyone's strategic plan at this time in 1987. The strategic plan that we developed for the University of Cincinnati included increasing our research from the mere $30 million per year to over $100 million per year over the next decade. It also included a plan to upgrade and modernize all of our teaching programs in the health-related colleges, with the hope of bringing the health professions' education programs closer together. Finally, it created a series of focused research areas where we could concentrate our investment and create program competition on the national scene.

I also established a number of other working groups and had regular meetings with all of the department directors, hoping to co-op them into a new practice organization. My intent was to establish a group practice organization with a faculty practice plan, much as we had at Stanford. The plan at Stanford that taxed clinical income for the departments at 10 percent provided a fund for the dean to develop new clinical and research programs. Though this was a system widely accepted in other medical centers, there was instant opposition here. John Hutton and I exhorted them to help develop a mechanism to support new program development, but it was to no avail.

It soon became apparent that my plan would not be possible, and if we tried to push this issue, the dean of the medical school and I would both have short tenures. We made a decision that an equally effective strategy would be to put all the expenses back on the clinical departments and allow them to retain a major part of their clinical income. Thus, a shift of expenses rather than an academic tax on clinical revenue brought us to the end that I sought. We maintained control of all of the state funds and endowment funds for the medical center, which could be allocated to departments where new research programs could be initiated. This plan brought less opposition and permitted me to reallocate funds to important areas for development, and to support the "Reaching for the 21st Century plan."

Hutton and I began this reallocation of state funds in a more equitable fashion, based on teaching contributions and the potential of the departments for research. Later, when I calculated the effects of this strategy, I found that the shifting of expense and the reallocation of state funds produced an effect almost equal to an academic practice tax of 10 percent on clinical revenue. This is quite similar to the impact of a practice plan employed at many academic medical centers. Practice income had over two decades become one of the largest sources of support for colleges of medicine, and was the basis for major growth in clinical departments.

As the medical faculty increased and state or private funds decreased or remained static, practice income became one of the major sources of funding for an academic medical center. By constantly pressuring department chairs to appoint younger faculty with active research programs, we initiated many of the programs proposed in our strategic plan.

In addition to participating in medical center activities, I was a senior vice president and provost for health affairs for the university. Soon I found myself deeply immersed in university-wide issues. In order to do university business, we had cabinet retreats that usually lasted for two days once a month, where we went away from the campus and stayed overnight. The cabinet was comprised of all of the university vice presidents. These meetings were very boring to me, and what we did in two days could usually be done in the medical center in one or two hours under my direction. There were a number of occasions at these retreats where people lost their temper and entered into shouting matches with each other, sometimes almost ending in fistfights.

The two women on the cabinet always felt that they were being discriminated against. On one occasion, when Thurmond Owens, the president's chief of staff, attacked the vice president for research, Eula Bingham, over a budget decision, she became enraged, threw her glass on the floor, retreated to her room and locked herself in, refusing to come back and join the meeting. After much persuasion, she joined the group again for dinner and an uneasy peace was made. The reason these sessions were contentious was that the university was going through major budget reductions, and the allocation of these reductions to administrative units was not always uniform. Budget reductions in our state funding caused much controversy among the vice presidents and their areas of responsibility.

I was always in conflict with the other vice presidents over budget issues. When I came to Cincinnati, I identified some new sources of funding, and the other vice presidents were always trying to reduce the medical center's part of state funding disproportionately. These university retreats focused on the decreasing support for higher education and how we could offset the losses. They were also devoted to developing a master plan for university rejuvenation. However, as we shared food and wine, we had a lot of late-night discussions of university challenges. The fact that I had a formal plan for advancing the medical center allowed me to gain and build trust with the other university officers as we negotiated the tough issues.

During these retreats, I made sure that the budget reductions did not fall disproportionately on the medical center. The center did have other sources of funds besides the state budget, and in the past, university reductions were offset by taking medical center funds. During these meetings, I became aware of how much President Steger wanted the medical center to succeed. He frequently supported my position, or would allow discussion for a prolonged period and then come forth with a compromise proposal. He seemed to disdain making preemptive decisions, and sometimes prolonged the discussion to the point of agony. He understood better than I the need for letting big issues percolate through a prolonged process before coming to final resolution. Such delays occasionally caused major problems such as the failure to dismiss inadequate performers. However, during these lengthy retreats, he and I bonded and he offered me some of his philosophy of management, i.e., "A general cannot succeed unless his troops support him, especially in a major battle." While I defended the medical center vigorously, it was clear that at times I needed to be a good citizen and support the general programs of the university with some of our financial successes.

On one occasion, we reallocated $1 million from the hospital budget to the general fund of the university to offset some the effect of drastic program reduction. On another occasion, the medical center funded the purchase of properties needed by the university to developing a new university office building and a campus hotel and conference facility. We provided $4 million for this purchase of land from the city of Cincinnati, since the development was to be built contiguous to medical center property and could be a valuable conference site for the medical center.

Initially, I had little knowledge of public university-related activities, and soon found that I needed to understand university budgets, faculty recruitment, and how to deal with a faculty union. The thought of a union of faculty members was foreign to me. President Steger assured me when I was being recruited that the faculty union would be no problem for me, but I soon found that not to be true when I vetoed the tenure promotion of four faculty members from the college of medicine. The union-driven process was for recommendations to be made at the department level, reviewed at the college level, responded to by the dean, and then come to the provost for recommendations to the board of trustees. Once I vetoed four who were proposed, and the process then took my negative recommendations to a faculty council grievance committee. After many grievance hearings that occupied hours of my time, I convinced the faculty council grievance committee that it was necessary to have outside peer reviews of these individuals. I selected the reviewers, and using that mechanism, I sustained three of the four vetoes. That was a major step forward in dealing with promotion to tenure, and from that time forward, few recommendations for people unqualified for tenure were sent by the departments to the dean and me.

In addition, we established a medical school tenure review committee, which was valuable in keeping some of the pressure off the dean and me for making negative decisions. The decision by peers, even from other departments, was more acceptable to the faculty. Tenure is less important for faculty in clinical departments than in the rest of the university. This is because the physician who leaves an academic setting can set up an independent practice and generally earn more than his or her academic compensation.

My relationship with the faculty union was always controversial, and I clashed with them on many occasions. I believe faculty unions lead to mediocrity, since this one tried to reduce every appointment to its lowest level. In fact, in many departments in the university, everyone who requested a promotion to tenure after having served the minimal number of years was promoted. I opposed this and became a nemesis in grievance hearings. The faculty member who acted as a lawyer for the union frequently became so enraged at me that I feared he might have a stroke during some of our hearings. After a few years, though, there were few challenges to my recommendations on faculty promotions to tenured positions.

My persistent challenge to the union leadership and the use of peer review for evaluating accomplishments resulted in most requests for promotion and tenure in the medical school being based on meritorious performance.

Some problems in sustaining long-term support for faculty in a college of medicine have developed in the past three decades. First, the number of faculty has more than tripled to more than 100,000 nationally. The faculty not only teaches but carries out funded research and delivers high-quality medical care. They generally fall into three classes or groups: clinicians, basic researchers, and teachers. Secondly, the state contribution to public medical school funding has proportionally decreased dramatically from 35-40 percent to 10-15 percent. Thus, the old process of awarding tenure to faculty, which virtually guarantees lifetime compensation, required re-examination.

Our approach was to establish alternate appointment tracks. A *clinical track* for those providing clinical service was used frequently, and the compensation was determined by the clinical income generated. A *research track* was used for those doing largely funded research, and 75 percent of their compensation was expected to come from their research grants by the third year after their appointment. Neither the clinical track nor the research track had tenure. We used these tracks for a large majority of our appointments during my seventeen years. The percent of faculty with tenure in the college of medicine was reduced from approximately 60 to 30 percent as more faculty retired and many new appointments increased the size of the faculty. This reduction in the appointment of faculty to tenure was resisted largely by members of the faculty union, which was under the auspices of the American Association of University Professors.

Once we had an alternate pathway well established with a review mechanism and compensation based on performance, the general faculty accepted our view that tenure was not necessary. This approach also permitted faculty members to have differential compensation based on their performance and contributions. Over the years, the resistance to the multi-tiered appointments in our college of medicine began to disappear, and many faculty members had the feeling it was equitable. Many other medical schools in the country also adopted alternate appointment mechanisms, with a reduction in tenure. This fact was well known by most of our faculty members, and helped make it more acceptable, although a few "diehards" still objected.

In addition to the college of medicine, I had responsibility for the college of nursing, the college of pharmacy, the Veterans Administration Hospital, and Hoxworth Blood Center. I was appalled at the lack of research interest in the college of pharmacy, and I included a number of its leaders in the strategic planning process to involve them in developing a research agenda. A similar lack of research emphasis was present in the college of nursing, where there seemed to be a strong presence of the faculty union. Over the years, we worked diligently to increase the research efforts in both colleges, and to integrate their programs more with the University Hospital and with the other health profession colleges.

In the last two decades, medical research has become more complex, and a nucleus of faculty with similar interests became necessary for successful research programs. Therefore, I encouraged all new appointments to the colleges of nursing, pharmacy, and allied health to have colleagues and areas of interest in the college of medicine, where the research ethos was well established. This was because the college of medicine had a much larger research-oriented faculty and building a core group of faculty with similar interests in any one of the other health colleges was really not possible with the resources we had available.

The banding together of research faculty throughout the medical center in the hope of breaking down some of the silo mentality and barriers with health professionals was also one of my goals. This was much more easily accomplished with the research faculty than with the teaching faculty, for reasons that still escape me. Research and research funding for the faculty in pharmacy, nursing, and allied health was much improved by pharmacy faculty members developing relationships with colleagues with similar research interests in the college of medicine. In actuality, the faculty in each college became more entrepreneurial during the years of my tenure. They developed new teaching programs that increased state funding, and levels of enrollment rose to meet the local demand for new graduates in nursing and pharmacy.

The Hoxworth Blood Center was part of the medical center and it supplied blood to more than forty hospitals in southern Ohio, eastern Indiana, and northern Kentucky. It has been in operation since before World War II, and was one of the best known private institutional blood banks in the country. The director of Hoxworth, Tibor Greenwalt, was in his late 70s when I arrived. Soon after, it was necessary to recruit a new director and I was fortunate to be able to recruit Tom Zuck, who had many years' experience directing blood banks in the military. He was a longtime career man who could not give up some of his military ways. He always addressed me as "Sir," and even when I asked him not to—he said, "Yes, Sir."

It was obvious we needed to begin to plan for a new facility, and over the next five years, a new clinical building was constructed near the University Hospital, resulting in a new high-quality home for the Hoxworth Center. The center had a community advisory board, and on many occasions they thought the director should report to them, and that they could dictate the programs of the center. From its beginning, the charter of the center called for its direction to be focused by the head of the medical center. I had to meet with that board on numerous occasions and point out to them that this was a university-based blood bank, and that it reported directly to me. Over a period of several years, I managed to work successfully with the advisory board, restructuring it to be more supportive of Hoxworth and to understand its role as an advisory panel.

Bill Schubert was the chair of the department of pediatrics, and was also the director of the Children's Hospital. Schubert was a tall, stooped-shouldered man who spoke softly and seemed to be a friend to everyone in Cincinnati. He was a staunch defender of children and Children's Hospital. As chair of the department of pediatrics and head of the hospital, he wielded great power in the community. Choosing Bill Schubert to chair the search committee for the job that I assumed was a brilliant decision on the part of University President Steger. By giving him the responsibility of recruiting me for the senior vice president and provost for health affairs position, it helped to give the board of trustees of Children's Hospital confidence that the university was working to build good relationships. The Children's Hospital began to feel that they had a major impact on the future direction of the medical center. Since the relationships between University Hospital and the Children's Hospital had been strained over the previous decade, this proved to be a very valuable step forward.

The Children's Hospital had been integrated into the university's programs in 1929 when James Procter, of the Procter & Gamble family, made a major contribution to build the Children's Hospital and insisted that it be located adjacent to the university's college of medicine. Initially, the relationship was quite cordial and worked quite well, but over several decades, problems with the administration of the university had arisen, and the Children's Hospital board was leery of the way the university faculty was developing teaching and research programs.

However, the medical staff of the Children's Hospital was the pediatrics department, and they all were faculty of the college of medicine. The Children's Hospital also had a research arm that was created as a foundation, and over the years, the foundation developed an endowment of more than $1 billion. The foundation's mission was to support Children's Hospital and its teaching and research programs. The department of pediatrics was critical to the college and its the largest department.

When I arrived it had almost 180 members, and it has grown over the past sixteen years to over 300 members. Children's Hospital has rebuilt the entire 1929 hospital, and the new building has expanded to 365 active beds. Pediatricians from the entire region for a hundred miles around refer their patients to Children's Hospital, and it serves as a major referral center for specialty and subspecialty programs throughout the central Midwest.

Bill Schubert was a very important person who helped improve the relationships with Children's Hospital, and helped facilitate my efforts to include the Children's Hospital and its board in our plans. I attended many of the meetings of the board and medical staff of Children's Hospital in an attempt to ensure a positive relationship with them.

During my recruitment, the best advice about meeting members of the board of trustees of the university and the kinds of questions I should be asking of the university president came from Bill Schubert. Several years later, he told me a story that on one of my visits I had worn a pastel green shirt with a rather bold tie. After all, I was coming from California— what else could be expected? When I was interviewed by Walter Bartlett, then chair of the university board, and he observed my attire, he called Bill Schubert to say, "I don't think this young man is interested in the job here. He didn't even wear a white shirt when he came to visit with me." I guess that, coming from the West Coast, I never regarded a pastel green shirt as a problem. It certainly would have been a problem if I had not worn a tie, but in Cincinnati, the old conservative image of a starched white shirt on any university official seemed to be paramount.

Over a period of years, the Children's Hospital has become more integrated into the medical center and in its relationship with the university. In many instances, it became the lead for the medical center in developing community programs and community relations. One of the most important was a program, "Every Child Succeeds," which helps disadvantaged children to access health care and educational opportunities. This program was initiated and directed by Judy Van Ginkel, who had worked as an integral part of my staff for eight years before starting this program.

Children's hospitals consider themselves as fragile players in academic medical centers. They frequently believe their best interest is to act independently. This was true in my early relations with the hospital board. I followed the advice given to me by my colleague Bill Kelley, then the director of the University of Pennsylvania Medical Center, who lost his relationship with the Children's Hospital of Philadelphia. His advice was, "Don, if they want you to lie down and let them roll over you, do it, to keep them as part of your vision."

The Shriners Burns Hospital was also an important part of the medical center and was one of the four Shrine hospitals treating children with major burns in the United States. When I came to Cincinnati, the Shrine organization wanted to build a new hospital to replace the current one, built in the 1960s. I worked closely with the national organization and the local administrator, in an attempt to negotiate an exchange of the old hospital as a gift to the university for designation of property on which the new Shriners Burns Hospital could be built.

I had no previous experience dealing with the Shrine organization, but soon found out it was quite strong in Cincinnati. One of their largest temples was located near the medical center. Many of the community leaders were part of the Shrine organization, and there was considerable pressure from the community and the board of trustees of the university to negotiate the transfer of property to the Shriners for building their new hospital. The Shriners totally supported the hospital and research relating to the treatment of burns. Children from all over the South and central Midwest were hospitalized at the Shriners Burns Hospital in Cincinnati, and it was important to keep the hospital as part of the medical center. One of the chairs of our clinical departments was a high-order Shriner, and in later years advanced to the 23rd Order, which was the highest order of the Shrine nationally. As our negotiations progressed, it became clear to me that I was under considerable pressure to negotiate a mutually beneficial relationship with the Shrine.

Talks had been ongoing for a number of years, without success. I remember a meeting at the Cincinnati airport with our university corporate counsel Melanie Newberg, and the senior officials of the national Shrine organization. This was an instance in which the old boys of the Shrine paid no attention to our female general counsel. After our meeting broke up without an agreement, Melanie made a number of suggestions to me. She suggested setting a deadline for a decision, and outlining in detail the value of the transactions to each party. We did this, and I took a very forceful stand, and told the Shrine organization, "Within the next two weeks, I either hear positively that you are accepting the position that we have laid out for you, or I will begin utilizing the designated property for your new hospital for other purposes within the medical center."

This was prime real estate on the main north-south street of the campus, and I knew that it would be used sooner rather than later for the medical center's development, if not for a new burn hospital. The Shrine organization capitulated, and an agreement was struck. They built a beautiful hospital facility that included nearly 50,000 square feet of important research space. This research space permitted several research units from the college of medicine to relocate on that site in new facilities. The medical staff of the Shriner hospitals are also faculty of the college of medicine. The Shrine supports several million dollars' worth of research here each year. This was viewed by the community as a major accomplishment.

Early in my tenure at Cincinnati, I visited many hospitals in the area to learn about their operations and how they might relate to the college of medicine and the medical center. One of the hospitals I visited was Drake Hospital, about ten miles from the main campus. It was the charity rehabilitation hospital for this region. I was intrigued with the concept of a dedicated rehabilitation hospital, and especially with the fact that the Drake facility was located on many acres of undeveloped land. However, I was in no position to acquire it. About two years after my arrival, Drake came under intense local and national scrutiny because a serial killer, an employee, had given lethal injections to at least forty-eight patients at that hospital. This became a national story, and created quite an outcry in the region.

Since the Drake Hospital was the responsibility of the Hamilton County Commissioners, they came under major criticism and were under intense public pressure to find a new course for the operation of the hospital. I then learned that Drake Hospital had a successful relationship in the 1930s and 1940s with the UC Medical Center, and that the college of medicine had supplied the medical staff for the hospital. Drake's nearly 100 acres of prime property could be incorporated into a component of the medical center if the funds to reconstruct the existing facility and build a new one were available.

It was clear to me that only the university and the medical center could restore the reputation of Drake Hospital and give assurance to patients and this community that it was now a safe place for rehabilitation programs. Recognizing the need for financial assistance to do the rebuilding and new construction, I sought the help of the county commissioners to help us fund the building of a new Drake Hospital. After a long series of negotiations, we came to an agreement that the university would take on the responsibility for Drake Hospital. A new governance structure, largely controlled by the university, would be put into place, and the county commissioners (with voter approval) would create a fund of $60 million to rebuild the hospital, and establish a tax levy to continue to subsidize the hospital for its charity patients in an ongoing way. These negotiations were my first with the Cincinnati political system, and required long hours of meetings lasting into the night in the cavernous back room of the administration offices at Drake Hospital. When the final agreement was reached, one of the commissioners was on vacation in Arizona. He refused to fly back to Cincinnati to sign the agreement unless we paid for him to fly first-class. I allocated this payment from my private endowed funds from the medical center to make this possible. Thus we entered into an agreement with the county commissioners to restore the reputation of Drake Hospital and to build a major midwestern rehabilitation center.

We passed the county tax levy, and it has been in place ever since. Now known as the Drake Center, it has prospered as a major component of the medical center with many of our educational and clinical programs centered there. Nonetheless, it took several years for the public to accept that Drake Center was a safe place, and that the quality of the programs there were as good as any other place for rehabilitation in the area. In recent years, Drake has become one of the finest rehabilitation centers in the Midwest, and in 2006, Drake was purchased by the health alliance and now operates as part of this system.

In my position as director of the medical center, dealing with department chairs turned out to be quite a challenge. Many of the department chairs in the medical center were prima donnas, and the organization had made them directors of their own corporations with little oversight. They were not in any way connected to each other as a unit, and in many ways felt quite independent from the college of medicine. This created a lot of petty jealousies among the chairs and a major problem for me. I was confronted with how best to bring the group together. The chair of surgery had been one of the major problems for the previous administration, and I viewed that as likely to be the case for me as well. In fact, even before I arrived, he became a problem.

Soon after my appointment was announced, I made an unplanned visit to Cincinnati because I had learned that Josef Fischer, the chair of surgery, was hostile to my appointment and was promoting faculty unrest in the college, and also upsetting physicians in the community.

I arrived in Cincinnati on a cold evening, was taken to his house, and we sat by his fireplace. Fischer was an imposing figure with a puffed-up chest accentuated by the fact that he always wore a vest when he was not in a green scrub suit. He spoke with great authority and imposed his will on others. He was a major national figure in the American College of Surgery, and brought prestige to the medical center. I wanted to entice him to be part of my team, but recognized the risk.

On that evening, after considerable conversation and being told what he would and would not do, I finally came to the conclusion that I must set him straight. My final comments of the evening were, "Joe, you will either play on my team and participate fully in the new strategic direction, or, if not, you had better find another team on which to play." He did not comment, only frowned and said that we had had a good evening together.

This ended a frank conversation, and the next week I learned that my threat had made him acknowledge that he would work with the new administration. Although he would prove to be a thorn in my side on some matters, he was totally devoted to building the best department of surgery in the country. Sometimes over the years he didn't play on the team, but I was able to keep him in line most of the time by insisting he talk with me any time he faced a controversial issue. Still, he remained controversial with the community physicians.

My first few years were a major learning experience in which I encountered challenges at every level. Each day was filled with addressing problems and with recruiting new leaders and staff for the medical center. One of my early recruitments was Robert Luke, to head the department of medicine, one of the most important teaching and research departments in a medical college. John Hutton and I tried to recruit several national figures, but were unsuccessful because we lacked the resources, and the rebuilding task for the department was so daunting.

Luke came from the University of Alabama-Birmingham, where he was head of nephrology. He successfully reorganized the department and corrected its financial difficulties. After accumulating considerable reserves, his Scottish nature hindered him from spending the funds necessary to recruit outstanding talent until his later years. However, success was coming and we were able to initiate our "Reaching for the 21st Century Plan," focusing on a series of new plans in heart disease, cancer, neuroscience, pediatrics, and early childhood development, which took advantage of our major Children's Hospital expertise and its faculty of then over 180 physicians and researchers.

While at Stanford as director of the cardiology division, I had always had a very active referral practice. As a physician, I've always believed that the major administrative figure in a medical center would have a much better understanding of the challenges being met by the clinical faculty if he practiced medicine on a part-time basis. By maintaining a clinical practice, one sees the deficiencies as well as strengths of subspecialty and ancillary services such as radiology, the clinical laboratories and billing, and can work with administrative personnel to correct problem areas. I knew that it was important for me to be seen as a major supporter of clinical practice, as I had been at Stanford. Thus, as I made my plans to move to Cincinnati, one of the early decisions I made was that I would continue to practice medicine and see patients with heart disease.

I had obtained my license to practice in Ohio, though with bureaucratic difficulty. First, I attempted to use my existing California license to reciprocate with Ohio. When a physician moves from one state to another a new license is required. Generally, a new license can be obtained through a process of reciprocity, with the new state accepting the license from the state from which one moves, as long as it is active and in good standing. I was told that the reciprocation process might take one year. California physicians coming to Ohio were not licensed quickly. California did not accept reciprocity for licensing from any state, but if you had passed national boards and applied within five years of finishing residency, California would accept you for direct licensing. They required anyone coming from another state using the reciprocity mechanism to take a written and oral examination. These exams were quite difficult for anyone who had been out of medical school for as long as ten years, and only a few passed the exam.

It was for that reason that most states either did not grant reciprocity on the basis of a California license, or they gave people an extremely hard time and required a long wait before approving them. I was then asked if I had a license in another state. I remembered that after my graduation from medical school I had acquired an Alabama license. It had been inactive for more than twenty years. I was advised to activate it and use it to ask for reciprocity. I had to write a letter to the licensing board in Alabama and pay twenty-six years' worth of back fees, which amounted to only $165. I did so, and in about three weeks I received a license to practice in Ohio.

My first patient encounter occurred when Joe Fischer called one late snowy afternoon to ask me to see a patient on whom he had done a thyroidectomy, and who was now having some problems with abnormal heart rhythms in the postop recovery room of University Hospital. My offices were located in a different building, so I had to struggle through the snow to reach the medical sciences building, which then connected directly with the University Hospital. The connections were through a complicated network of underground tunnels. I was not aware of the various side tunnels.

I began my trek over to University Hospital after dark, and found the tunnels poorly lighted and strewn with trash. Right then I made a decision to have them cleaned up as quickly as I could. But that night, as I wandered through the tunnels I lost my bearings, and it took me more than thirty minutes to find my way up into University Hospital, where I had trouble finding the postop recovery room. Better signage also found its way to the top of my list.

I finally found the patient, treated her abnormal heart rhythm successfully, and over the next sixteen years, this patient came to see me in the outpatient clinic and went through a whole host of medical procedures, including a knee replacement, a hysterectomy, and several major abdominal operations. She became my first patient and my patient of longest standing at the university. I continued to practice actively for all my seventeen years, seeing new patients and continuing to see patients who followed me from my Stanford practice. Many of these early challenges helped me to develop the skills to push for further reforms in the medical center. Furthermore, my successes gave me renewed courage to tackle even more difficult problems.

Chapter Forty-six

LAURA ADAPTS

I spent a great deal of my time with university and medical center activities when we moved to Cincinnati. Unfortunately, I had to leave Laura to make her own life in our new home city, which she did, after a rocky start.

Initially, both of us were extremely excited about the move, but became sad as we left California and our home of twenty-two years, watching all of our belongings being loaded into a large moving van. When we arrived in Cincinnati, our home at Seven Knolls was not available for occupancy, so for ten days Laura and I lived in a one-room apartment at the Vernon Manor Hotel near the university.

She was alone much of the time, as I left each day before daylight and returned well after dark. Frequently she said, "Will this job always take all of your time?" Finally, after twelve long days for Laura, we moved into our home in one weekend. Although we had labeled all of the boxes as they were being packed, we found our directions had not been followed by the packers, and everything, including soiled dishcloths and the trash, were loaded in some of the boxes. In our previous moves, we had not accumulated so many things. We did manage to quickly identify where the furniture would go in the new house, and our movers were very cooperative.

During our first week in the house, there was a violent rainstorm. Clogged drainspouts overflowed, and water poured into our basement. We were quite distressed, but soon found that the drainage system, which was built into the house sixty-two years earlier, drained the water away and there was no real damage or problem. During our third week in Cincinnati, Laura became quite ill. She was alone while trying to assemble the house and developed a severe upper respiratory infection. The days were gray, and I continued to leave before daylight and return well after dark. The grayness together with the problems created by the rain made it most unpleasant, and one dreadful evening she said to me, "I wish we had never moved here, and that you had never brought me to this place."

She was so ill during this period that I went out alone and bought a Christmas tree, something we had always enjoyed doing together. When our son-in-law, David Marks, arrived just prior to Christmas, his helpful hand and cheerful spirit were welcome. Laura's mood changed. From that point forward, she has almost always been quite positive about our move to Cincinnati. She immersed herself in developing lasting friendships and relationships.

We wanted to find a church compatible with both our needs, and after visiting several and finally settled on the Indian Hill Church, which is a combined church of the Episcopal and Presbyterian denominations. There is both an Episcopal rector and a Presbyterian minister. The services alternate, but each minister may lead several services before the change occurs. This was an "open door" for Laura, and she became very involved in activities in the church. She introduced the small group suppers concept, which had been part of our church activities in Los Altos, with eight individuals meeting in the home of one that is designated for each of four meetings during a four-month period. These are organized potluck dinners and a time for fellowship and getting to know other church members. This program continues with Laura's guidance, and is very popular with some members.

Laura soon became an elder in the Presbyterian Church and took the training course for the Stephen Ministry, after which she adopted the family of an abused woman with four young children. She has mentored this family over a period of more than a decade. She also served on the Episcopalian search committee for a new rector for our church, and continues to be actively involved in the outreach programs of the church. The combined denominations provide a unique ecumenical experience, which we both cherish. Laura has more acceptance of standard Christian doctrine than I, so the combined doctrines provide outlets for both of us. This church was formed as a combined congregation more than fifty years ago, and even though there have been some problems, there is no thought of separating.

One problem did occur in 1999 when the Presbyterian minister retired and the Episcopal rector was forced out.

One problem did occur in 1999, when the Presbyterian minister retired and the Episcopal rector was forced out. I was selected to be on a combined search committee, and we met weekly for over a year. We finally selected and recruited a rector, Pat Merchant, and a Presbyterian minister. They were not compatible from the start. After a year, the Presbyterian minister resigned. Pat Merchant has recently resigned as rector and a new search is underway. The church had a period of turmoil, and I was delighted not to be on the subsequent search committee to select a new Presbyterian minister. After a year-long healing process with an outstanding interim Presbyterian pastor, a great choice was made and successfully called. David Hawley has been widely accepted and has already shown the leadership necessary to help heal any remaining scars.

Through the church, Laura was also introduced to the Inter Parish Ministry, which is an organization serving people in need in eastern Hamilton County and Clermont County, to help them reach self-sufficiency. She has served as a member of the board, representing Indian Hill Church, for nine years. The number of needy in this community has waxed and waned with the employment cycles, and Laura has budgeted her time with the current increased need. Indian Hill Church is one of the largest supporters of Inter Parish Ministry.

In addition to her church activities, she became a board member of the Indian Hill Historical Society, and was soon elected to the position of vice president. She has continued to be active in this organization, and every year is responsible for one or two of its major programs. The historical society is devoted to preserving the history of the "village," which is the designation for our town. The society has published a number of books, and in one, Seven Knolls is designated as one of the fifty historic homes in the village. The book describes the homes, their architecture, and history.

She also joined a garden club known as the Dirt Daubers, and through this has developed many friends in Indian Hill and surrounding communities. Because of her own recovery from breast cancer, she has served as a member of Reach for Recovery, visiting patients with breast cancer after their therapy. More recently, she joined a P.E.O. chapter, an international organization providing educational opportunities for women, of which there are several chapters in Cincinnati and she has acquired many new sisters. Through this organization, she continues to expand her circle of friendship with other women throughout the area and other regions.

Laura has also been very interested in our philanthropic activities, and through our establishment of a charitable lead trust, she has worked with the funding agency, the Greater Cincinnati Foundation, to see that our charitable contributions are made to our chosen arts organizations, including the Cincinnati Art Museum, the Cincinnati Symphony, the university's College-Conservatory of Music, and the Playhouse in the Park. All of these roles in our general area have provided an opportunity for Laura to be involved in the life of this community in a most meaningful way, in addition to her activities supporting my career role at the university medical center. She frequently hosts luncheons and dinner parties at our house, and we attend many university functions together.

While we were settling into life in Cincinnati, Laura sought roles in other areas of philanthropy. In 1997, Laura was invited to join the President's Cabinet, an advisory board to the president of her college, which had changed names from Florence State Teachers' College to the University of North Alabama (UNA). The college is located in Florence, Alabama, in the northwest corner of the state, and since her graduation has grown to enroll about 7,000 students. The president's advisory board meets twice a year, and at one of the meetings, Dan Howard, the senior vice president for administration and development, presented Laura with several opportunities to make a contribution for the renovation of the college campus, based on plans developed by the Olmsted Company that designed

Central Park in New York. In 1999, we decided to support the development of a plaza and fountain to be located at the focal point of two new major walking streets, which were to be developed from streets that previously had auto traffic and parking. The funds to develop the latter were to come from the federal government, and we offered to provide the funds to build the fountain and plaza. It was to be named for Laura, and would have a garden area and a plaque explaining her reasons for the gift. Laura's primary reason for making the gift

THE FOUNTAIN AT THE UNIVERSITY OF NORTH ALABAMA.

was to encourage more students to choose UNA for their education, and to enjoy a much more beautiful and friendly campus. The presence of the new campus would inspire more students to seek a higher education in a better environment for teaching and learning. We approved the plans and the project began. Once it was underway, we were again approached by President Potts of the university and Dan Howard about creating a gateway from the town of Florence to the plaza and fountain. These plans were quite exciting, and we agreed.

The gateway is known as the Harrison Gate to the university, and represents a major access to the town of Florence. In order to fully understand our commitments to the UNA, I need to describe Dan Howard, one of the most enthusiastic persons we have encountered. He not only relentlessly sought federal funding, but our support as well. Once we agreed, he personally oversaw every aspect of this program. He went to Italy to see the fountain limestone being quarried, the fountain components carved, and oversaw its installation, and every detail of the dedication. During its installation,

UNA'S FOUNTAIN, A CLOSER VIEW.

we obtained a photograph of him standing atop the completed project with his arms outstretched.

Without Dan's total dedication it is doubtful this project could have been completed in the two-year period. In October 2002, our children and grandchildren joined us in Florence to attend the dedication ceremony. It was also attended by some of Laura's classmates from college, and a number of her Alabama relatives. The dedication of the fountain was the highlight of a two-day celebration. Over the past six years, the gardens around the Laura M. Harrison Plaza have matured nicely, and many couples choose to have their wedding photos taken there.

Laura is now "at home" in Cincinnati, and cherishes her involvement with these many organizations. She has many friends and has participated in a great variety of activities, both civic and altruistic. In many instances, she has introduced me to community leaders that have been beneficial to my career through her contacts with their wives and her contacts in the associations where she has participated. We have always worked as a team—utilizing each of our best capabilities. There could be no better partner, wife, lover, and supporter for me than Laura.

Chapter Forty-seven

HOLY GRAIL

One of my major objectives was to enhance the national reputation of the medical center by building a much stronger research program. Research accomplishment is the measure of academic centers and compares with reaching for a golden ring.

After examining the research activities in Cincinnati, I soon saw a clear need to stimulate research and its funding. This was a primary focus of our planning process during that first year. Our plan, "Reaching For the 21st Century," contained a platform for encouraging research, and earmarking funds for it. Our initiatives focused on specific areas where Cincinnati investigators possess research strength or potential to become nationally competitive.

As this plan unfolded, John Hutton, as dean, established incentives to apply for major research funding for the faculty in the college of medicine. The four areas that we chose as having base research strength or potential were cardiovascular disease, cancer, neuroscience, and perinatology and early child development. Our intent was to divert new funding into these areas, with the hope that our programs would become nationally recognized. For a medical center to achieve national recognition, the level of research funding is the most important parameter. The quality of the faculty is closely coupled with the ability to compete for peer-judged research funds.

ALBERT VONTZ MOLECULAR STUDIES BUILDING, I.E., THE GEHRY BUILDING.

One of the early successes that earned us national recognition was our successful entry into a national competition. We applied for monies from the National Heart, Lung, and Blood Institute for a program designed to train young investigators in biomedical science and career development in the cardiovascular area. In July 1993, we competed with thirty-five other institutions nationally for a seven-year program. I had been told we had a strong application by Claude Lenfant, the director of the National Heart, Lung, and Blood Institute, and due to my cardiology background, the reviewing committee believed I could successfully develop this program in Cincinnati, as I had at Stanford.

After a reverse site visit at the NIH in Bethesda, Maryland, we were selected as one of two winners, to the surprise of almost everyone in the country. The reverse site visit permitted us to present our program in face-to-face meetings with the approving committees. Site visits are generally held at the institution making a grant request, with visits by experts to judge the merits of an application. For a reverse site visit, the investigators from the institution go to a central location, such as the NIH, to meet with the reviewer. Few in the academic community believed that we could successfully compete with Harvard, Johns Hopkins, Baylor, Duke, and Stanford, but the reviewer believed we had the potential. The only other institution selected was a combination of the Massachusetts General Hospital with the Massachusetts Institute of Technology. I had many calls from my cardiovascular colleagues around the country, asking how we managed to be selected and congratulating us on our success. They were surprised, since at that time our total research funding for the medical center was only about $60 million.

They were surprised since at that time our total research funding for the medical center was only about $60 million.

Space is one of the important components to building research. The general concept is that research laboratories are to the investigators as stadiums are to professional sports teams. At Stanford, I had learned that acquiring space was one of the most difficult challenges for a leader in an academic medical center. Space was at a premium at Stanford, with a continuous struggle among investigators to acquire more space for their research programs. My initial assessment at Cincinnati was that we had enough space, but it was poorly used. Space was often assigned to investigators who had no current research funding. I also learned that to recruit researchers to Cincinnati, a late entry into the research arena, it would be necessary to provide more space than was required at Stanford. We had grand plans to grow, and therefore, needed to build more research space. To have a championship research program, one must create the appropriate research space, and that became a major challenge for me and my team.

In a state school such as the University of Cincinnati, the Ohio Board of Regents controls the funding to build new academic and research space. When I arrived in Cincinnati, the board of regents had never approved the building of research space at any of its institutions. Over a period of four years, I made several presentations in order to convince them that the quality of their academic programs would be enhanced if they supported the building of new research space.

This would enhance our ability to recruit well-known and respected researchers who would successfully compete nationally for funding. My presentations finally had their desired effect, and over the period of a decade, we managed to build three new research buildings for the medical center with state funds, and Children's Hospital built two research buildings utilizing private funds. These new buildings provided space for the growth of our programs and our new recruits.

The appropriate use of research space is also a matter of concern in a medical center. Investigators who are no longer able to generate research funding frequently want to hold their space, and since they have tenure, they are allowed to do so. I knew this had to change, and anticipated a battle. One of my and dean John Hutton's early goals at the University of Cincinnati Medical Center was to create a space committee and to convince that committee that all space should be controlled centrally.

Research space could then be allocated to researchers successful in acquiring external support and dollars for their work. This committee worked diligently over a three-year period and created a space formula. This long time frame for reaching a conclusion and presenting a plan illustrates how difficult the problem was in the minds of the faculty. This formula allotted a defined amount of space for a graduate student, for a postdoctoral fellow, for research technicians, and initially required $200 of research funding for each square foot of research space allocated. Over the past decade, this requirement has grown to $350 per square foot of research space. While this does not quite equal the formula at Stanford, where each square foot of research space probably accounts for more than $700 of external research funding, the formula has been widely accepted and is applied on a department basis rather than an individual basis.

Each department chair is responsible for allocating the research space for that specific department. Any change in the space assignment must be defended before a highly qualified committee of the faculty in charge of space allocation. The mechanism that we developed to control and reallocate space was an important step forward in effectively utilizing space at the University of Cincinnati Medical Center. Our formula for space assignment has been adopted in modified form by other medical centers.

As the field of life science research was expanding during the 1980s and '90s, John

Hutton and I recognized that many researchers used some of the same technologies as the basis for their research efforts. It seemed to us that creating a core research facility that U.C. investigators would be allowed to utilize would encourage much collaboration, and would likely result in increased funding success.

Transgenic technology was the first core technology we identified and committed to make an investment in. The mouse was used as a model. It was well known that mouse genes are closely related to human ones, and that abnormal human genes could be transferred into the mouse genome, which would then develop the abnormality similar to the human condition. It was also possible that certain genes known to be important in the development of certain organs or functions within the mouse could be "knocked out," and a mouse model of a disease created.

These models became important for studying therapy or disease mechanisms. Thus, in 1991, we created a core program for creating mouse models of human disease. Over the next twelve years, several dozen research grants at our institution were based on this technology. We were so successful in developing mouse models of cardiovascular disease that these have been sold world-wide to other research institutions. It might sound unreal but we now have more than 50,000 transgenic mice in our facilities within the medical center. The maintenance of a transgenic mouse facility is costly, and requires strict control. One must dress in a space-like suit to enter the facility, in order to avoid infection. This is to prevent the colonies of mice from becoming exposed to bacteria or viruses and possible infection. Clearly, those spooked by mice should not enter. This core technology has proven to be successful in attracting major research funding to Cincinnati.

Other such core technologies involve the $15 million we spent together with Children's Hospital creating a Center for Bioinformatics. Bioinformatics is the computer-based program that allows investigators to access the databases containing the sequences in the human genome and other gene-based data catalogues. Now over 200 investigators use this for their gene-based research. We also established a proteomics core, and several dozen investigators use this.

Proteomics is a study of the products such as enzymes, cell promoters, and hormones, synthesized at the direction of genes. These products will be targets for drug development in the next few decades. Our policy of building new research facilities, developing core labs to be used by a large number of investigators, and selectively choosing areas for additional funding where we have strength or potential strength allowed us to rapidly develop the research potential of the institution. We increased the externally funded research from $30 million upon my arrival to more than $260 million in the year I stepped down.

Faculty in the colleges need to feel that the university leadership supports and appreciates their efforts. In order to encourage and stimulate investigators and to reward top investigators, I developed a "Grants Party" for this special recognition. The first year for this event, which was held at my house with a dinner, planned wine tastings, and a short speech to thank the investigators, occurred in 1990. In California, we had always used our house for entertaining visiting guests, and as a place for celebrations and parties for my staff and my postdoctoral fellows, and we continued that tradition at Cincinnati. The house we purchased was just what we needed for the Grants Party and many other receptions and parties that we've held at Seven Knolls.

At our first Grants Party in 1990, we required a total grant holding by an investigator to be $150,000 per year to be invited to attend the Grants Party. We had about thirty-five investigators attend that year. The party was widely accepted as an occasion to honor research success. We held this party continuously for twelve years, and it created considerable enthusiasm among our investigators. In 2002, the last year that I held this event at my house, we recognized and honored more than 120 investigators with grant holdings over a level of $300,000 per year. This party was highly regarded by the investigators, and in years when the grant-holding level to qualify increased, people who missed by a few thousand dollars called and almost begged to attend.

Each September, we erected a large tent over the terrace to host the party. It was interesting to note that the annual party encouraged investigators to increase their research activities and apply for more than one grant to reach the year's required funding level. And, many of them were quite successful in doing so. From the beginning, the Grants Party turned out to be a stimulus for investigators to apply for and be successful in obtaining more external funding for their research.

The comments that I heard frequently from those who attended were, "This is the first time the university has recognized our important contribution to the colleges and to the medical center," and, "…we really appreciate what you are doing, and sharing your home with us for our Grants Party is a highlight of the year." Laura and I enjoyed meeting all of the investigators, many of whom we do not have regular contact with throughout the year. I always kept my formal remarks short, but clearly expressed thanks to all of those who were participating in making the research efforts of the medical center successful.

In addition to acquiring research space and grants, it is necessary to develop a plan to recruit and retain high-quality investigators. We wanted to focus the university's research in a few areas of strength, and to reward those who were successful in their research applications. During my tenure at Cincinnati we applied all these principles successfully. One of the hard lessons I learned was how difficult it was to recruit top-notch researchers from either the East or West Coast. On occasion, when we recruited and developed highly funded investigators, it was difficult to retain them. They were being attracted to and sought after by more renowned institutions. In order to compete, we had to provide more high-quality research space and compensation equal to that of the more desirable East and West Coast institutions. The advantage that we stressed was the much higher standard of living that the salary could support in our midwestern city. We understood, even so, researchers on the East and West Coasts had advantages over those in the Midwest.

An example of this bias for the coasts is how difficult it was to get members of our faculty inducted into some of the honor organizations for medical research. At Stanford, I had been accepted into the American Society for Clinical Investigation and the American Association of Physicians on my first application. However, in many instances, when I was recommending candidates from the University of Cincinnati faculty for admission to these organizations, I found that it was necessary for them to wait two or three years and to require upwards of twenty recommendation letters from peer investigators. The majority of the members of these organizations come from elite East and West Coast institutions. They are on the committees that choose and elect members, and thus we had an uphill fight to have our researchers accepted into these organizations.

John Hutton and I made a concentrated effort to nominate highly qualified faculty. We selected outstanding candidates, we recruited individuals from our old institutions of Stanford and Harvard to support these individuals, and we wrote many letters to others to get support for our candidates. I remember a specific instance of trying to get one of our outstanding cardiovascular researchers chosen to be in the American Association of Physicians. He was nationally recognized, was the principal investigator of our Centers of Excellence in heart failure research by the National Heart, Lung, and Blood Institute, and was publishing papers in many of the best journals in the country. I made a concerted effort for three years to write letters of support and to recruit people from outside the institution to support this individual. All of this came to no avail, and in this instance we failed.

In other situations, John Hutton succeeded in gaining national letter-writing support for our candidates and subsequently, many of our nominees were elected to membership in the American Society for Clinical Investigation. We were less successful with other organizations, but continued to try.

One of the most important activities of a senior vice president and provost in a medical center is the recruitment of talented colleagues. During my tenure at Cincinnati, this meant the recruitment of deans for each of the university's health colleges.

Upon assuming my job in 1986, it became clear to me that the colleague I most needed was a dean for the college of medicine. Since I knew many nationally recognized academic physicians, I made a strong effort to choose a nationally well-known person for this job. I went against all precedent at the university and decided to chair the search committee myself.

I chose John Hutton to be dean, and had to sell this to the search committee. He was not the choice of U.C. president Joe Steger or Norm Baker, the provost for the west campus, who was responsible for all colleges other than the health care group, but they acquiesced to my decision. The west campus was situated about a half mile west of the medical center campus, and housed all of Baker's colleges.

Steger told me, "He is your choice. You will have to make up for him in community appearances. Go ahead. Good luck." John Hutton became the most outstanding appointment of my tenure at Cincinnati. We became great colleagues, and almost always agreed on a direction for the campus development. He worked closely with the students and dealt with the multiple faculty and faculty issues on a day-to-day basis. I became more of the strategic planner, and he was the spark plug for getting things done.

We had an excellent fifteen years working together, longer than any other two individuals leading a medical center in the country during this period. We both had extensive networks within the national medical community that we could use to recruit. In addition, we had a common vision on where research in health care should be directed, and we shared the vision of making the medical college more prominent nationally. Most dean of medicine appointments last four to five years, but John was successful for all of his fifteen years.

About five years after my arrival, we needed to recruit a dean for the college of nursing. When the sitting dean reached the end of her contract period, Mary Jane Jesse, my associate provost, led that search. After considerable review of candidates on a national scale, we chose Andrea Lindell to lead the nursing college. Although she came from a nursing college that was not associated with an academic medical center, I was convinced she had leadership potential based on the success she had creating an outstanding nursing college in Oakland,

Michigan. I was right. Lindell was not the stereotype of a dean for a college of nursing. She was totally dedicated to creating an outstanding program. Many nursing-dean candidates were more interested in maintaining the status quo than in developing new quality standards for their educational programs. Andrea is tall, speaks with a commanding voice, and was always positive in her approach. She was an imposing figure in the university's Council of Deans, where she persisted in demanding excellence. She speaks slowly, and in a well-organized manner.

The nursing college needed substantive leadership change and program development. It also needed innovative new programs. Andrea Lindell initiated a Ph.D. program and acquired the nurse anesthetists' program from the department of anesthesiology in the college of medicine. These programs brought new students and allowed her to appoint several highly talented new faculty. She has led this nursing college to increase its research base, and certainly to improve its national reputation. She was the national chair of the board of the Deans of Colleges of Nursing, and achieved national prominence.

There are hundreds of nominees for the Florence Nightingale Awards. Only a few can be selected...

Dean Lindell had an occasion to meet the grandniece of Florence Nightingale on one of her trips to Australia. She brought her to Cincinnati for a visit, and convinced her to support the college. This stimulated the development of an annual Florence Nightingale Dinner to honor outstanding nurses in Greater Cincinnati. There are hundreds of nominees for the Florence Nightingale Awards, and while only a few can be selected, the stories about their dedication to and care of their patients brings a deep appreciation for what nurses really do in our health system. One poignant story I remember is of a nurse who cared for a patient badly injured from an auto accident, and who was extremely limited when discharged to home, where she had six young children.

The nurse from the intensive care unit went to her home daily for three months to care for the patient and her children, without any compensation. The reward for the winner is $1,000, but figuratively more important is a bronze bust of Florence Nightingale, which was cast for the college. I was given one on my retirement, which I cherish and display in a prominent position.

At about seven years into my tenure, I recruited a new dean for the college of pharmacy. Dan Acosta came from the University of Texas, where he was a division head in the college of pharmacy. Dan was a native of Texas, and spoke "Texas talk." He had a unique aptitude for spotting and seizing opportunities to create new programs. He had an excellent academic background, and has raised the standards in the college of pharmacy by recruiting individuals with research experience.

The national trend in pharmacy is to move from undergraduate programs to Pharm. D. programs. This is a professional degree, and allows these pharmacists to take a large role in helping patients with medical programs. Dan Acosta converted the college programs to the Pharm.D. by expanding class size and adding new faculty. This new program required an extra year of education, but met the present need for new pharmacists. I insisted that his faculty recruits have research interests that can ally them with researchers in the college of medicine, so they can be part of the Centers of Excellence for the medical center. This has proven to be quite successful for the college in that several new faculty members were successful in joining active research teams and obtaining their own peer-approved funding.

More recently, we formed a college of allied health sciences. Andrea Lindell was the driving force who accomplished what I had wanted to do for years. She served as the arm to make it happen. For many years, I wanted the many disparate programs in the health care professions, which were scattered throughout the university, to be brought together into a college. First, I brought some of them together in the Center for Allied Health Sciences and then, over the objection of the faculty senate, created a new college of allied health sciences with a new dean. This process took almost seven years to accomplish. I recruited Elizabeth King as dean in 1999 to lead this college, and it is off to a good start. The college is comprised of physical therapy, occupational therapy, radiologic technology, dental hygiene, ultrasound technology, and other health-related disciplines.

At the University of Cincinnati, the recruitment of deans requires following a very complex course outlined in the union contract of the faculty and within the rules of the university. It requires a search committee, and its membership make-up is defined in the contract. These committees are frequently comprised of people with diverse points of view, and it is difficult to coerce them into action.

However, it is the way in which department heads and deans must be recruited in this institution. When they were carefully selected, these committees carried out their recruiting successfully, following my requirements. Over the years, I learned that first you identify and recruit the brightest people; second, you check carefully on their ability to be team players; and third, you recruit people brighter and smarter than yourself. This was my way to build a talent pool and to appoint committees to do so. Many recruits to the colleges in the medical center met these requisite criteria during my tenure.

Chapter Forty-Nine

THE HASSLE

*All my previous career appointments were at private institutions, and
I soon found that I had a poor understanding of the role politics would play
in my developmental programs at the University of Cincinnati.*

Early in my tenure, I discovered that the city had previously owned University Hospital and it was then known as the Cincinnati General Hospital for over a hundred years. It had become a State of Ohio facility in the late 1970s, when the transfer of Cincinnati General to operations under the umbrella of the State of Ohio was necessary because the city could no longer fund the programs and facilities of an academic hospital. There had always been tremendous pride in Cincinnati for supporting its city university and the city hospital that served mainly an indigent population.

Many of Cincinnati's citizens did not favor the transfer to the State of Ohio and withdrew their private philanthropic support, which had helped maintain the facilities even when the city was unable to do so. This animosity among the citizenship took more than twenty years to heal. I have talked with many older citizens who had in the distant past been loyal supporters of the old hospital, who withdrew their support for twenty years after its transfer to the state.

A new hospital had been built with state funds in the mid-1970s, and the state government became the owner of the hospital. However, the city still owned the land on which the hospital resides and many of the long-term employees at University Hospital, former employees of the city, were still on a retirement program managed by the city. These newer arrangements created a maize through which one had to go in order to try and change any of the relationships.

After the new hospital was built, it was considered necessary to rename it, from the "old Cincinnati General," as everyone knew it, to "University Hospital." This occurred in 1980, although by common use, many still referred to it as "old General." With the name change, the hospital began to serve the entire medical community, rather than only the indigent, whch was its previous focus.

In addition, I was soon to learn that the indigent care in the University Hospital was supported by a property tax levy from Hamilton County. This system of support was unique in the United States when it was instituted in 1966. It still seemed like a novel idea to me when I arrived, as it was very helpful for the finances of the University Hospital to have at least a major part of its indigent care covered by public funds. Very few other municipal hospitals had this type of safety-net funding. There were restrictions on patients' qualifying, but in general, anyone living in Hamilton County could qualify if they fell below the poverty line, as defined by federal standards.

The tax levy had to be passed with a voter referendum every five years, and the hospital was already preparing for the five-year levy vote when I arrived. Having never been involved in a political campaign of this type, I learned a lot as we worked to pass that levy. I spent a great deal of time chairing a committee totally dedicated to passing the levy. We recruited two outstanding leaders from the business community who were recognized as supporters to chair a levy support committee. Perhaps most important, I learned that we could not use any public funds to support the tax levy campaign, and with the result that I had to solicit the business community for over $100,000 for this effort. I also learned that we needed to turn our entire employee base into ambassadors who would speak in favor of the tax levy in order to protect their jobs, and into grass-roots workers who would distribute yard signs to support the levy vote.

> *The expense for their care was a write-off at the University Hospital and became an increasing financial burden.*

We passed this tax levy in 1991, 1996, and 2001, with almost 60 percent approval. However, with each passing levy, it became more difficult to negotiate the contract for care of the indigent with the Hamilton County Commissioners, who had control of the hospital levy funds, as they adopted managed care reimbursements for their payment schedules. This program reduced reimbursement for many procedures and hospitalizations. Still, the levy was a great resource for the University Hospital programs, since most care of indigents from Hamilton County had reimbursement. Patients from other, surrounding counties who could not pay also usually came to University Hospital.

The expense for their care was a write-off at the University Hospital, and became an increasing financial burden. My relationship with the political leaders in Hamilton County was mostly cordial. I met with the county administrator regularly. When the county commissioners had difficulty with the Drake Hospital because of the actions of a serial killer and the ensuing lack of public support, I negotiated with the commissioners for the university to take over Drake. The serial killer admitted to killing several dozen patients over the period of two years without being detected. This was a "hot potato" for the commissioners, and the county residents blamed them for not overseeing the hospital administration.

It was a terrible scandal, with much national attention, and it put me in a good bargaining position to get support for a takeover of Drake Hospital. This also involved passing a new tax levy of a much greater magnitude than the one that had previously been supporting Drake. This was necessary in order to develop the funds to rebuild the hospital into a major regional rehabilitation center. The hospital was of the 1920s vintage, and needed to be completely rebuilt.

The campaign for the levy came with strong support from the county administration, and I have a vivid memory of an election night when the Drake Hospital tax levy was on the ballot. We held a vigil at county election headquarters, watching the results of the election. We watched with anxiety as the returns came. If we did not pass the levy, we would have no way to support the health care for the uninsured at Drake, and the university would not take over Drake Hospital. The lessons I learned about passing levies proved to be extremely important. We had recruited community leaders as co-chairs, who spoke out forcefully for the levy. They wrote op-ed editorials and made public appearances. Even more important, the employees became strong advocates.

Once we knew we had a majority vote for the Drake levy, we went off to a local restaurant for a celebratory dinner—at our personal expense—and we broke open a bottle of champagne. I had never participated in a political campaign of this type before, and was excited about the outcome. The campaign allowed the completion of the Drake transfer, and we considered it a great victory for the residents of the area who would come to need the services of the hospital.

The new Drake Hospital was built after I hired Earl Gilreath as director. Earl had long been a hospital director at several hospitals in Greater Cincinnati for twenty years. He was known as stubborn and uncontrollable but also as a tough detail-oriented manager. A gaunt man with a square jaw and receding hairline, he spoke rapidly and with force. His demeanor belied his past and impending success.

The rebuilding took place over a period of four years, and Gilreath looked after every brick that was placed. He was a hands-on manager who frequently visited the hospital in the early morning, often as early as 4 a.m., to be sure the hospital was functioning efficiently. He also checked out how his employees were working. Since he reported to me, we met frequently and his message to me was, "You have to always be watching over your shoulder—someone is trying to take away your opportunity." He certainly practiced this approach. Gilreath was intense, and frequently challenged me on my decisions for Drake. Sometimes he could be even more challenging than some of the department chairs in the medical college. We met weekly and had hardnosed discussions, but after we hammered out agreements, he followed through with implementation. After Drake was rebuilt, he challenged Drake's working relationship with the university and the county commissioners, and I felt he had to be replaced. I admired his will and continued to see him, although he had no further hospital affiliations. Later he managed a popular flea market in Kentucky. Drake continued to develop as a rehabilitation hospital and assisted-living facility under the able leadership of Bobbie Bradford, whom I hired in 1998. The county wanted to jettison the hospital in 2005 and after a protracted series of negotiations succeeded in selling it to the Health Alliance in 2006. Karen Bankston, a former member of my staff at University Hospital, was appointed administrator.

In the 1940s and 1950s, Drake Hospital had been closely allied with the college of medicine, with the staff appointed from the college. Its programs were separated from the university in the 1950s. We reunited Drake with the health colleges of the medical center and added major programs in medicine, nursing, and pharmacy as part of their health care delivery and training programs for the colleges at Drake. Drake became a nationally recognized rehabilitation center, and now almost anyone I see who has had a stroke or is in need of major rehabilitation, wants to be at Drake. I have the same feeling. If I need its rehabilitation services, I want to go there.

As Drake became more recognized, there were increasing visits by members of the political community. I distinctly remember one occasion in 1991, when president George Bush was visiting Cincinnati. I received a call from the U.S. Secret Service at 2 a.m. at home saying that President Bush wished to visit a patient at Drake Hospital, and we needed to be prepared. This young man, whom Bush was visiting, was a top student at Hughes High School, and he had been in Cincinnati six months earlier. The young man had been shot in the neck soon thereafter, and was a paraplegic now at Drake Hospital. Earl Gilreath, the director of the hospital, and Joseph Steger, president of the university and chair of the board of the Drake Hospital, were both out of town, and since I was the next senior person responsible for Drake Hospital, the call came to me. I arose, went to Drake, and started meeting with the staff to plan the president's visit for 10 a.m. the next morning. Arrangements were made by the Secret Service for intense security, and as planned, the president arrived at 10 a.m. He visited with the young man to express his sympathy. I accompanied President Bush through the hospital.

To the dismay of the Secret Service, the president chose to go elsewhere in the hospital and visit with other patients. He shook their hands and asked about their medical conditions. He seemed genuinely interested in how Drake Hospital was working with them on their rehabilitation. During this time I had an opportunity to chat with him about the health care system of the country. He asked many interesting questions about rehabilitation and about the prevention of the kind of horrible events such as the one this young bright student had encountered.

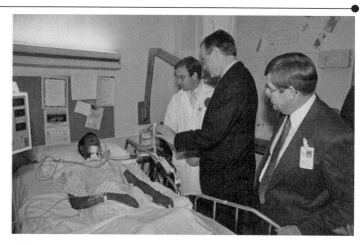

AT THE DRAKE HOSPITAL WITH PRESIDENT BUSH, SR.

The entire staff of Drake Hospital was most appreciative of the president's visit. Many of them had an opportunity to shake his hand and have a photograph taken with him. This event was one of the publicized highlights of that year in the annual report of Drake Hospital. Drake has continued to be a great force in the community, and in 2000, the hospital created an annual distinguished supporter award for someone who has made a significant contribution to it. I was fortunate and proud to be chosen for the award in 2003, the third year after its initiation. I felt honored for all my activities in the establishment of the "new Drake."

Since University Hospital is the primary care site for the indigent patients of Cincinnati, I frequently had to work with the elected officials of the city. Dealing with the city officials was always difficult for me, and quite different from my relations with the county commissioners. Early in my tenure, I met on frequent occasions with the incumbent city manager and each succeeding city manager on frequent occasions, to discuss the relations between the medical center and the city. We were involved with providing some medical services at the numerous city clinics and had a reasonable working relationship with the city's health commissioner. The medical center also expanded its role of providing specialty medical services for the city's six health clinics.

However, I found it almost impossible to plan the medical center's growth within the city. The major street providing access to the medical center, Martin Luther King Boulevard, needed widening because traffic in and out of the medical center had become terribly congested. Creating new access was necessary, and over my strong protestations, the university was required to provide the funds to pay for the plans and traffic-flow survey. I managed this with hospital funds. Later the city did carry out the widening and improvement of this major traffic bottleneck, and it greatly aided the growth of the medical center.

I have always wondered what made the city agree to our request, since in many other instances they seemed to have little awareness of the importance of the medical center in the Cincinnati "uptown" development, as the area was called, in contrast with their efforts in the downtown and riverfront development. This disregard by the city was also for the university and the hospitals. This was particularly difficult to understand, since the number of employees working in the medical center exceeded that of any other employer in the region. I have always believed that they responded to our needs only because of pressure brought to them by the community councils of individuals living in proximity to Martin Luther King Boulevard, rather than because of anything we did.

The board of trustees of the university was extremely supportive of the Martin Luther King Boulevard improvement effort, and also helped to bring pressure to bear on the city in another initiative. I tried for ten years to get support from the board of trustees and the city for creating an entrance and exit to nearby Interstate 71 off Martin Luther King Boulevard, a main artery running east and west through the city and through both the East and West Campuses of the university.

The board supported it, but the city has to this day resisted this effort, even though I pointed out that having all of the cars pouring out of the medical center through Corryville, an uptown residential neighborhood, might well result in a child's death or major injury. Almost all of the 13,000 employees of the medical center have to drive thorough this neighborhood of Cincinnati known as Corryville twice daily to reach the freeway south or north, and it creates traffic nightmares and danger to citizens. I had no luck with the city.

Another instance of the intransigency of the city occurred over acquisition of property needed to build the new molecular sciences building and the Kingsgate Conference Center and Hotel. We had purchased privately the thirty-six small and run-down homes occupying the space we needed for this expansion, utilizing a privately created corporation. This area was referred to as Tobacco Row, and was almost a slum. We worked in close collaboration with the Corryville Community Council in acquiring the property and developed a program to help relocate displaced residents.

The additional property needed for our expansion was about four acres, and included a softball field and small recreation center owned by the city. The field had been assessed to have a value of $1 million. However, the city insisted on receiving $4 million, enough to build a large recreation center elsewhere in the Corryville neighborhood, which the city could not and would not do. After much haggling, we finally made a bargain with the devil, the City Council, and paid the $4 million with the prerequisite for them to build a new recreation center for the community. The saving grace for me was that now Corryville has a great recreation center and health club built with our funds, something the city would not have provided.

One of the final and largest conflicts in my relationship with the city related to the privatization of University Hospital. The city was one of the complainants in a lawsuit filed against the university and against me when privatization occurred. While the city manager was never in support of a lawsuit against the university, one of the lawyers acting as counsel for the city seemed to have a vendetta against privatization of University Hospital. I have always thought that he was heavily supported by some of the hospital-based unions.

In any case, the lawsuit was filed in 1995, and the judge in the case insisted on many private negotiations with the parties, and the lawsuit dragged on over a nine-year period, and was finally resolved in 2004. Ultimately, the city agreed to drop the suit, and because the hospital had become a Health Alliance hospital, the Health Alliance had to provide funds for the settlement as part of the agreement and take on a larger role with the city's health clinics.

At the state level, my relationship with the political systems in Ohio started early after my arrival in Cincinnati. Within the first four months of my arrival, I was asked to attend a private dinner with Democrat governor Richard Celeste. This was to celebrate his reelection to a second term. There were so few Democrats in Cincinnati that I was selected because there was a dearth of people to attend and no one knew my political affiliation. I was seated next to the governor and had a very pleasant conversation with him during dinner.

Celeste was a good conversationalist and very knowledgeable about Cincinnati. He was handsome, with graying hair and a ready smile. I enjoyed much of my conversation with him, and we both enjoyed the food and wine. At the end of the dinner, he asked me what he could do to help medical programs in the state. I suggested that he could close two medical schools, since Ohio had six medical schools and needed only four. Ohio was training twice as many physicians as it needed for replacements, and many were establishing practices elsewhere. Almost half of the students receiving medical degrees in our state schools leave to practice in other states. Often, their loyalty to their alma mater and philanthropic financial giving diminish once they leave the state. Ohio is a net exporter of doctors.

Celeste looked quite shocked as he heard my opinions. Closing medical schools has the same connotation as closing military bases. No political leader in Ohio has ever proposed to close or consolidate any of the medical schools. Every time I met Governor Celeste after this event, he looked me in the eye and said, "You are the crazy guy who suggested that I close medical schools."

Soon after that encounter, I was taken to Columbus for my introduction to state government officials by M.J. Klyn, the university's vice president for governmental affairs. M.J. was a frail woman with red hair interspersed with gray. Her appearance, however, belied her demeanor as she spoke quickly, with intensity, and with full emotion. She had been a political operative for almost forty years, and represented the University of Cincinnati as a lobbyist for twenty years. She introduced me to the legislative leaders in the House and Senate, and then suggested that we go visit with Governor Celeste. We did not have an appointment, but we burst into his outer offices and M.J. Klyn said, "Is he here?"

The staff member replied, "Yes," and she bolted past the staff member and into the governor's office and conference room, dragging me along. He looked quite surprised, but she said, "Governor Celeste, I wish to introduce our new medical leader." We had a very brief conversation, I felt a bit chagrined for bursting into his staff meeting, and we left. Before we left, Celeste remembered meeting me and said, "You must be a bit naïve, or you would not have requested that I close medical schools."

In spite of my feelings, Celeste did everything he could to keep me from feeling embarrassed. Ms. Klyn was not embarrassed at all. Over the period of several years, I met with the governor's staff, and with the Ohio Board of Regents. The regents control state funding for higher education, and most important for me, the capital appropriations for new buildings. I also testified in both the House and Senate, most recently on the tobacco fund, which was part of the national settlement, and its allocation for biomedical research and economic development. We were successful in getting 18 percent allocated to biomedical research support in Ohio.

In spite of having six medical schools, Ohio has reasonably funded the medical programs in these schools, graduating more than 1,000 students each year. I did make a proposal to the Ohio Board of Regents to merge two sets of schools and end up with four. State money could then be allocated among four institutions instead of six. This was not looked upon favorably, either, and nothing has happened.

My relationship with the federal legislators from the Cincinnati area was relatively successful because, on several occasions, we were able to acquire earmarked funds for building renovation and programs. This required numerous visits to Washington, D.C. The most memorable one occurred when we were denied a major portion of our funding, or about $22 million, over a Medicare billings issue. We chartered a private plane because we could not get on a commercial flight quickly enough, flew to Washington, and six of us met with our congressional representative, Bill Gradison, who was a senior member of the House Appropriations Committee and a health care expert. That proved very helpful. He made one call to the Health Care Administration Organization with a suggested solution, and our problem was solved.

In order to try to obtain funding from the federal government for some of our building projects, Bill Keating, a member of the university board of trustees who had been most helpful to me in privatizing University Hospital when he was chair, and I made a number of visits to Washington to enlist support for our building program. Our primary contact was Representative Rob Portman, from Ohio Congressional District Two. He and his staff had always been strongly supportive and had helped us get earmarked money on several occasions. While we were not as successful as Alabama, Texas, and Alaska, these contacts helped us fund several of our activities.

Bill Keating had been a member of the House of Representatives for two terms in the late 1970s, and was well thought of. I remember on one occasion while visiting with him, we needed to go into the chambers of the Speaker of the House for additional meetings. This is an area that is closed to the general public, and there are guards to keep people out. As we approached the door, one of the guards broke into a big smile and said, "Mr. Keating, it is great to see you. We haven't seen you in almost twenty years." Bill was cordial, and said he was glad to be back. While Bill was wearing a pin that designated him as a former member, it was quite remarkable that he was recognized by some of the guards, even after nearly two decades of absence. We were, of course, escorted into the chambers, and had a meeting with the majority leader to lay out plans for funding.

Representative Dave Hobson, the senior Republican on the House Appropriations Committee, was also extremely helpful. He brought the Ohio legislative group together and worked to sponsor programs to provide us with earmarked money for an addition to one of our medical science buildings. Previously, the Speaker of the House in the Ohio Legislature, he had all of the appearance and actions of one of the "old-time major political operatives."

I once visited him in his Springfield, Ohio, office, which was on the top floor of a two-story bank. His office had a large desk, and cabinets around the wall with many commemorative gavels that had been given to him by various well-known and important political figures. Hobson retold his favorite story, one about his father, who attended the University of Cincinnati and dropped out to participate in World War I. There was supposedly a plaque dedicated to this group of students who joined the army, and he has suggested to me on numerous occasions that we find the plaque. We have searched everywhere without success, and I even jokingly considered having a plaque manufactured, and then made to look old, hoping to get more of Dave Hobson's support for some earmarked funds.

He was supportive and helpful to Rob Portman in obtaining such funds. Visiting the Halls of Congress in Washington is a lesson in serving the public and our democracy. Hundreds of people mill about, visiting various congressional offices, all for a specific purpose, hoping to fund some local proposal. Just riding through the tunnels on the train under the Capitol and meeting a whole variety of political leaders is worth the trip. Although I encountered both failures and successes in my political agenda, I did reach an understanding of how the system works. With all its checks and balances, it is functional and I enjoyed and appreciated being part of the system for that period of time, only wishing I had accomplished more to enhance our cause.

SYSTEM RESTRUCTURING

By the early 1990s, it was clear that managed care would alter the reimbursement for medical services in hospitals. While University Hospital became more market driven and profitable during my first seven years, it was clear that the recent past was not a mirror for the future.

We needed to reexamine the role of University Hospital in the community and to develop a business model for its ongoing success. This caused me to look back historically and view the future without rose-colored glasses.

University Hospital had existed as Cincinnati General Hospital for over a hundred years before it was converted in 1976 to a true university hospital serving not only the indigent but all citizens of the area. The public was not generally aware of this change, and when I conducted a public survey in 1987, more than 20 percent of Greater Cincinnatians were still referring to it as the "old General Hospital," and believed it served only indigents. This meant that many well-insured patients would not choose to be seen at University Hospital.

Meanwhile, we continued to restructure the hospital to be more efficient, and ultimately, profitable. I also launched a media campaign to educate the public about the excellent services available at University Hospital, in an attempt to change the patient mix to include more private patients.

In addition to the media campaign, we established two new programs during my first five years that did more than anything else to raise the community interest and awareness in the medical center and hospital. First, in 1987, University Hospital Air Care was developed. This was a helicopter-based pickup of critically ill patients at other facilities and from the scene of accidents or emergency injury situations throughout the Tri-State. University Hospital's Air Care served an area within a hundred-mile radius of the hospital, and the patients were brought to University Hospital emergency room.

The television media covered many of these accidents and emergency situations so that on almost a nightly basis, University Hospital Air Care was pictured in the TV coverage of the local news. During this period air care was becoming a more widely used service for accidents in large urban areas. The sound and sight of the Air Care helicopter overhead is recognizable now by everyone in the area. This brought attention to University Hospital to the forefront, and many of the citizens recognized they might have a need for such service someday. This may have been the seminal event for its recognition as a university hospital for all patients.

After air care, we established a cardiac transplant program. Together with surgeon David Melvin, we modeled this program on the one I had been involved in at Stanford for almost eighteen years. Human interest stories about heart transplant patients and the generosity of the families permitting donor hearts to be recovered have always been fantastic media events. The initiation of this program and its success brought extensive media coverage about University Hospital programs in transplantation not only of the heart, but the liver, the kidney, and the pancreas. Transplants made headline news on a regular basis, and the public began to be aware of the importance of University Hospital as a regional resource for the most advanced medical technologies and services available. We vigorously promoted both of these programs to make the community aware of the university's relationship to the hospital.

More than 150 community leaders attended these evening lectures and tours.

In addition to the air care and transplant programs, I organized a series of evening briefings and tours to bring business leaders of the Greater Cincinnati area to the medical center. I recognized that they would influence their medical insurance carriers in what medical services would be made available to their employees, and could support our new agenda for making the medical center more nationally recognized. I spent approximately thirty minutes updating the leaders on the history, background, and pathways for critical success of our strategic plan. I showed slides and allowed time for questions. The pressing issues were: How could we fund the new construction that I was proposing? How could we expect to recruit internationally known researchers from the East and West coasts to conservative Cincinnati? Why had I been willing to leave Stanford to come to Cincinnati?

All of these questions led to interesting discussions about how the business community could help to successfully invigorate the medical center. We then toured the hospital, so the business leaders could understand the unique role of University Hospital in training the future medical leaders for the region, and in providing the most sophisticated health care for its citizens. The groups were small, usually consisting of ten or twelve people, and after ninety minutes of lecture and touring, we concluded with time for informal discussion in University Hospital's physicians' dining room, and with a winetasting and hors'd'oeuvres. More than 150 community leaders attended these evening lectures and tours. I was pleased with my first effort to reach out, since the medical center became the topic of discussion at many meetings I attended. These approaches were not intended for fund-raising but to raise the awareness of a new approach at the medical center.

Another attempt to create an understanding of the importance of University Hospital and its medical services was made through meetings I held with the editorial boards of the area's two newspapers. I highlighted our accomplishments and our strategic directions within the scope of "Reaching for the 21st Century." We received several positive editorials that brought our strategic plans to the attention of many in the community.

Management of University Hospital under David Fine's and my leadership became more efficient and cost effective. We had comprehensive training sessions for the staff, and redirected their efforts toward a private-institution mentality. This was to encourage the staff to provide a high level of service and to focus on patient and family welfare. Once University Hospital became profitable, we began adding new technology to improve our patient care. We built a new emergency trauma center, neonatal intensive care units, cardiovascular and surgical intensive care units, and a new bed tower.

The original trauma center had been built to handle only 40,000 visits per year, and today we are seeing over 95,000, and are in need of a large addition. All of the intensive care units were twenty years old, and there was a great need to have updated and modern units. In order to function as a center capable of the newest medical technology, we had to have modernized intensive care units, operating suites, and a competent staff to care for critically ill patients.

Hospital rooms that would accommodate an increasing flow of private patients were required, and the renovation of all existing units was needed, and these things were carried out. In addition we built the Barrett Cancer Center, a regional center for evaluating and treating cancer patients in a single, specialized unit. For the first six years of my tenure, these projects went quite well, with University Hospital developing a large, positive bottom line to help support the academic programs of the college of medicine and to support the buildings and new technology. We incurred very little additional debt to complete all our hospital construction.

Still, the costs of medical care were increasing rapidly, and by 1992, the public was becoming concerned. The four largest corporations in Cincinnati, Procter & Gamble, General Electric, Cincinnati Bell, and Kroger commissioned a study on why health care costs were rising so significantly. This study, known as the "Iameter Study," by a company of that name from San Mateo, California, was carried out over an eighteen-month period. It laid the framework for what was to happen in the funding of medical care in Cincinnati for the next decade.

The findings were that there were excessive hospital beds and overuse of specialists, with a resultant rapidly escalating cost to employers for their employees' health care. It was recommended that managed care, which was already prevalent on the West Coast, was the solution to the dilemma facing these corporations. Managed care came to Cincinnati with a vengeance, and many employers signed up.

The managed care companies, Aetna, ChoiceCare (which later became Humana), United Health Care, CIGNA, and a number of smaller players made their first foray into health care by reducing hospital reimbursement through their contracts. Because of the excess capacity in hospitals and hospital beds, managed care companies were able to pressure hospitals into frequently reducing their charges to below their costs. This turned out to be a very difficult issue for University Hospital, where costs were higher than community rates because of its education and training mission for residents, the large number of indigent patients, and the high complexity of illness in its patients.

For these reasons, the managed care companies began excluding University Hospital from their panels of hospitals for reimbursement. University hospitals do have higher operational costs because of training of medical students, residents, and nursing students, but also receive greater reimbursement by the Medicare formula. That formula takes into account the number of residents and the percentage of Medicare patients. Managed care companies would only reimburse University Hospital at community rates, and would not provide the subsidy to cover training costs as Medicare did. With a higher cost basis, it was impossible for the university to contract with managed care companies unless the university was willing to accept a financial loss.

The managed care companies would not agree to these formulae from Medicare for the additional costs. By 1994, University Hospital had access to only about 10 percent of the patients covered by managed care contracts in Cincinnati. This greatly limited the patients who could be treated at University Hospital. The exception was emergency services at University Hospital, the only Level I trauma center service in the region. Up until this time, the managed care panels had not started their reduction in reimbursement to physicians, nor had they narrowed their panels of physicians.

The university physicians could now care for patients at other hospitals but could not admit their patients with private health insurance to University Hospital. There were a few exceptions to this. If University Hospital offered the only service in town, such as a Level I trauma center service or major organ transplantation, private insurance would cover it.

In addition, over an 18-month period, the number of admissions to University Hospital was declining; the university physicians were growing increasingly unhappy about being unable to admit patients to the hospital because of the managed care contracts. It was for that reason that we began to explore the possibility of merging with other hospitals to create a "system of care" like our original proposal for a new university-controlled system of health care (HERC), which had been proposed by my first hospital administrator, David Fine.

The Jewish Hospital was across the street from University Hospital, and was considered part of the "pill hill" hospitals. This designation was for all of the urban hospitals in Cincinnati because they were closely located on a central hill, thus "pill hill." I approached the board chair of Jewish Hospital first, since it was close by and was the most vulnerable to the managed care dilemma after the University Hospital. He was cooperative, and began to plan with us, but did not bring his administrative staff into the planning efforts. Ultimately, this created a split on his hospital board, and the board chair was forced to step down. There was no possibility of further negotiation with the Jewish Hospital system, since the administrators of the hospital were opposed to the idea of a merger.

The next discussion took place with Bethesda Hospital, a large and growing northern suburban hospital and a central city hospital, which strategically made the most sense for a merger with University Hospital and university physicians. Bethesda had both an in-town base hospital and a suburban hospital, but unfortunately, it was unwilling to close the base hospital in town, and negotiations floundered.

When I presented the concept of closing their base hospital, the senior administrator just stared out the window and said, "No way would my board accept this. We have been in that hospital for fifty years." In my view, it was necessary that they close the base hospital to reduce the number of beds and at the same time, reduce the competition with University Hospital. Our discussions ended. However, six years later, the base hospital was closed as consolidation continued.

In late 1993, after discussion with a subcommittee of the university's board of trustees, and internal discussions among University Hospital Director Terry White, John Hutton, the medical school dean, and Jonathan Lippincott, University Hospital's director of planning, we made a decision to approach Christ Hospital to consider a merger. Our plan then was to create a health alliance. Christ Hospital was a major referral center, and it competed with

University Hospital for specialty care. There was intense competition between its staff and U.C. physicians. The president of Christ Hospital, Jack Cook, was wary, but entered into the discussions, and over a six-week period we developed a plan for a merger to create a health system to accommodate the new managed care hospital environment. It was apparent that the board of trustees of Christ Hospital was initially not in favor of this idea, and I received several informal messages stating so.

One of the more interesting stories in my Cincinnati experience was the meeting I had with Bill Keating, the chair of the university board, a major proponent of this merger; Tom Laco, chair of the board of Christ Hospital; and Roger Howe, former chair at Christ Hospital. Keating was one of my major supporters and advisors as a member of the board of trustees of the university, and for two years as chair. He was tall and thin, had fair skin and freckles, and was known by everyone in Cincinnati from his past service as a city council member, a two-term member of the U.S. Congress, and publisher of the *Cincinnati Enquirer*, our major city newspaper. Bill played a pivotal role in many of my difficult decisions. We met one afternoon at the Queen City Club to negotiate with the Christ Hospital board, and I expected to be told that the merger would not be considered.

The Queen City Club, the city's preeminent downtown business club, is an imposing four-story structure with heavy, dark, wood paneling throughout. All U.S. presidents since Lincoln have attended meetings and spoken there. The walls are lined with art by famous Cincinnati artists, including Frank Duveneck, Henry Farney, Joseph Henry Sharp, Elizabeth Nourse, and 1800s vintage paintings of bearded past presidents of the club. Many major business deals in Cincinnati are culminated at meetings at the Queen City Club.

The room we met in was dark, and the mood of those attending matched its atmosphere. I had made extensive preparations for the meeting, with flip charts and overheads outlining the rationale for a health system. For the first forty-five minutes of my presentation, it was clear that I was making no progress, until Tom Laco, who had previously been vice chair at Procter & Gamble, began to understand the dilemma of managed care, and how it would affect Christ Hospital, as well as University Hospital. It was almost as if a light bulb went on in his head. Laco was a stern fellow with a chin that displayed power, and once he spoke, I felt our presentation had at least penetrated.

He said, "Roger, we had better listen to these folks. I think they are on to something that will affect Christ Hospital." From that point forward, we made considerable progress in gaining their understanding of the need for a new approach, but again, we did not come to a full agreement. Keating and I left the meeting and went back to the University of Cincinnati for a board of trustees meeting, which occurred later that evening. I needed one more vote by the board for approval of my plan. Someone told me that George Strike, a member of the board, was hospitalized at Christ Hospital for a hip replacement. I knew he was strongly in favor of the proposal. I needed his vote. I went to Christ Hospital, found a wheelchair, loaded George Strike onto it and into my car, and I then took him to the university and used the elevator reserved for evacuation, as this was the only elevator with access to the board room. With his vote, the decision was positive. I took him back to Christ Hospital. The nurses, having missed him, were frantic. I had not told them I was taking him away.

Later that evening, the Christ Hospital board met and also approved the merger. This had all been done in absolute secrecy, and on Valentine's Day 1994, we made the announcement of the planned merger, which would be completed over the next ten months as the details were worked out. The name we chose was the Health Alliance of Greater Cincinnati. In my opinion a better name emphasizing the university and Christ Hospital would have led to earlier recognition of this merger by the general public.

With his vote, the decision was positive. I took him back to Christ Hospital. The nurses, having missed him, were frantic. I had not told them I was taking him away.

A lot of work was involved to culminate this agreement, so we employed the services of a major consultant from the Booz Allen consulting firm. The legal paperwork required several weeks to complete. There were also audits and studies of past performance. Booz Allen's recommendation for governance of the new organization was an at-large board of community leaders, but this concept could not be sold to the Christ Hospital board, and therefore, we ended up with a representative board of equal numbers of members from each organization. I knew this was a mistake but could do nothing to change it at the time. I feared they would support activities for their respective hospitals rather than for the good of the merged organizations. This proved to be true, and was a problem for the Alliance from the beginning.

About a year after this merger was completed, members of the Health Alliance board were approached by St. Luke Hospitals, consisting of an East and West Campus in Northern Kentucky. These were community hospitals with few major specialty programs. After considerable negotiation, during which, in my opinion, the St. Luke Board did not fully understand the merger commitments they were making, the St. Luke Hospitals joined and received equal representation in the Health Alliance board, even though they were one-fifth the size in financial terms of the other two hospitals. I felt this was not a sound decision because in no instance in the business world would this ever happen. I had been left out of these negotiations and on learning of the decisions I was distraught, knowing we were setting the stage for major problems within this new health care system.

A year later, the Jewish Hospital approached the Health Alliance about the possibility of joining. I was included in these negotiations, since I was then chair of the board, and after lengthy discussion, they agreed to close their base hospital at a future date, and to begin plans for expansion of the number of beds at their Kenwood site, their northern suburban hospital. This resulted in a net reduction in the number of beds in the new system. This was the same kind of deal I had offered to Bethesda Hospital earlier. This suburban site had been acquired by Jewish Hospital a few years earlier, and was being rebuilt at the time of the merger. Again, the total Alliance board size was reduced, but everyone had equal representation.

About two years later, Fort Hamilton Hospital, a small community hospital in a northern suburb, was brought into the Alliance but was given less representation on the board. The structure of the board and parochial actions of board members to support positions favoring their respective hospitals made operation of the system complex and difficult. This became more apparent to me when I was the second chair of the board for an eighteen-month period. It was a difficult time for the Alliance, and since I supported the college of medicine's demands for its support, I was considered to have a conflict of interest and was allowed to be chair for only eighteen months, although I had been one of the major architects of the Health Alliance.

Still, there was considerable initial exuberance after the Christ-University Hospitals merger, both within the hospital staff and with the physicians, as leverage with the managed care companies was accomplished, leading to higher reimbursements. During the honeymoon period of the first two years, the Health Alliance was financially successful. Nevertheless, there were many problems over funding allocations to the college of medicine and how the mission of taking care of the indigent would be handled.

The senior hospital management and the board of directors were reluctant to live up to the terms of the agreement that we had carefully negotiated. Several committees were appointed to try to reach a compromise. Overall, there were strong positive feelings about groups of physicians getting together among the hospitals, and there was a lot of initial flourish to have combined groups of community and university physicians.

But in the long run this combination did not take place. Physicians began to fight among themselves, and the hope that they would join community and university groups together never materialized. This was especially true for the subspecialty physicians who were quite competitive for patients and their access to various hospitals. This competition among physician groups was intensified by the reduction in reimbursement starting in 1997. Reduction in reimbursement levels by the managed care companies had finally reached the physicians, after already having the major effect on hospitals.

After about thirty-six months, the initial blush of cooperation ended. The Health Alliance started to lose money, the board became contentious, and the university in many ways was designated the scapegoat for insisting on payment to the college of medicine. University Hospital was singled out for its higher costs and its need for increased spending for advanced technologies. In spite of the higher costs, University Hospital was profitable in the Health Alliance because of the Medicare subsidy for resident training programs and a higher level of patient illness, which also produced a medical subsidy.

However, over a period of five years, with considerable restructuring in the administration, and a new CEO, the troublesome adolescent hospital system matured and moved into the black financially. There were still problems about support for the college of medicine and its multiple community missions, but the board, which now has several nonaffiliated community representatives, has begun to work more effectively. After I stepped down from my university role, the attempt to restructure the Alliance had many roadblocks. Christ Hospital and St. Luke Hospitals have recently proposed a unilateral withdrawal. The issue is yet to be resolved. In my view, the early mistakes in not creating a nonaligned board led to many of the troubles that the Alliance is now facing. The failure to have a board that could act in the best interest of the Alliance, rather than the parochial interests of their representative hospitals, has been the major problem of this and similar mergers. Systems in which an independent board has been created have fared much better.

After the merger of Christ and University hospitals, it became apparent that part of the high cost of care at University Hospital was related to the resident training programs, which had almost 500 residents, as well as to the high labor costs of construction with a heavily unionized work force and many state regulatory requirements. After considerable planning and discussion, a proposal to privatize University Hospital was developed. I was chair of the board of the Health Alliance at the time, and in order to keep state officials in the governor's office informed, I developed a plan for the privatization initiative. This would result in a lease of University Hospital to the Alliance, and seemed essential, since the hospital was owned by the State of Ohio and could not be sold.

I wrote a memo, which as a code name I labeled "Batman Project," and distributed it in Columbus to the governor's office to keep them informed and ensure their support. This moniker on the memo proved to be a terrible mistake. In Cincinnati, the memo was kept totally confidential, but the governor's office distributed it to the media, and immediately we were facing a public relations disaster. The contents of the memo became public before we had a chance to inform our employees and present the plan for their continued employment. The leak created major concern among our employees, most of whom were unionized. Particular concern was expressed by the maintenance and housekeeping staffs. Their unions held meetings and made demands on me to meet with them. We offered reassurance about jobs, and about our efforts to do what was best for each individual employee, especially concerning their retirement options. Our human resources staff tried to work with several groups, but there remained a level of unease among our employees. Nonetheless, we moved forward with the plan and presented it fully to the staff.

We were required to have public hearings on the proposal, and in the fourteen hours of hearings, Bill Keating, then chair of the university board of trustees, and I maintained the spotlight position. I received a newspaper designation as "Batman," and Elliot Cohen, director of University Hospital, was called "Robin" for his part. A dissenter even showed up for the hearings in a Batman costume. There were over a hundred speakers, with only ten in favor of privatizing. One headline stated "Privatizing Handled Ineptly," and another called it "Batman Acrobatics." I was almost daily being depicted on the front page of the *Cincinnati Enquirer* as an arch villain, and demands for my resignation were made. The editorial page of the local papers contained letter after letter about our plans.

According to the newspaper, I was taking away more than a hundred years of University Hospital's historic mission as it had existed when it was Cincinnati General Hospital. And it soon became apparent that the community physicians also opposed the privatization of University Hospital because it made our physician practice group more competitive in their market for patient admissions. While it was uncomfortable for me to be pictured as a villain day after day, the media attention actually helped publicize a more comprehensive view of the role of University Hospital, and provided a forum to present our side of the health care programs of Greater Cincinnati.

Some of the quotes from articles about me were, "the essence of this case involved the zeal of a public official, Dr. Donald Harrison, whose single-minded goals for University

Hospital were allowed to override the legal processes" and constraints designed as checks and balances on government overreaching, and, "Harrison worked as an officer of U.C. and used university resources and personnel to convert the hospital into a private entity." The city also filed a lawsuit aimed at the university and me over this issue, as did three other groups. Because my picture appeared so frequently on the front page of the newspapers, I was easily recognized throughout the community.

Being recognized in the community because of what was taking place in the privatization of University Hospital had both a good and bad effect. The good effect was that I was now able to meet with all the political leaders and to make them aware of the plans and ambitions for the medical center. Among the many Republican constituents of Cincinnati, the fact that I was trying to privatize University Hospital was widely accepted, and the fact that they could recognize me helped me get support for other programs. On the other hand, the African American community and those living in the center city tried to make me out as the devil incarnate. It was clear that I would need to do much to overcome their hostility.

Thirteen-and-a-half hours of those public hearings were led by people opposing the privatization. This included city council members and representatives of the Ohio House. The staff writers of the *Enquirer* lampooned me daily. However, in the final weeks before a vote by the university trustees, the editorials in both daily newspapers supported the plan. The final word was, "Let University Hospital be reborn as a cost-efficient, not-for-profit teaching hospital, committed to indigent care, reasonable benefits for its workers, and to survive."

Once the privatization occurred, ironically, the employees accepted many of the options that we offered, which were in fact directed at what was best for each employee. For example, if they had been long-term employees, they were allowed to keep their pension plan with the city, which was very lucrative. If they were short-term employees, they were permitted to go into a much better 401K plan with the new system, with major matching contributions by the Alliance. In the long run we were able to convert almost 4,000 employees, without a single lawsuit over changes in personnel. This was a remarkable outcome, since the hospital staff was heavily unionized. The lawsuit that *was* filed by the city to block the privatization was a problem, however. It was in the courts for almost seven years. The lawsuit was finally settled in 2004, after I had retired, with University Hospital and the Health Alliance agreeing to help the city's health clinics by supporting physicians who provide specialty services.

The Health Alliance had a number of problems during my years at U.C., but in 2003 and 2004 it became successful financially and increased its market share in the Cincinnati region.

In 2004, it registered approximately 39 percent of all hospital admissions in the area. It has also been successful in negotiating higher reimbursement from managed care companies. This large system could not be left out of the panels for hospitals of the major managed care plans, because the employees of the major corporations would demand that they be seen at these premier hospitals.

As the ability of managed care to control health care costs has faded, the importance of large systems has been undermined. For University Hospital, however, the Alliance has worked well, for the hospital now has access to more than 90 percent of the managed care patients, and there has been a steady growth in the volume of patients seen in the hospital and ambulatory clinics. In 2005, University Hospital had the largest share of patients in the hospital market of Cincinnati. The University Hospital has finally been recognized for its role as the center that brings the latest medical advances to the region.

Many problems with the Alliance remain. When the Alliance had a negative bottom line, there was a decrease in capital expenditures, especially for new technologies. This situation can significantly hamper hospitals from staying current with new diagnostic and treatment options. Most medical technologies have a life cycle of approximately seven years, and when a hospital falls behind in capital expenditures, it generally loses competitiveness. Since the Alliance is now financially in the black, it has a policy in place to make up for the reduced capital expenditures over a four-year period. Also, to improve community relations, outside members who are not aligned have been added to the board, resulting in better recognition of the support necessary for the college of medicine. Overall, I would characterize the Alliance as being successful but tenuous. It will need to be nimble, and adapt to the ever-changing environment of medical reimbursement and the desire of components to withdraw.

While the Health Alliance as a hospital system has become more successful, the competition among physicians and the town-gown problems with the college of medicine faculty have intensified as the managed care companies begin to ratchet down on reimbursement for physicians. Once the hospitals were brought into line with managed care company objectives, reimbursement for the specialty physicians became their major target. Reimbursement to physicians was ratcheted down below Medicare levels in many instances. This has led to intense competition, much hostility on the part of physicians, and difficulty in getting their cooperation with the hospital system. Physicians have also banded into groups and created ambulatory centers for much of the high-reimbursement care.

These centers have had a major negative impact on the hospital systems. The patients taken away for procedures in an ambulatory center have the highest levels of reimbursement and profit for the hospital. When this happens, frequently the hospital systems are left with the most seriously ill and those with chronic conditions, where reimbursement is low, and becomes a reimbursement loss for hospitals.

In spite of the managed care companies' activities, health care costs in the Greater Cincinnati area, while they remained stable for about four years, have now started to rise quite precipitously. It is clear that there is no true comprehensive system of health care in Greater Cincinnati. Each component of the health care system is struggling for reimbursement, and there is no system that puts the patients' welfare foremost.

The major partner of physicians with the Health Alliance is the university physician group, with more than 450 physicians. With my full backing, they have formed joint ventures for developing a northern suburban campus in West Chester, now designated as University Pointe. West Chester is located in Butler County, the fastest-growing county in Ohio. Dan Gahl is the major driving force for this development. It is underserved for medical specialists, and the community has a high standard of living, with a high average wage.

In order to offset the fact that the college of medicine faculty takes care of a great many charity patients and Medicaid patients where the reimbursement is low or nonexistent, they welcomed having a practice site where specialists are needed, and where the reimbursement would be equitable and offset the time University Hospital physicians care for nonreimbursed patients. It is apparent that Butler County will continue to grow rapidly, and that having a medical base in this area is extremely important. I backed this activity because it would increase the presence of the university in a high-growth area, and would increase the financial stability of our departments that were heavily dependent upon clinical income. A major medical office building was opened, and an ambulatory hospital followed. The Health Alliance has planned and has under construction a full suburban hospital scheduled to open in 2008. It is hoped that as the Health Alliance matures, a better relationship will develop among the physicians, as well as a true health care system for a large part of the population.

Another area of health care that needed change came to my attention soon after I had become senior vice president of the university. This was the responsibility for the university's student and employee health system—36,000 students and 3,200 employees and faculty. The system was fragmented into one system for the medical center and one for the main campus. The facilities were antiquated, and the morale of the staff was extremely low. There was a budgetary crisis each year and no fix in sight.

Over a ten-year period we renovated the facilities, developed a student health insurance plan, and hired a dynamic new medical director, John Andrews, who had been a staff physician at the Center for Communicable Diseases. For the next several years, we developed a strategic plan to upgrade the system, to give it new facilities, and to provide full services that focused heavily on preventive care to the large student population. Several new programs were also initiated for employees, although most kept their private physician relationships.

As the major building programs on campus evolved, several sites were considered for locating the new facilities. A fortuitous decision was made to include the student and employee health service in the building plans for the new university athletic building. Donor support for this facility was strong, and the center is now located on the third floor of this centrally located building. Services for general medicine, psychiatric care, women's health, and a host of preventive services are available in a state-of-the-art unit. I have not visited a campus that has a more functional and comprehensive program. On a recent visit to the site, I was overwhelmed with the staff's thanks to me for my persistent efforts over many years.

The business of being CEO of the university's medical center occupied most of my time, but for my free time I adapted to a more leisurely country living style in Indian Hill. Indian Hill, referred to as "the Village" by its residents, is an independent eastern suburb of Greater Cincinnati.

When we moved to Cincinnati, Laura and I wanted to continue to be able to use our house for entertaining university visitors, and as a place to bring faculty and staff home for social affairs, as we had at Stanford. This created the specific need for a house that met the

requirements for us to do that. After accepting the position of senior vice president and provost for health affairs in Cincinnati in August 1986, I made my plans to come and begin work in November 1986. As soon as the decision was made, finding an appropriate house in Cincinnati became a priority.

THE HOUSE AT SEVEN KNOLLS.

We wanted a house where we could entertain relatively large groups of people from the medical center, for we were not accustomed to using country clubs for our entertainment, as most people in Cincinnati did. We also wanted a pool, and a reasonably sized yard and garden. Initially we had ruled out Indian Hill because of its distance from the medical center, although we knew this was the premier location for housing in Cincinnati. Overall, the price of houses in Cincinnati seemed reasonable to us, since they had not escalated like they had in California. The house we had purchased in California for $38,000 sold for over $500,000, allowing us to make a sizable investment in our next home.

We carefully identified our needs, and searched other areas of Cincinnati extensively. We made a bid on a house in Hyde Park, but it was not accepted. We also evaluated several possibilities in Clifton, but all needed extensive renovations. We finally found the ideal house and purchased it in Indian Hill. Our house was built in 1925 by the Morgan family, who were the owners of the U.S. Playing Cards Company. The architect was Guy Burroughs, who designed several houses in Indian Hill. It had been built on thirty-six acres and is an estate known as "Seven Knolls." The house is an English Tudor, has a full basement, and three floors. There are nearly 12,000 square feet in the house. It had six-and-a-half bathrooms, a servants' quarters that we could turn into offices, and the house could accommodate our family and grandchildren when they were born. It had a large living room, but most impressively, a large great room with cathedral ceilings of almost 1,000 square feet.

The house had a free-form slate roof and copper gutters, and the entire property was covered with exotic trees. While the gardens needed considerable work when we moved in, it was clear that this could be a beautiful place. About fifteen years before we purchased the house, acres acres of the land had been given to the Greenbelt Conservancy of Indian Hill, and three five-acre lots had been carved out and sold to other individuals. There were just seven acres for our house, yard, and the gardens. The house had a large slate patio, an orchard, a large swimming pool, and fountains with marble statues. The division of the lots for other houses had been shielded by a row of evergreen trees, which meant that in no direction could you view another house from ours.

SEVEN KNOLLS, A CLOSER VIEW.

While we were delighted with the purchase of our house, we did not recognize how little furniture we had until we began to move into the large house. Initially, we walked about the house, examining each room, and its multitude of built-in cabinets and bookshelves. We recognized then the wonderful architectural detail that was built into the house as we made each new discovery.

Two adjacent kitchens and a pantry had been built and furnished with stainless steel cabinetry. This area was extremely functional for large catered affairs, which we looked forward to hosting. The floors in the kitchen and pantry were the original asphalt tile. We replaced them with hardwood floors similar to the ones we had in California.

We made other discoveries in the house, such as the secret wine cellar, which had existed during prohibition, and the finished third floor of the house, which had been the nursery and the quarters of the supervisor of the house and properties. Two bedrooms off the kitchens, used for the servants in earlier years, were converted to highly functional offices, one for each of us.

GARDEN AT SEVEN KNOLLS.

We explored the grounds and found the original landscape plans that showed five zones of planting. The botanical names of many of the rare plants were still legible. Most of these, however, were overgrown or extinct, and were not identifiable. As we explored, we found an orchard with many apple, pear, and peach trees. There were also lots of blueberry plants, several rows of raspberries, and a few hazelnut trees. A vegetable garden area contained the deep-rooted asparagus that came up each spring and satisfied our desire for asparagus for about six weeks of each harvest season.

There was a large pool measuring forty-four by twenty-two feet and it even had an old heating system, though no longer functional. We discovered that the pool had been the first heated one in Cincinnati, and utilized oil as its fuel. This outdated heating system could not be repaired, but since we liked to swim in cold water such as the 68-degree water at Lake Tahoe, we started to swim usually around the first of May and were able to swim until mid-October. This was surprising to us because most people in Cincinnati opened their pools after Memorial Day and closed them the first week in September. The swimming was great exercise, and I found this form of exercise one of the best for me.

After we identified the large gardens and about five acres of grass that needed to be cut frequently, we knew we needed to find some good help. A man named Marvin Lingerfeld was recommended to Laura by the gardener of one of our nearby neighbors. He was a small, muscular man with a deep voice and great strength. Marvin had worked for Milacron and had been laid off, and was eager for work. Initiall,y we employed him almost full time, and after about twelve years he wanted to retire, but we convinced him to work three half days a week. Marvin became the manager of the property and looks after it like it was his own.

All of the service people came to know Marvin since he gave them strict instructions about what they should, and could, and could not do on the property. Marvin became great friends with our grandchildren and almost everyone else who visits with us, and everyone who visits with us always asks, "How is Marvin doing?" Without Marvin, I am not sure we could have survived and cared for Seven Knolls as we have.

In the winter, Marvin worked for a few days inside the house, but had a great distaste for doing housework. However, Laura convinced him that things like polishing the copper screens, which were on all of our windows and had been corroded for sixty-five years before we moved into the house, was a job he could do well. They shined and returned to a beautiful copper color after his work. Marvin continues to look after the trees throughout the property. We've had several trees struck by lightning, subsequently coming down in the windstorms. These had to be cut, and the wood stacked for the fireplace. We had a large grove of trees separating our property from a neighbor's, and in a very dry season these trees began to show signs of distress. We paid a small fortune to have them fertilized and deep watered, but they made a great recovery and still form a screen, maintaining a feeling of privacy.

Having come from California where we had a redwood hot tub adjacent to our pool, we sought to find a way to have a Jacuzzi. Not wanting to put it outside exposed to ice and snow, we found the ideal place for a Jacuzzi was in our oversized garage, and accommodated it between our parked cars. To make it seem more pleasant, we put a canopy above it, but almost everyone who visited with us looked at this Jacuzzi in the middle of a garage as a strange operation. Several years later, when talking to a city maintenance man, Laura was told that the garbage collectors who entered our garage each week labeled us "the family with the Jacuzzi in the garage," rather than by our name. This does not keep me from using the Jacuzzi once or twice every day all year round.

Indian Hill is a rural area, where 35 percent of the twenty-three square miles that supports approximately 6,000 total people is committed to the Greenbelt Conservancy space that surrounded our property almost completely. When we moved here, we were delighted to see an occasional deer; however, over the next seven years, the deer population expanded in number and began to feast on our garden plants. To protect our vegetable garden, we erected a six-foot high fence, but the deer could still jump that and eat the beans, which they seemed to delight in just as the new leaves would come on. Over the past twenty years, the deer have become bolder and more numerous. They will walk on the terrace, and in winter, when there is snow on the ground, eat the yew and other base plants next to the house. It has become impossible to deal with them, and we often find as many as fourteen wandering on our lawn, jumping and playing like gazelles on the Serengeti Plains in Africa.

Since I had grown up a hunter, I looked into ways to decrease the deer population, and found that the law in our town allowed hunting with a bow and arrow by a property owner, and permitted me to kill five deer in each season for our own use. I bought a crossbow, got a hunting license, and set up a target practice. I hunted for several winters, but was unable to kill a single deer. They seemed to sense me wherever I was hiding, and stayed just out of my range. I took a shot at several, but never brought one down. In an attempt to thin the deer population, Laura wrote many letters to the mayor of the town, but there was always the counter support group for preserving the deer and not "shooting Bambi." We were allowed to permit hunting on our property by those approved by the Rangers of Indian Hill, who are our police, and during several winters, we did have hunters who killed deer on our property and often shared the venison with us.

The deer population continues to grow, though, making it difficult to find plants the deer will not eat. However, after careful study and selection, we have identified some plants that the deer will not eat, and they now fill most of our garden areas. We have given up our vegetable garden—the hard work in the garden lost its pleasure when everything was eaten before we could harvest it.

We also had a problem with raccoons. They began to dig through the yard for grubs, completely turning over the lawn; and they climbed the trees and onto the house roof. Laura and Marvin decided to use a Havahart trap and turn them out across the Little Miami River about five miles away. One summer they trapped twenty-three raccoons, and I was sure they kept coming back to our place the next day after they had been released. I sprayed one with red paint on the foot, and it never turned up again, so I might have been wrong about that. Marvin said, "Doc, those darn raccoons can't come back from where I take them."

Recently the state passed a law making it illegal to release a raccoon, for fear of rabies. They now must be killed if caught. Chipmunks also were very prevalent, and seemed to enjoy eating through the ropes that pulled our pool cover, and digging throughout the yard and garden. I once trapped thirty in one year with large gopher traps. We had woodchucks and rabbits, which also ate the garden plants. The rabbits seemed to come out every spring and disappear by winter. I believe they are eaten by the foxes in the area. Our favorites, though, are the squirrels that do no real damage. They jump through our trees, and play in our yard. We also have bird feeders and attract many species of birds just outside a garden room window. The feeders are particularly successful in attracting the cardinal, which is Ohio's state bird and a beautiful species during the wintertime when the white snow covers the ground.

In the past ten years, moles became our greatest nemesis for the yard, because they plow through flower beds, raise large mounds of soil in the lawn, and excavate tunnels throughout the yard. They invade from the woods, and one mole can dig 150 feet of tunnel a day. Over several years, I attempted to poison the moles, and to flood their tunnels, but to no avail. When they became so disruptive to the lawn that it looked like a mine field, Laura happened to mention to me a local man known around town as "the Mole Man." He had developed a new mole trap, which he stated worked very successfully. Laura purchased six, and an accompanying video on how to use them, and gave them to me as a Father's Day gift.

Marvin and I learned to set the traps, and in the summer of 2003, we caught twenty-five moles. I promised Marvin a $10 bonus for each one he caught. I received no bonus, but caught twice as many as he did. At the end of summer, 2003, we had a nice lawn with no mole mounds. But in 2004, we began again since over the winter they returned. Mole trapping continues each summer, and in 2004 I caught forty-two, in 2005 I caught twenty-eight, and 2006 was a big mole summer, with forty catches.

We do love some animals, and our first pet was a cat named Mittens. Mittens was a stray who wandered into our lives after we had been at Seven Knolls about five years. Initially the cat was shared by us and one of the neighbors. Both of us were traveling extensively, but one of us always seemed to be in town and the cat knew to go back and forth to the two houses where it could be fed. After these neighbors moved, the cat moved in with us. The cat was not a house pet, and when it was young it loved to hunt and bring in ground squirrels, lizards, and snakes, to show us its prowess. As the cat got older it became gentler and wanted to be patted and rubbed, but still was not one that would get in your lap. The cat would climb on the Jacuzzi, stick out a paw and wave it in the air to be patted.

If you did not pat Mittens, he put his paw out, and patted you on the head as you sat in the Jacuzzi. When we were traveling, Marvin came and fed the cat, and although he never really liked the cat, he tolerated it. The cat was a great favorite of our grandchildren, and when they visited, he would play with them for a while, but then scurry away to exert its freedom. At age 13, Mittens became ill with diabetes, thyroid disease, and old age. After a stay at the vet's it was recommended that we euthanize the cat. Two years later, we acquired a second cat. He was also a stray that came to a friend's house, who gave him to us. He is gray with stripes, and very playful. We named him Lucky—he spends much of his time in Laura's lap. He is very different from Mittens, but fits our lifestyle much better. Too bad he is not a hunter.

We used the house almost like a country club, hosting eight to ten parties a year for the university, and we also enjoy hosting charity events, supporting the heart association, the Indian Hill Historical Society, the symphony, and the public radio stations through the wine auction. The organizations have sold, at auction, dinners prepared by us, and visits to my wine cellar, to raise money. Initially, on our children's visits with us at Seven Knolls, we designated bedrooms for each of the families. With six-and-a-half baths, we have enough for everyone. And with eight grandchildren now, there are often sixteen of us in the house, which we can handle comfortably with everyone having their own space. The grandchildren enjoy the pool, the outdoor swings, and the grounds, and we are delighted to have them visit. Though our social life was largely related to my official university functions, we consciously tried to keep time for ourselves and for our children and grandchildren to visit. Our family visits and social time with grandchildren have increased since stepping down from the university position.

Probably the thing that helped us get settled in Cincinnati most was our house at Seven Knolls. The only time I surprised Laura about a function at home was about three months after we moved in. There was a call from the Indian Hill Historical Society (IHHS), asking to put our house on the house tour they had each May. I said yes, without checking with Laura. I did not recognize that we then needed to get the house furnished within a very few months. This decision probably caused us to acquire much of the furnishings for the house in quick order rather than take several years. The tour took place without incident, and we later hosted the IHHS house tour a second time, when it was more completely furnished.

We love the house, we love the grounds, we have a wonderful time here, and as we contemplate our retirement and needs for living in a retirement community, we have great ambivalence about leaving the house, and only wish that some of our children lived in the area so they could inherit this wonderful place that has been our home for the past twenty years.

Though I was always very busy, I have enjoyed being a "hands-on" property owner, working around house and grounds as much as I could. Laura has enjoyed it even more, and has been the hands and brains behind the gardens.

Chapter Fifty-two

PARADE *of signataries*

During my tenure at the university, I have had the opportunity

to encounter a number of individuals who were prominent on the national

and international stage.

Among several who played key roles in what I was attempting to accomplish or who were patients in my practice were Frank Gehry, the architect, Robert Mondavi of California wine fame, the emir of Bahrain, the Kwok and Cha families of Hong Kong, and Edward Teller, Henry Kissinger, Linus Pauling, and Milton Friedman. The details of these relationships are already highlighted. In my role at the university, I was also asked to participate with a group of medical center directors in Hillary Clinton's planning for a universal health system in 1993. We spent two Saturday mornings at the White House office building. These sessions were led by Hillary. Her major objective was to design a health care system that included everyone. She presented statistics to document the shortcomings of our present system. We debated the proposals she presented and expressed our concerns for the programs that would impact our health education programs. The sessions were intense but fruitful. A more comprehensive plan was a result of her persistence. We were photographed with both Mrs. Clinton and the president. Our concern was what role academic health centers would play in such a system. Of course, it all came to naught when the plan failed.

DON WITH PRESIDENT CLINTON IN 1993.

We had major speakers on the campus each year. Some of my favorites were Colin Powell and Bill Cosby. These individuals were selected because of their accomplishments, but also because the university was attempting to upgrade the quality of its commencement speakers. Bill Cosby gave a presentation peppered with humor, but also focused on how a college education could improve the life opportunities of the graduates. Colin Powell highlighted the importance of dedicated service to our country as a worthy mission for the young graduates. I also worked with the two-time governor Bob Taft on several programs to promote economic growth in Ohio, and met John McCain with the governor on one of his visits to our state.

At Stanford, I had participated in a medical conference at my alma mater in Birmingham, Alabama, with Albert Sabin, who developed the oral polio vaccine. His work had all been done at Children's Hospital in Cincinnati. Once I had settled in Cincinnati, I had an opportunity to visit with him and his wife, Heloise, where they lived in Washington, D.C. Mary Sue Cheeseman, of the university's development office, joined me, and we convinced them to leave his memorabilia

DON WITH HILLARY CLINTON, AT THE WHITE HOUSE.

to be displayed in the lobby of our new Molecular Science Building. This has been a major attraction for tours of schoolchildren as they learn about the devastating disease of polio and Dr. Sabin's work here to eradicate the disease. Since Sabin's death, his widow, Heloise, visits here often. We enjoy sharing time, memories, and dinner with Heloise.

Chapter Fifty-three

MEDICINE *and wine*

I grew up a Baptist in Alabama, so it might seem surprising that
I developed a love of wine—it is likely that the Baptist imprimatur never
really fit me. For many years, I have studied wine, visited wineries and wine
regions worldwide, and have seen winery owners as patients. I have also explored
the medical benefits associated with wine consumption. I am interested in its
production, and also have a broad ranging desire to sample and taste as many
wonderful wine products as possible.

My first experience with wine was in Boston, where fellow residents and I had an opportunity to do some tasting and share our opinions of the only wines we could afford at the time—low-priced California jug wines. Almaden was our largest product to sample. Later, in Washington, D.C., and Bethesda, I had a number of colleagues who were interested in wine and knew a great deal about it. There were many excellent wine stores nearby, and in the District of Columbia one could purchase in a store in Georgetown, known as "Plain Old Pearsons," and get descriptions of the wine and sampling tips from knowledgeable employees. Though this is common today, wine stores of this type were not then. The prices were very reasonable, and there was also an opportunity to sample excellent wines in a number of high-quality and ethnic restaurants.

ROBERT AND MARGRIT MONDAVI WITH DON.

My move to California allowed me to develop a deeper interest in the production of wine, and an opportunity for me to sample extensively. Once we had purchased a house in

Los Altos, I found an old Italian winery that had been in business for almost ninety years, not more than two miles from our house.

Gemellos was a small winery in Mountain View, California, producing Italian-style wines and particularly focusing on Zinfandel. Laura and I were still on a tight budget, but I found I could take my two-gallon jugs in the side baskets of my bicycle to Gemellos and fill one with white wine from one of their barrels, and one with red wine. This often became my "Sunday ride." I would then rebottle these and have the wine for two weeks, and even some for visiting guests. They were excellent wines for their price. Gemellos also made some high-quality wines—not those I sampled directly from the cask. And I had an opportunity to observe their production, aging, and bottling. During my first few years in California, we found multiple opportunities to visit in the Napa Valley. It was certainly not as busy as now, and we were welcomed at visits to many of the wineries and invited to sample their wines at will. We visited Beringer, C.K. Mondavi, Heitz, Buena Vista, and others.

During this time, I became acquainted with Ray Baldwin, the national and international marketing manager for Paul Masson Winery located in Saratoga, California. He was my patient and also became a close friend. Ray permitted me to buy wine directly from the winery, and it would be delivered to my house in eight- or ten-case lots. It was almost like I was a retail outlet. With these great wines we hosted parties for my postdoctoral fellows and faculty. One of the most memorable occasions of welcoming new postdocs and faculty was hosting a winetasting on our patio at the beginning of each new year.

The new year for our program began in July, and we enjoyed these midsummer winetastings on warm evenings. For many years, we drank Paul Masson wines. Their sparkling wines and their Grey Rieslings were our favorites. After a couple of years, we found that we could enlist wineries from the Napa Valley to provide wine for this event as part of their public relations and marketing, and they would provide a host for a true winetasting, with an educational discussion of each of the wines they poured.

We continued to host these parties at our home for many years. The most memorable events occurred when the Ridge Winery hosted us rather than at home. They were located at the top of the Santa Cruz Mountains and looked out over the whole Bay Area valley. They hosted the new postdocs and faculty with a tasting and a sumptuous picnic for several years. The road up was a rise of 3,000 feet, with about thirty sharp S-curves. It was always a wonder that no one missed the road coming down the mountain after the winetastings and picnics at the Ridge Winery. There were a number of other small wineries in the Santa Cruz Mountains. Most produced small quantities of wine in the Italian style. We visited them on weekends, sampling from a number of the wineries. These familyrun wineries then made only 3,000-4,000 cases a year, but have increased their output substantially as Italian-style wines have grown in popularity.

During our California years, as I refined my taste for wine, and I became acquainted with many of its better wines. My most memorable visit to a winery in Napa occurred when I had been on a trip to make a presentation at Lake Berryessa in California and noted a newly built winery in Oakville. This winery was the new Robert Mondavi Winery, which had just opened three days before my visit. It was an eye-opener, and exciting to see this beautiful winery and to taste some if its first vintages. I have no memory of meeting Robert Mondavi at that time, but fast-forward a few years.

One Sunday when I was president-elect of the American Heart Association, I arrived at the San Francisco Airport about forty-five minutes before the departure of my flight to Dallas for a meeting. I was seated in my coach seat, when a woman with a child came along and informed me that I was in her seat. We had duplicate boarding passes, and the cabin attendant moved me to first class and gave the coach seat to the mother and child. Soon thereafter, a man sat down by me and in a friendly way asked me where I lived and what I did. I told him that I was at Stanford as chief of cardiology. He informed me that he had visited Stanford and had lunch with the president just the week before. I asked him what he did and where he lived. He mentioned Napa Valley and said he was in the wine business.

I instantly acknowledged that he must be Robert Mondavi, and I figured that because the president of Stanford University would not have had lunch with just anyone from the Napa Valley. We laughed over this, and lots of other stories, a great deal, and sampled a number of wines on our way to Dallas. He insisted that the airline personnel bring us several to try.

During the trip he told me that he had had a diagnosis of a cardiac condition and he needed consultation. I suggested to him that when I got back to the Bay Area that he get in touch with me, and I would evaluate the problem, but I never believed that he would call. Several days later he did, and I saw him in consultation at Stanford and delivered the good news that I found no evidence of significant heart disease. Over the next few years, I saw him in consultation at Stanford and was invited on several occasions to stay in his guest house, visit the winery, and attend some of the concerts at the winery in Oakville. We soon developed a friendship that lasted until his death, and we frequently visited with him and his wife, Margrit, in the Napa Valley.

During these same years, I also had an opportunity to visit Chile, Australia, New Zealand, France, and Italy to sample their wines. In South Africa, I was able to visit the Stellenbosch area which was making great wines using the viniculture techniques learned from California. When I moved to Cincinnati, I found Mondavi was well known by people here who had wine interests. I was asked to invite him to Cincinnati to meet some of the owners of wine stores and restaurants, and to participate in the First International Wine Festival (IWF) in 1990. Mondavi agreed to come, and the IWF planned several events in connection with the Festival. One was a dinner for community leaders that I hosted at our house, for which he supplied the wine and during dinner gave a short discussion of each.

The chef of the Palace Restaurant, Paul Dagenbach, cooked in our kitchen, bringing almost all of the things needed for a multi-course dinner from the Palace for the setup in our house. The Palace Restaurant was the secondmost respected to the internationally known five star Maisonette in Cincinnati in this period. This event is so well remembered that almost every month, someone speaks of it to me. There was also a Sunday afternoon tasting hosted by the Mondavis on our terrace, at which about fifty people sampled the latest of the top-rated Mondavi wines and heard his lively discussion of each.

The International Wine Festival in Cincinnati was organized to be a fund-raiser for the local public radio station and other related charities. There were judgings of the wines submitted by the wineries. Gold, silver, and bronze medals were awarded, and then tickets were sold for a large public event for open tastings. The festival also had dinners hosted by the winemasters from some of the famous wineries in California, Oregon, and overseas. I was asked to be a judge, and, along with twenty-five or so other people, we judged the wines a week or two before the open tasting, awarding the gold, silver, and bronze medals that were displayed at the open tastings. This has been great fun, and I have participated thirteen of its sixteen years. We have training with experts, and this has certainly sharpened my ability to judge wines. The judges compete for the opportunity by participating in a "tasting challenge," and are selected based on their scores closest to those of the experts. If one's scores compare poorly with the expert, or if one is frequently giving scores distant from those of their peers, they are excluded from the tasting competition.

The Mondavis returned to Cincinnati on another trip at my invitation. We visited Findley Market, an old-style European Market, which has operated for almost 150 years, where Margrit said she had shopped for years when living here and that it reminded her of home in Europe. Margrit Mondavi had lived in Cincinnati for five years just after World War II, when she was married to a former pilot in the Air Force, whom she had met in Switzerland.

Over the years, we have been with the Mondavis in Napa when they have hosted their Italian partners and held their Great Chefs cooking school. We laughed a lot, and sampled a lot of excellent wine together.

To complement my wine interest, I always wanted a wine cellar. In Los Altos, my house had a basement where after a few years I decided to build one. There was an external excavated entrance to the house, which was underground, and by putting a roof and ceiling over this, I converted it to an appropriate wine cellar.

GENE AND ANNE FIFE WITH LAURA IN THE HARRISON WINE CELLAR.

I built all of the racks myself, and began to collect wine. My main focus was in California Zinfandels and Cabernet Sauvignons.

My house at Seven Knolls in Cincinnati had a basement that I thought could accommodate a wine cellar quite adequately. When I began my move to Cincinnati, I wanted to be sure I had plenty of California wine, and not only moved about twenty-five cases from my cellar, but went out and purchased another ten cases to put on the truck for the move.

I did not know it when I purchased the house, but later found a false door with a six-foot safe behind it, leading into what obviously had been a wine cellar in earlier days. It had ancient wine racks, but no temperature control. It obviously had been used during prohibition for storing wine behind the closed door of the safe. For several years, I considered building a proper wine cellar with temperature and humidity control, but had not acted on my plan.

One evening at a dinner party, I met a Cincinnatian, Jim Diekebok, who was then the owner of the largest producer of wine racks in the country. He had his designers come and design a cellar for me that is twenty feet by fourteen feet, and it incorporates the old safe door and the cellar that was already in the house. The new cellar has redwood display racks, and storage racks, and can accommodate up to 4,000 bottles of wine. I only have about 990 now, but that varies from time-to-time depending on the number of parties we host. We use our wine cellar for frequent tastings among our friends and business associates, and we also sell opportunities for tastings at several charity events in Cincinnati. We have hosted these events for the International Wine Festival, the Cincinnati Symphony, and the American Heart Association, and fund-raisers for the Inter Parish Ministry.

It has been exciting to sustain my interest in wine, and to visit wineries in South Africa, Chile, Australia, Portugal, France, Italy, Sicily, and New Zealand, all areas of California, Oregon, and Washington. The quality of wines all over the world has improved tremendously. An exciting trip for Laura and me was to participate in the International Pinot Noir Celebration in McMinnville, Oregon. We had three days of tasting directed by experts, and sampled several hundred of the world's finest. As do many physicians, I believe that wine, used in moderation, has a place in promoting heart disease prevention. While I cannot explain the "French Paradox," I think wine accounts for much of it.

The paradox is that, in spite of the rich, cholesterol-laden diet of the French, they have a very low incidence of coronary heart disease. There are now many studies that show a reduction in heart disease mortality rates in wine drinkers as compared with those of non-drinkers. This has led to some people classifying wine as medicinal. There may be a physiological explanation, in that wine drinking increases the "good cholesterol." There are many other theories as to why this occurs. For my part, I adhere to the adage that "A day without wine is like a day without sunshine." But always used in moderation. Also, on one of the couch pillows at our Tahoe house is the slogan, "Life is too short to drink a bad wine." I try hard to follow this advice.

Chapter Fifty-four

WITH FRANK GEHRY

When I arrived in Cincinnati, the buildings at the University of Cincinnati were all of dark, purple-brown brick. The Medical Science Building, which housed the college of medicine, looked dark and had small windows and I characterized it as looking like a prison.

The building contained 960,000 square feet, however, and was highly functional to support the teaching and research missions of the college. It had that institutional look, with all gray walls, and the halls smelled of the chemicals being used in the laboratories. It was clear to me that much needed to be done to change its appearance, both inside and out. I had the walls in the halls of each floor painted with a different pastel color to give the building a new warmth and character. The grounds around the buildings were bare, frequently cluttered with debris, and the parking garage was a solid cement structure, with no lawn or trees around it. We planted trees, cleaned up the debris, and enhanced the appearance of the buildings.

THE GEHRY BUILDING.

Much of the old space in University Hospital, particularly the patient rooms and support areas, needed major renovation. Also, support functions for my office were scattered throughout the medical center campus, often in different buildings. New or renovated space was needed to expand and enhance the efforts of these support functions. The old medical school building of 1919 was designated Health Professions Building, known as HPB, and had been "gutted," but no renovation had been planned.

One of my early aims was to bring the various support functions together in one building, to be able to create more interaction among the planning and construction group, the public relations group, the development, and the financial services components. HPB, a 1919 building, which had housed the medical school until 1974, had been designated for teardown after it was "gutted." This had not yet occurred, and it appeared to me that we could renovate three floors of this building and bring all of our functions together. Jonathan Lippincott, the head of medical center planning, and I worked with a local architectural firm and the university planning group, and we came up with a plan to renovate this building, which we did for a total cost of about $70 per square foot, as compared to the building I had recently built at Stanford that cost over $250 per square foot.

We created space for the functions of all of my day-to-day reports, and created a senior vice president's suite that included up-to-date conference rooms and a mini-kitchen. I worked with Jonathan Lippincott to ensure that people would identify the senior vice president and provost's area as one of authority. He designed a unit with curved walls and etched glass that mirrored the pattern of etching that had been on the large front doors of the medical school in 1919. It certainly let people know where they should come for decisions. He also used this design for the large tabletops in the new board room. The highly functional board room was used by many departments from the health colleges for their events. When the construction project was completed, I was able to consolidate the administrative units under my control from throughout the medical center.

During my tenure at the medical center, almost $1.5 billion of construction was completed. The first large project, a 3,200-car parking garage, was an urgent priority. For the first six months after my arrival, I received about two dozen letters each week with complaints about parking problems. The medical center had grown considerably, but new parking facilities were not created.

Next, we dealt with the inadequate clinic and office space. In the ten years before I came, multiple plans had been made for building an office building where the faculty of the college of medicine would practice. Soon after my arrival, working together with David Fine, we developed a plan to build what became the Medical Arts Building, and we arranged financing. We needed approval for long-term leases from the department chairs, for their clinical activity to support the project. After much bickering on the part of department chairs who were hesitating to invest their reserve funds, we assembled all department directors one evening in a single conference room and laid out the full plan, together with the financial options. We refused to let anyone leave before signing a long-term lease for their space in the new building. It worked and all signed.

The building was constructed adjacent to the University Hospital, and connected with it through the Barrett Cancer Center. The building plan identified a potential capacity of approximately 120,000 patient visits per year. But now, since this number has been far exceeded, the clinical practice offices of general internal medicine and family medicine have been relocated to another new building, the Hoxworth Center, constructed later by University Hospital and now part of the Health Alliance.

Since University Hospital had been built during the 1970s, it lacked many of the features of an upscale university hospital, and in my early years, we began planning major expansions and renovations. Over a four-year period from 1991 to 1995, we built a new bed tower, new surgical intensive care units, and new coronary care units. They were part of a new addition that also housed a neonatal intensive care unit, and a much-enlarged emergency room suite.

The new neonatal intensive care unit, or NICU, as it is called, was built to take care of thirty-six incubators for premature infants. It is now one of the most impressive units for neonatal care throughout the country. Over the next eight years, the entire university Hospital was renovated floor-by-floor. There were conversions of two-bed units and five-bed wards to single rooms, which became the norm for hospitalized patients during this time. In addition, University Hospital planned a new clinic building, the Hoxworth building, since by this time the Medical Arts Building was already filled to over capacity. Two floors are occupied by the Hoxworth Blood Center; one floor is occupied by the BIOSTART Incubator for small company development from university technologies. The BIOSTART Incubator was designed by John Kornberg, an architect from Menlo Park, California, whom I had previously known. BIOSTART has vivid and multi-colored painted walls. The floor has a design of a flowing river on its surface, which is referred to as the Ohio River flowing through our unit. This was to give meaning to the fact that we were creating an area for innovation and company development here along the Ohio River. This space is still regarded as some of the most upscale clinical research space in the area.

The Hoxworth building was completed in 1993, and it has provided space for the family and internal medicine practices, and recentlys the dermatology practice and the ophthalmology practice were relocated to this building. It has also accommodated the growth of the Hoxworth Blood Center and the incubator.

Much of the building in the medical center took place at the Children's Hospital. A much-enlarged hospital, outpatient building, two research buildings and an educational building, two new parking garages, and new administrative space were included in making an entire campus for Children's Hospital. The Children's Hospital complex is one of the most up-to-date clinical, educational, and research facilities that I have seen at any academic medical center in the United States. The building programs there accounted for more than half of all the construction in the medical center during my tenure.

As we began to contemplate construction of research buildings, we became engaged in a university-wide planning process to develop a campus master plan. This plan was to be the work of the president and all vice presidents. The university chose George Hargreaves from San Francisco as its campus planner. He is a tall, gaunt, fast-talking individual with very fixed ideas for campus planning. He is well known because of his faculty position in the School of Architecture at Harvard. Over the next eighteen months, all officers of the university spent many days in retreats with Hargreaves, developing the plan. During this time, I was frequently going to California for company board meetings, and often returned on a "red-eye flight" overnight from San Francisco to Cincinnati. George Hargreaves was often on these flights, as well, on his way to our officers' retreat.

I once asked him why he, a well-known master planner, would participate in the University of Cincinnati planning effort. I knew that he was not being paid a large fee. His comment was quite interesting: "I have never seen such an ugly campus, and anything I can do to make it look better will be a feather in my cap."

The working planning sessions with George Hargreaves and his associate Mary Beth were very intense two-day sessions, much like the retreats of the president of the university and the president's cabinet. There was continuous controversy about where buildings should be located, how they should be financed, and what the traffic pattern flow might be. Such controversial items as closing many of the streets meandering through the university, making them walking pathways, and reducing parking lots to make way for green space, would in many ways change the face of the entire university.

The planning not only involved the West Campus of the undergraduate and graduate academic programs of the university, but also the East Campus, known as the medical center, where the colleges of medicine, pharmacy, and nursing, and University Hospital were located. Our hospital planning was not always congruent with the master plan, and I had to intervene in many cases, to bring about a compatible solution. One of the best examples of this was where to locate the Hoxworth Center, which we insisted should be connected directly to University Hospital. But the Hargreaves planners wanted it located in a more distant off-site area because of the potential need for more space for academic programs. Hargreaves lost this one—of only a few of his recommendations. The planning sessions were quite intense, but in the end, very productive.

We ultimately agreed upon a master plan and decided to choose internationally-known architects to design buildings on the campus. For the first two research buildings, I chose not to seek internationally-known architects, because I knew the costs would be greater and I wanted to quickly acquire as much laboratory space as possible for the money available, in order to attract highly funded investigators with national reputations. We built the cardiovascular building and the environmental health sciences building as standard brick buildings on the medical campus.

However, we did have a major laboratory consultant, Earl Walls, work with us on these projects, and came to an agreement on standardized open laboratories with core cold and warm rooms, and instrument rooms to support each side of the open laboratories. This became our standard laboratory design, and it was similar to that of many major research-based universities and companies in the 1990s. We chose warm colors, not so much in vogue then, for the hallways and laboratories, to make the building more friendly.

DON AND FRANK GEHRY IN BILBAO, SPAIN.

In the meantime, I was observing the building of major projects on the West Campus, which were designed by well-known or "signature" architects. These projects received considerable praise. Signature architects almost always design buildings to enhance a city or a campus image. In 1994, when we were planning to build a molecular science building on Martin Luther King Boulevard that would become the gateway to the medical center, Dale McGirr, the university's vice president for finance, convinced me to consider a signature architect.

Together, we interviewed four architects by spending a whole day with each and seeing their work. First, we interviewed Richard Meier, who at that time was building the Getty Museum in Los Angeles. His buildings were all white, and we determined this would not fit well in Cincinnati. We visited Robert Venturi, who was responsible for many of the buildings at the University of Pennsylvania and at Princeton. Personally, I liked him, but did not think he would design the innovative building that I was seeking to be our gateway. We next spent more than a day with Frank Gehry. This was before he had completed the Guggenheim Center in Bilbao, Spain, though it was under construction at the time. I had a feeling that he would provide us with a unique building, and his personality and mine seemed to be congruent. He liked to ask questions about my philosophy of science, what I wanted to highlight, and described several of his projects to us. In his studio he had models of the Bilbao project and the Disney Symphony Hall in Los Angeles. They were exciting projects to me. I wanted a building that represented the new spirit of the medical center, that of encouraging entrepreneurship, and that of being innovative.

So we chose Gehry's firm to do our building. I had quite a task in convincing him to use the standard laboratory design that we had already chosen. Even before Gehry, the idea of open laboratories did not get an overwhelming acceptance by the research faculty. In order to convince them that this was the laboratory design of the future, we took several of the physician and research leaders to visit other centers and companies that had built open laboratories, in the design from Earl Walls's proposal. He had first instituted open laboratories at the Scripps Institute in La Jolla, California, and the design had been adopted by a number of other academic centers, as well as by a number of pharmaceutical industries. Open laboratories are quite different from the closed modules of four hundred or so square feet that had been the standard laboratory design for many years. The openness provided easy access to core facilities such as cold and warm rooms, and special areas for cell culture, as well as a mechanism for more interaction among the faculty and research students. Faculty offices were located in adjacent areas, while the desk areas for postdocs and graduate students were located on the window side of the open laboratories.

I well remember one of the discussions I had with Gehry over the issue of open laboratories and the design of the building. He said to me, "Don, I want to be in full control of how this building is to be built because we have design staff that can give you new and exciting space."

I replied, "If I remember correctly, you have never built a science building. We have already made a major study of open laboratories, and believe they are the wave of the future." After more discussion, Gehry believed that he could build all of the other components of the building around the standard laboratories and still come up with an architectural masterpiece.

I then told him about the Scripps Institute Laboratories in La Jolla, and invited him to meet with Earl Walls, the man who designed the open laboratory concept. The two men met, and Walls convinced Gehry that the open architecture was the research laboratory of the future. The next iteration of the plans for the molecular science building that were sent to me contained the idea of open laboratories.

All of the office space and conference space in the center of the building had the typical Gehry design, with no single unit looking like another. In fact, we had to have a New York firm design special modular furniture that could be modified to fit irregularly designed offices. The faculty accepted the idea of individually designed offices much more readily than they had accepted the open laboratory design. The partnership established by Earl Walls with Frank Gehry became the cornerstone of our building, allowing it to become an architectural masterpiece as well as a highly functioning science building.

During the planning, we had many visits to Gehry's studio in Santa Monica. I developed a warm and personal relationship with him, and when the Guggenheim Center opened in Bilbao, Spain, my wife and I were invited as his guests. What a wonderful trip that was! That building captured the attention of the art world, and Gehry became even more renowned. I was overwhelmed with the exciting design of the building in the dark, smoke-filled industrial city of Bilbao, Spain. It is unlikely that we could have recruited him to be the signature architect for our building after the completion of the Bilbao project, with the publicity he received. However, his fame as an architect helped us obtain financial support for the building. Albert Vontz, owner of Heidelberg Distributing Company for southern Ohio, really appreciated Gehry's work. He made a large donation to support the building, and it was named the Vontz Center for Molecular Studies.

The building Gehry designed for U.C. has curved exterior walls and looks like a series of biologic cells pulled together. While most of Gehry's building had extensive curved walls, they were not built of brick, but with metal, which could be molded to curves for the walls. In order to match the other building exterior finishes in the medical center, brick was chosen as the material for the building. This was the first major brick building for Gehry, and his first biological science building. He spent several days in Cincinnati just looking at other buildings, to choose the color of the brick to be used.

We could not afford the original titanium he wished to incorporate, so the final decision was for an all-brick building. Office suites were in the center of the building. There were huge windows for each of the laboratories, and an interstitial floor to carry all the utilities, which permitted rearrangement of a laboratory within the matter of a day or two. Interstitial floors contain all of the utilities, which are then accessed to each laboratory by special conduits. These can be changed without moving walls or ceilings. While the interstitial floors cost extra money, they also save at least six months in future renovation project time and many dollars, which occurs on average every three years.

One of the interesting challenges in the planning stages of the building was how to build the curved brick walls Gehry wanted. Bill Vetovitch, the president of a building firm in Toledo, met with Gehry and after a day of persuasion, Gehry convinced him to build these walls in great panels, then bring them to Cincinnati to be welded into a steel frame for the building.

Vetovitch told me a story of leaving the day after Gehry's visit to go fishing in Wisconsin. While he was there, after a day or two, he stood up in his boat and said, "I don't know how in the hell I am going to ever build those curved walls." Nonetheless, he developed a plan, it worked, and all of the panels fit the metal frame except one, which was dropped during the installation process. Watching Vetovitch in action, screaming at contractors, suggested to me that his blood pressure must have increased because of his decision to be engaged in this project. He retired afterwards, and I have always wondered if this was due to the stress of working for Gehry.

I had to settle a number of controversies during the construction, and I had to carefully monitor the costs. Laura Fidler, of our planning group, followed the construction day by day. Gehry's buildings all have a history of large cost overruns, so we monitored costs on a weekly basis. The building was constructed over a three-year period. During this time, many people would come to my office and say, "Are you sure they know what they are doing? Nothing seems to be straight, and all of those windows seem to be misshapen."

We kept our costs in line with great difficulty, settled the controversies about the landscaping around the building with George Hargreaves, and kept the program on schedule. These activities required weekly reviews of the buildings by the university architecture staff and my staff. Laura Fidler was my representative, and did a great job of keeping the construction on schedule and on budget. I almost always attended these reviews as well. Once the building was finished, the opening was cause for a big celebration.

We invited two Nobel Prize winners who had been my colleagues at Stanford. They were Paul Berg of Stanford and Ferid Murad of the University of Texas in Houston, for the opening celebratory research conference. Charlie Rose, the TV talk-show host, accepted our invitation to emcee the show and to host an interview describing the building on his nationally televised program. There was an open house the weekend that the building opened, and while we typically have about 200 attend these openings, over 6,000 people came through the building because of the publicity it had been given in the Greater Cincinnati area.

This was the most unique building in Cincinnati at the time. Even people not connected with the medical center wanted to see it. There were strong supporters for what we had done, and strong negative feelings regarding its visual impact as well.

In addition to the opening ceremony and the open house, I decided to host my past Stanford doctoral fellows, to attend and make presentations of their latest research and business accomplishments. More than fifty attended. The presentations were exciting, and I was proud of what they had accomplished and the positions they now held. We hosted a dinner at Seven Knolls, which was highlighted by an old-fashioned "roast" quite similar to the ones we had at farewell parties at our house in California. We all looked a bit older, but everyone was in high spirits from being together again.

From my standpoint, the Gehry building captured what we wanted, a symbol to demonstrate the new direction for the medical center, now placed in its gateway. Subsequently, this building has been featured in the national architectural press and is visited by architects from all over the world. We also have requests to use the lobby of the building for wedding receptions, and we have a regular program for visitors who are interested in architecture to visit the campus and see the building. It has accomplished all that I had hoped, and yet it remains a highly functional research science building.

FELLOWS AT GEHRY OPENING.

There are always challenges to building state-owned buildings in Ohio. The design must be approved by a state architect who is usually not knowledgeable about academic buildings. The bid process is lengthy, and one is required to accept the lowest bid. This process sometimes results in using inferior companies on important projects. The failure to be able to use a general contractor for all the work also drives the costs up by approximately 30 percent. However, building costs in Cincinnati were about 30 percent less than what I had experienced at Stanford for comparable buildings. So one might consider it a bargain. The construction of these new buildings was one of the great pleasures of my job, and was essential for my plan to change the image of the medical center.

Chapter Fifty-five

FOR A DECADE

As the decade of the '90s drew to a close, everyone was aware that our strategic plan of 1988-89, "Reaching for the 21ˢᵗ Century," needed updating. In 1998, Congress announced that it would double the budget of the NIH over a five-year period from $13 billion to $27 billion per year for 2003.

This became one of the driving forces for us to create a new plan so that we could share in this potential research funding bonanza. We called our new plan the "Millennium Plan." The idea was that this would be a plan for the first decade of the new millennium, not a one-thousand-year plan, as this name might indicate, and the name was common to similar plans of many other organizations in this country.

Planning for more than five years into the future for a medical center makes one question the sanity of those making such plans because of the rapidity of change in funding sources and in medical reimbursement. In 1998, we brought together more than a hundred leaders from throughout the many units of the medical center and set about over the next eighteen months making a plan for the first decade of the new millennium after 2000. We reviewed our successes of the 1990s, during which our research funding had gone from $30 million to $142 million. On the medical center campus, we had built five new research buildings and had recruited several hundred new faculty.

We benchmarked our activities against national standards and found that in research, our funded investigators were in the top 10 percent, based on total amount of funding for each investigator as compared to national peers. They were receiving, on average, more than $350,000 per investigator each year. This suggested to us that in order for us to acquire our share of the doubling of the NIH budget, we had to add new investigators. We could expect our current investigators to increase their productivity by 10 or 15 percent, but not 100 percent. We chose a goal for the medical center of $300 million of funded research by the year 2010, and did the necessary calculations, which showed that we needed to add approximately 300 newly funded investigators at more than $450,000 each to make this occur. This raised questions about the space to support the laboratory programs, the funds to recruit them, and the focus areas on which we should concentrate to highlight the strengths of research in our institution.

I evaluated the strengths and barriers to success of a number of research areas in which we had expertise, and then appointed subcommittees to work for several months evaluating each opportunity. In the end we chose to again focus on the four areas that had been our strengths in the 1990s: Cardiopulmonary; cancer; neurobehavioral, which included stroke, degenerative neurological diseases, and behavioral diseases such as addiction and obesity; and perinatology and early development, strong research areas of Children's Hospital. We also added diabetes as a fifth focus, since we recognized that we had some strength in this area, but needed major additions for success.

Our next task was to determine how to create new laboratories for these investigators. We began planning for major renovation of the Medical Sciences Building and the addition of a new research building as a connecting wing on the west side of the Medical Sciences Building. This building soon had an acronym, CARE, which stood for Center for Academic and Research Excellence.

We also acquired seven research buildings in Reading, Ohio, which were gifts from the Aventis Corporation. In these facilities, we created a new department, and the Genome Research Institute. David Milhorn, the chair of physiology, became its first director. These buildings had previously been the center for research for the Merrell Dow pharmaceutical company and later its merged companion, Marion Merrell Dow. In 1998, these companies merged into Hoechst, and the research programs were transferred to New Jersey. I approached Hoechst about giving the Reading facilities to the university. Since they were a German company and could not benefit from tax credits, they refused.

When another merger resulted in Aventis Pharmaceutical, I made another attempt, with the help of Laura Fidler, Director of Facilities Planning, and was successful. The negotiations took several months, and were culminated with the company making an outright gift of the buildings and property to the University of Cincinnati Foundation, an independent 501(C)(3) foundation. This designation was necessary for the company to receive its tax credits, since it would not occur if the buildings were given to the State of Ohio, the parent of the university.

For the Millennium Plan, our greatest challenge was to find the funding to do the recruitment and to support the 300 investigators until they were able to acquire national funding for their research. Dale McGirr, chief financial officer and vice president for finance for the University of Cincinnati, came to our rescue. Dale thinks fast, but sometimes talks in riddles. He helped devise a plan to use the increase in overhead return from new research to support the recruitment of the new faculty and to support the research space to house them.

The plan was to borrow funds in advance with payments after the researchers had been recruited. It was an ambitious, imaginative plan, and took a major risk. It required considerable negotiation with the university's Grants Administration officers, and the more focused use of research overhead. With all of this in place in 2000, we launched the Millennium Plan.

Three years after implementation of the Millennium Plan, it was going quite well. We had moved expeditiously to sell the plan widely in the community and in the state, as having potential for economic growth by the commercialization of basic research into spinoff companies taking advantage of our incubator, BIOSTART, and some of the new possibilities for venture capital funding. In these first three years, we increased our research support to more than $260 million, well ahead of our projected plan for the ten years; we recruited sixty of the new investigators; completed the renovation of the Aventis space in Reading, Ohio, and established the Genome Research Institute in that space. We also finished the planning and potential funding for the CARE building.

The new decade had commenced with a very detailed plan for further success for the University of Cincinnati, recognized both locally and nationally. This was a good start for the ambitious long-range plans that we had developed. Things were going well, and the medical center had enhanced its national recognition. It was at this point that I made my decision to step down and to accept an emeritus appointment. I had long outlasted the five years most directors of medical centers survived, and we were at the height of success. In 2007, the Millennium Plan was still in place, and hopefully, will reach its goals by 2010. The reduced pace of research expenditures by the NIH, however, may limit its full implementation.

Chapter Fifty-six

AT CINCINNATI

As I reach the end of my career at the University of Cincinnati, it seems worthwhile to consider my impact on the institution and what legacy I leave. The difficulty here is to be objective, for I recognize that my ego about the changes I brought about may interfere with that objectivity.

When I arrived at the University of Cincinnati, the general attitude was that it was a reasonable place for educating medical students and residents who serve the needs of the region for practicing physicians. The prevailing attitude was: "Oh, yes, we do a bit of research, but we are part of a conservative Midwest." There seemed to be little thought of any national recognition of the medical center's components.

My charge in coming to Cincinnati was to change this attitude, to provide a new emphasis on growth of clinical programs and research, and to have higher national aspirations for the medical center. Not knowing much about the institution, one of my first tasks was to learn as much as I could about its culture and past history. Now, in retrospect, I try to sum up my own assessment of the changes that I brought about with the plans "Reaching for the 21st Century," and the "Millennium Plan."

The 21st century plan was published and circulated widely. It was the focus of all of my annual "State of the Medical Center" addresses, and it was the constant message espoused to the community. Our successes were far greater than we had first imagined possible. We did restructure the clinical practices, and became a more unified operation.

We had a "turnaround" at University Hospital and over a six-year period built a new bed tower, surgical, medical, and cardiac intensive care units, a state-of-the-art neonatal unit, and a new emergency facility, still the only Level I trauma unit in the area. We also built a new practice building, the Medical Arts Building, and the Barrett Cancer Center.

We created a new home for Hoxworth Blood Center, making it more of a community resource, responsive to an advisory board, but still under the senior vice president of the medical center. It is an independent blood bank, supplying forty hospitals, and I always regarded it as one of our major assets. We also acquired Drake Hospital and turned it into a regional rehabilitation center and a site for educational programs for the four health colleges. These were the initiatives that occupied my everyday thoughts. I persisted in discussing and presenting them at every opportunity.

In order to enhance the research capabilities, we needed major research renovation and construction. My initial enthusiasm convinced the university administration to put research buildings at the top of the capital needs with the Ohio Board of Regents' capital allocations. Unfortunately, the state had never provided funds to build research buildings, and it took two biennia and hours of presentations to convince the Board of Regents that research was an important mission of its top-rated universities.

With new support, we proceeded to build three new research buildings. The environmental health building houses one of the largest departments of environmental health in the country. The cardiovascular research building allowed us to move multidisciplinary cardiovascular programs into one space to create synergisms and enhance the research funding capabilities for each of the groups. The Vontz Center for Molecular Studies is the highest level research facility. With these new facilities,

The research programs at CHMC were among the fastest growing in the nation. During my tenure they grew from less than $10 million to almost $100 million.

we recruited top-level investigators, which soon bore great fruit in terms of our research support and our national ranking.

During the same time, the Children's Hospital Medical Center, which is an important and integral part of the overall medical center, developed two new research buildings, and also fully participated in the change of attitude that we perpetuated throughout the medical center. The research program at Children's flourished with the addition of many new investigators in the department of pediatrics. Tom Boat was recruited as the new chair of pediatrics and president of the research foundation to lead all the changes at CHMC. The research programs at CHMC were among the fastest growing in the nation. During my tenure, they grew from less than $10 million to almost $100 million.

The enhancement of the research effort occurred in large part because we created programs of excellence that could be shared as core facilities and core operations throughout the Center. The most prominent of these was in the mouse transgenic models, a bioinformatics center, the proteomics core laboratory, and in enhanced biostatistical support.

We pioneered the development of research institutes, and created the Health Policy and Health Research Institute of the university, similar to a school of public health. Faculty from many departments spend part of their time working in this institute, and it has begun to have a major impact on health policy throughout the region. The second institute that we created was the Genome Research Institute, which was to occupy all of the space in the property that Aventis had given the U.C. Foundation in the city of Reading.

With the help of many individuals, we created a new college of allied health sciences. This brought together many of the other health professions' educational programs throughout the university into one college. We renovated the then vacant old Shriners Burns Hospital into a marvelous college facility for this group of new health professionals. In the end, we needed much more research space on the campus, and during my final three years, we laid the plans for the CARE building, which will be completed in 2008.

On the clinical side, we acquired property in Butler County for our new clinical campus, known as University Pointe. The first building opened before I stepped down and plans are now progressing for a hospital on the campus, as part of the Health Alliance. This will be a northern comprehensive campus for the medical center, which will develop over the next ten years.

In order to change the attitudes of complacency, new deans were recruited for each of the colleges. All department chairs in the college of medicine except one were new appointments during my tenure. We moved from a lackadaisical, "we're okay" attitude to one that can be expressed as "can do." We took calculated risks to move forward in our attitudinal changes, and in our development. We needed to interact more closely with the community, especially in educational and clinical programs. In addition, we needed to build mechanisms for the basic research to be commercialized, to lead to economic growth of the region. The creation of BIOSTART, the incubator for small companies, in the Hoxworth Building, filled this void quite well. This concept of providing subsidized space for spinout research opportunities for the faculty, to provide business advice, and core facilities that could be shared at a reasonable price, led to a more entrepreneurial spirit.

In order to capitalize on the federal government's Small Business Administration investments for research programs, we created Emerging Concepts, Inc., which allowed researchers with commercially viable ideas to obtain funds without having to create a company, but with full aim of commercial development. We also revamped the Intellectual Property and Technology Transfer offices at Children's Hospital and the university. As part of convincing the community that we are an economic engine, I contracted with a national firm doing economic impact assessments to carry out two studies, which demonstrated more than a $3 billion impact on the economy of the region. The medical center employed over 13,000 individuals, and in support roles throughout the community another 15,000 involved with construction, supplies, and other health-related functions.

As I evaluate my contribution to the University of Cincinnati, it also is important for me to mention lost opportunities and mistakes made along the way. There are several, but I will highlight only a few. From my standpoint, one of these was that I did not get involved in enough state politics to influence state funding of programs at the medical center. Ohio has been remiss in not recognizing that the strength of its universities ultimately helps to keep commercialization in the state viable. I believe I could have helped make a better case for this.

Another mistake, even though I tried desperately, was my inability to sufficiently convince the Cincinnati business community of the importance of the medical center in order to receive their enthusiastic and active backing. Finally, my failure at an early date to convince the University of Cincinnati board of trustees to support the risky idea of a community comprehensive health system, Health Education and Research Corporation (HERC), focused at the university, was a large failure. It led to the subsequent resignation of the first director of University Hospital during my tenure. The creation of the Health Alliance came several years after our attempt to create a university-based health system throughout the region—HERC. HERC would have permitted us to have an area-wide health system, with the university as its center.

Chapter Fifty-seven

RETURN to my roots

Birmingham-Southern College had been quite important to me in providing the educational framework that I had missed in high school, and in providing an underpinning for my successful career. This task fell to a few dedicated teachers who were willing to spend time and to help a student whom they regarded as having potential. I can probably never thank or appreciate them enough.

After my graduation from Birmingham-Southern, I always appreciated the liberal arts education that I had received, and the socialization that occurred with college. This was important to set me on the course of growing from a redneck Appalachian to becoming a physician and a well-recognized academician. From the time of my graduation in 1954 until 1972, I had only passing activity with the college through receiving its alumni newsletter and publication.

While at Stanford, I began to reassociate myself with Birmingham-Southern, and received considerable recognition. By 1970, I had become nationally known because of my activities with the heart transplant program at Stanford, and I was invited back to the campus to speak with students and faculty. My presentation went quite well, as I encouraged them to consider careers like my own. I was also inducted into Phi Beta Kappa as an alumnus member because I had met the criteria for membership as a student, but because of then present quota limitations, was not chosen.

In 1972, I was chosen to be a distinguished alumnus of the college, and returned to Birmingham for the ceremony. I was quite impressed with the new president, Neal Berte, and with how well the college was doing. Over the next few years I spoke with Neal on several occasions, and began to contribute to a scholarship fund and to a major building fund for the campus. I received frequent letters from President Berte, and was accustomed to receiving calls from him, asking for support and advice. I was also invited to be a member of the selection committee for the Distinguished Alumnus, a very prestigious award from the college. I continued this for five years.

After coming to Cincinnati, I had further opportunities to reconnect with Birmingham-Southern College, my undergraduate alma mater. Over the Christmas holidays in 1996, I received a call from President Berte, asking me if I would consider being a backup speaker for their commencement the next May. This seemed unusual, and being a bit curious, I asked whom I was backing up, and he told me that it was President Clinton. I thought it acceptable to be "second fiddle" to the president and I said, "Yes."

In February, I was told I would be the speaker since the president was not going to be able to make the appearance. I worked hard on a speech, wanting to make a good impression on the graduates. Laura and I returned to Birmingham, visited the college, and renewed our acquaintance with Neal Berte. I made the presentation at the Civic Center with a large crowd of students and parents in attendance. The title of my talk was, "Lifelong Learning: Challenges for Re-engineering Society," and it received a very warm reception from the students and parents attending the graduation ceremony. I was awarded an honorary Doctor of Law degree, of which I am quite proud and upon re-reading my commencement speech today, I am convinced that I gave the students good advice, but don't know whether or not they accepted it.

In 2004, Neal Berte reached the thirty-year milestone as president of the college, and there was a Thirtieth Anniversary Celebration honoring him. A number of distinguished speakers were invited back, and I was honored to be chosen to speak for the biomedical sciences. Other speakers included a retired senator from Alabama, the executive editor of *The New York Times*, and several distinguished theater and musical performers.

A large number of alumni returned to the college to honor Berte. I also went back for my Fiftieth Class Reunion during that same year. I met many of my classmates and I recognized some of them, in spite of all our aging. We shared stories of our lives since graduation fifty years before, and also remembered stories from our years in college, but I have a sneaking suspicion that many of these never happened.

Birmingham-Southern College played a major role in my development from an Appalachian to a leading cardiologist, a leader of a large medical center, and my life as a physician.

Chapter Fifty-eight

RETIREMENT
emotions

During the months prior to my official retirement, Laura and I talked about what I would do to occupy myself. She was strongly in favor of the decision to retire, since she had always warned me to step aside while I was "on top." However, she made it clear to me that she did not want me home on a full-time basis, where I would expect her to be my secretary.

She was concerned that I would become depressed, because I might not successfully adapt to a less hectic and directed schedule. Yet, she wanted us to have time to do things together without such restricted time constraints, usually coupled with some business agenda. It was with these goals that I enjoyed our New Year's celebration welcoming in 2003.

I was about to move into a new phase in my life, and I was uncertain what it would bring. I sought to continue to find meaning and profit from what I had observed with many of my patients as they entered this phase of their lives.

As January 2, 2003, dawned, and I was stepping down from heading the medical center, I remember two strong emotions. The first was one of relief from the everyday challenges of being in charge of a major academic medical center and the multiple people problems that emerged on a daily basis, but the second was the more important feeling of being adrift without an anchor on any major issue to occupy my time. As we celebrated the New Year, my mind vacillated back and forth between these two emotions. I knew I would face new challenges in moving to a new office, but since my successor had not been selected, I had not faced the inevitable challenge of downsizing my multiple filing cabinets, many journals, and large files of reprints and materials, some of which I had even brought from Stanford University and accumulated over almost fifty years.

In the days following my official retirement, Marie Blum, my long-dedicated secretary for seventeen years, and I started to sift through the more than twenty filing cabinets containing much of the paperwork that I had accumulated in Cincinnati—my patient records, which dated back to my earlier time at Stanford, and my personal and business transaction records as well. We had large trash bins brought in to take care of the discharge material, and in many instances found that the filing system had long contained items that were no longer of use to anyone. We sorted the records that needed to be maintained for my successor when he or she arrived, and left these carefully marked in filing cabinets.

We knew that we had space in our new office setup for only about six filing cabinets, and we sought to sort the material down to that level. This allowed me to keep many things that I had preserved over the many years and could not find a way to part with at the time. We embarked on a program of gradually moving the material that we selected to keep to my new office, which was in the pharmacy building on the ground floor. An unoccupied suite had been completely refurnished and new furniture had been installed. The pharmacy building is an older building, and the windows to the outside of my office were of a shutter type that had been recently replaced. The building itself was much smaller than my senior vice president office complex, and contained an office for me, with a large credenza behind my new cherry wood desk, a small conference table, and an antique sideboard, which the contractor purchased at an antique sale. This is a marvelous piece of furniture, at least 100 years old, and became a perfect accompaniment to the new furniture in the office. The suite was also set up with a new telephone and computer system, which was installed in the credenza behind my desk. The outer office contained a desk and work area for my secretary, the filing cabinets were arranged around the work area, and a small two-seat waiting area for my visitors was available inside the door leading to the main hallway.

We also had a work room with coffee maker, our photocopy machine, and all of our supplies and additional filing cabinets were housed here. Each of the rooms seemed to have a temperature-control mechanism, but we soon found out that this seemed to not assure us of a warm environment in which to work. It seemed that we were on a central heating system, and our thermostat in the offices did not function very well. During much of the move and while we discarded piles of material, I often felt as if part of my life was being taken away. Sometimes it was an uneasy feeling, as I remembered the events and the people, many of them dear friends, surrounding many of the items we were discarding.

In spite of its small size, the office complex proved to be quite serviceable as we continued to move ourselves into it. Other than not having to meet a daily work schedule and to shoulder major responsibilities, my days at the office were not too different than before. I had the services of my longtime secretary Marie Blum, who thought of every aspect of my business activities in an all-encompassing way, better than even I. She had reached the age of 80 years, did not desire to retire, but wished to work only two days per week. It was almost fortuitous that Jean Morrison, who had been the executive assistant for Jack Cook (president of Christ Hospital and the first CEO of the Health Alliance), had also decided that she wished to retire from her position at the Health Alliance, and was delighted to be able to work with me three days per week. So my secretarial services were outstanding, probably with almost eighty years of experience between the two of them, with the added bonus that they knew each other and almost everyone in the city with whom I might be interacting.

There was much for Jean to learn about my daily activities, and especially my business relationships, but with my help and the kind assistance of Marie, she soon caught on, and this working relationship came to be quite smooth within the first few months. I was quite relieved to have people who knew and understood my activities, my travel, and my relationships to many people in the community. Laura was especially relieved that I had adhered to her wish not to move home and set up my office there, and expect her to provide secretarial services.

Since my retirement occurred at the New Year, 2003, the retirement party that was planned to honor me was delayed because of the holiday season until mid-January. Laura Fidler, who had been one of my right-hand people, was responsible for organizing this event, which was held at the Kingsgate Hotel and Conference Center on the campus. The plan was for all of my family, children, and grandchildren to attend, and for invitations to be sent to many in the community, including our congressman, Rob Portman, with whom I had worked on many occasions. A series of speakers were selected and recruited to outline my contributions and career at the University of Cincinnati. My family was offered an opportunity for one person to speak, and my youngest daughter, Donna Marie, was selected for this role.

While my colleagues, Joe Steger, president of the university, Gene Fife, a dear friend and one of my patients, and Representative Rob Portman gave accolades to my performance, my daughter, Donna Marks, was much more focused on family relationships and on some of the comments I had made when I first decided to leave Stanford and come to the University of Cincinnati.

She gave tribute for much of my success to my wife, who had been a loyal supporter and was willing to move with me to Cincinnati. She also reminded the audience that I had stated that I could do the job that was in my plan for Cincinnati in seven to eight years, and would then fully retire. Donna's point was that I was a slow learner, and it had taken seventeen years for me to reach the point where I was willing to step down from my position. The whole affair was joyous, and the three beautifully presented remembrance books of letters and comments from my colleagues from Cincinnati, my postdoctoral fellows from Stanford, and many, many friends gave me reading material for many weeks. As I read all these complimentary letters, I tried not to let the accolades get too imbedded in my psyche.

During those first few months of retirement, I found that having more time at home with Laura was pleasurable, but in some ways was also challenging. I had always been one to be fully occupied at all times. Now, not going to work for early meetings, and coming home earlier in the afternoons provided time in which I needed to find activities to fill.

Fortunately, Laura had ideas of things for me to do and urged me to take up more food preparation, particularly for dinner, and to work with her to plan more travel to keep me occupied. I think she was delighted that I was not home all the time, and that I did go to the office every day.

My plan was to keep moving, keep busy, and not to develop any withdrawal symptoms due to not being in charge at the medical center. I made a major effort to withdraw myself, to be nothing but an observer of how things were progressing in the medical center. I continued to meet with Dan Gahl, head of the university physicians' practice plan, Jim Wesner, general counsel for the university, and Jim Tucker, vice president in charge of physical plant management, parking and student housing. I met with these individuals for the purpose of listening to what was happening, but in no way engaging myself with any of the day-to-day decision making. I knew how difficult it was to not interfere, but I made an absolute decision to not do so.

As part of keeping busy, I began to do more exercise, especially focusing on biking along the bike trail near our house known as Rails to Trails, when the weather developed to spring. During the first few months, when it was still winter, I increased my exercise at the Cincinnati Sports Club and began to swim more often, starting with a quarter mile, and building up to a half-mile per day. After six months, I believed I was succeeding in retirement and emotionally I felt good about my progress.

During the summer of that first year after retirement, Laura and I spent three weeks in August at Lake Tahoe, at our vacation house, and I did a backpacking trip with Donna and her family into the Desolation Valley wilderness area along the crest of the mountains on the west side of Lake Tahoe. This was the first of this type of challenge. Donna, her husband, David, and Ruth and Jonathan, the two oldest grandchildren, planned this event in minute detail. Laura remained at our home with the two younger Marks children.

Desolation Valley is in the high Sierra Mountains and has a series of pristine lakes, which provide great camping sites. Our trip started with the distribution of what each person would transport on their backs. For this trip, I started with approximately thirty pounds, but insisted I carry much of the food. I knew it would be eaten, and my load would diminish. Everyone carried his own sleeping bag, ground pad, clothes, and raingear. Jonathan and I shared the lead up and down the trails for most of the trip. He was frightened on one section when we ascended over 9,000 feet and walked along a narrow ledge for several hundred yards.

I coached him along, having him face the mountain and advised him not to look over the ledge. We camped at two lakes, had great food, swam in ice-cold water, and viewed great star constellations, as Jonathan and I slept out without a tent. The trip was a learning experience for us all. It was an opportunity I had missed for more than twenty-five years, and I captured the feelings of how small we humans are in the great scheme of the universe.

After our Tahoe time, we entered the fall of 2003, and I began to search for other potential activities, and was offered an opportunity to join a venture capital group to begin what would become a fourth career.

Nine months into my retirement, and after consulting with numerous friends about what I should or could do, I made a decision to join with a group from Palo Alto, Californiia, to form a new first-time venture capital fund, which we named Charter Life Sciences (CLS). I knew my proposed partners from earlier business experiences. I had previously worked with Barr Dolan, who was the principal founder of an earlier venture capital firm, Charter Venture Capital, which had operated for almost twenty years. Charter Venture Capital was a fund supporting the development of advanced technology companies. There were life science companies and high-tech companies in their portfolio.

A decision had been made to split the companies from four previous funds into a group of the life science companies and a group of high-tech companies. The life science companies were to be managed by CLS as they were going forward. There were almost twenty companies in the CLS group, and their direction was to be determined by the principal directors of CLS. Members of CLS were on the boards of most of them, and several of them had been founded by CLS members when they were supported by Charter Venture Capital. In addition to Barr Dolan and me, the other directors were Fred Schwarzer, who had previously been the CEO of one of the life science companies in the Charter Venture Capital portfolio, and had also worked for the largest investor in Charter Venture Capital; and Nelson Teng, who founded four companies funded by Charter Venture Capital and was a professor at Stanford.

The partners' first objective was to raise capital for CLS investments. We, too, created a business plan outlining what we would do as a group and what type of companies we would fund. This is known as a Private Placement Memorandum (PPM) which is used to explain CLS plans to potential investors. Over a period of two months, this document was drafted. Our unique features were to be an early stage fund directed by individuals who had worked together before and had considerable medical, technical, and business experience. We agreed to focus on devices and biopharma companies for our initial investments.

We decided that a unique characteristic would be to have an Ohio office as well as the main office in Palo Alto. I would direct the Midwest office, and seek to identify potential technologies and companies in the Midwest that we could fund. Once our PPM was completed, we circulated it to pension funds, fund managers, endowments, and wealthy individuals. Over the next eight to nine months, we traveled the country making presentations to groups in Ohio, Michigan, Pennsylvania, Virginia, Massachusetts, Illinois, Los Angeles, and San Francisco, and ultimately, we acquired the services of a placement agency in Europe. Members of our group made presentations in Denmark and Switzerland. Presentations were also made in Singapore, Hong Kong, and Taiwan. The fundraising was far more difficult than I had expected, and it took us eighteen months to raise $67.5 million. We had our first close in 2004, and after a first close we could begin to fund companies with the money raised from investors.

This is a labor-intensive process, and one that requires considerable consultation with individuals who are knowledgeable…

Because of Barr Dolan's long history as a venture capitalist in California, many opportunities for funding are presented to him by individuals with new ideas seeking funding. In addition, because we had a Midwest office and visited many of the universities and early stage company incubators throughout the region, we began to have numerous business plans presented to us for funding. In order to handle the large number of business plans and presentations being made to us we developed an initial screening mechanism that utilized the eight characteristics that we thought were most likely to yield a successful company development and commercialization.

Based on a scoring system, if a score of 70 was achieved by a company, we then took a closer look at its potential for funding by CLS. After a presentation by the principals, and an opportunity for us to discuss with them in detail, we could then make a decision as to whether or not we should enter due diligence. Due diligence resulted in us consulting experts in the field, the inventors of the technology, and seeking further information about the intellectual properties status, and perhaps looking into a market survey for the potential commercialization value of such a company. Since 2004, we have reviewed more than 1,350 business plans. Our initial screening process has screened out nearly 1,150 of those.

We have had presentations by more than 180 companies, have entered due diligence on about sixty, and to date have funded ten. This is a labor-intensive process and one that requires considerable consultation with individuals who are knowledgeable about the technologies. For me personally, it has been like going back to medical school. I have extensive medical knowledge and have kept up well in the field of cardiology. I also have had a smattering of experience in drug delivery and in women's health programs, but I have had to do extensive study about orthopedics, neurology, infectious disease, cancer, and many other areas of medicine, since opportunities come to us in almost all of these areas. These challenges occupied much of my time but still left opportunities to plan activities with Laura.

Once we decided to have an Ohio office, it was my job to determine a site for the office. Having been one of the founders of BIOSTART, an incubator for start-up life science companies associated with the University of Cincinnati and Cincinnati Children's Hospital, the BIOSTART suite seemed like an ideal site for our Ohio office. It would put me near people developing early technologies aimed at commercialization. I chose an office area large enough to have a colleague join me and to be able to accommodate students from the business graduate school as interns, and to have my secretaries work with me. Over the next two years, I maintained an office that had been provided to me at the pharmacy school as well as the Charter Life Sciences office at BIOSTART.

In order to choose a colleague to work with me, I began to interview people in Cincinnati. After interviewing several individuals, Karen Morgan, who had worked with the Senmed group, a Cincinnati venture firm that had recently disbanded, came into my office and asked if I would have an interest in her joining me. She was interviewed by my group in Palo Alto, and once she was approved by all, she joined us as an associate to help establish and manage the Cincinnati office, making sure that it was completely integrated with the operating systems in Palo Alto, establishing a video conferencing area to permit us to work actively with the CLS office in Palo Alto.

On our weekly four-hour partners conference call utilizing internet video communication, we discuss all of the new business plans we have screened in the previous week, and discuss each of the companies with which we are doing due diligence and in which we have already made investments. The length of these conferences allows for intense discussion of each of Charter's opportunities, and keeps all partners apprised of issues about each of them.

Companies chosen to make presentations from Cincinnati or from the Palo Alto area can video conference presentations from the Charter office to the other site. This arrangement of video conferencing by internet is inexpensive, and permits us to minimize travel from Cincinnati to California. We do hold quarterly reviews of each funded company, and a once-a-year meeting of our science advisory board is held in California as well as an annual meeting for our investors. Six to ten trips per year are made to Palo Alto by those of us working in Cincinnati.

In addition to presentations by potential companies, we attend numerous meetings where multiple companies make presentations, and where other VCs attend. These provide networking opportunities and an opportunity to see early stage companies in which we might have an interest.

One of the companies we have funded, EnteroMedics, Inc., which focuses on vagal nerve blockade to treat and prevent obesity, was developed in an incubator in which I worked with a group of scientists in Minneapolis. Two other companies are developing cardiovascular products, and I serve as an advisor to each of them and have recently been elected to the board of CoRepair, one of the two.

Charter Life Sciences invested initially in an asthma company, a cancer company, a macular degeneration company, and an Alzheimer's company. We have continued to follow each of these actively since we made the initial investment, and have set aside money for follow-on investments in each case. Raising a second venture fund for Charter Life Sciences is now in full swing, and began in earnest in September 2007.

It is anticipated that this fund will be larger than our first fund, hopefully $150 to $200 million. The small size of the first fund limited the type of investments we could make and the scope to which we could invest, ranging initially from $1 to $3 million with a set-aside of up to $6 to $8 million for later-stage investments in the same companies. Since all investments are made by consensus, it is necessary for extensive discussion to take place among all of the partners on a regular basis.

I have enjoyed this experience, and have learned a great deal about the venture capital process. It has been educational for me to learn of many new technologies outside of cardiology. There have also been many opportunities to become acquainted with other venture capitalists with whom we jointly invest in some of our companies.

While there are reasons to criticize venture capital it has been the driving force for entrepreneurial activity in life science fields. Many of the advances in medicine have been initiated by capital infusion from venture capital. For me, the opportunity to be on both the receiving and giving side has been eye opening. I like the opportunity to continue to be actively involved, and yet have the time to pursue my other more socially important activities. I plan to continue on a part-time basis for the next several years.

As I continue to work in my fourth career as a partner with Charter Life Sciences, it consumes only about half of my time. This half-time activity does not preclude other activities on my calendar, since it only requires me to be in contact with my Charter partners by phone, computer, or internet.

Since stepping down from my university position in 2003, I have increased several activities in my life that are very meaningful, and in many instances, downright fun. One of the most important objectives for me is to spend time with my children, their spouses, and eight grandchildren. First, for Laura's and my Fiftieth Anniversary in 2006, we took the entire family to the Galapagos Islands for a ten-day trip. It was organized by Lindblad Expeditions and our venues included a visit to Ecuador. We spent eight days on the Lindblad ship, the *Endeavor*. We cruised around to seven of the Galapagos Islands, with daily trips onto the islands or into the sea around them for snorkeling or

GALAPAGOS WITH FAMILY FOR OUR 50TH WEDDING ANNIVERSARY.

beach trips to view the various animals. Educational and inspiring, the trips provided me time for activities with each of the grandchildren. The opportunity to visit the place that stimulated Darwin to develop the concept of evolution was very educational for all of the grandchildren. They were particularly impressed with how close we could get to the many varieties of animal life.

Second, we attempt to have the grandchildren visit us at Seven Knolls, at least one each year. In 2005, 2006, and 2007, they all visited for several days around the Fourth of July weekend. We typically attend the Indian Hill Fourth of July parade, spend hours around the pool, and of course, a great deal of time sharing food. This past year, five of the youngest grandchildren spent another week with us after their parents had gone home. This was "Gran's Camp," i.e., Laura's Camp. There were organized educational activities in the mornings, fun activities around the pool, and field trips in the afternoons. The children produced a short play that they presented to us on one of the evenings. I made a video of this and it is a much anticipated highlight as all of the grandchildren gather to view their and their cousins' parts in this production.

Third, for the past four summers, I have accompanied at least one of the families on four back-packing trips in the Sierra Nevada Mountains. On two of the trips, I accompanied Donna's family. The first trip, into the Desolation Valley area on the west side of Lake Tahoe, was exciting and made me want to do more. The other trip with the Marks family in 2005 was into the Lakes Basin, near Graeagle, about fifty miles north of Lake Tahoe. In 2006, we revisited this area again with Beth's family, but took a different route. Beth's husband, Peter, organized the trip. It was one of the most arduous hikes we have taken, and there were times when I was not certain we would make it over the next mountain.

Laura joined us on the trips in 2005, 2006, and 2007, so she could spend additional time with the grandchildren. These trips teach the children perseverance, since on a backpack trip you are carrying your food, as well as all your other necessities. Much organization takes place, and the older grandchildren help distribute what goes into the backpack of each individual. The trips have been arduous but quite fun-filled, and all of us will have memories long into the future.

GRAN'S CAMP.

A fourth way we enjoy having time with the grandchildren is during the holiday periods, particularly Thanksgiving and Christmas. Each of these holidays in the last three years has been spent with one or other of the three families. We attempt to fairly distribute our time with each of them. We also visit their schools on grandparents' day, letting Ruth Marks, our oldest grandchild, drive with us when she visits, now that she has reached the driving age of 16.

My free time has allowed me to be more supportive of Laura's role with her college at the University of North Alabama in Florence. My role mostly takes on the form of being

A CHILDREN'S THEATER PRODUCTION.

her chauffeur since we generally drive there for her activities. In 2005, she was one of the individuals who suggested and helped organize UNA's first alumni celebration. It included all of the classes of the 1950s. The college had no alumni registry before this event, and Laura was the stimulus for its development.

She has continued her role as part of the President's Advisory Council and being a board member of the UNA Foundation for fund-raising. In the fall of 2006, she began a one-year term as chair for the advisory board and I foresee more chauffeuring activities for me during this time. These trips to UNA allow us to visit the Laura Harrison Plaza, to see the growth of the landscape around it and review its impact on the college and city. It is a great joy for both of us to realize the impact of giving back to an institution. These trips also give us an opportunity to visit with my only known relative in Alabama, Betty Harrison, a relative by marriage, since

LAURA AND DON BACKPACKING NEAR LAKE TAHOE.

she was married to my cousin Laurence Harrison. She lives in a small community on the banks of the Tennessee River near Athens, Alabama. It is always great to visit with her and to recall memories of old times with our family in Alabama.

In retirement, one seeks to find an avocation

for which there is now considerably more time. Having been involved in bicycling and bicycle trips for a number of years prior to retirement, I am delighted that I have more time for it now. The Little Miami Bike Trail is only a mile and a quarter from our house and has recently been extended to be more than eighty miles long. It is a Rails-to-Trails biking route almost completely off-road. In the spring, summer, and fall I find time to ride this trail on twenty-, thirty-, or forty-mile trips several times per week.

I consider this a substitute for golf, which I have not played since my early years at Stanford. Laura often rides with me and on weekends when we can take longer trips, we frequently take lunch breaks to eat at some of the restaurants along the trail. In addition to almost daily biking during the nice weather, we have continued to take organized biking trips.

In 2004, we took a Vermont Bicycle Tours trip for a week through the Canadian Rockies. The mountains were beautiful and the rides quite arduous. In 2005, we took an REI trip to the Gulf Islands off the coast of Vancouver Island in British Columbia. This trip started in Victoria, and we biked on three of the islands for two days, each time staying at

BIKING THE DANUBE WITH ELDERHOSTEL.

wonderful hotels and seeing some of the most beautiful scenery in the Pacific Northwest.

In 2006, we took our first bike trip with Elderhostel titled "Bicycling Along the Danube." We biked from Munich to Vienna on bike trails following the route of the Danube River. We stayed in small hotels along the route where we enjoyed educational lectures, musical concerts, and opportunities to visit numerous churches and cathedrals.

In 2007, we took another bike trip with Elderhostel. Laura and I spent the first four days in Berlin before the bike trip began. Then, for thirteen days, we biked along the Elbe River ending our journey in Prague. It was educational and permitted us to extend our friendship with two other couples from our 2006 trip.

Our biking trips provide an opportunity to meet wonderful new friends, and as long our physical stamina permits, we will continue to do at least one or two trips per year, as well as keeping up our local biking activities on the Little Miami Bike Trail.

Chapter Sixty-one

AND VULNERABILITIES

Throughout my life, I have maintained a very active exercise program. For years, I jogged five to seven days per week, from five to fifteen miles per day, and ran two Marathons when I was in my 40s. I found that jogging gave me the "runner's high" and also helped me control my weight.

After jogging for more than thirty years and reaching the age of 67, I began having pain in my left hip. This was aggravated by my jogging, although in the three or four years before this I became a more active biker, which did not seem to aggravate the hip pain. I consulted one of my close friends who was an orthopedist, and without doing any examination, nor doing an MRI, he told me that I had probably worn out some of the cartilage in the hip, and probably had some scarring and fibrosis in the bursa around the hip. He informed me that I could continue jogging and in two or three years they would replace my hip, or that I could stop jogging and the pain would probably go away in a month. This seemed quite serious to me— I stopped jogging, and, as I was advised, the pain disappeared, only to come back occasionally when I had been on my feet or taken a long hike.

In order to substitute a new exercise program, I increased riding my bike on the Rails-to-Trails path near our house, on as many days as possible. I also started being a regular at the Cincinnati Sports Club, where I am able to work out on a stationary bike, a treadmill, and a group of machines to strengthen my upper body. I also started to swim almost five times per week in a very serious program, moving up to a half-mile per day. These new exercises continued to give me the high that I got from jogging, and substituted quite well for the fact that I could not continue. I did try on several occasions to start back jogging, and after a short period of time my hip pain returned. Recently, I had an orthopedic consult and a series of x-rays on this hip. The cartilage is fine, but I have bursitis caused by some spurring on the bone. A physical therapy program has alleviated the problem.

As one ages, other vulnerabilities of health begin to emerge. I have not been spared some of these, even though I remain very healthy. The more important ones affecting me in minor ways include an enlarged, but benign, prostate, a transient benign cardiac arrhythmia, and chest pain probably as a result of gastrointestinal reflux. This was initially thought by me to also be cardiac in origin but later refuted. While these ravages of aging are annoying, they have not compromised my active lifestyle.

These episodes have reminded me of my vulnerability, and I believe are all due to the aging process. My approach to thwarting these aging effects is to adapt a vigorous counterattack.

Having reached the age of 74, I awaken each day believing that I am in a race to outrun the onrushing aging of mind and body that comes to all of us. Some of the approaches which I have taken may seem unorthodox, but so far, in my own personal case I believe they are clearly working. Each day I am aware of the aging of my mind, and I clearly see it happening when I try to recall names of individuals that I have met in the recent past or when I am unable to distinctly recall recent events, phone calls, and some of my daily tasks that need to be accomplished. So far, these memory lapses have not affected my ability to function successfully. On the other hand, my memory of events that occurred long ago seems to be quite sharp, and as I work on this manuscript, memories from the distant past seem to just well up in my mind. To combat this aging mind syndrome, I have adopted a number of strategies, which I believe to be helpful.

First, I keep notes of events that occur, and when traveling, keep a careful diary with Laura, a practice we began years ago. In addition, each day I write out tasks to be accomplished, even for weeks and months ahead.

Second, I make a point of trying to dial phone numbers without looking them up. I also try to keep my calendar in my head, without having to refer back to specific notes. Third, I am continuing to read three newspapers daily, *The New York Times, The Wall Street Journal,* and *The Cincinnati Enquirer.* I try to remember the articles that I read and discuss them with my office staff and with my wife. This tests my memory almost on a daily basis. I also continue to read five major nonmedical periodicals, *The Economist, Fortune, The New Yorker, Science,* and the *Wine Spectator.* I try to abstract and clip interesting articles to read while traveling on planes, and for discussion with individuals. In addition, I attempt to keep up with publications in my field of cardiology. On a regular basis, I read the *Journal of the American College of Cardiology, the American Journal of Cardiology, the New England Journal of Medicine, Circulation,* and *Circulation Research.* I find that I have time to review more manuscripts sent to me by editors of various journals, a task I enjoy. Last year, I reviewed more than ten articles for publication in the *AJC,* two in the *NEJM,* one for the *Journal of the American Medical Association,* three for the *International Journal of Clinical Practice,* and two for *Drugs.* Finally, I am attempting to read widely as I always have, particularly focusing on religion, autobiography, biography, and carefully selected fiction.

All of these avenues continue to challenge my mind, and I believe it is still keeping the aging process at bay. How long this can continue is not abundantly clear to me.

On the ability to perform physical activities, I have also noted that aging is a relentless process. Having been forced to stop jogging at age 67, I have continued to notice the decreasing capabilities for heavy physical exercise. In order to keep my body as strong as possible, I have adopted a number of approaches. At the beginning of each day, I go through a series of stretching exercises that are almost yoga-like in appearance. This relates to deep breathing and stretching extensive muscle groups.

At least five times a week, I visit the Cincinnati Sports Club to carry out an hour-and-a-half workout. This usually begins with a stretching exercise, a static bike ride for more than twenty minutes, a workout with the medicine ball, and one with a series of exercise machines. These exercises are followed by swimming one-quarter or one-half mile in a twenty-five-meter pool.

I occasionally employ a trainer to help me sharpen up some of my exercise activities. In addition to these daily exercises, I make every effort to do outdoor biking, trying to keep a speed of fourteen to sixteen miles per hour. Since Laura rides with me most of the time, it is another opportunity to do more things together. In addition, while at Lake Tahoe or traveling to many places in the country, I continue to bike on a regular basis. At Tahoe, with elevations of 6,200 feet, it takes several days of acclimation to be able to ride the twenty or thirty miles. When traveling in San Francisco, Southern California, Arizona, Georgia, and elsewhere, Laura and I rent bikes and ride extensively. Another element of trying to maintain my physical status is the never-ending struggle of keeping my weight under control. I tend to gain or lose five to seven pounds quite easily but have maintained my weight at about a standard place of being slightly overweight for the past fifteen years.

In addition to trying to outrun aging of mind and physical body, I have adopted some unorthodox eating and drinking patterns. I do believe that keeping one's cholesterol as low as possible, particularly the low-density lipoproteins (LDL), is a good idea. However, I have not seen much evidence in my medical practice that dietary control of cholesterol is possible. A small number of individuals are extremely sensitive to diet, and are able to lower total cholesterol and the low-density lipoproteins. These people are the exception, and I have found that statins work much better.

Since I do not believe in a low-fat diet, I have continued to enjoy all manner of cheeses. I do limit my consumption of red meat and eggs, but that is just dietary choice rather than belief in a low-fat diet. Even though I think that most people who eat a balanced diet really do not need a vitamin, as I have aged I have begun taking a daily multivitamin.

One of my important beliefs is that wine in moderation does improve health and decreases mortality. Many studies of this have been made and while the limits of wine consumption to ten or so ounces a day has proven to be beneficial, I frequently exceed this amount, and as of yet, in all of my medical exams, have failed to see any deterioration of function. My experience as a cardiologist is, if one exceeds 120 grams of alcohol per day, one is more likely to have an alcoholic cardiomyopathy. Since most wines contain either twelve or thirteen percent alcohol, this would mean that any consumption greater than twenty ounces would be excessive and would lead to this increased risk. It has been difficult to determine this with precision, since most people do not give accurate accounts of their alcohol intake. Taking wine with food has long been one of the mechanisms to prevent its ill effects. This has been well proven by the French, who on average drink more wine than any other population in the world, while at the same time consume a high-fat diet.

I continue to hear the ogre of aging chasing behind me, and perhaps not far behind that, the grim reaper. However, running as fast as I can, I am trying to stay ahead and hope for many more healthy, happy years.

Chapter Sixty-two

AND GIVING BACK

If you live long enough, many honors may come your way. In 2008,
a number of honors and opportunities to "give back" have come my way,
and they make a difference in my life. In February 2008, I attended my
fifty-year medical class reunion in Birmingham, Alabama, and recalled,
with my surviving classmates, many memories from our medical school days.
This helped to solidify many of the memories about my education written
in the earlier portion of this book.

In May of 2008, I was honored by my college, Birmingham-Southern, by being chosen as one of the representative students showing the major impact the college had on their lives. This program was to start a major capital campaign for the college to expand its programs and image. The ceremony and program for the kick-off of this campaign was held on the campus and was attended by more than 350 guests. During the trip, Laura and I met with a number of the honors students and faculty and heard their presentations. This inspired me to sponsor and endow the student honors program for Birmingham-Southern College. This is a new and expanded program that will appoint thirty outstanding students as Harrison Scholars each year. They will do honors work and write a thesis during their college years. The first class of Harrison Scholars entered the college in August 2008. In the future, I hope to participate annually in the presentation of their honors theses.

In June of 2008, the Board of Trustees of the University of Cincinnati approved the naming of the newly constructed health sciences library the Donald C. Harrison Health Sciences Library. Its dedication was a memorable affair, attended by a number of my colleagues and friends from California. This was a tremendous honor for me. It represented the culmination of my desire for the University of Cincinnati Academic Health Center to have a top-flight academic library and computer-training facility for all of the health sciences.

In July of 2008, I was informed that the Donald C. Harrison endowed professorship will be filled, after being vacant for several years. This professorship was established when I stepped down as senior vice president and provost for health affairs in 2003. The award will be given to Professor Randy Seeley, a renowned investigator who focuses on obesity and metabolic diseases. Over the years, he has been one of my favorite faculty members. I'm delighted that he will be the Donald C. Harrison Endowed Professor.

In November of 2008, I was honored at an award ceremony as the founder of the University of Cincinnati College of Allied Health Sciences. This college was formed from a number of disparate programs in health sciences from those existing in many colleges of the university. Dean Andrea Lindell of the college of nursing was my collaborator in making this a political reality. The present dean, Elizabeth King, has done an admirable job of adding new programs and enhancing the reputation of the college. I regard the formation of this college as one of my major educational accomplishments as the leader of the health sciences programs at the university.

As is apparent, 2008 was a rewarding year for me and has provided an opportunity to "give back" for all of the successes that have come my way over the past fifty years.

Chapter Sixty-three

SUMMING *up*

My life has been centered on utilizing my creative energies to balance several careers, family activities, a successful marriage, and the challenge of living through a rapidly changing period of history. The challenges and opportunities to move from a humble birth in Appalachia to a much larger national arena are a reflection on what is possible in our great country.

I was very fortunate that I was able to successfully have multiple careers as a physician, a scientist, an inventor, a consultant, a businessperson, and a venture capitalist. The rewards of being a physician caring for many patients still stand out as a wonderful part of my career. The research in which I participated with many of my colleagues and postdoctoral students helped in the development of a number of new diagnostic and treatment approaches for patients with heart disease.

Based on concepts that I learned as a scientist, I was able to become an inventor, and filed and had issued a number of patents in my later life. My activities as a consultant gave me a number of business opportunities that proved to be challenges, but provided opportunities for financial independence. Becoming a venture capitalist after my physician and administrative careers ended gave me an opportunity to continue to learn about the many new diagnostic and therapeutic advances that will be finding their way into medicine in the next decade or two. One of the most rewarding of my career choices was to be the CEO of the medical center at Cincinnati, to redirect it, and to watch it serve the patients of Cincinnati and become nationally prominent.

As for my family life, there was a delicate balance of finding time for family as our children grew into teenagers and adults. This required continually updating how we interacted as a family unit. I am very pleased with their career developments and interest in civic and charitable pursuits, their choices of spouses, and now in particular, with the eight wonderful grandchildren they have brought into my world. It is a marvel to me to see how the lives, education, and opportunities of our grandchildren are so different from when I grew up in central Alabama. I have no doubt that great challenges lie ahead for them, but also great opportunities.

My marriage to Laura, and the understanding we had for each other, having grown up in the same rural background, was the wisest choice that I ever made. She has been a continuous helpful supporter of my careers, and at the same time the bulwark for family development.

She has guided me on many occasions with wise decisions, and always in my despair comforted me and encouraged me. We have been through our challenges together, and have maintained our mutual respect and love for each other. Our lives continue to be totally intertwined as we go forward to the later stages of our lives. We really believe in giving back, and in our waning years, we plan to be even more charitable by establishing and using our Family Foundation to fund programs to help those who are disadvantaged.

For my own direction, I have never found a time without many opportunities, and in meeting the associated challenges I have never found my life to be dull. Using my creative energy, I have had more successes than failures. I have been fortunate to cross paths with the movers and shakers of this fifty-year era of my adult life. While I faced a number of adversities, I always believed in an old country adage, "When one sees a pile of manure, always look to find the pony nearby."

From here forward, my task is to keep a rational balance. To give up those things that in the past might have seemed irreplaceable, to search for meaningful replacements to keep my mental enthusiasm and activities on an upward trajectory. I remember another old adage from the south, "Those that look under many rocks will find many worms," which applies to my life.

I continue to strive to find the good and to reject the bad. In many ways, I remember my Appalachian roots, those lessons from my mother to strive for perfection, those from my dad to persevere. I hope to live out the rest of my life enjoying more time and adventures with Laura, and especially, finding more time to be with my children and grandchildren as they mature as teenagers and adults. It has been a great life, and I hope it endures for many more years.

*During my twenty years as chief of cardiology at Stanford,
I maintained an interest in the development of medical technology
and was particularly keen to learn how these technologies were
commercialized and made available to patients.*

In my role as a consultant to medical technology and pharmaceutical companies, I had gained an understanding of how important new technologies were to improving patient care. This interest was only heightened after Laura and I established Medical Education and Consultation Inc. and began to work with medical innovators to establish programs for educating physician groups about new technologies and pharmaceuticals.

I had previously been an advisor to several venture capital companies, including the Mayfield Group. Thus, in 1985 when I was approached by Barr Dolan, a partner in Charter Venture Capital, to evaluate two opportunities that the company was considering for funding, I was well-prepared to become actively involved with the companies.

With Michael Franz, one of my postdocs, and Barr Dolan, I became the co-founder of EP Technology in 1986. The initial product was a special catheter inserted into the heart for recording monophasic action potential in a beating heart to help with the diagnosis of abnormal rhythms. As we developed this concept, it became clear that it was not a great commercial opportunity. However, working with Roger Stern, a Stanford graduate engineer, we developed the new concept of using radiofrequency energy delivered through a catheter to treat conditions that lead to cardiac rhythm abnormalities. By using the radiofrequency energy to ablate aberrant pathways of conduction, this technology permanently prevented the abnormal rhythms.

After safety studies were carried out in animals, several clinical trials were quite successful in showing the effects of treatment. However, because of difficulty in obtaining the necessary funding to complete trials that would satisfy the FDA, the company was almost bankrupt. Alan Kaganov, who was then the CEO of EP Technology, made a very successful presentation to the Warburg Group of New York, who agreed on a $10 million infusion into the company. This led to great success, and in 1995, the company was bought by Boston Scientific and continues to be a market leader.

In 1986, Charter Venture Capital funded the work of an inventor/entrepreneur in a company known as Vasocor. I joined the company as an advisor, board member and interim

CEO. The company developed technologies to identify atheromatous lesions, or the lesions in coronary arteries that will lead to heart attacks. The approach was to develop immune markers of the atheromatous lesions. Monoclonal antibodies were developed to attach to the obstructions. The monoclonal antibodies would be labeled with radioactive tracers that could identify patients at risk for heart attacks. The company had a remarkably strong scientific advisory board, including Edgar Haber, chief of cardiology at Massachusetts General Hospital, and Russell Ross, chair of pathology at the University of Washington. Ross was the initiator of the concept that atheromatous deposits in coronary arteries produced an immune response.

The company's name changed from Vasocor to Scotgen when it acquired additional technologies. The company was funded by two venture capital firms from California and two from the Boston area, but unfortunately, the financial condition of the company deteriorated. As chairman of the board I spent a great deal of time mitigating the war among the various venture funding groups. After several years, it became apparent that the technology was not reliable enough to sufficiently allow the identification of lesions in coronary arteries. The concept of the immune basis for atherosclerosis went into hibernation for a number of years, but recently Russell Ross' concept has been vindicated and is now one of the prominent theories for the development of atherosclerosis. Scotgen was put into "mothballs," but the technology is still available. However, it has not been bought by any other company to date.

I remained on the board of both of these companies after I moved to Cincinnati in November 1986, requiring many trips back to California. I became a regular "red eye" overnight air passenger returning to Cincinnati. I had little time to pursue other company formation. However, in 1994, I was again approached by Barr Dolan, Nelson Teng, and Roger Stern of Charter Venture Capital about becoming a co-founder of a women's health company known as Vesta. This company was again using radiofrequency energy for ablating the endometrium of the uterus in women who had excessive bleeding. The technique allowed this common condition to be successfully treated without removing the uterus. Vesta remained a virtual company with only two full-time employees. After successfully demonstrating safety and effectiveness in ten patients in Mexico, an opportunity to sell the company developed. The company was purchased by Valley Laboratories, a subsidiary of the Pfizer pharmaceutical company. While I wanted to see the technology further developed for commercialization, it was clear that the venture capital concept of creating the greatest value for investors was more important. This was a lesson well learned about venture capital: never pass up a highly profitable opportunity.

Although I remained extremely busy as the CEO of the University of Cincinnati Medical Center, I continued to look for opportunities in the world of medical technology development. In 1990, I received a call from Dale Spencer of the SciMed Corporation in Minneapolis, Minnesota. Dale was seeking a board member who was a medical cardiologist. He agreed to meet me for an interview luncheon at the Greater Cincinnati Northern Kentucky International Airport. Dale was a well-organized and no-nonsense CEO who knew exactly what he was seeking and allocated only two hours for the interview. I was convinced that this would be a good position for me and agreed to become a member of the five-person board. We met in Minneapolis and had frequent conference phone calls on strategy. The company was developing rapidly and was commercializing a technology for opening obstructed coronary arteries with a balloon-type device on a catheter.

There are two highlights of my time on this board worthy of mention. The first was how I ended up with frostbite on my face during a severe winter in Minneapolis. The day started for me in San Diego, where it was a warm 80° in January. I had a long swim before departing for Minneapolis for a board meeting. It was 25° below zero with the wind blowing about 35 mph when I arrived at the airport. I took a taxi to the hotel, and since I was late for dinner, I gave my luggage to the bellman and asked for directions to the restaurant. He said that if I walked four blocks I would be there. Unfortunately, I missed the restaurant and walked several blocks too far, only to turn around and come back. By that time, I had frostbite on my face. At dinner, I learned that we could get back to the hotel via an indoor skywalk. After that, I was quite careful about how I confronted the winter in Minneapolis.

My second memory is of SciMed's shareholder meetings. In most companies, a shareholder meeting attracts very few people, but in Minneapolis a number of angel investors had been involved in the early phases of funding SciMed. Thus, the annual meeting consisted of an evening affair and a dinner attended by up to a hundred people. They asked very penetrating questions, and I learned a great deal about how shareholders view a company.

SciMed was very successful and was bought by Boston Scientific in 1995. It has been maintained as a subsidiary division in Minneapolis as one of the major interventional cardiology companies.

In 1996, I was invited to join the board of a company called InControl, whose medical director, Jerry Griffin, had been one of my postdocs at Stanford. The company was located in Seattle, Washington and was developing a device to stop abnormal rhythms in the atrial chambers of the heart. At that time, I became acquainted with Mark Knudsen, another board member who was a cardiac physiologist and a serial entrepreneur from Minneapolis.

While the technology that was developed proved successful, over a period of several years it became clear that the company could not stand alone. The CEO of the company, Kurt Wheeler, developed a great team but spent money with abandon. In 1999 the company and technology were sold to the Guidant Corporation. That decision required my input while I was traveling in Berkeley, California, and I had to participate in that board meeting from a phone booth on the edge of a park in Berkeley. There were no reliable cell phones yet.

Soon after the sale of InControl, I was asked by Mark Knudsen to join Venturi Medical, a partnership and an incubator that he was developing in Minneapolis for the purpose of funding and commercializing medical technology. The first technology developed was to treat snoring and sleep apnea. The company, Restore, developed inserts to be placed into the soft palette of patients, thus stiffening it and preventing the snoring and airway obstruction. After a successful initial public offering (IPO) and several years of minimal sales, the company was sold to the Medtronics Corporation.

A second technology was being explored in the Venturi incubator, development of a technology for treating obesity by a company called EnteroMedics. It was known that when the vagus nerve was surgically interrupted to treat ulcers, patients lost weight. Thus, the idea of blocking the vagus nerve to treat obesity was developed. The vagus nerve controls: 1) satiety or the signal to the brain that causes one to eat; 2) motility of the stomach, which, when slowed, decreased food intake; and 3) the enzyme secreted from the pancreas, which causes the uptake of nutrients and calories. Blocking the vagus nerve altered all three of these and seemed like a successful mechanism for treating obesity.

The technology to block the vagus nerve was developed by constructing a sequence of signals from an implantable transmitter to a series of electrodes that had been placed on the vagus nerve. Over a several year period a large number of pigs were studied to demonstrate the safety of this technique. The company was funded by venture capital firms from the West Coast and carried out initial clinical trials in Norway, Mexico and Australia, demonstrating effective weight loss when the electrodes were placed in patients by minimally invasive surgery. The company had a successful IPO in 2007, and I was happy to be a minimal co-founder of the company through my work at Venturi.

In the mid-1990s, I was asked to join the board of two other public companies. Novoste, located in Atlanta, Georgia, was a company that produced radiation of the obstructive lesions in coronary arteries after they had been reduced with balloon angioplasty, which prevented the redevelopment of stenosis or blockage in the arteries. The second company was Pharmaceutical Products Development Inc., or PPD, located in Wilmington, North Carolina, a contract research company that carried out large scale drug trials for pharmaceutical companies. Because of other commitments at the University of Cincinnati

Medical Center that resulted in my inability to get to board meetings, I remained on these boards for only a short period of time.

I was also on the board of Heart Stent, an early-stage medical development company in Minneapolis. The concept of a stent from the inside of the ventricle to the obstructed coronary artery did not prove viable, and the company failed.

Due to time constraints, it became clear that if I wanted to be involved in these ventures, the companies needed to be located in the Cincinnati area. I considered several opportunities, and in 2000 I was invited to join the board of Enable, a device manufacturing company located in West Chester, a suburban area of Cincinnati. This company had been founded by Mike Hooven, who soon became a friend. The company was profitable but was only outsourcing its products to be sold by surgical instrument companies. Mike believed that Enable had only limited growth potential.

Mike came to me one day asking what cardiovascular diseases would be amenable to treatment with new surgical instruments. We drew diagrams, researched information, and debated possibilities. I suggested that heart failure was an important area needing a solution, but he did not believe he could develop any technologies for its treatment. During this period, I became aware that atrial fibrillation could be treated by electrically isolating the pulmonary veins feeding into the left atrium of patients who developed atrial fibrillation. The original studies had been done with catheters using radiofrequency energy, but they demonstrated limited success.

Mike's solution was to use specially designed clamps for applying radiofrequency energy. They would hold the tissue between them and allow complete electrical isolation by ablating the heart tissue. This seemed like a great idea, so we formed AtriCure. Norm Weldon and I guided the company's early development. Several venture capital firms from the West Coast funded the company to successfully launch extensive clinical trials and have a successful IPO.

With 235 employees and a very sophisticated engineering team, AtriCure has become successful and is the market leader for the surgical treatment of atrial fibrillation. In 2004, Dave Drachman became the CEO of the company and has directed an annual growth rate of more than 30 percent each year since that time. He has developed an outstanding team and has a very supportive board chaired by Dick Johnston. I am quite proud of being one of the co-founders of this company and believe that the technology, which has been used to treat more than 50,000 patients with atrial fibrillation, will become even more successful in the future.

After resigning from PPD International in 2000, I was approached by Candace Kendle, the founder of Kendle International, whose headquarters are in Cincinnati. The company, like PPD, was a contract research organization (CRO), performing clinical trials for major pharmaceutical companies. Candace convinced me to join her board of directors and to work with her and her husband, Chris Bergen, in actively expanding and growing Kendle International.

I have been a member of the board for eight years, and during that time the company has expanded its scope. It is now the fifth largest CRO in the world, expanding its activities into Eastern Europe, South America, and Asia. In recent years most pharmaceutical companies have outsourced their clinical trial work for to the CRO's, and Kendle has been very successful in capturing this.

The last company in my parade is Uterine Muscle Disease, Inc. (UMD), formed in 1997. The concept for this company resulted from a conversation I had with Jim Liu, a professor of gynecology at the University of Cincinnati Medical Center and Wolfgang Ritschel, a renowned professor of pharmacy. We had become aware that the vaginal mucosa was very permeable to pharmaceutical agents and could be used as a transport mechanism for pharmaceutical products into the body.

We focused on one disorder in women, dysmenorrhea, which is the pain that occurs with menstruation and is severe in up to five percent of all women. Our concept was to use a tampon coated with an effective pain killer. The tampon would absorb the menstrual flow and the drug would be delivered selectively to the uterus, where the pain originated.

Our first objective was to obtain the intellectual property, or patents, for these ideas. Over a period of several years we developed a large patent portfolio. I have had seven patents issued as either the primary founder or co-founder, and there are five others still being prosecuted. UMD formed a corporate relationship with Kimberly Clark; however, after several unsuccessful years, Kimberly had a change in management, which impacted on its relationship with UMD. The company is now having difficulty raising money and has been placed in hibernation by its CEO, Rick D'Augustine.

As founder, co-founder, or board member, my parade of companies has allowed me major involvement in the development of new medical products. I have been a member of the board of directors of twelve companies, and I have learned a great deal from each experience. I have been fortunate to have outstanding colleagues in these companies, and almost universally the companies have developed products that are of value in treating patients with medical disorders.

INDEX

Acosta, Dan, 287
Al Khalifa family, 166
Alderman, Edwin, 132
American College of Cardiology, 124
American Heart Association, 124, 190, 196
Andrews, John, 312
Appalachia, 2, 370
Aravelli, Joe, 236
Ascension, Paraguay, 176
Asian-Pacific Cardiology Meeting, 184
Astra Pharmaceutical Company, 158, 182, 218
AtriCure, 376
Avenue of the Giants Marathon, 113

Bahrain, 166
baptism, 29
Baragwanath Hospital, 200
Barnard, Christian, 145, 147
Barondes, Samuel, 66
Batman Project, 309
Berg, Paul, 337
Bergen, Chris, 377
Berte, Neal, 348
BIOSTART, 332
Birmingham-Southern College, 31, 38, 39, 46, 348, 368
Blum, Marie, 350
Boat, Tom, 345
Boyes, Barrett, 160
Braunwald, Eugene, 80, 85, 88
breast cancer, 211
Buenos Aires, 177
Burchell, Howard, 125
Burkhart, Clara Mae, 35
Bush, President Sr., 294

Buttrick, Charles, 74

Cairo Museum, 203
Cannon, David 132
Cardiac Arrhythmias, a Decade of Progress, 218
Carlsmith, Wendel, 173
Celeste, Governor Richard, 296
Center for Academic and Research Excellence (CARE), 341
Cha, Johnson, 184, 224
Cha, Chi Ming, 184
Cha, Mrs., 231
Charter Life Sciences (CLS), 356
Cheeseman, Mary Sue, 323
Chezov, 193
Children's Hospital Medical Center, 257, 266, 332, 345
Church of the Holy Sepulcher, 246
Cincinnati General Hospital, 300
Clark, Dave, 156, 157
Clinton, President, 322
Clinton, Hillary, 322
Cooley, Denton, 210
Cosby, Bill, 322
Cruickshank, Robert, 192
Cuban Missile Crisis, 90

Democracy Wall, 186
Dexter, Lewis, 78, 92
Dillingham, Lowell, 221
Dimick, Alan, 47
Dolan, Barr, 356
Donald C. Harrison Endowed Professorship, 368
Dolan, Barr, 372, 373

Donald C. Harrison Health Sciences
    Library, 368
Drake Hospital, 268, 269, 293

Eastwood, Clint, 233
Enable, 376
EnteroMedics, Inc, 359, 375
EP Technology, 372
evangelical revival, 28

Falk Cardiovascular Center, 150, 221, 241
Favaloro, Renee, 178
Fidler, Laura, 337
Fiene, Thomas, 96
Fife, Gene, 204, 352
Fine, David, 257, 259
Fischer, Josef, 270, 272
Fitzpatrick, John, 191
Fogarty, Tom, 137
Folsom, Big Jim, 10
Forbidden City, 186, 226
Forrest Gap, 2, 4
Fountain at North Alabama, 277
Friedman, Milton, 108, 322

Gahl, Dan, 353
Galapagos Islands, 360
Garden City, xvii, 8, 11, 22
Gehry, Frank, 322, 334, 335
Genome Research Institute, 341
Gilreath, Earl, 235, 292
Glaser, Robert, 128
Gran's Camp, 361
Grants Party, 284
Great Hall of the People, 226

Hamilton County Commissioners, 291
Hancock, William, 124
Hargreaves, George, 333
Harrison, Sovola, xvii, 2

Harrison, Ann, 9, 19, 20, 33
Harrison, Tinsley, 55, 56, 60
Harrison, Beth, 75, 92, 106, 110, 113, 114,
    155, 170
Harrison, Doug 74, 94, 106, 110, 114,
    170, 205
Hawley, David, 275
Haymarket Square, 72
Health Alliance of Greater Cincinnati, 306
Hesa, Sheikha, 167
Hewlett Packard, 120, 123, 181
Hillman Hospital, 52, 53
Holman, Hal, 91, 98, 100, 102, 128
Hobson, Dave, 298
Howard, Dan, 277
Hoxworth Blood Center, 264
Hultgren, Herb, 129
Hunt, Sharon, 140
Hutton, John, 258, 270, 280, 282, 286, 304

InControl, 374
Indian Hill Church, 274
Indian Hill Fourth of July, 360
Indian Hill Historical Society, 320
intern match, 61
International Wine Festival, 327
InterParish Mission, 275
Irwin, William G. Endowed Professorship,
    142

Jerusalem, 246
Jesse, Mary Jane, 194, 233, 286
Jones, Frank, 238
Johnston, Dick, 376

Kaganov, Alan, 372
Kaiser Health System, 118, 136
Kapany, Narinder, 180
Kaplan Award, 195
Keating, Bill, 298, 305, 309

Kendle, Candace, 376
King, Elizabeth, 288, 369
Kingsgate Hotel and Conference Center, 352
Kirkland, John, 160
Kissinger, Henry, 206
Klyn, M.J., 297
Kupferberg, Cyril, 250
Kwok, T.F., 210

Lake Tahoe, 110, 214, 361
Laura Harrison Plaza, 362
Ledbetter, Ray, 51
Lederberg, Joshua, 120, 135
Levine, Samuel, 70
Liao, Zheng Zi, 185, 226
Lindell, Andrea, 287
Lingerfeld, Marvin, 316, 319
Lippincott, Jonathan 304
Little Miami Bike Trail, 363
Lorenzi, Nancy, 250
Lu, Ping, 187
Lucky the Cat, 319
Luke, Robert, 270
Lyons, Champ, 54

Machu Picchu, 178
majlis, 169
Malaysia, 236
Marks, Donna, 92, 94, 111, 114, 174, 252, 352
Marks, David, 274
Mason, Jay, 132
Massachusetts General Hospital, 57
Mauna Kea Hotel, 173
McAnnally, Clark, 43
McCain, John, 323
McGirr, Dale, 334
Medical Education and Consultation (MEC), 216
Merchant, Pat 275
Merigan, Thomas, 98, 134

Millennium Plan, 341
Mittens the Cat, 319
Mondavi, Robert, 322, 326, 327
Morgan, Karen, 358
Morrison, Jean, 351
Morrow, Glenn, 88
Mulberry River, 9, 21, 25, 32, 44, 61
Murad, Ferid, 337
mushroom poisoning, 101

National Institutes of Health, 78
Ngorongoro, 202
Nogoya, Gladys, 212
Novoste, 375

O'Connor, Sandra Day, 220
Old Silk Road, 229

Pasteur Institute, 154
Pauling, Linus, 206, 322
Peter Bent Brigham Hospital, 57, 64, 67
Pharmaceutical Products Development Inc., 375
Pickens, Boone, 195
Playhouse in the Park, 276
Popp, Richard, 132, 139
Portman, Rob, 299, 352
Potts, President, 277
Powell, Colin, 322

Queen City Club, 305

Reaching for the 21st Century, 260, 280
Redwood National park, 164
Roberts, Bill, 239
Rosenberg, Saul, 91, 96
Ross, Richard, 131
Rowe, George, 34
Russell, Richard, xviii, 70
Rytand, David, 100

Sabin, Albert, 16, 323
San Francisco Marathon, 113
Sanservino, Don, 114
Schroeder, John, 132, 141
Schubert, William, 248, 256, 267
Schwarzer, Fred, 356
SciMed Corporation, 374
Seven Knolls, 274, 284, 315, 316
Shanghai Thoracic Hospital, 225
Shapiro, Harold, 240
Shriners Burn Hospitals, 267
Shumway, Norman, 128, 144, 186, 221, 241
Stanford Chapel, 108
Stanford doctoral fellows, 337
Stanford University Hospital, 96, 121
Steger, Joseph, 250, 263, 352
surrogate parents, 156

Taft, Bob, 323
Teirstein, Paul, 255
Teller, Edward, 108, 205, 322
Teng, Nelson, 356
Teton National Park, 162
Tew, John, 256
Thorn, George, 57, 65, 70
Treister, Bernard, 159

UAB Medical School, 63
University Hospital, 302
University Hospital Air Care, 300
University of Cincinnati Medical Center, 256
University of North Alabama (UNA), 276
University Pointe, 312
Uterine Muscle Disease, Inc., 377

Valley of the Kings and Queens, 203
Van Ginkel, Judy, 267
Vasocor, 372, 373
Vermont Bicycle Tours, 175, 363
Vesta, 373

Vontz Center for Molecular Studies, 345
Vrh, Irv and Bessie, 207

Wafa, Jamil, 166, 169, 171
Weber, Buddy, 57
White, Terry, 304
Wiley, Mary, 232
wine cellar, 328
Winkle, Roger, 132
Wiot, Jerry, 256
World Congress of Cardiology, 192

Xinjiang Province, 226

Zug, Switzerland, 246